GEORGE BIDWELL.
(From Photo. by NUMA BLANC, Paris, 1872.)

Forging ∵ His ∵ Chains.

THE AUTOBIOGRAPHY

OF

GEORGE BIDWELL

AN AUTHENTIC HISTORY OF HIS UNEXAMPLED CAREER IN AMERICA AND
EUROPE, WITH THE STORY OF HIS CONNECTION
WITH THE SO CALLED

£1,000,000 FORGERY

ON THE BANK OF ENGLAND,

AND A COMPLETE ACCOUNT OF HIS ARREST, TRIAL, CONVICTION, AND
CONFINEMENT FOR FOURTEEN YEARS IN
ENGLISH PRISONS.

With Numerous Illustrations.

Fredonia Books
Amsterdam, The Netherlands

Forging His Chains:
The Autobiography of George Bidwell

by
George Bidwell

ISBN: 1-4101-0052-9

Reprinted from the 1888 edition

Fredonia Books
Amsterdam, The Netherlands
http://www.fredoniabooks.com

In order to make original editions of historical works
available to scholars at an economical price, this
facsimile of the original edition of 1888 is
reproduced from the best available copy and has
been digitally enhanced to improve legibility, but the
text remains unaltered to retain historical
authenticity.

PREFACE.

THE early chapters of this volume were written at a time when I had some misgivings as to the propriety of placing it before the public. It seemed to me likely that such a book would be misunderstood and misjudged by a class of readers, and the real purpose of its publication ignored. My friends disagreed on the subject, and gave dissimilar advice. I was placed in a position not unlike John Bunyan's:

> Some said, "John, print it;" others said, "Not so."
> Some said, "It might do good;" others said, "No."

But by far the greater number of my friends insisted that I *must* publish the book; and it now goes forth upon its mission, I trust, for good. I sincerely hope that no one will regard it as a mere record of crime. It is not a contribution to "flash" literature, or designed for the edification of the vicious. It is intended for honest people, and, I may add, as an enduring injunction for them to remain such.

I believe it to be a duty, which I owe my Creator and mankind, to occupy the remainder of my days in "works meet for repentance." I have come also to believe that in no way can I do so much to atone for past misdeeds as by giving the true story of my life to the world. The most critical reader will scarcely claim that my physical punishment has been insufficient; and yet, through all those weary years, my mental sufferings were by far the greatest.

In all ages men have fallen and reformed. If this book shall tend to convince the people of my native land of my own reformation, one of its objects will have been attained. If it shall prove a timely warning to any young business men or those occupying places of trust, who may be startled into a recognition of their own danger, I shall feel that my labor has not been in vain, and that my new life and liberty will not be altogether useless.   G. B.

CONTENTS.

CHAPTER VI.

CHAPTER VII.

CHAPTER VIII.

CHAPTER IX.

CHAPTER X.

CHAPTER XI.

CHAPTER XII.

CHAPTER XIII.

CHAPTER XIV.

CHAPTER XV.

CHAPTER XVI.

CHAPTER XVII.

CHAPTER XVIII.

CHAPTER XIX.

CHAPTER XX.

CHAPTER XXI.

CHAPTER XXII.

CHAPTER XXIII.

CHAPTER XXIV.

CHAPTER XXV.

CHAPTER XXVI.

CHAPTER XXVII.

CHAPTER XXVIII.

CHAPTER XXIX.

CHAPTER XXX.

CHAPTER XXXI.

CHAPTER XXXII.

CHAPTER XXXIII.

CHAPTER XXXIV.

CHAPTER XXXV.

CHAPTER XXXVI.

CHAPTER XXXVII.

CHAPTER XXXVIII.

CHAPTER XXXIX.

CHAPTER XL.

CHAPTER XLI.

CHAPTER XLII.

CHAPTER XLIII.

CHAPTER XLVIII.

CHAPTER XLIX.

CHAPTER L.

CHAPTER LI.

20568 B
4,5771

Order of Licence to a Convict made under the Statutes 16 & 17 Vict.,
c. 99, s. 9, and 27 & 28 Vict., c. 47, s. 4.

WHITEHALL,

18th day of *July*   188*7.*

HER MAJESTY is graciously pleased to

grant to *George Bidwell*

who was convicted of *Forgery*

at the *Central Criminal Court*

~~for the~~

on the *18th* day of *August,* 18*73*, and was

then and there sentenced to be kept in Penal Servitude for ~~the term of~~

Life

and ~~is~~ now confined in the *Woking* Convict Prison,

Her Royal Licence to be at large from the day of his liberation
under this order, during the remaining portion of his said term of Penal
Servitude, unless the said *George Bidwell*

shall, before the expiration of the said term, be convicted of some
indictable offence within the United Kingdom, in which case, such
Licence will be immediately forfeited by law, or unless it shall please
Her Majesty sooner to revoke or alter such Licence.

This Licence is given subject to the conditions endorsed upon the
same, upon the breach of any of which it will be liable to be revoked
whether such breach is followed by a conviction or not.

And Her Majesty hereby orders that the said *George*
Bidwell be set at liberty within Thirty Days
from the date of this Order.

Given under my hand and Seal,

Signed, *Henry Matthews.*

TRUE COPY.

Licence to be at large.   }

for Chairman of the Directors
of Convict Prisons.   }

B & S (23,576a) 500 4—87

George Bidwell

AFTER IMPRISONMENT. (From Photo. by STUART, Hartford.)

CHAPTER I.

DURING the past twenty years, hundreds of columns have been published in the newspapers throughout the world regarding myself and my transactions. Having been so freely commented upon by press and public, while it was beyond my power to reply, now that I am again free, I feel it incumbent on me to publish the true story of my life, which will not only correct all mistakes or false reports which may have been circulated, but serve as a perpetual warning to the young men of America to avoid the temptations by which I was beset, and to restrain that inordinate thirst for gold which seems fully as insatiable to-day as it was a score of years ago.

The alleged $5,000,000 Forgery on the Bank of England, in 1873, is now a matter of history; and as I have been regarded the principal character in that transaction, I feel sure that no reader will question my ability to "tell the whole truth, and nothing but the truth," regarding the gigantic fraud. My capture, and subsequent incarceration in English prisons, are facts as widely known as the forgery itself. Before commencing the narrative proper, I desire to picture a few of the realities of my prison life, and to explain my presence in America, a *free* man.

Before I had been six months in prison, heavy band-irons were riveted around my ankles. These were connected by a chain, and I was condemned to wear them day and night, in bed and out, for six months. I was also forced to wear a parti-colored dress, one-half of the jacket and knee-breeches

2 (17)

being yellow and the other buff. I will hereafter describe in full, with illustrations, both the ordinary and the punishment suits worn by prisoners in the English prisons, and give the alleged reasons for my punishment, with an account of what I did to incur such a fate. The ultimate consequence of this treatment was that, throughout the next thirteen years, I was unable to stand upon my feet. During the first five years of that period I was never out of the cell in which I was confined, except once a month to the bath-room in the ward. After the expiration of the five years, I was taken out into the yard for an hour each day. This continued for a month, after which I was again in the solitude of a cell for the space of two years. All this occurred at the Pentonville and Dartmoor prisons.

In the month of November, 1881, I was removed to the Woking male prison, twenty-two miles from London, and confined in a cell about three years longer.

Throughout these various periods of solitary confinement, I never saw the blue sky, the sun, or the twinkling stars.

During the last five years of my imprisonment my friends had been making untiring efforts to obtain my release, but all petitions to that end had been rejected by the English government. It will be seen that it is exceedingly easy to get into an English prison, but almost impossible to get out again.

I had been incarcerated since March, 1873. On the 18th day of July, 1887, I heard hasty steps approaching my cell door. The key grated in the lock — the door opened — and a prison officer, stepping in, said:

"You are free! and I am going to London by next train with you! A dispatch has come that you are to be sent at once!"

This was about 1 P. M. Officers hurried about to get me fitted with a suit of citizen's clothes, shoes, hat, etc. My photograph was taken. The medical officer was sent for in great haste to examine into my physical condition. In about one hour I was on the railway. Can the reader imagine my delight at this sudden resurrection from a living grave?

More than fourteen years! Few can form an idea of what that means. Fancy yourself being obliged to remain shut up in your own house until you had read the Bible through three and one-half times, at the rate of one chapter a day. It would take 5,231 days. Though I began those years a black-haired, robust young man, at the end I found myself a gray-headed cripple; yet, on this first opening of the world anew before my ravished eyes, how beautiful everything appeared! Even dull-looking old London seemed glorious. And the throngs of people in the streets! I could not tire of looking at them. I thought to myself: "These streets have been thronged the same each day through all the years that I have been in solitude; the lives of these people have been running on in various phases, while mine has been standing still!"

The English authorities sent two officers in citizens' clothes with me to Liverpool. They were very civil and attentive on the journey. They had orders to make the trip without attracting attention. I was taken by them on board the steamer, and they remained on the wharf until she was under way. The Government apparently feared that I, crippled as I was, might give them the slip and remain in England, and these officers were obliged to report that they saw me sail, and to bring a certificate signed by the captain to that effect.

On the voyage from Liverpool to Queenstown, I saw a man who landed at the latter place whom I believed to have been sent along to see that I did not leave the steamer there. But I was only too glad to take my last look at the coast of Ireland, and to see the good steamship Wisconsin in the broad Atlantic with her prow turned toward the loved land of my nativity, so often visited in dreams through all my years of desolation.

Capt. Bently was the only one on the steamer who was informed of my history, and I think he kept the secret. When I arrived on board, the warder gave me the first saloon ticket which my friends had purchased and given to the English authorities. This was taken under a false name, as it was not desired that my release should become known to the public. It was done without my own wishes having been consulted on the subject. This proceeding placed me in a false position, and for some time I did not feel like joining with the other passengers in the various plans for whiling away the time at sea. For the time of year the voyage was a very rough one, and we were greatly delayed by fogs, so much so that the fog-horn was going most of the time for four or five days. The waves washed the length of the deck, and at times poured down upon the steerage passengers. On such occasions the women and children would scream with terror, believing that the ship was going down.

I passed most of my time during the voyage in writing out from memory some thousands of lines of verses which I composed in Woking prison. The nature of my occupation had been observed, and on the occasion of an evening concert got up among the saloon passengers, I was asked to compose some verses for the occasion. This request resulted in the production of the " Steamer Wisconsin Squibs ", the same being received with unexpected favor by the good-natured audience. At a subsequent entertainment I was again called upon to take a part. I had sent the committee several pieces to select from, and they put me down for three recitations. I recited " The Sleigh-Ride " and " King Alcohol ", both selections from poems composed by me at Woking, which were vehemently applauded. Passengers at sea are very easily pleased.

Upon my arrival in New York, August 4, 1887, I found the question was being considered whether so dangerous a man should be permitted to land on his native soil. The conclusion appears to have been that, if I once set foot on shore, I could make a fight of it to prevent expulsion and exile.

I was arrested on board the steamer at the Guion line wharf as I was about to land, in the presence of my wife, son, and sister. The two former had journeyed from New England to meet me; the latter had accompanied me on the voyage from Liverpool. The officers had no warrant for my arrest, but had been ordered to bring me to the police headquarters on Mott street. They performed their duty with as much consideration as the nature of the case permitted. They assured my wife that I should not be long detained. But their protestations gave her no confidence. While waiting for the steamer, she had read the articles published in the papers previous to my arrival, and declared they would never let me go free again. She believed that as soon as it became known that I was released, the commotion already excited by the papers would create such a feeling against me that I would be again placed in confinement. It was in vain that I assured her that I had expiated my crime and paid most dearly for my wrong-doings — that I was, according to the law, a free man, and that no one had a right to molest me. It is impossible for me to depict the disappointment and anguish of that faithful, long-suffering wife, who, after a separation of nearly twenty years, believed it was to be indefinitely continued.

My wife, sister, and son accompanied me to the police headquarters and stood bravely by me. On our arrival there the sergeant in charge said to them, " You can all go now, we are going to keep him here until to-morrow." They refused to leave me; but at last being assured they would be permitted to see me at 4 P. M. (it being then noon), they reluctantly departed.

About 2 o'clock I was taken into a brougham by two detectives, driven to a back entrance of the Jefferson Market Police Court, and taken through into a private room. In a few moments Justice Duffy came in from the public court-room where he had been holding examinations, and promptly interrogated the officers as to the cause of my arrest. Upon discovering that there were no charges against me, except that I was considered too dangerous a man to be left at large, the judge spoke substantially as follows :

"That is no ground or reason whatever for depriving a man of his liberty; it is known that the prisoner committed a crime in a foreign country, and has paid the penalty by more than fourteen years' imprisonment. It would be against every principle of justice to interfere with him, so long as he conducts himself like a good citizen. A man may have committed a crime, and while suffering punishment determine to lead an honest life in the future. How unjust, then, as soon as he is free, to arrest him as a suspicious character. Instead of encouraging a man to lead an honest life, such a course as has been taken in this case is the sure way to drive him back into crime. It is bad policy, and I trust no similar case will occur again.

"For these reasons, I order that Bidwell be forthwith discharged from custody, and be allowed a fair opportunity to take a fresh start in life!"

What a friend I had in that righteous judge!

I was obliged to return to police headquarters to await the arrival of my friends, as I did not know at what hotel they were staying. At the appointed time they came, and I was at last reunited with my family, from whom I had been separated so many years.

The following editorial article, which appeared in the "New York Herald" of August 4, 1887, will serve to show in what manner my arrest was regarded by unprejudiced, influential journals:

AN OUTRAGE.

The arrest of George Bidwell on his arrival at this port yesterday, by two detectives, as related in another column, was a gross outrage.

He was charged with no offense, and, as far as appears, suspected of none. There was no legal ground for his arrest, which was made without lawful warrant or authority. The man is an ex-convict just released from a British prison, where he has served a long term of confinement for forgery. That is no excuse for his arrest here.

The only explanation of their action the detectives had to offer in the police court where they took their victim, was that they " wished to show him to the members of the force so that they would know him in the future if he attempted any ' crooked ' operations." Justice Duffy quickly saw that the prisoner was illegally held, and at once discharged him. But he should not have let the detectives off without a scathing reprimand that would serve as a salutary warning to like offenders in the future.

There have been too many instances of high-handed doings of this sort on the part of detectives. These officers should be given to understand that arrests are to be made in accordance with, not in violation of the law, and that even an ex-convict has rights that are to be respected.

The press dispatches detailing my return and illegal arrest, though containing numerous errors, did much, however, to excite sympathy for me throughout the country.

While I was detained at police headquarters, my photograph was taken by the instantaneous process, without my knowledge. In the papers the following day, I read of the theft, and that the picture had been given a place in the " Rogues' Gallery." My photograph had never before appeared as a star in that ill-omened galaxy. But, after becoming a thoroughly repentant man, it was then surreptitiously obtained and I suppose placed there.

The portraits of myself which appear among the illustrations in this volume will show that I no longer shrink from the gaze of honest people.

I was discharged from prison in a badly crippled condition, and suffering from great physical exhaustion, the result of a long and terrible incarceration, one almost unexampled in modern times. However, the good blood and strong constitution which I had inherited from a long line of pure-living Puritan ancestors, endowed me with the power to undergo sufferings which would have proved mortal to the majority of men.

The ensuing pages will contain a cursory history of the circumstances which surrounded my early life in Michigan —

an account of my removal to New York city — my marriage to the noble and devoted young lady, who has been spared and preserved to care for and educate our children through all these long years of undeserved mental suffering, brought upon her by my misconduct — my connections with wholesale houses, and business success in New York, and how I over-weighted myself in aiding others — my temptations, and the gradual undermining of my honest business principles, up to and including a true account of the great forgery on the Bank of England, with the events that followed, up to the present time.

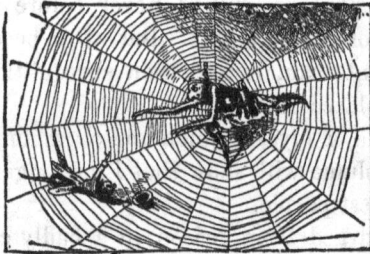

LEAVING LIVERPOOL.— GEORGE BIDWELL'S FAREWELL TO JOHN BULL.

CHAPTER II.

POSSIBLY some readers may desire to know something about the antecedents of my family. There are hundreds of Bidwells scattered over the United States, and it is generally believed that the name is derived from Bridgewell (the well by the bridge).

The ancestors on my father's side emigrated from Norfolk, England, and were among the first who settled in New England. In the Doomsday Book, compiled by order of William the Conqueror, between 1066 and 1100, will be found a record of the family and the coat of arms, which is among the most ancient.

Whatever may belong to hereditary descent, I have had one practical benefit from it, the sound bodily health before referred to.

My ancestors left England, like the other Puritans, not on account of poverty, but to obtain religious freedom, and all down through the generations those of the family who remained at the homestead or in its vicinity, attended the old Congregational or Puritan Church.

My great-grandfather, Capt. Zebulon Bidwell, was in the Northern Army during the Revolutionary war, being killed in one of the fights which preceded the capture of the British General Burgoyne, at Saratoga.

I pass along down to my father, who, in 1832, married and moved to Bloomfield, Orleans County, New York, where I was born.

When my father was a very young man, the Methodists opened a small chapel not far from the homestead; he became a convert, forsook the old family church, and joined them. My mother also joined them at about the same time, and thus two congenial spirits met.

My parents cared but very little about this world, believing it but a place of preparation for the next. From about the time their children could "toddle," they were forced to go to church and sit out hour-long sermons; and woe to the child that fell asleep. I could not have been four years old when, on one occasion, I fell asleep and was instantly taken out of church by my father and well spanked.

Yet, in matters not pertaining to morals and religion, they were ever most loving and indulgent. Sunday was observed by them in the old Puritan way. We children must read only the Bible, Sunday-school books, Baxter's "Saints' Everlasting Rest," or Bunyan's "Pilgrim's Progress"; and indeed Sunday was a "slough of despond" to us.

We were debarred from playing with a kitten or a doll. A pack of cards in the house would (we were told) have brought down a judgment from Heaven upon us. Even the game of checkers was looked upon with suspicion, and regarded as a temptation of the devil.

Dancing was considered an almost unpardonable sin, and the violin an especially diabolical instrument. Everything in the way of amusement was regarded as time lost in making preparations for eternity.

Am I exaggerating? I am only reproducing from my memory an exact picture as left upon my mind by the events of those days; and I write with reverence, only desiring to let the attentive and thoughtful reader judge what effect such teaching probably had upon my character and life; and whether the rebound did not at last carry me as far in the opposite direction.

I have endeavored to describe thus briefly the religious atmosphere which surrounded me in childhood. But, had I lived up to the religion which my parents believed in and taught their children, I should never have been forced to undergo so much disgrace, nor to have passed so many dreary years within the gloomy walls of a prison.

In 1837 my father went to the then paper village of Lanesville, Mich., which was situated about fifty miles west of Toledo, Ohio; the Michigan Southern Railroad was afterward built between the latter place and Chicago, passing through the village. It is now the thriving town of Hudson. He there purchased land, and built a house and shop; then returning east, he took his family by the Erie Canal from Medina, N. Y., to Buffalo; then by the steamboat "Erie" to Toledo. The Erie was the first steamboat, I believe, that ever ploughed the waters of Lake Erie. At that time the run from Buffalo to Toledo took more than three days; a journey which is now made in double that number of hours.

During the first year after our arrival, all of our family of six, with the exception of myself, were prostrated with fever and ague. As nearly all the other settlers were alike afflicted, it was not possible to hire any one to care for the sick or render any other assistance; in consequence I, a lad of six years, was the "working force" through the greater part of that long year of deprivation and misery. It seemed miraculous, under the circumstances, that any recovered; but all did, except the youngest, a two-year-old brother.

At the end of the year my father found himself so deeply in debt that his property was all sold for about one-fifth its value. Having had our fill of Lanesville, we removed to Adrian, in the same State, at that time a growing village. We arrived there penniless, but my father soon got a little start and opened business in a small way. After I was fifteen years of age, my father seemed to rely entirely upon me.

As before stated, my parents were religious people. Religion was everything to them, all worldly affairs comparatively nothing. Yet through all their lives both worked very hard, and would make any worldly sacrifice for what, in their opinion, was for the benefit of their children. They believed it a religious duty to divide their last crust with the suffering, and preferred rather to make friends with the poor and down-trodden than with the prosperous.

My father belonged to the old abolition party. Adrian was a station on the " Underground Railroad," *i. e.*, the line of travel between the Ohio river and Canada by which fugitive slaves escaped, these being carried by wagon-loads in the night from the house of one abolitionist to that of another, and there secreted during the day.

It was often a desperate race for liberty, or chains and death, until they had got one hundred and fifty miles north of the Ohio river. In a village the wagon-load of fugitives would be hastily distributed at the houses of the abolitionists. I remember hearing some of those secreted at our house tell about their marvelous escapes — how they were chased by bloodhounds, etc., before they reached the Ohio.

My father seemed to possess no business qualifications whatever. He was honest, simple-hearted, and confiding. He would no sooner get a business established than some stranger would come along, worm himself into his confidence, and soon have everything in his own hands, leaving my father penniless. One of these recurring events happened when I was nine years of age; and as my father was in poor health at the time, I took to peddling molasses candy and apples in a basket, and for a long time brought in enough money to support the family. On the occasions of these periodical downfalls, neighbors would say to me: " Your father is too honest to live in the West." It was not that he was too honest, but too confiding, and deficient in worldly wisdom. Through long years of solitude, while lying crippled in a prison cell, the thought often entered my mind that, had my parents been more worldly-wise, my fate would have been different.

In my eleventh year, I bargained with a rich man of the

place to saw four-foot wood twice in two and split it, for fifty cents a cord. I was attending school at the time, and one Saturday I set to work, and by noon had so huge a pile sawed that, when my employer came home to dinner, he, with his wife and daughters, looked at it from the kitchen door with astonishment. Soon afterwards this gentleman offered to take me to his home, give me an education, and start me in a business. His name was Ira Bidwell, a distant cousin. He was well known, especially in Michigan, and in St. Paul, Minn., later, as a merchant and banker. He was, like my parents, a Methodist. His kind offer was not accepted, however, my parents believing that the religious training of their children necessitated their presence at home. I believe this was an unfortunate decision for me.

When I was about twelve years of age, my father was again " taken in and done for " by a sharper from Buffalo. Believing there was an opening for him in Toledo, Ohio, in 1845 he removed with the family from Adrian to that place. There I set up a street stall for the sale of periodicals and apples, trashy novels and candy, lemonade and pocket-knives, small-beer and steel watch-chains, etc.

I succeeded in supporting the family until my father got into business again, and continued in trade until I had a capital of nearly fifty dollars. With this I bought an old steamboat clinker-built yawl, twenty-three feet long, and had it half-decked and fitted out as a sloop. My father being then in more comfortable circumstances, I passed my summers on the Maumee river, making occasional excursions into Lake Erie. I was so fond of sailing that I used to go off alone, and, after sailing all day, remain in the sloop nights, while she lay anchored near the shore, sleeping in the folds of the sail.

When I was about fifteen I took my beloved sloop to a ship-carpenter to get the hull sheathed over. The bill was about eighteen dollars. I had invested all my money in her, but as the carpenter was an old friend of my father, and had always treated me kindly, I had not a doubt but that he would trust me for the repairs. To my surprise and mortification he said I must pay the amount at once. As I could not do so, he had the boat sold at constable's sale without delay. My father refused to interfere or advance me anything, and so I lost my dear old "Mayflower." I had no suspicion at the time, but I have since thought there was an arrangement between my father and the carpenter to get the boat away from me, and thus turn my energies in another direction.

Soon after this event a New Orleans boarding-house and hotel "beat" ingratiated himself into my father's confidence and soon became his right-hand man. It was not long before my father was again moneyless and out of business.

I had by this time picked up some knowledge of candy-making, and we heard there was a good opening for the business at Grand Rapids. The last "ruin" had left us with but a single horse and wagon. My father borrowed a little money, and in December, 1849, he and I left Toledo for Grand Rapids. As the country was deeply covered with snow, and the roads but little traveled, and only by sleighs, the track being too narrow for our wagon, it was hard dragging one hundred and fifty miles. However, we arrived at Grand Rapids a day or two before Christmas, rented a small shop, and by working day and night, we made up a stock of sugar toys. We had brought with us a small stove and the moulds in which to cast the toys. On Christmas day we had sold a quantity, which left us a profit of thirty dollars, quite a little fortune in our pockets. Our next step was to sell the horse and wagon for one hundred and fifty dollars.

We then rented a larger store, and in five years from our humble start we were doing a large business in confectionery, fancy goods, and jewelry. The business devolved on me alone, my father deferring everything to me because of his belief in my superior judgment in business matters.

All others with whom I came in contact seemed to place

a like confidence in me, and I began to consider myself capable of conducting a much larger business enterprise. It may be that this conceit and overestimation of my abilities puffed me up considerably. It needed but a little imagination to picture to myself a near future in which I should become a rich merchant. Up to our arrival at Grand Rapids in 1849, every enterprise of my father's had resulted disastrously. Now that I was at the helm, everything certainly prospered; home comforts increased; better educational advantages for the younger brothers and sisters were enjoyed.

I was highly respected by those members of the community whose good opinion was worth having; all of whom had unbounded confidence in my integrity and business capacity. I was observant, anxious for improvement, quick to grasp at new ideas, and to ascertain what was in them that might aid me to reach the " El Dorado " of which I had dreamed, since, when in my ninth year, I began to sell apples and candy in a basket. The reader may smile to learn that at this time I was but sixteen years of age, although I looked much older. At eighteen I sported a beard and moustache. Like most boys, I was anxious to appear older than I really was, and the sturdy frame with which Nature had favored me helped out the innocent deception.

Our business steadily increased, and in course of three years our credit became so well established with the merchants of New York, and other trade-centers, that we could get all the goods required. We now began to run wagons to supply goods to the dealers within a circuit of one hundred miles. Although this system worked successfully in more populous localities where the roads were good, it proved a failure in the newly-settled State of Michigan. The towns and villages were widely scattered, and sparsely populated, the roads almost impassable; and the wear and tear of horses and wagons, with occasional damage to goods, was to us appalling. With no knowledge of business save what I had " picked up," I could not understand the necessity of an annual inventory, and had no means of judging what our profits were, except by the ease with which money came in to meet our bills.

After having run the trade-wagons a long time, money matters appeared to tighten up with us, and it became more and more difficult to make payments. I began to investigate, and, to my dismay, discovered that our assets scarcely equaled our indebtedness. If at this juncture I had consulted with an experienced business man, instead of relying upon my own immature judgment, I should have learned that an established business with good credit is in itself a capital for a young man of energy. To stop the trade-wagons would have been to me a great mortification. But that is exactly what an older head would have advised; and, as the rest of the business was profitable, it is likely I should have remained in Grand Rapids to this day. My parents had no suggestions to offer, as they were, like myself, quite overwhelmed by the result of our six years' energetic work. I consulted with a lawyer, who had lately opened an office next door, but as yet having no practice. When I explained the state of affairs he evidently saw that his opportunity had come, and he made the most of it. He advised me to put all the property into the hands of an assignee, the same to be sold and divided as follows : those creditors who had shown me some attention when I had visited their places of business were put in the first class, to be paid in full out of the assets. The second class was composed of those who had favored me less. These came in next if enough were left to pay them. Under such an iniquitous arrangement the third class could of course receive nothing. Experienced readers need not be told the result of such an assignment. As my lawyer doubtless expected, the second and third classes of creditors began law proceedings to break the assignment and get all the creditors put on an equal footing. As a matter of course the lawyers got all that the creditors did not. My lawyer skillfully arranged about two years' practice for himself, which estab-

A NEWGATE SCENE.—DON'T WANT HIS PICTURE TAKEN.

lished his position at the bar, and he is to-day one of the wealthiest lawyers in the State of Michigan.

That assignment invented by the lawyer has unquestionably affected my whole life. Ever afterwards, when trying to get into business, I was haunted by the idea that some claim would be brought forward before I was able to pay it. At the time of the assignment, I had given up some valuable real estate, my own private property, also my gold watch and chain, to pay firm debts. I have gone into this matter somewhat in detail because there are many persons still living who, doubtless, believe I acted dishonestly. I look back to this assignment as the direct starting-point of all my misfortunes.

My parents also gave up every thing, leaving themselves and children destitute. Amid all, my parents never lost one tittle of their faith in God's providence. In fact, despite the many adverse instances in which the answers to their prayers appeared to " go by contraries," I always had a latent, deeply-rooted conviction that because of their prayers nothing very bad would ever happen to me, and this belief became consolatory after I began to grow " crooked ". Many times when lying in the cell of a foreign prison, undergoing dreadful and long-continued tortures, I would say to myself : " O, would that I could believe all that my parents did, and possess the same faith and confidence in God ! I should be happy even here." Well, they are gone ; and if they are not now enjoying such a state of everlasting bliss as they anticipated, they richly deserve it. Through all the years of my incarceration it has been a great consolation to feel that, as long as they lived, I did all in my power to assist them, as well as my younger brothers and sisters.

After I had turned over all the property into the hands of the assignee, I left for New York city, determined to seek my fortune in a place where so many others had acquired theirs. I felt that I possessed energy, perseverance, and physical capacity to undergo more hardships and to accomplish more work than most young men. Besides this, I was strictly temperate, and not addicted to any of the vices so common in large cities. In my various trips to New York and other cities for the purchase of goods, I had learned that the theaters and bar-rooms were well patronized each evening by young business men. I had also been told that many were addicted to gambling and other vices. I thought to myself: "If such young men give satisfaction to their employers and get on in New York, why cannot I?" At this time I was 23 years of age. I felt that I ought to succeed. When I turned over my own real estate, I received $300 of its value, which enabled me to go to New York.

On my arrival in that city I purchased sugar and shipped it to a younger brother in Grand Rapids, to enable him to carry on the manufacture of confectionery, and thus support the family while I was getting into business. Before he had got fairly started, the creditors of my father and myself attached the sugar for our debts, and he was forced to submit to the loss, which broke up his business.

Thus, the family were left destitute in Grand Rapids, and I was in New York, without employment. I rented a small room in Greenwich Street, and eked out my money at the cheapest eating-houses, seldom spending more than twenty or twenty-five cents a day for food. Day after day I went from one wholesale house to another, applying for a situation of some kind, but in vain. My money began to run low, and I lived on ten or fifteen cents a day.

About this time I made myself known to Mr. J. Milton Smith, Secretary of the Home Fire Insurance Company. I had met this gentleman when on a visit in New England. He proved a true friend to me as long as I remained in New York. If all merchants and business men who are rich and prosperous would treat young men, especially those just from the country, as this gentleman and his excellent wife did me, fewer of them would get among bad associates and be led to ruin. Mr. Smith invited me to his home in Brooklyn, and his hospitable wife insisted that I must dine with them. I had eaten only a ten-cent breakfast that day, and they must have been astonished at the quantity of food which disappeared. However, I suspect those benevolent, noble-hearted souls understood the situation, and afterward I had frequent invitations to their house. Mr. Smith exerted himself to find an opening for me, and at last succeeded in getting me a position in the wholesale grocery house of C—— O—— & Co. I knew nothing about the business, but very soon I was directed by the firm to make a trip to New London, Norwich, Willimantic, Hartford, and New Haven, all in my ancestral State. As the grocery men in those places were all strangers to me, on my first round I only introduced myself and left my card. Three weeks later I made the trip again, and found that all remembered me. This time I received several orders. I now went around regularly once a month, and the number of my customers and the amount of orders constantly increased. The orders by mail also increased. Every dealer who gave me an order became a regular customer. In 1857 the firm of C—— O—— & Co. failed ; and as the business was wound up, I had to transfer myself and customers to another house. By this time I had the control of considerable trade, and had no difficulty in getting into the wholesale grocery house of Messrs. B—— & H——.

Upon leaving Grand Rapids, I had arranged with my parents that they should remain there with their other children until I had pushed my way into a position whereby I could support them. But they were induced to remove to the village of Muskegon, to assist in organizing a new society of Methodists, and build a church.

Muskegon is now a very pleasant city of about 30,000 inhabitants, and one of the lumber emporiums of this continent. In 1857, it was a village of wooden huts, cabins, and small houses, inhabited principally by lumbermen and those " tough and rough " characters usually found on the outskirts of civilization. Whisky-selling, gambling, dog-fighting, and more brutal animal bipeds bruising each other, was the order

of the day. On hearing about their removal, I was much
troubled, but at the time it was out of my power to do anything. They were not long there before they found out their
mistake. In order to live, they opened a hotel; some of their
customers would come and stay a few days, and when my
father asked them to pay up they would invite him out into
the street to fight. Evidently they were used to fighting
landlords, but I do not think my father ever had even an
angry dispute in his life. The account that reached me of
the state of affairs hastened my determination to get them
out of the place, and I could think of but one way, which was
to bring them on to New York. This was a very rash undertaking for a young man not yet receiving more than six
hundred dollars a year. But I had a fatal confidence in my
own powers to carry any burden. Besides, I expected to get
my father a situation of some kind, and my young brother,
then a lad of twelve, into an office. I sent for the family,
and at the same time hired part of a house in South Brooklyn.
They came, and affairs ran smoothly for some months.

My income rapidly increased. In 1858, I transferred my
business to the house of J—— H—— & Co. I had hitherto
been working on a percentage; I was now on a regular salary,
with the promise of twelve hundred after October 1st. On the
strength of this expectation, I married a young lady with whom
I had made acquaintance while visiting the old homestead in
Connecticut. The remarkable prudence she has shown in all
affairs of her life — her success in bringing up our children
through all the years of separation — and her adherence to me
under circumstances which would have irrevocably estranged
most women—prove that I made a good choice, if she did not.
Her age at that time was seventeen and mine twenty-six.
I was already supporting nine persons besides myself, and
though sanguine of success in business, I felt almost afraid to
assume another responsibility. But I was deeply in love, and
I feared that by delay I might lose the dear object of my

affections. Therefore, I rashly cast all prudential considerations to the winds, a customary proceeding among lovers.

I have never been a believer in signs and omens, but on my voyage from Rio Janeiro to Marseilles, just previous to the great catastrophe of my life, I lost a valuable diamond ring overboard. Thirty years since I gave the young lady who is now my wife an engagement ring with an opal setting. Owing to a family affliction, she was married in black. While in an English prison, I read in one of the library books that each one of the incidents referred to was ominous of misfortune.

CHAPTER III.

AFTER my marriage I took still more active measures to
help some members of the family into a position where
they might be able to earn something towards the general
support. A man of some means went into the confectionery
business with my brother, but the copartnership soon resulted
in a failure. This enterprise, instead of easing my financial
burdens, only increased them. During this time I was hard
pushed for means to pay rent and supply food for those
dependent on me. As my account with my employers was
kept balanced or slightly overdrawn, on one occasion, after
returning from a trip, I purposely withheld fifteen dollars
from my collections. Goods were sold on thirty days' credit,
any dealer in good standing being allowed that time. On my
trips it would frequently happen that I collected the money
for goods which had perhaps been purchased only a week
instead of a month. It was one of these advance payments
that tempted me to retain the amount before mentioned, as a
temporary relief for pressing necessities.

Previously, when on my trips, in case I made use of any
portion of the money collected, for special expenses, I always
had the deficiency charged to my account, and this had been
satisfactory to the firm. I argued to myself thus: "My
brother is now in business, will no longer need my assistance,

(38)

and if I overdraw my account, it will place me in a bad position with the firm. This money is not due for three weeks yet, and the firm will not look for it before. I am really doing them no harm if I pay it over when due. My expenses being reduced, I will be in condition to do so, and will be careful not to get myself into such a predicament again."

I was ashamed to tell my bride of three months that I had not money to purchase food for her. Had I frankly explained to her exactly how matters stood, all would have been well.

As previously stated, my brother did not succeed in his business, and instead of replacing the fifteen dollars at the end of the month, I felt obliged to increase the deficiency. As the firm had the utmost confidence in my integrity, no inquiry was ever made into the accounts of my customers. Therefore, although during the next few months the deficiency gradually increased until it reached the sum of two hundred and fifty dollars, no discovery was made. Through all this time my mind was filled with apprehensions of exposure, and I made desperate efforts to extricate myself from the gulf into which I was slowly but surely sinking.

My position was becoming unbearable, and I looked about for some honest means to raise money to make good the amount I had embezzled. One day a man whom I had known at Grand Rapids came into my place of business and showed me a "Patent Globe Coffee-Roaster," of which he owned one-half the patent-right. He said he had come from the West to sell the right, but had not yet been able to do so. He was no business man, and I saw at once it was a thing I could sell, and told him so. He eagerly accepted an offer which I made, and I at once had a cut engraved and some bills printed. I also took the sample coffee-roaster to the wholesale hardware houses, and in a short time had orders for several gross.

Soon after I met Mr. Wilcox, of Roys, Wilcox & Co., Berlin, Conn. He saw there was money in the roaster, and I sold him the half right for one thousand five hundred dollars. The owner was greatly pleased at the price, and gave me the two hundred and fifty dollars I required to square matters with my firm. This I did at once, and found that the deficiency had not been suspected.

Now, for the first time in several months, I breathed freely, and felt that the state prison was no longer staring me in the face. If, at any time throughout those months of trouble, I had applied to any one of several friends for advice, explaining my position, I should have been at once relieved, and the calamities which followed would no doubt have been averted. But at that period of my life I could not bring myself to confess to any one that I had committed a dishonest act.

While engaged with the coffee-roaster, I had neglected, a good deal, my grocery business, and had gone to the store as seldom as possible. As soon as I had made all square, I gave up the place, preferring to abandon it and make a new start in life, rather than remain there with the risk that what I had done should accidentally be discovered — of course a wrong decision.

Mr. Wilcox, who had purchased the coffee-roaster, gave me temporary employment in the house of his agents in New York. Shortly after, I received a letter from one of my customers, stating that the firm had dunned him for ten dollars that he had paid me, and for which he held my receipt. I could not recall the circumstance, but suppose it happened in this way: On my rounds, the train from Norwich to Hartford stopped ten minutes at Willimantic. I had two customers there, whose places of business were located opposite the depot. When the train arrived it was my usual plan to run across, take the orders, give a hastily-scrawled receipt for any money paid, and then rush for the train; in the car I would look over the collections, and enter the particulars in my memorandum-book. I must have neglected to do this with the ten dollars — if that was the exact amount of the account

Hilton.

IN FORT LAFAYETTE, NEW YORK HARBOR.

paid — or if, as is more probable, the amount was several hundred, I had accidentally entered it ten dollars less.

When I received the letter from Willimantic, my father happened to be in my place of business; I at once gave him ten dollars, with which he went to my old grocery house, to adjust the discrepancy. But Mr. H. had also received a letter from Willimantic, informing him that the ten dollars had been paid to me. This fact caused him to suspect that other sums might have been retained by me in the same way; he therefore refused to receive the ten dollars, and stated his suspicions to my father, who stoutly maintained that he knew me too well, and that such a thing was not among the possibilities. Poor, mistaken old father! To the day of his death, he never had the least idea of my struggles, deceptions, and (I may as well call things by their right names) crimes, throughout the previous months.

A day or two later a constable arrested me on the charge of defalcation. Mr. D., the head of the firm, immediately said to me, " In case you are held and want bail, send for me at once." I thanked him, and accompanied the constable to the Tombs police court-room. I was taken into a private room, where, a few moments later, Justice Connelly came and began an examination into the charge. The prosecutors, Messrs. J——, H—— & Co., my former employers, were not present, but were represented by an attorney. I related to the justice the circumstances which must have caused me to make the oversight — for it was an oversight. The lawyer had nothing to say against me, except that the ten dollars was unpaid. I explained to the justice that I had tendered payment, and as the lawyer could not dispute the fact, I was discharged.

In the course of the examination, no allusion was made to any previous deficiencies; but I have no doubt this affair caused the firm to make a comparison of dates on which I received money, as per my receipts, with those on which I paid it in, as shown by their books. Happily, I had paid all of it in before any discovery was made.

The head of the house where I was at the time employed, surprised that I should be arrested by my former employers, held a consultation with them, and then discharged me.

Thus, I very soon began to reap the fruit of my first dishonest acts.

This book will doubtless be read by some who are "in the same boat." Both in and out of prison a great number of similar cases have come under my observation; though the defalcations usually originated from contact with vile associates, fast living, or by "putting on style" out of proportion to the income.

As a rule, young people will not listen to the warning advice of their elders; therefore, each in his turn, as they grow old, have to regret that they did not profit by the experience and advice of others. Let me conjure all, who find themselves in a position similar to mine, to lay aside all pride, fear, or shame, and at once seek the counsel and assistance of an elder friend, and give the facts without reservation. It is treating such a friend unfairly to ask for advice and assistance unless a full and frank exposition is made, to enable him to look upon the matter in all its bearings. All that I have seen convinces me that this is a subject of the utmost importance, and that the space devoted to it cannot be better occupied.

Every person who does a wrong act, or commits a crime, from the least to the greatest, believes at the moment that he or she is justified in so doing. Every man who contemplates doing a "doubtful" act, in case he is strongly desirous to do it, has a way of "putting" things before his own mind which blinds him to its real nature. At the same time others, who notice the action, see clearly that it is wrong. Now, this principle in human nature holds good, no matter how low we descend into the ranks of the countless millions bound in the chains of vice and ignorance.

Prisoners placed in circumstances where they can talk, do so incessantly; and, as they know little else, their conversation naturally reverts to the events of their past lives, in which stories of robberies, and revelry on the proceeds, predominate. No matter what may be their demeanor towards the authorities, servile or otherwise, they are generally frank, manly, and honest in their intercourse with each other. While in prison they lead a quiet, regular life, and are not exposed to the temptations which surround them on every side when free. Under such circumstances, while much of their natural predilection to evil and crime comes to the surface, a great majority act like well-disposed men, and, so far as they have the opportunity, are kind and obliging.

It has been my good (or ill) fortune to have heard the life histories of all varieties of criminals, from the area thief or the petty pilferer to the men who have perpetrated atrocities as monstrous as any recorded in the annals of crime. Yet I have not seen one who had not found a salve for his conscience — reasons which, to his own mind, rendered his act justifiable to himself. In too many instances the excuse was that they were drunk; indeed there are few convicts who do not trace their fall to drinking habits, or to their having been left by parents who neglected every duty, and sacrificed every other object in life for drink.

The word "circumstances" is perhaps the most important one in the language. It is the circumstances which surround from birth that make the difference between the judge upon the bench and the prisoner at the bar. To exchange each at birth into the other's circumstances, hereditary taint excluded, would have reversed the present position. And until this fact is accepted, and duly considered, but little progress can be hoped for in the reformation of the great mass already entangled in the meshes of crime. I feel deeply the importance of this, for I have seen so many instances of naturally good men — young men — who were in prison the second, fourth, or even the fifth time. I knew of one who, after undergoing seven years' penal servitude, was free only twenty minutes. This man was sent from the Chatham prison to the

Millbank prison, in London, to be discharged. The next morning he was set free, and hurried down to the Westminster bridge to cross to the Southwark side of the Thames, to visit his old haunts, and such of his former companions as might be out of jail or prison. While crossing the bridge, twenty minutes later, he espied a woman carrying a hand-bag. As it was early in the morning, and but few about, he snatched the bag from the woman and made a run to escape, but at the end of the bridge rushed into the arms of a policeman. He was taken at once before the police magistrate, who committed him for trial. The grand jury was in session, a true bill of indictment was found the same morning, and in the afternoon he was tried, convicted, and sentenced to ten more years penal servitude. The next morning he was transferred to Millbank prison, having been away just twenty-four hours from the time of his discharge. This is an extreme case, but a great majority of the convicts who are discharged from the English public-works prisons are not free more than an average of one month.

My object at the present point is to impress upon the mind of any reader who is tempted by pressing needs, however brought about, to take the first plunge into the abyss of crime, the importance of avoiding the first step in the downward path, the end of which he is not in the position or state of mind to foresee. That path and its end I know but too well. I have trodden it to where it embouches within the gloomy walls of a prison.

Would you be a slave of slaves? Before this book is ended, you will see what I mean by that expression.

The condition of the slaves on Southern plantations was most enviable when compared with the lot of prison slaves. Many of them had their little homes, not shut in by high walls, and the windows not latticed with iron bars. They were not precluded from having their wives and children around them, and thus were not cut off from giving vent to some of the affections common to all humanity. They were not obliged to restrain their smiles, their laughter, and their tears, under penalty of three days' bread and water. After the day's labor was done, they could sit at their little cabin doors and watch the children playing, or listen to the music of the fiddle and banjo, while the younger people joined in the merry dance. The air they breathed had a smack of freedom, untainted by contact with gloomy walls. At Christmas-time they could have some relaxation from labor, and take a part in enjoyments unknown at least to English convicts. For these there is no relaxation and no change. The same dreary round from day to day — the days dragging slowly into months — months into weary years, which wear heavily on both mind and body, and still no change — no hope save in prospective freedom.

No young man who occupies a respectable position in life, or creates one for himself, ever plunges deliberately into crime. On the contrary, the progress in that direction is so slow, so gradual, that, like the hour-hand of a watch, it is unnoticed. The deluded victim, blinded by conceit and confidence in his own abilities, makes such good excuses to his conscience before taking each faltering step that, while still regarding himself an honest man, as the world goes, he has already reached the brink of the abyss and can no longer save himself from the plunge

> Which lands him where the venging furies are;
> Remorse slays Hope, then hurls him to Despair.

At that stage he says to himself: "I cannot live under this degradation and shame. The power that created and rules the universe will justify me in putting an end to my life." But you won't die! At the last moment latent hope will spring up and prevent you from carrying out your determination. In my own case, the first night after the sentence (and on several occasions afterward, when numerous petitions for my release had been refused), I felt that I could not endure life longer. Once I got an improvised rope fastened in a ventilator above the door, piled some books on a rickety stool, and mounting on top put my head into the noose, and let my weight tighten it, until the blood was surging tumultuously. I was about to kick the books and stool away, when, like a flash of lightning, a voice seemed speaking in my buzzing ears: "If you do this, all is finished! Live, and you may be of benefit to your family and mankind!" With difficulty I removed the noose from my neck, and sank down horrorstricken at what I had attempted.

CHAPTER IV.

AFTER the ten-dollar affair had thrown me out of employment, I was ashamed to have recourse to any of my
friends, and being unable to pay rent longer, I sold the lease
of my house in Brooklyn, together with a part of the furniture, and removed to a suite of rooms in a tenement house in
New York. I was at that time scarcely able to provide food
for those dependent upon me. Before long I found a person
willing to join me in reopening an old-established bakery in
Grand Street. It had been closed for some time, a result of
the death of the former owner, who had made a small fortune
out of the concern. As we did not understand the business,
it was not many months before it had to be closed, and I was
again seeking employment. Having acquired some knowledge
of the business, I took charge of a bakery for a sale-agent, and
having within a month found a buyer, I received one hundred
and twenty dollars commission.

I now purchased a confectionery business in Broadway,
mostly on credit. That was a business which I understood,
but I foresaw that the rent — $3,000 per year — would eat up
the profits, although the business was making money, as I
was assured by the owner. On account of the debts still
hanging over me from the Grand Rapids failure, I was obliged
to do business in my wife's name. This confectionery busi-

(47)

ness having been, as stated, bought mostly on credit, I was just in a condition to take chances, and did not investigate very closely. I was only too glad to take hold of anything on terms which would, if only temporarily, give support to my own and my father's family. A few months' trial showed me that it was very close work to pay the rent, and that the location was too far down town. I therefore found a vacant store farther up Broadway, near Bleecker Street, at that time considered one of the best locations for retail business in New York.

I had taken this store the 15th of September, the rent of seventeen dollars for each week-day to begin on the 1st of October ensuing. This interval was allowed me in which to put in the fittings and remove from down town. On the day of removal I had but sixteen dollars, and was in debt several hundreds for labor and material in fitting up. By the terms of the lease I was bound to pay the rent monthly in advance. How was this to be accomplished? On the first of October, the day on which the new store was opened, I had, nevertheless, not only paid the rent but also part of my other indebtedness, and had as fine a place as any of the kind then in New York. I will now explain the nature of the financiering which enabled me to meet those liabilities. It will be seen that my plan was not the newest in the world, viz: Paying off one debt by making another elsewhere a little larger. Some readers may have heard of such a process even as late as 1888. I found a young man with six hundred dollars who offered to loan it to me on the security of my store fixtures, provided I would employ him at fifty dollars a month as long as I held the money, to which I agreed.

From October 1st to January 1st, the business was so prosperous that I had paid off more than four hundred dollars of the old debt, and the six hundred to the young man, as I did not really require his services. The net profit for the three months was over one thousand dollars. This was the retail trade alone; and as I contemplated selling at wholesale

1 Austin Bidwell. 2 Geo. McDonald. 3 Officer. 4 Geo. Bidwell. 5 Officer. 6 Edward Hills. 7 Mr. Straight, Q.C.

McDONALD SPEAKING TO MR. STRAIGHT, Q. C., DURING THE TRIAL.

in a short time, it seemed clear that I had struck a mine. Now let the reader see how I lost that finely-established business. It may be remembered that I had some bills printed to advertise the " Coffee-Roaster." I had by accident ordered them of a printer named Hilton ; and as he seemed to me a fair-minded and honest man, our acquaintance ripened into a warm friendship, at least on my part.

On the first of January, after paying off the six hundred dollars, I saw that I needed the use of a like amount for a while longer, but believed I could obtain it for less than fifty dollars per month. My first intention was to borrow it from a wealthy New England relative, but on explaining the situation to my friend Hilton, he immediately proposed what he held to be a better plan. He had only enough means to carry on his own business, and as I felt a prejudice, as did my wife, against letting any relative know that we were obliged to borrow, I accepted his plan, which was as follows : I was to give him my notes signed in blank ; he was to purchase goods to the amount of one thousand dollars from whoever would accept my note in payment.

It was proposed that the goods should be purchased on six months' credit ; these I was to sell, at perhaps a small loss, and have the use of the money until the note or notes became due. The plan on paper looked fine ; but as I afterwards discovered, it not only ruined my reputation, but got me " taken in and done for" in an exceedingly " clever way " (as the English put it). The reasons Hilton gave for wanting more than one note, and those signed in blank, were, to give his own words, " I don't know what amount I shall buy at one place, and can fill out the note accordingly. Of course the people to whom I give the note will think it is one which you have paid out in the regular course of business. If they come to ask you about it, tell them it is all right, and will be paid when due." I had no objection to doing this, for I had not a doubt of my ability to meet the obligation. The next day a gentleman called and showed me my note for five or

4

six hundred dollars, and asked me if I expected to pay it at maturity. I replied, "Certainly," and he went away. I saw Hilton the same evening and asked him if he had received the goods for my note. He replied: "The merchant was not satisfied, and concluded not to accept it in payment for the goods." "What did you do with the note?" I asked. "I tore it up," he replied. Having complete confidence in his integrity, and above all in his friendship, I did not distrust him. The next day another note was brought to me with precisely the same result.

Hilton came to me for more blank notes, and I gave him a number, but, as a business precaution, required him to give me the same number of his own signed in blank. The readiness with which he complied increased my confidence that he was acting toward me in good faith.

For the next month, gentlemen frequently came to me with my notes for various sums; and, incredible as it may seem, I continued to swallow down Hilton's assurances that the parties, after making inquiries, had refused to complete the transaction. With childlike simplicity I also accepted his assurance that he always destroyed the notes. Owing to circumstances, I did not ascertain the entire truth until several years afterwards, or just before I left for England — an excursion which cost me the best years of my life. These are the facts: Hilton had discovered the names and addresses of my references, who were business men of high standing in New York. He did not make the purchases in person, but through a broker. This man paid for the goods with my notes, giving the names of my references, then delivered them over to Hilton. When I left New York, later on, to sell my new invention (see next chapter), he still had a number of my notes signed in blank, and, on the strength of the references, continued to "buy" goods — how long, and to what amount, I have never known to this day. At all events, money represented by the amount of the notes brought to me for only a month, before I left New York, must have been twenty thousand dollars, and from facts discovered later I am satisfied that Hilton received goods, of all kinds, to the amount of thirty or forty thousand dollars.

Some months later I called on Mr. Erastus Titus, one of my references above mentioned, to pay a balance of twenty dollars due him. He not being in, I paid the amount to his son, Erastus Titus, Jr.—still a resident of New York—and subsequently I had frequent occasion to recall a remark which he made when I handed him the money: "I always said that you would pay us."

At the moment the remark seemed to be *apropros* to nothing, and I let it pass; but occasionally afterwards, when I came in contact with those who had known about my Broadway business, I could perceive from their manner that something was wrong. These had doubtless heard of the huge swindle which Hilton had perpetrated in my name, and supposed that I, being the chief actor, of course "knew all about it," and thought any reference to the subject might hurt my feelings; therefore I obtained no clue to the truth until long afterwards, as explained elsewhere. It was in some degree the inexplicable "cold-shouldering," as above intimated, that helped me onward in the path which led ultimately to the great catastrophe of my life.

In all such cases it would be better to state frankly to a friend what is causing one to regard another coldly, thus giving an opportunity for explanations which would relieve or confirm the suspicions.

The "goods" comprised furniture for a four-story, brownstone front in upper New York, where I afterwards called on Hilton; horses and carriage, printing machinery and material, etc. He conducted this matter so skillfully that, for years after, although I saw his style of living was wonderfully improved, I never even suspected that he had received anything for the blank notes I had put in his possession. Indeed, I felt so confident he had destroyed them, that in turn I destroyed those he had given me, although some years after I discovered one which had been overlooked. All this occurred in the year 1862. During the Rebellion, this man Hilton went into the manufacture, in New York, of blank notes and bonds for the Confederate government. Of course he had to do all this secretly, and get his productions smuggled through the lines.

I was not aware of this till I called at the Ludlow Street jail, in 1864, in response to a letter he had written me. He was then confined by order of the United States government. He had been imprisoned at first in Fort Lafayette. The means acquired by the negotiation of my notes had enabled him to enlarge his printing establishment, and open a book printing and publishing house. He had soon after begun printing Confederate notes and bonds, and had thus made a good deal of money. He had previously so much faith in my verdant simplicity, combined with stupidity, that he — up to the time I left for England — told me all his secrets without reserve, and especially after he became aware that I had taken to " ways that are dark " to obtain money. When I saw him in Ludlow Street jail, or " House of Detention for United States Prisoners," as its numerous inmates called it, I found him seated in the interior court-yard, tipped back in his chair against the wall, with his heels up in true Saratoga style. At that time I had never been imprisoned, and my ideas of the internal management of jails and prisons were as crude as those of ordinary outsiders. Finding him in such a place, apparently so comfortable, about the following conversation ensued :

"Well, old fellow, you don't seem to be in such bad quarters, after all. I thought they had you behind the bolts and bars."

"Oh," he replied, "I make that all O. K. I have only to give the keepers a proper 'douceur' to do as I like. I am out here or walking about the place all day, and in the evening, after there is no longer danger of a visit from any of the government authorities, one of the keepers goes home with me. You see I take supper and breakfast at home, and get back here in good season in the morning."

" But what about your dinner, cigars, etc. ?"

" My dinner is sent to me from a restaurant, and I send out for cigars, fruit, or anything else I want."

" Does the time hang at all heavy on your hands ?"

" Oh, no ; I read the papers, have a game of billiards with one of the deputy marshals in the officers' quarters, see any friends who may call, adjust and arrange business matters connected with the printing-office, and before realizing it the time has come for me to start home."

" But how did you get into this scrape ?"

" I had a contract from the Confederate government to engrave the plates and print fifty million dollars of their blank notes and bonds. I purchased the tools and material required, and had some reliable men — I mean good rebels — who understood engraving, printing, etc., sent to me by the Confeds. These men worked all night in my establishment, while I carried on the usual business in the daytime. They came to the printing-office after my day workmen had gone home. I let them in from a side street, and they left early enough in the morning to avoid any contact with the day hands. Everything connected with the Confederate job was locked in a room of which I held the key. I struck off several million dollars, and smuggled all through the lines safely to Richmond. The Confederate government had agreed to pay me in gold, but they were so hard up that I received nothing."

" Well, what did you do then ?"

" I found that the two skilled workmen sent me by the Confederate government were quite willing to take part in a new scheme which suggested itself as soon as I found the Confeds had gone back on me, and that was to fill in our blank bills, notes, and bonds, with the names of Jeff. Davis and others, in exact imitation of the genuine signatures of which I had specimens."

" But, my dear fellow, that was forgery, was it not ?"

"Forgery be ——! Why, it was aiding the government to squelch its enemies and to put down treason and rebellion, by weakening their credit! Don't you see that by flooding the South as I have done with the counterfeit, that the rebels themselves have begun to distrust all the genuine paper issued by their own government? Can't you realize that I have done more than the armies to break the backbone of the rebellion? And see how I am served!"

At this point he became very indignant; and I may remark that my pseudo friend was not the only one who, in those stirring times, was changed from a warm rebel sympathizer into a good patriot by imprisonment in the casemates of Fort Lafayette.

"By some means," Hilton continued, "the U. S. Marshal got an inkling of what I was about, and had my place watched until he was satisfied of the truth of his information. He then made a descent on my printing-office, and carried off every thing connected with the engraving and printing of blank notes. At the same time he had me arrested, and consigned to pace the ramparts of Fort Lafayette by day, and sleep in one of its bomb-proofs by night."

"That was rather rough on you, but you had put your foot into the trap in the first place by supplying the rebels with the sinews of war, and I am rather of the opinion you have got your just deserts; but tell me how you got transferred from Fort Lafayette?"

"By using twenty thousand dollars in lubricating the wheels of the law machine, the same as I use oil to make my printing-machinery run smoothly."

"Very good; but how are you going to get out of the fix?"

"Oh, I have made that all O. K., and will be free in a few days; but it has all cost me a mint of money, and I shall be hard up again for some time, especially as I can't run the 'Confederate' any longer."

I have recounted this conversation of Hilton's as an example of how men in their own estimation never do wrong, and how they plaster that word over in their consciences. Readers who are skilled in the science of casuistry may solve this problem: Was it right for Hilton to forge the names of Jeff. Davis, Benjamin, and other Confederate government officials, if he really intended to flood the rebel States with counterfeit bank and treasury notes for the ultimate purpose of crippling that government?

CHAPTER V.

WHILE Hilton was trying, as I supposed, in vain to get me the small amount I lacked to make my business easier during the dull months of January and February, I had evolved out of my brain an improved steam-kettle; and as soon as I saw the Hilton plan was liable to fail, I determined to raise the necessary capital from my invention.

I left the store in charge of a brother-in-law, before then out of employment, and, with his family, living at my house. He was an utter failure as a business man, though a " plodder " who afterwards became rich in the " turtle " way.

I learned subsequently that, when any one came into my Broadway store and asked where I was, or any other question, he would not look at them, but remain in stupid silence. I doubt not but some of those to whom Hilton paid my notes called to see me, and being thus treated thought I must have ran away, and later conferred with my landlord. At all events *he* called to see me, and being thus received, went straightway and let the store for the following year to another party.

In the meantime, with no suspicion of what was passing in New York, I was having unexpected success with the sale of my steam-kettle, and sent home several hundred dollars to

(56)

HILTON READING ON THE PARADE—FORT LAFAYETTE.

pay the next month's rent and other expenses. Of course I was in high spirits, believing that I was, after all my struggles and vicissitudes, fairly settled in a money-making business, and that I should be no longer cramped for means to carry it on.

I wrote to my wife frequently, but as I was going from place to place I could not tell definitely where a letter would reach me. At the end of four weeks I had received none, and I started for home triumphant, having cleared above expenses more than one thousand dollars. On my arrival in New York I was utterly dismayed at finding the store closed, and a placard in the window which read thus: "This store will be occupied by Messrs. ——, with a full assortment of Mourning Goods of the latest Parisian styles. Opening day on Wednesday, May 1, 1863."

During my absence the business had been grossly mismanaged; and it appeared that my brother-in-law accepted of a small sum from the new lessees to vacate the store at once — a transaction on a par with his other business achievements.

I learned that the gentlemen who had rented the store while I was absent, paid four hundred dollars for the privilege of possession before the first of May. Had not the store been closed on my arrival, I could in all probability have held possession.

Thus, I found myself once more afloat, and for a few days was greatly depressed and discouraged. Very soon I left New York with my only remaining hope, my steam-kettle. Those who had been victimized by Hilton with my notes, after the Broadway store was closed did not know where to find me, and as the notes became due I received no notice from the holders of my paper. Had 1 received a single notice I should have discovered all the facts. If I had remained in New York, the gentlemen who acted as my references would have informed me; although Hilton had taken every precaution to cover his connection with the business by the employment of a broker, I believe there was sufficient evidence to have shown up the whole affair.

The breaking up of my Broadway business started me on the journey which brought me in contact with one of the most skillful commercial swindlers ever known — Frank Kibbe, of whom the reader will learn more about hereafter.

Within a few months, I had made several thousand dollars from the sale of my steam-kettle, and I began to think of establishing myself once more in business.

During my travels, I had made a short stay in Toronto, and had ascertained there was an excellent opening there for a wholesale confectionery business.

I soon hired a large warehouse well suited to the purpose, and fitted it up in proper shape. I sent for my family to remove from New York, and soon after their arrival I had the factory in operation. Now for the first time in my life I had started a business on a safe foundation, with ten thousand dollars to carry it on. People conversant with my previous mishaps said: "Surely, Bidwell has the thing right this time." But he did not have it right. It would be difficult for the reader to imagine how I was obliged to abandon the business almost at the start.

When I first concluded to make the venture, gold was at a premium of about twenty per cent., greenbacks being worth about eighty cents in gold. I reasoned thus to myself: "There is no better security in the world than a United States greenback, and it is absurd that it should not command its full value in gold. Other people must look at the matter in the same light, and see that it is nothing but the operations in Wall Street that put greenbacks below par. Such an unnatural state of things cannot continue, and it will not be long before the good sense of the majority will predominate and the bills be worth their face."

That sort of reasoning shows how "fresh" I still was in financial matters. I kept on investing in the Toronto business, holding my capital in greenbacks to exchange for Canada money only as fast as became necessary. Gold kept going up, up, till by the time I had my factory ready for successful operation it had reached above two hundred and eighty.

To exchange my ten thousand at the rate current in Toronto would leave me with only about three thousand dollars capital. I regretfully abandoned the business, with the loss of three-fourths of my capital; for, in order to close up matters, I was obliged to sell one hundred dollars in greenbacks for thirty dollars in Canada currency, which was the equivalent of gold. At this time, I sent my father, with the others of the family, to Chicago, and for the first time since marriage my wife and I were living by ourselves.

Previous to the Toronto fiasco, while staying at a hotel in Buffalo, engaged in the sale of my patent kettle, I had gradually fallen into the habit of passing a part of my time evenings either in watching the game of billiards, or in playing myself. On several of these occasions I had noticed a man playing, who was also a guest at the hotel. His general appearance was that of a business man. He was above the medium height, slim, with auburn hair, light complexion, a blonde mustache, and a pair of noticeably large, light-blue, restless eyes. He, like myself, seemed to be alone, and to have considerable leisure. One evening I was watching a game, when he came forward and asked me to play. I accepted the invitation, and had several games with him before I left Buffalo.

Some months after this, I was staying at the old Fountain Hotel in Baltimore. I found the restless, shifty-eyed man, whose acquaintance I had formed in Buffalo, stopping at the same hotel, and on the strength of the former meeting we passed our leisure time in playing billiards. He led me to believe that he was traveling on some kind of mercantile business, and it was not long before I told him about my steam-kettle. He gave me his name as Frank Kibbe, and my acquaintance with that man proved the most unfortunate event of my life. With the exterior and manners of a business man — active and indefatigable in the prosecution of his projects — insinuating in his demeanor toward strangers — plausible and fluent in speech — in private life uncommonly dissolute — fickle and false toward those with whom he became in any way connected,— he did not possess even the redeeming trait known as "honor among thieves." Frank Kibbe, who came to be known as "The Rogue," would resort to any means to obtain money with which to conduct the worship of his god and goddess, Bacchus and Venus. He was a most detestable coward, although among acquaintances a blatant braggart.

I have known but one other man who resembled "The Rogue" in personal appearance, being his opposite in every other trait except that of cowardice. In this George Engles was the former's equal, and up to the time I got into an English prison he had evaded paying any legal penalties for the forgeries which had brought him in several hundred thousand, and secured him the title of "The Terror of Wall Street." Later on I shall have something more to say of this man and his operations in Wall Street and elsewhere.

After a few days Kibbe saw fit to take me into his confidence. He told me that he had a commission office in Baltimore, and after some skirmishing about, finally divulged that he was afraid to go to his office for fear of being arrested by his creditors.

"I received some goods from New York," said he, "and have turned them over to Messrs. —— & Co., commission merchants, to sell for me. I have not paid for them yet, and am afraid to go to collect the proceeds of their sale. Now, I will give you an order for the goods, and if you will take it and collect the money from —— & Co., I will give you one-half."

I saw that there was no risk in accepting and executing the offer. During my connection with New York houses, and in the struggles of the previous few years, the strict business integrity which I had brought from Michigan to New York had been slowly but surely undermined, so that I had become satisfied that if I lived up to *legal* honesty, it was all required of me by the generality of men. I had reached the point where the only question which presented itself was : " Shall I get into trouble by doing so and so ? " Not, " Is this thing right — shall I be doing as I would wish to be done by ? "

I recalled how Mr. O——, a partner in the house where I was first engaged in New York, then esteemed an honorable man, and now one of the magnates in Wall street, who, when his house failed, and I had located with B—— & H——, brought in one of his former customers, and recommended him for credit. With the goods thus obtained the customer paid, as doubtless previously agreed between them, an old debt he owed Mr. O——'s house, then failed himself, and the house of B—— & H—— got nothing. Although that man was not my customer, and I had no acquaintance with him, the fact that I was then with B—— & H—— was what influenced Mr. O—— to bring his debtor there. At any rate the firm regarded the matter in that light, and it was a prime cause of their unfair treatment of me after that occurrence.

I agreed to Kibbe's proposition, and on presenting the order at the commission house, I was at once paid the proceeds of the sale, about one thousand dollars. Instead of keeping the whole amount as Kibbe would have done, I returned to the rendezvous and paid him one-half as agreed. He seemed, evidently, a good deal surprised at my good faith in handing him the money. All this time I was doing well with my steam-kettle, and slowly accumulating capital for a fresh start. After I had paid Kibbe the five hundred dollars he revealed to me how he managed, without cash payment, to get the goods shipped in large quantities to any address and place he desired. Had I not just returned from collecting one thousand dollars for goods acquired in that manner, I could not have believed it possible ; but, as will be seen, the scheme was not only possible, but not at all difficult. After he had let me deeper into the secrets of his business I could not restrain the thought, " Surely, Kibbe's method of doing business beats my steam-kettle all to nothing ! "

It has been a question with me as to whether revelations regarding the *modus operandi* of swindling in its various forms would be productive of more evil than good. On the one side there may be some who will imagine that they have only to go and do likewise, in order to sweep in money without stint. On the other will be merchants and business men, especially the inexperienced, who will learn how swindlers operate, and be placed upon their guard.

To any who may be already reduced to that state of mind and laxity of true business principles which would prompt them to apply anything they read here to aid in obtaining money dishonestly, I will make a few observations. First, whatever success you might have at the start, the result can only prove disastrous; that you may rely upon. I go farther: no person can commit a moral or physical wrong without in some way paying for it thereafter. For striking examples of the truth of this axiom, see other chapters.

When I first joined Kibbe, the plans of swindling here revealed were unknown to the police, and so far as they were concerned, we had little to fear; still it will be seen that we got into trouble occasionally. Though we caused merchants to lose goods amounting to hundreds of thousands of dollars, we lost the proceeds of their sale in one way and another; and I think I may safely make the assertion that but one swindler ever known to me escaped final punishment in a prison. That man was George Engles, the bank forger, who, through not being imprisoned, and giving full reign to indulgences, died prematurely; whereas incarceration at intervals, where he must have lived steadily, would have given his physical system an opportunity to recuperate, so that he would have survived, perhaps, to old age.

The last sentence contains a truth applicable to the lives of all criminals, and the question it suggests is worthy to be considered by our legislators and reformers.

While in prison myself, I took every opportunity to question prisoners of all classes, from the sneak thief to the bank

and jewelry burglar, as to the chances of escaping imprisonment.   The reply was generally to the following effect:
" Well, we all get there, first or last.   Some fellows have better
luck than others.   The most of us are no sooner out than we
are ' copped,' sometimes the very first time we try to ' pull a
swag.'   After a man has been in once, he seldom keeps out
more than twelve or eighteen months, and but few so long as
that.   It depends a good deal on the ' booze'; if a man boozes
much, he 's safe enough to be on the wrong side of the bars
within a few days or weeks.   Most of us would have been
killed long ago by drink and dissipation, if we had been let
alone; but they run us in, and by the time the ' lagging' is
done we are free of disease and ready for another splurge."

CHAPTER VI.

AFTER a few days had elapsed, Kibbe suggested the idea of going to another city and opening a "commission house." I readily agreed to his proposition, and very soon we "dropped down" in Providence, R. I. We rented a large store immediately without payment in advance, for when I went to see the owner he appeared satisfied that everything was all right and gave me the key. We had a magnificent sign put up, and furnished the office with desks, a set of books, and a full supply of stationery. As soon as we were ready for business, we sent several small orders to New York and other places. Before leaving New York we had purchased and paid for one hundred barrels of flour, and other saleable bulky goods, enough to make a show in our new store.

We opened an account at a bank and deposited two or three thousand dollars. All this had been accomplished without giving any references, and under false names. False names! I had, up to the hour of meeting "The Rogue" in Baltimore, considered that any man who would resort to the use of another name than his own, was beneath contempt. Alas! that I had sunk so low and taken such a stride into crime in so short a time!

In addition to Kibbe's specious arguments, and the more substantial influence of the $500, which fell to my share in

ONE WHO HAS BEEN ROBBED IDENTIFYING THE THIEF AT NEWGATE.

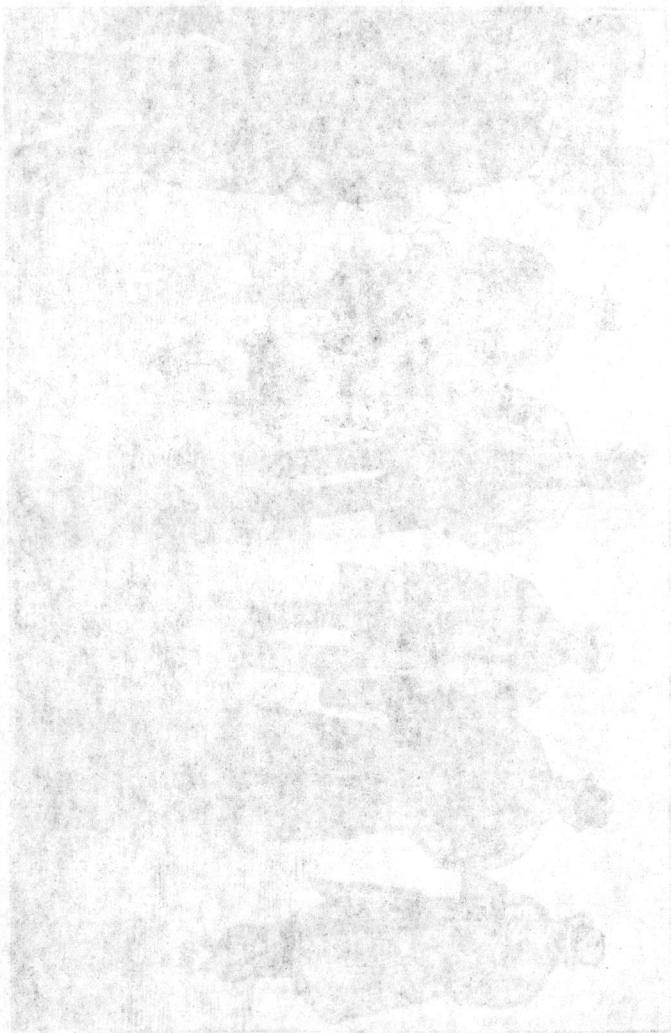

Baltimore, I attempted to justify my actions to my conscience in this wise: "It is dishonest for a man to obtain goods on credit when he has a doubt of his ability to pay for them; and still worse if he purchases with no intention to pay. But the first is done every day by firms that are in a shaky condition, with the hope that they may tide over their difficulties. The second is also of frequent occurrence, where firms know that they are going to fail and expect to make a settlement with their creditors at, say, twenty cents on the dollar. In regard to those loose merchants who deliver their goods to strangers, without references, they deserve a lesson on 'how to do business,' and the loss of a few hundred dollars is but a fair price to pay for their schooling." Of course this was false reasoning on my part, but it shows again how prone men are to argue in a way that makes the conclusion coincide with the desire.

All the small orders we had sent by mail were shipped and duly received by us. We soon sent checks to pay for these, and ordered at the same time a larger bill. Our store was soon crammed full of goods, which we sold, paid for, and then made still larger orders. These were filled, and while some of the shipments were on the way, Kibbe arranged with me to go to New York. He was to remain behind and sell some of the goods, but the bulk of them were to be shipped to me. Accordingly I left for New York via Boston. On arrival I found neither goods nor letters, as had been agreed. Becoming suspicious, I took the first train back to Providence, and arriving the following morning, found the store closed. On inquiry I ascertained that Kibbe had sold out the stock to a wholesale grocer at a considerable discount for cash, and had left for parts unknown. I found about two thousand dollars' worth of goods at the depot, which I sold — and then followed his example.

The result of this operation was, that I left with about the same sum that I had when we started the swindle. This was but an example of how swindlers occasionally "beat" each other.

5

As Kibbe and myself were passing along Broad Street the evening before I left for New York, he halted in front of a jewelry establishment, and pointing out a cross set with dia. monds said: "I am going to have that; just wait here a moment." He entered the place, and through the window I saw him present our business card to the proprietor, who then came to the window and taking out the cross handed it to him. "The Rogue," after a little delay, came out, and show- ing me the cross exclaimed triumphantly: "Everything is lovely, and the goose hangs high; he is coming down to the office in a few days to get a check in payment for this $400 cross." As we had closed our place of business before he came, not again to reopen, it is superfluous to remark that the jeweler called in vain for the check.

Kibbe, having "left me in the lurch," as stated, in com- pany with a friend I started on a hunt to find him and make him disgorge the $20,000, or all he had. We first went to New York, but could find no trace of him anywhere in the city. I now procured a false beard for my friend, and having shaved off my own, we thought ourselves so thoroughly disguised that Kibbe could not recognize us. We took the Hudson River steamer for Albany; but there we could see nothing that looked like a bogus commission office. Our plan was to go through the business streets, and wherever we saw a new sign to satisfy ourselves that Kibbe had nothing to do with it; also to visit the principal hotels at the dinner-hour and watch, one of us the public, the other the private entrance. Finding no clue in Albany, we decided to start for New Orleans via Buffalo, Cleveland, Toledo, Detroit, Chicago, and St. Louis. We stopped over at Rochester and one or two other of the larger places on the line of the New York Central Railroad, at length reaching Buffalo. In passing along Main Street I suddenly exclaimed:

"Hello! see that new sign across the street, 'Henry Harvey Short & Co.' I think it has a Kibbe look."

"Oh, don't flatter yourself with any such good luck," replied my friend.

"Well, let us make an investigation of the establishment," said I. We soon found a suitable place for him to put on his false beard, and he started on a reconnoitering expedition, while I remained at some distance away, but yet in sight of the suspected place. He went into the store, and very soon came back and joined me.

"Well, friend, what did you see?" I asked.

"I saw no sign of Kibbe," he replied; "but there was a young man sitting in the office, who pretended to be very busy writing when he saw me enter. There was a set of new books. and the place had a new look all around. The store runs back to the next street, and is about one hundred and fifty feet deep, with no merchandise in it."

"Very well, my boy," said I; "it is now one o'clock, and the young man will soon be going out to lunch, and if he is with Kibbe, will go to meet him, for he seldom goes to his place of business. You keep me in sight, and when the young man comes out I will follow him."

I had not waited long before the young man came out of the store and went straight to Bonney's Hotel, which was at that time a high-class commercial place. After he had disappeared within, I walked carelessly into the office, examined the register, and thought one of the names entered looked like Kibbe's writing. I left the hotel, and sent back my friend to inquire if Mr. Kibbe was in. The hotel clerk said he thought not. I afterwards learned from Kibbe himself that he was at that identical moment in the dining-room, and that as soon as my friend had retired, the clerk went into the dining-room and whispered to him that a suspicious-looking man with a bushy beard had just inquired for him.

In the meantime I had hastened to the police headquarters near by, and got a detective to come with me to the hotel. When we arrived, he went into the office, while I hurried to the corner, where I could watch the door of the private entrance Just as I reached the corner, I saw Kibbe step out and, without seeing me, hasten down the side street in the opposite direction. I ran and called the detective, who rushed around the corner after him — my friend and I acting as Kibbe's rear guard on the "double quick," he having about one square the start. It was a quiet part of the city, and as there were but few people in the streets, we had the fun all to ourselves. Fun! Well, some people might call it fun; but, although in those days I had good wind and speed, for a long time it was all I could do to hold my own with the quarry. The detective was a short, stumpy man, and as I passed him he was blowing like a porpoise. After a mile or so I caught up with "The Rogue," who had given out, exhausted. I said to him:

"Kibbe, you served me a dirty trick after my bringing you the five hundred dollars for the Baltimore job, when you know I could have kept it all! You had better settle at once, before the officer comes up, or it will be worse for you!"

"George," he replied, in the most cringing, cowardly manner, "I have only six hundred dollars by me. I will give you that amount, if you will let me go, and settle the balance to-morrow."

"I don't believe you," I replied. "You have the money; it is in the breast-pocket of your vest. Don't I know something of your ways and your rascality?"

But he insisted that he had but the sum named. My friend and the detective now came up. I told the detective that the man owed me a large sum, and that he was trying to put me off with six hundred dollars, which I would not accept. At this time I was an "innocent" regarding the ways of so-called detectives. While we were walking to headquarters, Kibbe was in great consternation. On our arrival there I still refused to settle with him for the six hundred dollars, and he at last offered to go with me to a friend of his and borrow the balance. In the meantime the detective had a consultation with the chief-of-police, in his private office. They then came into the room where we were, and when I explained what Kibbe had offered to do, the chief said: "We want our commission, and the best way is to let the officer go with him, while you wait here." I at once acceded to the arrangement. Kibbe and the detective left, and in half an hour the latter came back alone and went direct into the chief's office. In a few minutes they came out, and I asked, "Where is Kibbe?" The chief answered: "He has gone where he likes, and you had better do the same at once, or we will show you what it is to get us to arrest a man without a warrant. Come, clear out — quick!" I arose and started to leave, he following me, and as I reached the door, literally kicked me out. Such an indignity had never been put upon me before — or behind. Considering the circumstances, I saw that this was another occasion where discretion was the better part of valor, and therefore my friend and I quietly walked away. I was beginning to reap some of the harvest which surely ripens for all who enter into the conscienceless strife for gold, more gold.

> We read traditions in the storied page
> Which give us glimpses of a better age —
> That fabled time when, in the days of old,
> 'T is said men had no raging thirst for gold;
> But, when all ancient history we read,
> We find them tainted by the same fierce greed
> That now-a days sends thousands, in despair,
> To prison cells, and all the tortures there,
> Because, in their engrossing strife for wealth,
> They lost life's truest aims and moral health.
> Alas! 't is fearful madness, madness wild —
> In strife for gold to be misled, defiled.

My friend and I immediately began anew our search for "The Rogue," resolved that when once more in our power, we would employ no detective. We visited the store of Henry Harvey Short & Co., and interviewed the young man, whom we discovered was the owner of the triple name. I at once revealed the story of my acquaintance with Kibbe and its sequel. I informed the youth that he was being used for a tool, as I had been, and that I had no doubt it was "The Rogue's" intention to gather up all the proceeds of the swindle, and

leave him in the lurch. It was not long before I won his confidence completely, and he told me his story in substance as
follows :

"My father carries on the painting business in the city of
Brooklyn, and is now a man of some property. He gave me
a good education and on leaving school got me a place as
assistant bookkeeper in New York. I got on very well for
three or four years, until I fell in with a set of fast young
fellows, stayed out late nights, visited the theaters, billiard-
rooms, and other places less respectable. To cut the story
short, my employers became tired of my lax way of doing
work, and after repeated warnings, discharged me. I had
been living at home some months when I met Kibbe at a bil-
liard-room, and he told me if I would come out here with
him, I should make a good many thousand dollars, without
risk, in a few weeks."

The young man having informed me that "The Rogue"
had written him a note asking him to cross the Niagara river
at Black Rock into Canada, and meet him there, I persuaded
Mr. Henry Harvey Short to write an answer, stating that he
would meet him across the river next day. An hour before
the time appointed, my friend, H. H. S., and myself took the
street-cars to Black Rock, crossing the river on a ferry-boat.
While on board the boat my friend and I kept in the cabin,
our companion remaining outside on the bow. As soon as
the boat touched the Canada shore, Kibbe came out of a house
near the landing to meet his partner, who said to him as my
friend and I approached, "Mr. Bidwell and a friend have
come over with me, for I thought it best that you should see
them and settle."

Kibbe looked scared and disconcerted, but stood his ground.

I asked him "How did you arrange matters with the
detective ?"

"You refused the six hundred dollars," replied Kibbe,
"but as soon as we were outside the door, the officer said it
was enough for him, and if I would give him the money, he

and the chief would kick you out of the office. I thought," he added with a grin, "it was a fair offer, the closing part of it in particular, so I handed it over and came here to keep out of your way."

"Well, you have thrown away six hundred dollars for the luxury of having the chief kick me out of his office. Now, Mr. Kibbe, if you don't settle at once I shall return the chief's compliment with interest." I knew where he carried his money, and he convinced me that he had but a little over two thousand five hundred dollars on his person. He then said: "I will give you two thousand four hundred dollars cash, and turn over bills of lading for goods now at the depot and wharves to the amount of eight thousand dollars, consisting of flour, beef, pork, lard, oil, butter, etc."

To this arrangement I agreed, and we all returned to Buffalo. After arriving in that city we concluded the business, and the same evening "The Rogue" and his partner took the train for New York. The next morning I got an inspector to brand the flour, and took his certificate of inspection, together with samples, to a commission merchant. He took the samples "on change," and returned in a few moments, having sold the entire lot, and upon being handed the inspector's certificate, he gave me a check for the whole amount, less his commission. I got the check cashed at five minutes to three. I state the time merely to show that, had I been five minutes later, and obliged to stay over till next day, it is more than likely I should have had some of the parties who shipped the goods on my hands. Such an occurrence might have cost me all the money in my possession.

I close this chapter with a newspaper article, detailing a somewhat remarkable series of small, swindling operations.

[From The New York Tribune, 1867]
FALSE PRETENCE EXTRAORDINARY — ARREST OF TWO SKILLFUL OPERATORS.

Last night Detective Officer Richard Field apprehended George Hayes and John Howard, and took them to the Leonard Street police station, where they were detained by Capt. Petty. The operations of these prisoners are the most remarkable that have come to the knowledge of the police for many a day. About two years ago they opened an office on the northwest corner of Broad and South Streets, the business being transacted under the name of H. K. Clinton. Clinton (alias Hayes) purchased $150 worth of carpeting of Messrs. Humpfell & Hamlin, of Broadway, and of Messrs. Allen and Brothers, of No. 88 Leonard Street, $260 worth of silk cloaks. and these were delivered, with bill, at Clinton's office. Of course Clinton was not in at the time of the delivery but would return soon, and of course Howard received the goods, and the messengers who had delivered the goods were requested to call within an hour. When they did call they found an empty room, the goods having been removed and the firm having taken French leave. The couple next opened shop at No. 62 Broadway, and transacted business under the name of W. A Stewart. While here Hayes (now Stewart) bought $600 worth of furs of Mr. M. M. Backus, of No. 532 Broadway, and gave him a worthless check therefor; bought $500 worth of cloths of Messrs. Abernethy & Co., of No. 23 Warren street, and gave that firm a worthless check; purchased wagons valued at $585 of Messrs. Brewster & Baldwin, of Broadway and Tenth Street, and defrauded them, and many other tradesmen whose names have not been made known. The business was next resumed at No. 81 Beaver Street and there the chief was known as Wallace. They here defrauded Mr. John J. Smith, of No. 183 Broadway, having bought of him $1,857 worth of umbrellas, and of Messrs. J. F. Smith & Co., of Broadway and Catharine Lane, they got $345 worth of coach harness. Next they opened an office at No. 15 William Street, and Hayes became R. M. Kingsland, and as such victimized Mr. John B. Dunham of No. 111 East Thirteenth Street, to the tune of $1,200 for pianos, and Messrs. Betts & Nichols of No. 349 Broadway, to the amount of $275 for harness. Moving again, they adopted a new name, and opened an office at No. 61 Broadway, as W. S Hyatt & Co. Here they defrauded many merchants, among them Messrs. Lacy & Maker, of No. 27 Chambers Street, $124; Mr. M. A. Coburn, of No. 152 Fourth Avenue, $175, and Messrs. R. W. Tinson & Co., of No. 50 Broadway, $123

The next exploit of Hayes and Howard was at No. 106 South

INTERIOR OF AN ENGLISH CONVICT PRISON.

Street, where Hayes became W. A. Stewart. While here, Hayes bought $500 worth of harness of Messrs. Townshend, Baker & Co., of No. 46 Lispenard Street, and gave the firm a worthless check, ordering the purchase packed and directed to a firm in Texas, and delivered at No. 106 South Street. But unluckily for Hayes and Howard, Mr. Baker followed his harness, and finding everything wrong at No. 106 South Street, sent his check to bank to ascertain whether Hayes's check was good. On the clerk's return, the check having proved worthless, Mr. Baker seized his goods, and the rogues fled. The firm's business was next under the name of William H. Martin, and their office at No. 6 South Street. While here, Hayes bought $500 worth of flour of the Messrs. Hickman, of the New York Flour Mills, and the flour was delivered to his partner, as usual. But the game was blocked there, and Hayes, and Howard, his partner, were arrested. The entire firm was indicted by the grand jury, and six months ago a bench-warrant for their apprehension was intrusted to Officer Field; but Hayes and Howard kept out of sight until last night.

When captured in Bleecker Street, near Wooster, Hayes offered resistance. but the exhibition of a pistol quieted him, and changed his tack to a tender of his watch and $500 for his release, but Officer Field chose to deliver him to Capt. Petty.

Howard went quietly to the police station, and sullenly to a cell. He was once a clerk for a Boston dry goods firm. Hayes has been in the false pretense business in other cities, and in this city he has disposed of large quantities of spurious bank notes. It is believed that this precious couple have defrauded more than one hundred of our tradesmen, always, either by worthless checks, or by having goods delivered at their office, wherever it happened to be, and removing them therefrom as above described. They are young men of about thirty-two years of age, of exquisitely genteel address, and have been boarders at our fashionable hotels Capt. Petty will detain the prisoners in the Leonard Street police station for identification by tradesmen whom they have victimized.

It is almost unnecessary to explain that Clinton, *alias* Hayes, *alias* Stewart, was none other than the Frank Kibbe of my previous acquaintance.

Chapter VII.

PARTNER-SWINDLING — "DOCTOR" SAMUEL BOLIVAR — HOW HE "RAISED THE
WIND"—UP A TREE—THE WAY HE ROPED IN GREENHORNS—THE BOGUS
REFERENCE "DEAD BEAT"—JONES'S GRAND PIANO—THE EMPTY BOX—THE
ELM CITY ENTERPRISE COMES TO AN UNTIMELY END—MUSICAL "NOTES"—
DIAMOND CUT DIAMOND—BEATEN BY AN EX-ASSOCIATE, WHO DISAPPEARS
INTO OBSCURITY.

THE occurrences related in the previous chapter caused
considerable reflection, and after my return to New York
I looked about for openings into an honest business.

I saw an advertisement for a "partner wanted, with five
thousand dollars in cash." I called at the place designated,
and found a man seated in an arm-chair. He had a long,
heavy, brown beard, curving eyebrows, squinting bluish eyes,
rather coarse features, but on the whole not an unpleasing
countenance. He was below the medium height, and thick-
set. I afterwards found him rather gentlemanly in his address
when doing business, and able to tell a good story on all
occasions.

This man was Doctor Samuel Bolivar, as he styled himself.
He was very free in speaking to me of his antecedents after
we became acquainted, and I learned that he and his wife
boarded up town with a sister. Her house was filled with
young medical students. Bolivar had chummed in with them,
attended some of the lectures, and on several occasions had
been admitted to the wonders and horrors of the dissecting-
room. On account of an after episode in the "Doctor's" life,
it may be well for the reader to bear in mind just how he
obtained the handle to his name. He was the illegitimate son
of a Massachusetts man, and had been left to get through the

(74)

world in his own way ; and the result was that at thirty, when I met him, he possessed an amount of self-esteem, assurance, and impudence, that quite astounded me. He had been everything, and nothing very long. As a lad, he was a farmer's boy, match-peddler, newsboy, and bootblack. A little later he became a canal driver, then attempted to become a circus tumbler ; and when that aspiration was squelched by an involuntary double somersault, which landed him on his head and left a twist in his neck, he turned printer's devil. While performing the duties of this black art, he took to study, and picked up considerable knowledge of the art entitled " How to get into business on a small capital." After various experiences and adventures in his native New England, at the age of twenty he landed in New York, where he believed the goal of his ambition was in plain view. The " Doctor " had many excellent qualities, was a tender, considerate husband and father, amiable, generous, and faithful to his friends, but he was blind to the moral obliquity involved in easing strangers of their surplus money by sharp practice. I say strangers, for swindlers of his class are usually as scrupulous in their dealings with each other, or rather when they unite together to " beat " outsiders, as any class of business men. But generally speaking there is not much of the " honor among thieves " left of which we used to read in novels.

Bolivar informed me that he knew of a flourishing business to be sold, and having but five thousand dollars, which was not sufficient capital to make the purchase, he wished to find a good man to join him as partner. I told him that if the affair would bear investigation, I was ready to invest the necessary amount.

The fact that a man was willing to put in capital himself, naturally gave me a good impression, both of the man and the proposed business. He then accompanied me to a large retail grocery and provision store, and introduced me to the surviving partner. He appeared to be about sixty years of age, worn and sickly. On an examination of his books, I found that the business was really in a flourishing condition. He stated that since his partner's death, he had concluded to retire from business altogether. The price of his lease, fixtures, two horses and wagons, and the stock necessary to keep the business going, would be about ten or twelve thousand dollars. He had made an offer to Bolivar, which would give him a good business at a bargain.

So far, all seemed as satisfactory as possible; Bolivar gave me references, who spoke well of him, but knew nothing as to his means. As a precaution, I sent a friend to the place, who, accosting the proprietor, told him he was looking around to find a good business for sale, and thought he might perhaps know of one. He was informed that the place he was in was for sale, he himself intending to retire from business. After considerable conversation, my friend asked the price of the place. The proprietor offered the place to him as it was, for five thousand dollars. When my friend reported, I saw there must be a " take in " somewhere.

I called on Bolivar and said to him : " Come, Doctor, let me into your little secret, I am myself involved in speculations. I fancy we are both engaged in extracting an elixir from the ' root of all evil ' by similar processes."

After some farther parley, I told him of my friend's call at the provision store. He was at first nonplussed, but soon began to laugh, and said :

" This reminds me of a little story. Many years ago, a friend of mine went out to the Rockies to make his fortune by the discovery of a gold-mine. The first thing he discovered, after he arrived, was that his pork and flour were all consumed. He had succeeded so well in isolating himself, that, with the exception of his two pack-horses, there was not a civilized living creature within a circuit of one hundred miles. Taking his rifle, he started out to kill anything edible, from a rattlesnake to a buffalo, and before going far he caught a glimpse of some animal, and fired. He said to himself as he went through the underbrush in pursuit : ' That is a bear, and if I can make him take to a tree he cannot escape; once treed, he is my meat, and I'm sure of my dinner.' Suddenly he came to the edge of a small prairie and saw the bear crossing the open space. He did not know it was a grizzly, and taking good aim fired again. The grizzly turned, reared himself on his hind paws, and as soon as he saw his assailant, dropped down on all fours and ' went for him.' My friend took in the situation, and throwing away his gun ran straight towards a tree, which he reached just in time; and thus, instead of having treed the bear, he was himself treed. Well, neighbor, I guess instead of treeing you as I expected, you have got me up a tree."

" Doctor, tell me how you manage to make any money out of this partner business," I said to him a few days later.

" There are several ways of operating by which I rope in greenhorns," he replied; " the one I was trying on you is the best. I find a really paying business which the owner is anxious to sell for cash. I then ascertain the very lowest figures for which he would sell it. Then, I say : ' Now, Mr. Blank, I can get you a cash customer on one condition. You say that your place is worth seven thousand dollars, but that you will take five thousand dollars in cash. At your highest estimate you are not charging much for your good will, and you ought to know that the good will of an established trade is worth more than the fixtures, lease, and stock in trade. Yours is worth three thousand dollars. That would bring the value of your place up to ten thousand dollars. Now, sir, you set your price at that figure; I will get a man to go in partnership, who will pay his half, and I will give you a check for my half — five thousand dollars — which after its delivery you are to hand back to me in private.'"

" So far, very well, but in case your profit is tied up in the business, and you are bound to devote your time to it, what about that?" I asked.

" In the course of a month," he replied, "I manage to make my partner dissatisfied with me; then I get him to make me an offer of how much he will give or take. Whatever it is, I accept, get all the money I can down, and make an agreement secured by a mortgage on the place for the balance, in small payments. The result is that I get my pay or the place comes into my hands, in which case I have no trouble to get the money out of it."

In return for "Doctor" Samuel Bolivar's confidence, I related to him the little plans and devices for getting other people's money, into which Kibbe had initiated me. He thought each one of them a splendid way to make a fortune, and quite superior to his partnership operations. As a consequence he wished me to go into business with him, right away.

It will be perceived that from the moment I gave way to the seduction of Kibbe's offer of letting me make $500 so easily and safely at Baltimore, I became an apt pupil, thinking to let myself into such a way of obtaining money only so far as to get enough to enable me to establish a legitimate business. Certainly I believed that one or two months would do it.

Not long after our first meeting I directed Bolivar to hire an office, or suite of offices, on the ground floor at the corner of Beaver and Broad Streets. These were tastily fitted up and a large sign placed over each front. After this, I took another man with me to New Haven, Conn. Before leaving New York I had purchased an old sign (I have forgotten the name of the firm on it — call it Smith, Brown & Co.), and shipped it to New Haven. On our arrival there, we rented a store and put up the old sign.

Leaving my assistant at the New Haven store, I returned to New York and found everything ready to begin operations. I took the fourth and last member of our party — call him Jones — and went around with him. When we came to a wholesale place, that I had selected as likely to fill our order, I sent him in and told him what to buy, and to what amount. I remained near by while he made the purchase in the name of the New Haven firm, of which he claimed to be the head. After the purchase was completed, on the usual terms, he gave as reference Messrs. L—— & Co., our bogus New York firm. If any one called on L—— & Co., to inquire as to the responsibility of the New Haven firm, Bolivar would say, " We should not hesitate to ship them goods to the amount of $5,000 to $10,000, and all their dealings with us have been satisfactory." This was sufficient to cause the shipment of the first order. There is a saying common among merchants, or was twenty years ago : " A buyer who is ' crooked' always pays his first bill in order to get a bigger shipment afterwards." I found the most successful plan of merchandise swindling was to make but a single purchase, and then to convert the goods into cash at once, or reship them to a place where they could be easily and safely disposed of. The police are so well posted on this kind of swindle at the present day that such an operation would scarcely be attempted by the most foolhardy " crook."

After going around with Jones as described, until he had purchased from ten to fifteen thousand dollars' worth of goods, I concluded to stop at that. All the purchases had been of staple goods, such as butter, cheese, pork, hams, sugar, tea, coffee, etc. Now comes the funny part. Jones was something of a musician, and wanted to buy a piano to send home to his sister at the old homestead. I said to him : " These piano dealers are being so constantly imposed upon by sharpers that they have their eyes opened very wide. You can much easier procure articles which command ready money, and pay cash for your piano." But Jones wanted a piano at the cost of freight only; besides he did not like the idea of paying for what he believed he could get for nothing.

He went to the warehouse of the New York Piano Company and selected one of their grands, price $1,000. for which he tendered a draft at six months on L—— & Co., the New York bogus reference firm. This draft was taken by the treasurer of the Piano Company to L—— & Co., who promptly accepted it. As most of the goods were ordered to be shipped by the New Haven boat, which left Peck Slip at 11 P. M., Jones and I went there and saw the piano and a large quantity of goods delivered on board. Jones had no eyes for anything but the big box containing "my grand piano."

But my dear fellow, said I, " it is not yet in the old home-stead, and the music to be drawn from it may yet enliven some other ears than those of the ' old folks at home.' "

" But haven't I given a draft at six months, and hasn't it been accepted ? " said he eagerly.

There was no use trying to dampen his ardor; there was the box on which appeared his false name in big letters. We took the cars for New Haven, in order to be on hand when the boat arrived. The next morning we were up bright and early and went to the store. A few minutes after our arrival, in came two men, whom I felt sure were detectives. They asked some questions about the business, to which I carelessly replied to the effect that we were just about opening. I paid no further attention to them, and they soon left. We then went to the post-office and found letters containing invoices for most of the goods purchased the day before, also one from the managers of the New York Piano Company, as follows:

MESSRS. SMITH, BROWN & Co., New Haven, Conn.

GENTLEMEN: — A man purporting to be Mr. Smith of your firm called on us to-day and stated that he was just furnishing his pri-vate residence in New Haven, and purchased from us one of our best grand pianos, giving a draft at six months on L—— & Co., of this city. After calling on L—— & Co., and getting the draft accepted we made some further inquires which convinced us that the location of your Mr. Smith's private residence must be, not in New Haven — but in Wethersfield. [Note — the State's prison is located there.] A friend in New Haven, to whom we sent a dis-patch, replies: "No such men, firm, nor private residence in New Haven." Concluding that you are trying to "come it" on us, we beg to call your attention to the piano-case, which, on opening you will find to contain the exact equivalent to your draft accepted by

PRISONERS WAITING TRIAL, AT NEWGATE, RECEIVING VISITORS.

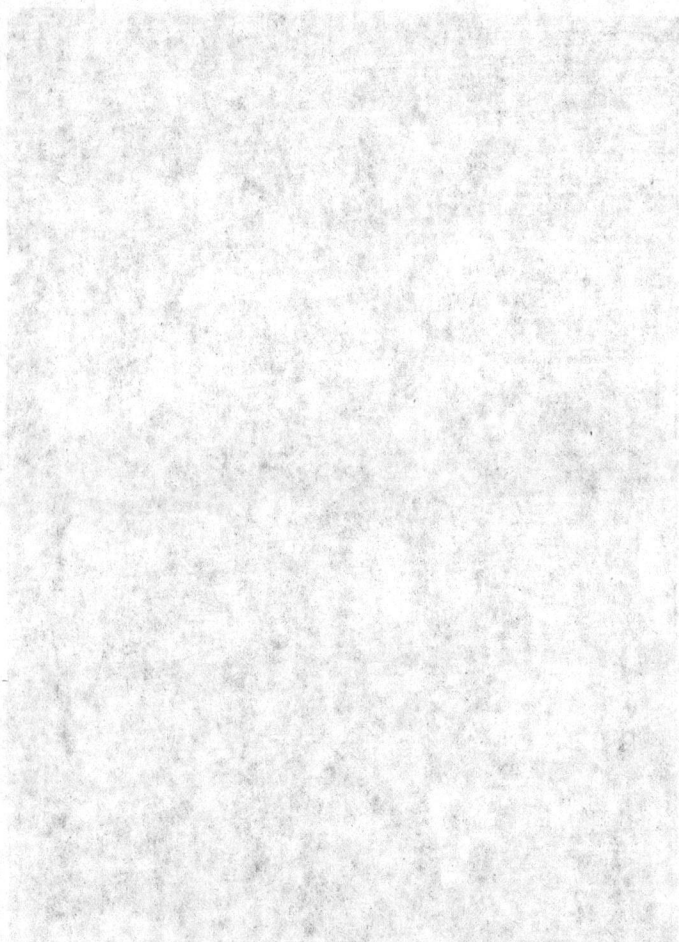

L—— & Co., viz. : $0,000. This draft we herewith enclose, so that if you are dissatisfied with our valuation of the document, you can reship us the piano-case, thus making matters square between us — saving the trouble, and say $4.00 freight and cartage for the empty case. Of course we feel satisfied as it is, but will feel more so, if you choose to send us the four dollars and the case.

From the events which followed, I have no doubt but that the manager of the New York Piano Company had communicated with the New Haven chief-of-police. After leaving the post-office I sent a man to the wharf, and while he was gone, we found that the two detectives were following us about. After the man returned, he said : "I saw the piano and a lot of goods on the wharf, and as soon as I spoke to the freight clerk a man came up and asked if those were my goods. I said they belonged to the firm in whose employ I was. I then asked the clerk for the freight bills, which he gave me, saying the piano-case was empty."

After taking the whole matter into consideration, I concluded to abandon the enterprise, for I saw that while there would be no trouble about getting the goods into the store, the moment I attempted to dispose of them the detectives would ascertain the places where they went. In case I reshipped the goods, the detectives would learn the addresses of the consignees, and notify by telegraph the New York creditors, who would arrange to have the goods attached on arrival at their destination. We waited until evening, and then took the train to New York. The next day I purchased several bills of goods in the name of L—— & Co., which were delivered in the way before described, then closed up the New York office, removing everything but the sign, and came out of the attempted big swindle with the product of a small one — just enough to cover expenses.

Arrived in New York, Jones was inconsolable at the loss of his piano — "My grand piano." "The scoundrel !" he exclaimed — "after I had paid him for it with an accepted draft — to play me such a trick ! Why, I have been dreaming

6

nothing but new music ever since I set eyes on it; my head was an entire Italian opera company and the Vienna Opera House Orchestra combined! Talk about Orpheus and Eurydice! the Furies resisting Orpheus's entrance into Hades! Bah! When I waked up this morning, I had my head full of something that would have cast all that into the shade, and could have played it all on my grand piano! And only an empty case! It is enough to make a fellow tear his hair all out!"

I could only laugh and roar at his rhapsodies and lamentations. At last I got breath to say: " Oh, Jones, my boy, do stop, or you will be guilty of homicide! Don't you see that it is only a case of diamond cut diamond? They have been too sharp for us; that's all."

After my friend Jones had recovered from the first effects of his disappointment, I sat down and wrote a letter substantially as follows:

MANAGER NEW YORK PIANO COMPANY:

DEAR SIR, — I take the utmost pleasure in handing you the enclosed four dollars, which you say will make you "feel more so," *i. e.*, quite satisfied regarding your transaction with the late firm of Smith, Brown & Co. of New Haven, Conn.

As I wish to keep the document you enclosed, I adopt your suggestion as to the piano-case, and have sent an order to the wharf agent in New Haven to reship it to your address. As to my friend Mr. Smith, *alias* Jones, *alias* Brown, *alias* anything, you are not so far out of the way about the location of his private residence — that is to say, you are only a few months behind, as he left Wethersfield less than a year ago. There is some excuse to be made for his error regarding "the fine New Haven residence" in which he was about to place the grand piano. It is this: He has an extremely strong imagination, and no sooner had he run his fingers over the keys of your fine instrument than he saw it all — the fine residence, elegant furniture, pictures by the old masters, and everything heart could wish, except a grand piano. Now, sir, let me congratulate you on the good taste and artistic appreciation of the state of affairs which led you to send him an imaginary grand piano. He does not just yet appreciate the action in its true light, but I have no doubt he will do so as he recovers from the paroxysm brought on by his disappointment. I am, sir, your disappointed

CUSTOMER.

Four or five hundred dollars' worth of goods had been shipped by rail, and were lying at the freight station in New Haven. I thought that the detectives were so deeply engaged watching the goods at the steamboat wharf that those at the railway station would remain unnoticed. Therefore I went to one Frothingham, who had been a salesman in the grocery house with me — a man with no particular conscience as to how he made money, so long as he kept out of the clutches of law — and told him about the goods, offering him one-half the proceeds of their sale if he would take an order, run up to New Haven, and reship them to New York. He accepted my offer, went to New Haven the next morning, returning the same afternoon, and coming to meet me at the International Hotel, Park Row, said:

"Well, you have got me into a pretty scrape! As soon as I presented the order signed Smith, Brown & Co., I was arrested, and had to let them know who I was. Then I could not get off without paying the detective fifty dollars, and as I had but twenty, I had to get him to come to New York with me. He is waiting over at the Astor House for me to return and pay him the thirty dollars."

Without thinking, I gave him the sum demanded, and he departed; but after considering the matter, I concluded that his entire story was false, and that he had really obtained the goods, taking that method to throw off suspicion of his transaction.

Some time after, I was in Albany, and calling on a liquor-dealer who I knew was a friend of Frothingham's, I said: "Mr. F—— wished me to call and get a sample of the whisky he sent you the other day to sell for him." The dealer said, "All right," took me up stairs, and showed me all the casks of liquor and oil for which I had given Frothingham an order.

This man was at the time connected with a wholesale grocery house in New York.

Since my return from England I have visited the quarter in New York where, as previously related, I had been engaged in the grocery trade. Nearly all the old firms had disappeared, but after looking about I discovered two old grocery men, from whom, among other things, I ascertained that Frothingham's conscienceless sharpness had never carried him higher than the position of a salesman, and that for a few years past he has disappeared into such complete obscurity that my informant did not know what had become of him.

CHAPTER VIII.

SOME months after the occurrences last recorded, I left the
home where I was living happily with wife and child,
having arranged with "Doctor" Samuel Bolivar to go West in
search of a good place to open a swindling commercial house.

Right here let me explain that during all this time, I
deceived and studiously kept my wife in ignorance of the true
nature of my business.

Young man! if you are in possession, as I was, of Heav-
en's choicest blessing, a good wife, reveal all your troubles to
her, and make her your confidant in business affairs.

Bolivar and I were unsuccessful until we reached Wheeling, W. Va.; there we found a wholesale tobacco business,
which had been conducted by Mr. Ott, who had reduced his
stock, and was about to close up that he might give his entire
attention to the hardware establishment which came into his
hands by the death of his father. The "Doctor" and I purchased the stock and goods on thirty days' time without being
asked for any references, intending of course, to obtain all the
goods we could within the month and then to leave. We
ordered a considerable quantity of tobacco from the manu-
facturers of whom Mr. Ott had purchased; this was promptly
shipped, and it would have been well with us had we adhered
to our original purpose of running the place but for a month,
or less. We sent out a young man, who had been in Mr.

(85)

Ott's employ, to travel for orders among the old customers of the house. Our firm was S. S. Bovar & Co., I was known by the name of Cole, and Bovar was the French form of the name of my partner.

Before the end of the month we found we were engaged in a really good and profitable trade, and began to regret that we had not gone into it under our right names. Had we done so, we might have taken advantage of the opportunity to settle down into permanent business, which through all had been my ultimate aim. We gave up our original plan and determined to keep on for a time, hoping to find a solution to the difficulty. At the expiration of the month we paid Mr. Ott in full as agreed.

Shortly after this a man, represented by his business card to be " J. M. Eldridge, dealer in Choice Groceries, Teas, etc., Cumberland, Md.," went to Baltimore and purchased goods at several wholesale houses.

The orders were promptly shipped, and in three or four days he had received nearly $4,000 worth of teas, sugar, etc. He sold the sugar in Cumberland, but not finding a ready sale for the tea, he reshipped it to Wheeling, to which place he then came. Offering it at a low price I purchased it for S. S. Bovar & Co., taking an invoice which he receipted. We shipped it by steamer to Bishop & Co., wholesale grocers, Cincinnati, with whom we had an account, to be sold and credited to us. One fatal chest, however, was retained in our store. Eldridge also sold us a lot of tobacco, which we added to our stock.

It appears that he had not paid for these goods, and after waiting a little time for the expected remittances, the Baltimore firms became suspicious that all was not right, and sent an agent to Cumberland. This agent had not much difficulty in ascertaining that something was really wrong, but could find nothing of Eldridge or the goods shipped to him. At last he discovered that a lot of teas, corresponding in number of chests to those sold by his firm to Eldridge, had been reshipped to Wheeling. He at once came on to that city, and being a shrewd, sharp individual, soon traced them to our store. Then he made inquiries regarding the house of S. S. Bovar & Co., and could only learn that the members of the firm appeared to be good men, and paid their bills. Supposing the teas to be still in our store, procuring a writ of replevin and a search-warrant, he came with a constable and obtained the single chest of tea so thoughtlessly retained. This encouraged the constable, Pender, to undertake a little in the detective line. He arranged with the Wheeling postmaster to deliver to him all our letters, which he opened by steaming, and after reading returned them to the postmaster, who then put them in our box. As these bore no evidence of irregular treatment we did not suppose they had been tampered with. The postmaster committed a felony against the United States postal laws — a State's prison offense — in order to uncover what was at that time (1864) a simple misdemeanor, the penalty of which was confinement in the county jail.

The constable Pender then went to the telegraph office and arranged with the superintendent for a copy of all dispatches addressed to S. S. Bovar & Co., or to Bovar or Cole. This was a mode of uncovering fraudulent operations at that time new to me, and against which I naturally took no precautions. In the meantime Eldridge had gone to some place in Ohio, but kept up a correspondence with me at Wheeling. Of course his letters addressed to me (Cole), care of S. S. Bovar & Co., fell into Pender's hands, giving him the whereabouts of the writer. Pender at once went to the Governor of West Virginia, who resided in Wheeling, at that time the capital of the State, procured a requisition on the Governor of Ohio, went on to Columbus, had his papers signed, and the proper warrant issued by the Governor. He then proceeded to the town where Eldridge was staying, caused his arrest, and after putting on hand-cuffs, took him on board the train bound for Wheeling. Eldridge was gentlemanly in his manners, of a generous and sociable disposition, one who made friends everywhere, especially since he had been able to procure plenty of other people's money to spend. They were not long in the train before he had quite gained the confidence of Pender, but not sufficiently enough to induce him to remove the handcuffs. After passing the town of Belmont, Ohio, Pender went to the rear of the car for some purpose, Eldridge sprang to to his feet, raised the car window and threw himself out headlong. The train was running about twenty miles an hour, and Eldridge after rolling over two or three times regained his feet, and found that although he had received a good shaking up, no bones were broken. The reader may think that such a leap in handcuffs could not be taken without serious results, but in the course of my story I shall give the cases of two men, one of them handcuffed, who leaped from trains in England going at the rate of more than forty miles an hour. Both of these men I became subsequently acquainted with in Woking prison, and heard the remarkable story of their lives from their own lips.

As soon as Eldridge shook himself together he started as fast as he could go across the country. Pender had taken the precaution to strip him of his money, watch, and other valuables, but he was happy to escape, handcuffed and moneyless as he was. Every effort to free himself from the irons proved unavailing, and after walking through the woods all night long, he came to a clearing and in sight of a comfortable log farm-house, about sunrise. He secreted himself in a clump of bushes at the edge of the clearing, and watched until the farmer came out with his axe and dinner-basket and went into the woods. In a short time Eldridge heard the steady strokes of an axe, apparently half a mile distant. He managed to tear off a portion of his shirt and wrap it around his hands, concealing the handcuffs, then went boldly toward the house and pleasantly accosted the woman who stood at the door surrounded by her children, as afterwards detailed by himself:

"Good morning, madam. You are no doubt surprised to see a stranger in such a condition as I am at present."

"Poor man," replied the woman, "what is the matter? Come in and rest yourself. Have you hurt your hand?"

"The fact is, my dear madam," replied Eldridge, "I am the victim of unfortunate circumstances. My father, at his death, left me a large amount of property. Some of my envious relatives, by misrepresentation and the bribery of dishonest physicians, had me pronounced insane, and an order issued to place me in the County Insane Asylum. They were taking me there yesterday, handcuffed, but as I had rather die than go to such a place, I seized an opportunity to jump out of the car window, and have been in the woods all night. Just look at my hands!"

The good woman had listened attentively to Eldridge's piteous story, and when he held up his hands, all swollen and bleeding from the cruel irons, she was utterly horrified, and moved to that deep compassion which is so characteristic of her sex the world over. She hastened to bring a hammer, a flatiron, and a file. With these she quickly removed the irons from his wrists, and then cooked for him a generous breakfast. During his stay, this angel of the wilderness mended his clothes neatly, put a silver dollar into his hand at parting, and he left this humble home in the woods in a comfortable condition.

If this good woman be still living, she may have an opportunity to read this record of her own sweet charity dispensed long years ago to a suffering man, whose sins she could know nothing of.

He now for the first time since his escape knew exactly where he was, and was able in the course of the day to reach the town of Steubenville on the Ohio River, which is less than fifty miles from Wheeling. It was a great wonder to him how Pender had ascertained his whereabouts, never dreaming that the post and telegraph offices had been tampered with. Therefore he used part of the dollar given him by the woman to send a telegram to me at Wheeling, asking me to come to him with a supply of money.

In the meantime, after a useless hunt for his escaped prisoner, Pender returned to Wheeling very much crestfallen; and throughout the next day he was the subject of numerous "hard rubs" from some of his friends, whose remarks were very soon related to Eldridge: "Hello, Pender! Have you lost your mule?" "What's the price of new handcuffs?" "Thought you were too old a head to accept leg bail!" etc., etc. Therefore it may be supposed he was overjoyed when a dispatch addressed to me was placed in his hands by the telegraph operator. After Eldridge sent his dispatch he waited about for the arrival of the train which would have brought me to his rescue had I received it. Instead of myself, Pender took the train, and as it drew up to the platform he saw him looking for me. He left the train and walking up to him, unperceived, said: "Well, Eldridge, how do you feel after the header? I knew you had no money, and did not wish to leave you out in the cold such weather as this."

Eldridge turned, stupefied, and before he recovered his usual presence of mind the handcuffs were again upon him, and this time Pender succeeded in lodging him safely in the county jail at Wheeling, where we leave him for the present to reflect over the result of a first step into crime.

Chapter IX.

THE firm of S. S. Bovar & Co. secured the services of a
young man named Wesley, who could be trusted to act
as porter. Of course he had nothing to do with the management, and was not let into the secrets of our business. Yet
it will be seen that he suffered equally with Eldridge, Bovar,
and myself.

During all this time we remained quietly in Wheeling
attending to the tobacco business. Because of my fictitious
name, "Cole," I had kept aloof from almost everyone, and
made no acquaintances among the merchants and business
men, but Bovar had made a great many. When it became
known that Eldridge was arrested, Bovar came to me in a
panic. I told him that I did not think they would dare to
molest us, and to guard against any possibility I decided to
go away for a few days. I was greatly puzzled at the apparent ease with which Eldridge had been twice captured, having no suspicion even yet that the postal and telegraph
service had been "worked."

It did not require a great amount of penetration to see
that matters were getting badly mixed, and I left for Evansville, Indiana, there to await events. Bovar was to write or
telegraph me in case of necessity, and in the course of a day
or two sent me a telegram, a copy of which was at once given
to Pender, by which means he ascertained my whereabouts.
He telegraphed to the authorities at Evansville, directing

them to have me arrested (which was promptly done) and
held to await a requisition on the charge of felony, a charge
which, as will be shown, could not be sustained.

The next day Pender arrived at Evansville with the requisition, took me in charge, and we at once started for Wheeling.
His experience with Eldridge had made him cautious, and he
kept me handcuffed during the entire journey.   This was my
first experience of such an indignity, and I felt the disgrace
keenly.   Arriving at Bellaire, the junction of the Baltimore &
Ohio R. R. and the Wheeling branch, we found that we should
be obliged to remain there over night.   Pender secured lodgings, or rather a small bedroom, and after eating supper with
shackled hands, I lay down on the bed, while he sat close by
me to keep guard.   Neither of us slept during the night, and
throughout the tedious hours I watched incessantly for a
chance to regain my liberty, and he, suspicious of my intention, sat by my bedside all night long with a revolver in his
hand.

In the morning the rain was pouring down in torrents,
but Pender would not wait for the train.   He hired a couple
of horses, which we mounted, and started for Wheeling, four or
five miles distant, I being still handcuffed.   After a time we
came to a level section with thick woods bordering the highway.   I formed a plan to gradually fall behind, and then rush
my horse to the fence, leap off, climb over, and take to the
woods.   When about one hundred feet to the rear — the rain
coming down in "buckets-full" — I turned my horse's head
towards the fence, digging my heels into his sides, but could
not make him go fast.   As soon as Pender saw my movements, he whirled his horse around, and by the time I had
covered half the distance to the fence, his horse had gained so
much on the skeleton which carried me that he was close
enough to open fire.   Through fear of hitting the horse, I
suppose, his shots were all too high.   I at last reached the
fence, but owing to my shackled hands I could not leap from
the horse's back directly over, and dismounted to climb it.

By this time Pender had got close to me, and I was obliged to surrender or risk a bullet at a yard's distance. Well, I surrendered! During the rest of our journey, amid pouring rain, he kept me just in front of him, and in another hour I was lodged in the same den with Eldridge.

This success emboldened the creditors of Eldridge to arrest Bovar and Wesley at the store, and to proceed against all four of us for a conspiracy to defraud. We were tried together, the jury brought in a verdict of guilty, and the judge sentenced us all, including the clerk Wesley, to two years' confinement in the county jail, the utmost limit permitted by the laws of the State of West Virginia for a misdemeanor. Had we not been strangers the result might have been different for all save Eldridge. At that time, in most of the States, the longest term of punishment that could be inflicted for a misdemeanor was one year in the county jail. What is the moral difference between obtaining goods under false pretense, pocket picking, or any other kind of stealing? There is but one — the petty thief or pickpocket often gets all the money that a poor man or woman has in the world.

Up to the time of my escape, to be described later on, I passed eight months in this West Virginia county jail; and as it was a type of a state of things still existing in many parts of the Southern States, as I judge by what I have read in the papers since my return from England, I conclude to give some description of life in that " reformatory institution."

Alas! does the constitution of society require that those who never had a proper start in life — permitted to grow up ignorant, amid brutalizing surroundings — should suffer the severest penalties, and become the scapegoats of shrewd, avaricious men? I refer to all unfortunates, white or black, who are now passing wretched lives, the victims of Society's neglect amidst what are denominated civilized Christian communities.

This Wheeling jail was a two-story and basement structure, solidly built of stone. The front was occupied by the jailor and his family. The rear building had a boiler for steam-heating purposes in the basement, the first floor being occupied by male, and the second by female, prisoners. Corridors about twelve feet wide extended from a large, iron-barred window, which looked into a back-yard surrounded by a high wall, to the front part occupied by the family, from which it was separated by a grated or barred iron door, the entrance to each story being from the residence. The stone stairs, leading from the basement to the top floor, were over each other in the same part. There was a porch over the front entrance, which was reached by a flight of stone steps. The flue leading from the fire-place under the boiler in the basement ran up in the wall near the large window at the rear. On each side of the corridors was a row of cells about five feet by ten, which were closed by double doors, that inside the thickness of the wall being of iron bars, the outer one of solid plank. In the wall was a small window, near the ceiling, about six inches horizontal width by two feet in length, affording but dim light even in fair weather. Six-inch closet-pipes ran through the rear of the cells near the floor, the openings to which were closed with cast-iron covers weighing thirty or forty pounds. These in course of time had become loosened from the original fastenings — a fact which had a decisive bearing on my escape, as will be shown.

West Virginia, in 1864, had no State prison, and in consequence all persons convicted of felony served out the terms of their sentences in the various county jails, associating indiscriminately with prisoners of every degree of guilt, from those awaiting trial or doing a month for drunkenness, to others sentenced to a life imprisonment for murder. In the Wheeling county jail were three of the latter sort, and very good, quiet men they were. There were also three confederates — Weston, a master builder, Charley Meredith, a Baltimore saloon-keeper and gambler, and Marks, a carpenter — who were doing respectively four, five, and seven years, for robbing the Adams Express Company's office at

Parkersburgh, W. Va. As usual, the most guilty escaped with the lightest sentence.

The master builder, Weston, was carrying on a large business in his line, but was dissatisfied with the rate at which his wealth was increasing. He had frequented Charley Meredith's saloon, passing many evenings in playing billiards, poker, etc. It is probable that losses at gambling caused him to concoct the scheme which he did for refilling his purse. He went to Cincinnati, made up a package, purporting to contain $35,000, and addressed it to himself at Parkersburgh. This he sent by the Adams Express Company, taking therefor the usual receipt given by the agents for money packages. On the arrival of this bogus package at Parkersburgh, the agent put it in the safe over night, a fact which was known to Weston's confederates, Charley Meredith and the carpenter Marks, who the same night entered the Express office, broke open the safe, and took away the $35,000 package. The next morning the agent was completely wild, and the whole town in excitement over the robbery. No clue could be found to the perpetrators, who remained quietly in town, engaged in their usual avocations. Weston came forward and demanded his package of $35,000, and although the company had no actual suspicion, before replacing the amount of the supposed robbery, they had Mr. Weston make affidavit as to all the circumstances relating to the money which had been sent to him. He, supposing the company would be satisfied with his declaration without investigating farther, made a statement which the company soon found to be false in some particulars. This aroused them to a more rigid investigation, which resulted in bringing the whole plot to light, and the trial and conviction of the confederates.

The male ward of the jail was so crowded that each cell contained two to four men — if four, these had to pack in the bed, heads and feet; and the same was the case with the female ward up stairs, the cells being even more closely crowded. The place swarmed with Mark Twain's " chamois."

These — not the chamois — were all let out into the corridors of their respective wards.

During the greater part of the day, the place was a veritable pandemonium. Laughter, singing, gambling, varied with occasional fights, washing and drying of clothes, kept the place rather lively. By the sides of the steam-pipes which passed up through the stone floor of the cells, the women had dug out the cement to make a hole through into the cells below. By these they would sit, or lie on their faces, and exchange ideas, not of the most refined nature, with some of the male prisoners underneath. The cells were divided by partition walls of stone more than a foot in thickness, yet holes had been made through these, enabling prisoners to talk or pass small articles back and forth.

Our advent among the prisoners was hailed with rejoicings, because they supposed we had some money — their own being exhausted. They were allowed to send the jailor's children out to purchase tobacco, fruit, pies, cakes, etc., the jail food being composed principally of corn-bread and potatoes. Especially delighted was Charley Meredith, who was good-natured, gentlemanly in his manners, full of jokes and fun, in fact an invaluable assistant in helping to pass away the monotonous hours in a jail — and to get away one's surplus cash by gaming. I did not at first suspect gambling to be his special calling, nor had I ever practiced it; but he soon initiated me into the game of poker, and some of the hands which he dealt himself were to me truly wonderful.

One Shelton, who was doing a term of fifteen years for horse-stealing, had become very — and I believe genuinely — religious. He was of small size, but like a bundle of steel wires — could twist and double himself into any shape, and was a complete acrobat. One day, three or four months after my arrival, he came to me and divulged a plan of escape, which I did not think was a feasible one. I said to him: "But, Shelton, you are now a religious man; you must believe that you were sent here providentially, and how can you think of attempting to escape?"

"Oh, I have been a very bad man, and committed more than one murder; but God has brought me to see my evil ways, and has pardoned me, and with His help I am bound to lead a new life. I had a great power and capacity to work for the devil, and am going to use the same qualities the rest of my life in working against him. I believe God has put it into my heart to escape from this place, and I believe, also, that He will assist; therefore I have put my life at His disposal, and shall execute the plan with which He has inspired me, even if I go alone."

Finding I would have nothing to do with it, he let Eldridge, Green, and Morgan into his plan. Green was doing five years for larceny, and appeared very well educated. Morgan was a good specimen of the Southwestern rough, desperado, and horse-thief — ready for any daring enterprise, from sheep-stealing to murder, provided there was any money in it. He was now doing ten years for horse-stealing, and was fond of boasting about his wild and lawless adventures. His last exploit had nearly ended his career, for an irate party of farmers had captured him on a stolen horse, put a rope around his neck, thrown the end over a limb, and pulled him up; but he was cut down by the sheriff, who arrived just in the nick of time. These three prisoners agreed to join Shelton in his project, and a night was fixed upon to make the attempt.

It was in the latter part of July, 1865; and as the weather was very warm, Mr. Jones, the jailor, an ignorant but kind and humane man, directed that the outside, solid wooden doors to the cells, usually locked, should be left open at night, that the air might circulate through them. The inner door, before described, was fastened by a bolt and spring slide on the wall of the corridor, beyond the reach of the occupant of the cell. Shelton's programme was to reach the slide and remove it, then get out of his cell, let the other men out of theirs into the corridor, and then dig a hole through the brick wall into the flue — all without being heard by the night watchman. How this was effected will be shown in the next chapter.

CHAPTER X.

I BELIEVE Eldridge to be the only survivor of the daring
escape, and the subsequent events were related by him to
me some months later.

Wesley and I were confined in the same cell, and on the
night that Shelton and his party had agreed upon, we lay on
the straw-bed listening attentively to catch every sound.
About one o'clock A. M. Shelton began operations. By means
of a tool which he had contrived, he reached through the
bars of the inner iron door—the outer wooden one being
open—and after some careful manipulations succeeded in
withdrawing the slide and pushing out the bolt. After listening a little, he cautiously opened the iron door of his cell, and
then those of two other cells in which his associates were
waiting and watching. All four now crept along the corridor
in the dark to the flue previously described.

With a jackknife blade fastened to a wooden handle,
Shelton began to dig the mortar out from between the bricks.
After an hour's work, each moment expecting to be interrupted
by the night watchman, he had made an opening into the flue.
All then let themselves down, Shelton being in advance.
When he had reached the fire-hole under the boiler in the
basement, where there was more space, he waited for the

others. Some noise had been made in coming down the flue by the falling of a brick, which had been heard by the night watchman, whom they saw through the furnace door enter the basement with a lantern, armed with a horse-pistol and accompanied by a dog.

They wore but shoes, trousers, shirts, and caps, and the passage down the flue had torn their shirts nearly off, and begrimed them with soot. In appearance more like demons than human beings, they sprang out upon the watchman. The unexpected appearance of so frightful-looking a quartette, unnerved the watchman, and a few threats caused him to drop the pistol in terror. The dog seemed to take part in his master's trepidation, and neither dog nor man offered any resistance to the flight of the fugitives. The noise aroused Jailer Jones, who was sleeping in a room, the door of which opened opposite to and about eight feet from the foot of the stairs which led to the second story. He sprang out of bed, seized a revolver, threw open the door, and stood awaiting events. In a moment the fugitives rushed up the basement stairs and around the corner to reach the stair-way which led to the second story. As soon as they came in view Jones began firing. Shelton led the way, passed within a few feet of the jailer, rushed up the stairs, unharmed by the bullet fired point-blank at him. Eldridge, who came next, had a like salute and the same lucky escape.

Morgan then attempted to run the gauntlet, but as he made the first leap up the steps he fell backward on the floor, groaning and cursing horribly. Green, who was just behind him, without the slightest hesitation, leaped over Morgan's body and flew up the steps with a bullet whizzing past his ear.

The window over the front porch was open, and Shelton, followed by the two survivors, made the leap of about twenty feet, and although severely shaken landed in the street with unbroken bones. When young Eldridge sprang from the roof of the porch one of his shoes fell off, but, expecting to see the front door open and to hear the pistol pop again, he dared not stop to pick it up, but sped on in the darkness. It was not long before all three were out of breath and obliged to stop, completely exhausted by their exertions, the excitement, the leap for life and liberty, and the run. After a hasty consultation they took the nearest route to the woodland, which was not far away from the suburbs of any town in West Virginia at that time. After what seemed a long time, but in reality only a few minutes, their faltering strides brought them into the forest. So far they had kept together, and now for the first time they dared to rest a little.

Shelton and Eldridge asked each other in the same breath: "Where is Morgan?" "Did you see him?" and peered back into the darkness, listening anxiously to hear the sound of his approaching steps. Green at last recovered sufficient breath to speak, and informed them of Morgan's fate.

But to return to the jail. We who were locked up in the cells cognizant of the attempt, heard the slight sounds made by Shelton in getting out of his cell, and letting his associates out; then came the light scraping of removing the mortar, the rustle made in getting into the flue, and the falling of the brick which aroused the watchman. For a few moments we strained our ears in vain to catch any further sound, but all was silent; then suddenly came a pistol shot, then another, then a third and fourth, followed by the terrible noise of the wounded man. All was now in an uproar; Jones and the watchman rushed into the street to raise an alarm; his wife and children were in a tremor of apprehension; and soon the jail was surrounded by an excited crowd.

We soon gathered from the conversation that some one had been killed, and were told by one of the Joneses that it was Eldridge. As he had endeared himself to all in the place, there were general expressions of grief, and Wesley and myself could not restrain our tears. It was not long, however, before we ascertained that the murdered man was Morgan.

We left the fugitives recovering their breath in the edge

of the forest, which extended to a great distance, unbroken save by the occasional clearings of the settlers. It was growing light, and each one began to take an account of stock and to realize his physical condition by an examination of the torn and grime-covered clothes, the cuts and scratches. There was little left of the shirts and pants with which they started out on that memorable morning. Young Eldridge's shoeless foot was lacerated and bleeding ; to protect it in some degree from the stones and briers, he tore off strips from his dilapidated shirt and bandaged the unfortunate member that must perform its share of locomotion. During the day they made but little progress, concealing themselves in the densest thickets, not daring to speak above a whisper or hardly stir a step for fear some treacherous twig might snap under their feet. At last, when the long summer day was ended, and darkness spread a veil over their movements, they took up their lonely and fearful tramp through the pathless forest, resolved on placing as great a distance as possible between themselves and Wheeling jail.

Their intention was to keep to the northeast and cross the boundary line into Pennsylvania. Thus they wandered courageously on through the night, with nothing to relieve the pangs of hunger save the leaves and twigs they chewed, or an occasional draught of water from a pool left in the dried-up bed of a watercourse.

Resting and sleeping through the days, avoiding all signs of civilization, they traveled three nights, and as the fourth morning dawned they felt so certain they were in Pennsylvania, and were so nearly starved, that they held a consultation and decided to send one of their number forward to a clearing near which they had halted, to ascertain their whereabouts, and, if possible, to obtain food.

Eldridge volunteered to do this, and after borrowing a shoe, and putting himself into as presentable shape as possible with the best tatters remaining among the party, he advanced to the edge of the clearing and found himself on the brow of a hill looking down into a valley in which was a large stream of water beyond gleaming in the distance. He beckoned to his companions yet within view, who hastened to the spot where he stood. They were more familiar with the country, and as soon as they looked down into the valley exclaimed simultaneously:

"That is Wheeling! and yonder is the jail!"

It would be impossible to describe their feelings — their chagrin, astonishment, and disappointment at this unexpected return to the near proximity of the very jail, the memories of whose iron bars and gloomy walls had spurred them on to superhuman efforts and to endure those weary miles of travel, all for naught! Starved, covered with bruises and sores, almost naked — what could they do? That was indeed a serious question, one involving liberty, very possibly their lives. Should they take to the woods again, perhaps to wander weary days and nights in vain? One thing was certain, they must get away from where they were, and without delay.

Wheeling being situated on the eastern side of the Ohio River, across which lies the State of Ohio, the fugitives reasoned that if they could cross the river they would be beyond the jurisdiction of the State of West Virginia. They retired to a thicket and held a " council of war," deciding to make the circuit of the city, reach the bank of the river some miles above, and find some means of crossing. This plan they proceeded to put into immediate execution, for they were literally starving, and fully aware that their strength would not hold out much longer. Shortly after, while plodding wearily onward, they came to a piece of marshy ground covered with huckleberry bushes, the fruit of which was just ripening. They eagerly gathered the berries which satisfied the cravings of hunger. Then, selecting a place of concealment, they lay down to rest a little while — not to sleep.

Unconsciously they succumbed to Nature's great restorer, and the three *miserables* became fast-bound in the arms of Morpheus, oblivious to all surroundings.

A farmer's wife with her children came into the patch to gather berries. Soon the children strayed from their mother and gradually came near the sleeping trio, who were at last aroused by the chatter and laughter. In the confusion attending their sudden awakening they did not recognize the nature of the disturbance, and, supposing they had been observed while picking berries, and that search was being made for them, they bounded to their feet to make another run.

The sudden uprising of the men was observed by the children, who, with cries of terror fled pell-mell down the hill. The mother heard the cries, and supposing they had been frightened by a snake, followed rapidly after them. The escaped prisoners took in the situation at a glance, and were satisfied there was no immediate cause for alarm, but decided to move on and get as many miles away from the spot as their weary feet would permit. Eldridge and his companions watched the fleeing group with some amusement. The former had now assumed the leadership of the party, and as he was taking a general survey, he espied a tin-pail — abandoned by the children in their flight — and asked one of his men to bring it, for with that pail he conjectured many possibilities in the way of foraging and cooking. The man soon returned with it, partly filled with berries; then all hands set to work, filled the pail and departed.

When night overtook them they crept into a barn, which proved a grateful shelter and a boon to men who had passed so many nights in the woods, their almost naked bodies exposed to the bites of insects.

Eldridge said afterward that he never enjoyed lodging in any first-class hotel in America or Europe as he did his bed of soft sweet hay in that barn.

They all awoke at dawn new men, and after an early breakfast on the berries, started with renewed courage on the tramp for liberty. It was not long before the pangs of hunger again reminded them of their lack of food, and set them to cogitating upon ways and means to obtain supplies. They resolved to reconnoitre at every farm-house until they found one where no dog was kept, conceal themselves until night, and then make a raid on the pantry, for they were still too near Wheeling to venture openly to ask for food of the hospitable Western farmers, who are ever ready to feed the hungry wayfarer if they do not believe him to be an idle vagabond.

The part of West Virginia where they were then traveling was quite thickly settled, and it was not long before they came to a place which Eldridge thought would answer the purpose. After dark they went into the barn and slept upon the hay-mow. About midnight they proceeded to the kitchen, and Shelton quietly raised a window, drew himself in, and soon reappeared with a large loaf of bread and a pan of milk. These they took to the barn and there enjoyed the greatest feast of their lives. After the banquet, it was daylight. Being shirtless, they " borrowed " a horse-blanket, tore it into three pieces for coverings, and then departed with all speed.

They were nearing the Ohio River, and by noonday were again famishing. The first eatable thing they saw was a goose. They got between the goose and the distant farm-house, and after a long, crooked (at any other time laughable) chase, their dinner was won. The goose was quickly killed, plucked, and cut up ready for cooking. The trio were so hungry, however, that they could not await the slow process of boiling; so, hastily collecting some leaves and dry sticks, Shelton lighted the pile with a match he had brought from the farm-house, and the party were soon swallowing pieces of the goose just about warmed through. About half the food was saved and carried along for another meal, and on reaching the bank of the Ohio River they built another fire and supped off boiled goose. They little thought it was the last time they should eat together.

The river, where they were about to cross, is more than a quarter of a mile wide, with a swift and treacherous current, the eddies and swirls of which tend to draw a swimmer under.

ENTRANCE GATE OF DARTMOOR PRISONS.

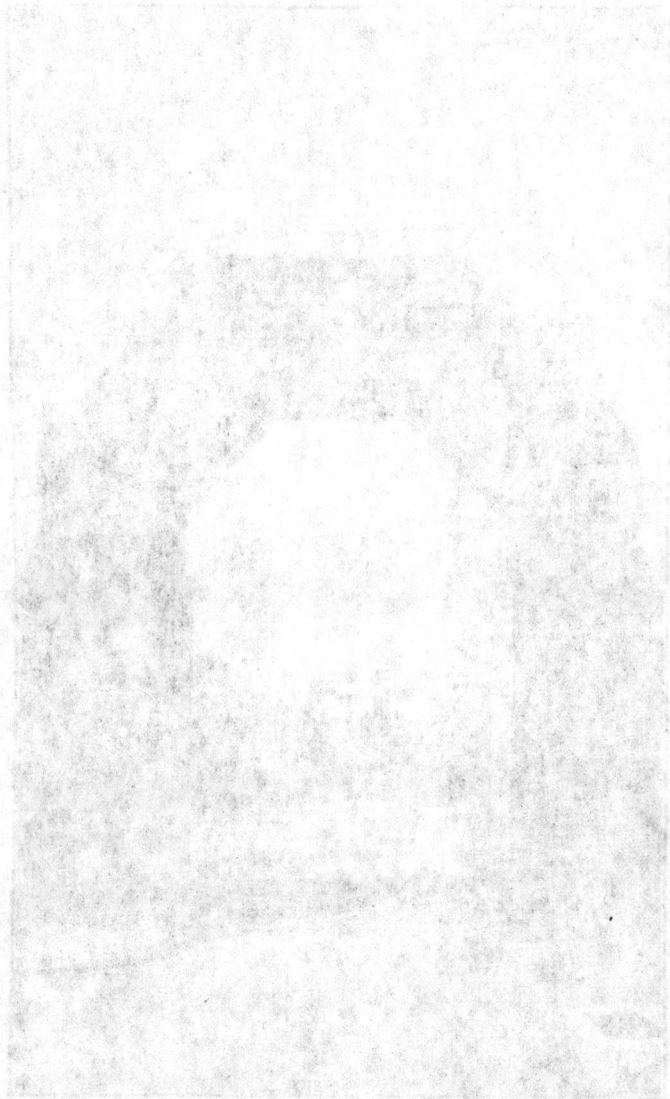

As they did not dare to cross by daylight, they lay quiet till dusk. Each had pulled a board from a fence, to aid in crossing the turbulent stream. Launching boldly into the river, for a time they kept together, but as they were whirled about in various directions, Eldridge soon lost sight of his companions, who were having a struggle to keep their heads above water, and, indeed, that was exactly his own case. But at last he could descry, looming up in the darkness, the high bank of the Ohio shore. This encouraged him to greater exertions, and he got within a few feet of land when the rapid current drew him under a flat-bottomed scow which was moored to the bank. After struggling under water for what seemed to him an age, his head striking the bottom of the boat during the time, he became insensible.

When he regained consciousness, he was lying on the shore, with his legs still in the water, and the morning sun shining in his eyes. He could never understand how he came to be saved. He lay for a time, too weak and exhausted to do more than pull his legs out of the water.

Becoming somewhat revived, he spread the piece of horse-blanket and the remains of his trousers out to dry, while he lay in the sunshine. The hot summer sun soon dried his scanty raiment and warmed him into life. He saw a collection of houses in the distance, toward which he proceeded, in the hope of finding a railway station, for he had heard the rumbling of trains, and determined to steal a ride if possible, as he was not more than twenty miles from Wheeling.

When near the village, he crept into a field of corn to wait till night, and appeased his hunger by gnawing the green corn off the ears. About ten o'clock he made his way to the vicinity of the station to await an opportunity to board some train. After a time a locomotive without a train came along, and while stopping to take in wood and water, he stole up behind and seated himself on the fender-block. Away rumbled the engine at high speed toward Pittsburgh, and Eldridge found himself in a position he had not bargained for. The space on which he was sitting was very narrow, and the lurches of the engine nearly threw him off repeatedly, it being only by the exertion of all his power that he managed to keep on. When he thought he could not hold out for a moment longer, the engine came to a stop just outside of Pittsburgh, and Eldridge was enabled to leave his dangerous position, unobserved.

He "levied" upon a scarecrow for an old coat and pair of trousers, but was still barefooted. This genteel young man, being reduced to the condition of a tramp and cadger, got on as far as Harrisburg by means of freight and cattle trains, sometimes traveling along the track or on the highway. No longer fearing recognition, he boldly applied at the farm-houses for food and lodging, and, despite his dilapidated appearance, he was generally not long in a house before he became a welcome guest.

At Harrisburg he was obliged to apply at the police station for a night's lodging, but he was now nearly at the end of his hardships. While in that place he had an opportunity to read the papers, and for the first time saw an account of the escape from jail, detailing the death of Morgan, and that a reward of $500 was offered for the recapture of himself and each of his companions. He never heard of these since he saw them struggling desperately for life in the turbid waters of the Ohio. It is certain they were never recaptured, and Eldridge has always believed they were then drowned.

Soon after leaving Harrisburg, on foot, he came to a large country villa, and applied for food. The master of the house happened to be at home, and something in the appearance of Eldridge attracted his notice. He immediately invited him in, and after hearing a part of his story, called in his wife and daughters, and all became greatly interested in listening to the recital of his experiences, which he recounted just as they happened, except that he played the part of an ex-Confederate soldier, instead of an escaped civil prisoner. The ladies showed great sympathy for him, and when he left, gave him money to pay his fare to Philadelphia, and a substantial luncheon to carry with him. He ascertained that the gentleman was one of the Harrisburg city magnates.

He reached Philadelphia without further adventure, and as he had no acquaintance nearer than New York City, he set out for a tramp through New Jersey. On the second day, when a few miles from Trenton, he called at a large farmhouse which proved to be the residence of a wealthy widowed Quaker lady. She gave him a bountiful dinner, but previously (his travel-worn looks and dilapidated apparel not according with her Quaker ideas of neatness) the old lady selected a complete suit from her departed husband's wardrobe, and told him to take it — with a bucket of water, soap, scrubbing-brush, and towel — to the barn, and tidy himself up. This he was only too glad to do, and after doing justice to the dinner, and with some money in his pocket, he left the kind-hearted Quaker lady, clothed in the habiliments of an honest man, and a few days later he was in New York among friends.

Eldridge was a man who had been religiously brought up, but had gradually and imperceptibly fallen into ways of obtaining money whereby not only his liberty, but also his life, had been placed in jeopardy. Does any one believe that if he had foreseen the ultimate dangers attending a first false step, he would have taken it?

CHAPTER XI.

A FUTILE PLAN — AN "OLD SAW" — A NEW CONSPIRACY TO ESCAPE — A TRAITOR —
I AM "BUCKED" AND HORSEWHIPPED — TO HEAL MY WOUNDED SPIRIT I SET
THE JAIL ON FIRE — CHRISTMAS DINNER IN JAIL — MY PARTY ESCAPE — CROSS
THE OHIO IN A "BORROWED" BOAT — A STOLEN RIDE — A "TRAMP" — GOOD
LUCK AND GOOD SAMARITANS — MEET PENEY IN NEW ORLEANS.

THE events recorded in the last chapter, up to the moment when the fugitives leaped from the porch, created a great commotion among us who were left in durance. The death of Morgan made but little impression upon us, compared with the fact that three had escaped and were at liberty. Each prisoner said to himself: "What a fool I was not to go with them!"

Jones, the jailer, allowed the prisoners to read his paper — a small sheet published daily in Wheeling — otherwise there was no provision made to supply them with reading matter. The master-builder's friends sent him an occasional book, which I borrowed. One of these was the prose and poetry of Edgar Allan Poe, the "Byron of America," and I committed to memory "The Raven," and other pieces.

I had soon tired of card-playing, especially poker, for I soon discovered that Charley Meredith, in one way or another, was certain to win whenever I played with him. I then whittled out a set of chess-men, but all who played with me soon became discouraged with their "hard luck." Therefore, much of the time hung heavily on my hands, and as this was the first time that I had been under lock and bolt the sentence of two years seemed as hard to bear as did the later one of "life" in England. In consequence, my mind dwelt constantly on the question of how to escape; but for three

(108)

months after Eldridge and party had taken " French leave" I could settle upon no feasible way, although one plan had suggested itself to me. It was customary for some prisoner to bring the rations contained in a large wooden tray into the corridor, the wife or daughter of the jailer unlocking the iron gate for that purpose when Jones himself was absent, which was frequently the case. I induced one of the prisoners, whom I thought reliable, to volunteer to bring in the tray; also letting three or four others into my plan, which was as follows: In October at the usual supper hour it began to grow dusk. We were accustomed to gather at this gate to look out into the street through the front entrance, and merely made way for the man to pass with the tray. When I saw a favorable opportunity I was to have my party posted near the gate, and as our confederate entered he was to " accidentally " drop the tray, so that the gate could not be closed. We were then to rush out, hasten to the front entrance, which was fastened only by a bolt during the day, open the door, and dash up the unfrequented streets to the same forest which Eldridge and party reached. It was a run of about a mile, the last of it up a steep hill; but as it would be nearly or quite dark, I considered that those of us who were county prisoners, dressed in citizens' clothes, stood more than an even chance of success.

On two occasions I had everything arranged, but at the critical moment the heart of the man with the tray failed him, and I was obliged to abandon the project.

It may have been fortunate for me that the plan failed, and I insert here the summary of an account which shows how an exactly similar plan proved abortive at the Rochester jail, on the 10th of September, 1873: " When Mrs. Beckwith, the jailer's wife, opened the iron gate leading into the corridor where the prisoners were walking about, four of them made a rush for liberty, bearing Mrs. Beckwith back. The intrepid woman fought nobly. She seized two of them by the hair and screamed. Just at this moment constable Suits happened to come into the jail on business and went to the rescue. Mr. Beckwith also hastened to the spot with a revolver, and presenting the muzzle, threatened to fire. The prisoners seeing that he meant 'business,' withdrew, and Mrs. Beckwith was released from her unpleasant position."

One of us prisoners, a Welchman, was a bricklayer and plasterer, and had been taken out daily to work about the city. One day while delving at a foundation, he picked out of the rubbish an old, rusty caseknife, which he slipped into his pocket and brought to his cell, thinking it would be better to eat with than his fingers. One of his comrades mentioned the find and I got him to procure it by stealth, for I *saw* I could make a *saw* which would *saw* through the bars, and in imagination *saw* liberty in the near future. I hid the knife away in a crevice, and waited to see if any inquiry was made for it. After a few days I gave it to Marks, one of the Adams Express robbers, who made notches in it with a jackknife blade he had procured. I then took charge of it again, and Wesley and I rubbed it by turns for two or three days on the stone floor of our cell, until the blade, which was of good steel, was as thin at the back as at the front.

I did not dare do much myself, as the jailers, male and female, watched me incessantly, but paid little attention to what the others did. I directed Marks and Peney to take turns in sawing with the notched knife at the bars of the back window, which were of one-inch round iron. There were usually eight or ten persons walking about on the stone floor, which would partially cover up the noise made by the sawing, but this made so penetrating and unusual a sound that I feared it would attract attention. I therefore directed two of the men to bring a bucket of water, procured a zinc wash-board, which I gave them, and told them to take some dirty clothes and rub away with all their might just in front of where the sawing was going on. This completely deceived the jailer and his family, for on more than one occasion they came to the gate to see what caused the singular noise, and on seeing the men rubbing briskly, went away satisfied. I knew that the night-watchman examined the bars of the window every night, so I mixed up a black dough of soot and soap, and when the sawing was done for the day, I had the men cover up the evidences of their work with this mixture.

In each cell was an iron bed-frame, hinged so as to turn up against the wall in the daytime, but when let down occupying nearly the whole space. With the knife-saw I cut nearly in two one of the bars which ran across the bed-frame, so that I could wrench it off to use as a lever in case of necessity.

Marks and Peney insisted that one bar cut out of the window would give sufficient space to get through, and I could not convince them of their error until I got four strips of wood and fastened them into a square just the size of the hole they intended to make. As the smallest could not get his shoulders through, they were satisfied, and in four days had two bars cut nearly through at the bottom end, and half through two feet higher up; all this had been accomplished without discovery. At least a dozen prisoners were cognizant of what was going on, and at last one of them plucked up courage enough to betray the plot, in the hope of thereby currying favor with the authorities — a common trait among the vilest-minded prisoners of all countries, as I have learned.

Neither of us conspirators suspected this treason, and all who intended to escape if they could, retired to rest happy in the belief that they were passing their last night in that place. The next morning the cell doors were not opened at the usual time, and I felt at once that there had been a traitor among us, and that our plans had been unveiled. About 8 o'clock the sheriff, jailer, and two or three men came into the corridor, the cell doors were opened, each man ordered out singly and "bucked." Perhaps some of my readers do not know the meaning of that word. The hands are tied together at the wrists; the man then sits down on the floor and draws his knees up to the chin; his arms are then forced down over the knees so that a stick can be thrust through above the arms and beneath the knees. This renders a man completely helpless, so that he may be tumbled about at will. After all engaged in the plot had been thus "fixed," Jones came to me, and striking me heavily across the hams with a rawhide several times, demanded "that knife." I told him it was unlawful for a jailer to strike a county prisoner, and since he had not asked for it before striking me in my helpless state, he could take it out in "rawhide." He was about to proceed to greater extremities, when Wesley very sensibly said : "I will give it to you if you will untie me." This was done, the knife given up, and all were released from "buck."

Wesley and I were ordered into our cell, both doors closed and locked, and directions given that we were not to be permitted to leave the cell day or night. Until our final escape, two months later, we were never out of that stifling dungeon —for it was nothing less.

This treatment made us ugly, and thenceforward we did everything we could to annoy the jailer — on one occasion nearly destroying the place by fire. We had procured some matches, which we lighted, dropped through a hole in the stone floor into the basement, which was filled with bedding-straw, and when we saw this was on fire we stopped the hole so that we might not be suffocated. Before the fire was discovered it had made such headway that it became a difficult matter to subdue it and save the place. Wesley and I were suspected, but when they interrogated us we would answer no questions, and heard no more of it afterwards.

My mind was more than ever made up to escape, for there were still seventeen months out of the two years to stay, and I felt sure we two could not long survive confinement day and night in a cell which, according to modern scientific ideas, was but half large enough for one man. After we were shut in as above, we had no means of communication with the other prisoners save through a small hole that had been drilled through the wall into the next cell, which Peney occupied.

BLACK MARIA CONVEYING THE FORGERS THROUGH LONDON IN CHAINS.

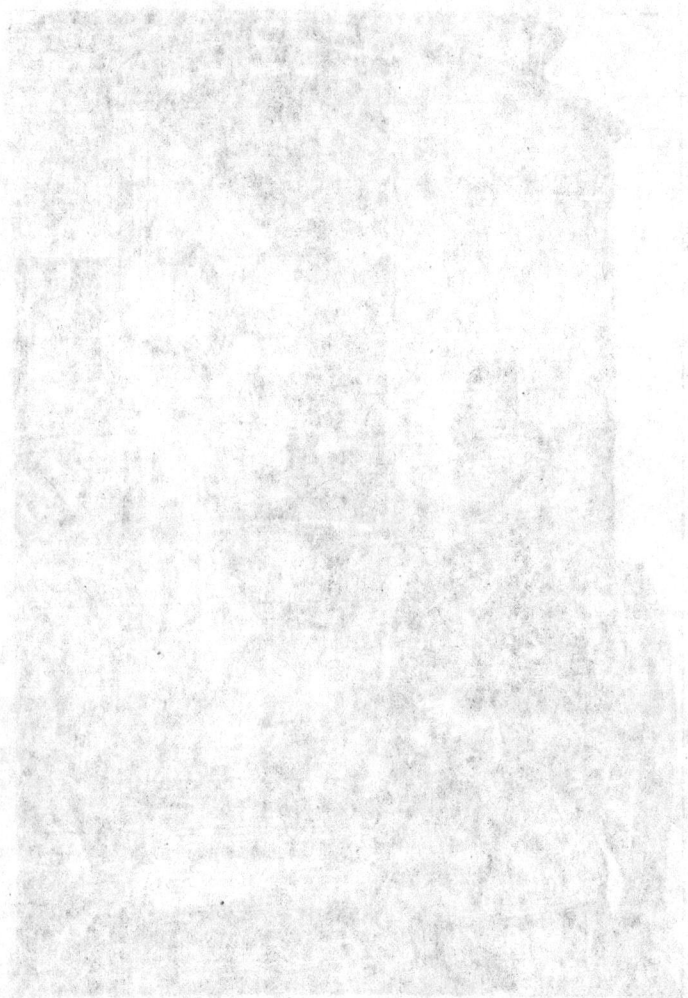

As he and Marks were the ones on whom I depended to carry out my plan, I had only to whisper my directions through the hole, and Peney would communicate them to Marks. After the discovery of the sawed bars, a blacksmith had come there and, without removing them, had put over the space heavy clamps and bars, which were fastened with nuts and screwed up tight. Some pieces of wood and strips of copper had been hoarded up and concealed; of these, Marks, with his knife-blade, managed to make a wrench, by cutting a square hole in a piece of the wood, and binding it with the strips of copper. This he finished, and on trial found it would unscrew the nuts. That fact proved, the wrench was hidden, and Marks tried his hand at making a key to fit the lock of the outer door of my cell, so that when the time for action should come we could be let out. In a few days the key was finished, and found to do its work admirably. We had kept the new plan as secret as possible, only six of us being aware of it.

Now all was ready; but the next day was Christmas, and as Mrs. Jones had promised all her unwilling boarders a good dinner, I thought we had better stay and eat it, especially as on that day there would be a better opportunity to leave the premises, everyone being engaged in preparation for the evening's festivities.

Accordingly Mrs. Jones, with the aid of her daughter, gave us a really good Christmas dinner of turkey, the prisoners, except Wesley and myself, being allowed out in the corridor all day — the man who I felt certain had betrayed us, being one of the favored ones; but as the whole work at the window would occupy only a few minutes, I relied on the surprise and consequent irresolution to keep him and others silent until we were gone.

There had been much noise and confusion in the corridor all this Christmas afternoon, the jailer and his family being in too jolly a condition to take notice of what was transpiring, especially jailer Jones, who was rather fond of his whisky. At half-past four it was dusk, and, as arranged, I passed

8

the iron bar through to Peney; Marks took his wrench and soon removed the clamps and bars from the window; Peney unlocked my cell door, and I handed him the heavy sewer-pipe casting before mentioned as rusted loose. While this was transpiring, Wesley and I remained in the cell, not daring to show ourselves in the corridor, for fear some of the jailer's family might notice us.

With a few blows of the casting Peney broke out the partially sawed bars of the window, and popped through into the back-yard, followed by the three other conspirators. Then Wesley and I started; he passed through the hole, but I, expecting we should be obliged to break the lock of the yard gate, delayed to put the casting through, so as to have it ready in case Peney failed to wrench it off with the bed-frame bar. I then got through, picked up the casting, turned around, and, to my astonishment, saw none of them except Wesley, who stood on top of a heap of rubbish, trying in vain to reach the roof of a small out-house that stood in a corner of the yard. I saw how matters stood, ran and boosted him up, then he pulled me up, from thence easily reaching the top of the wall, from which we dropped safely about twenty feet to the ground. We found ourselves in a narrow lane, which led in one direction toward the business portion of the city upon the river, and in the other to the quiet streets reaching out into the suburbs and to the woods. Our four associates were nowhere in sight, and we conjectured they had gone toward the woods. We took the opposite direction, walked down the lane, crossed two streets, and came to Water Street, which was thronged with people. We turned down this, and after walking a quarter of a mile, passed the station and came to some passenger cars standing on a side track. We entered one of these, thinking to stay till later in the night; but a watchman seeing us, came into the car, which we left by the other door, and walked on down the track, he following us for some distance, then turning back, greatly to our relief. About a mile below the town we came to a sawmill, and looking down from the high bank, saw a sight that made our hearts thrill with joy — a boat glinting in the moonlight, hauled up on a raft of timber. Creeping down the bank, upon the raft we found a large flat-bottomed skiff, which we quickly and silently pushed into the water, and getting in, with two pieces of board in lieu of oars, we were soon slowly propelling our stolen bark across the Ohio. We heared the opposite bank about two miles below, when suddenly hearing men's voices, we ceased paddling, and heard some one shouting: "What are you doing with that stolen boat?" Instead of replying, we silently turned her bow toward the middle of the river, and as we were disappearing in the darkness, could distinguish the words, "Wheeling jail," "escaped prisoners," etc. We floated down about a mile, and the clouds having veiled the moon completely, ventured to paddle to the shore, where we disembarked and pushed the boat as far out into the river as possible, so as to leave no indication that we had landed at that point.

We found ourselves, at about eight o'clock P. M., half a mile above Bellaire, Ohio — the railway junction before referred to. As it was quite dark, we ventured into the outskirts of the village, and coming to a small grocery I sent Wesley in to get some crackers and cheese — this because, being the one on whom Jones would wreak revenge if caught, it was incumbent on me to take no risk of recapture.

We then skirted the town and struck the railway, which runs west by the way of Zanesville, Columbus, and Cincinnati, to Chicago, which latter city was the point we desired to reach. After walking along the track at a rapid rate for perhaps ten miles, we came to Belmont station — near which Eldridge had escaped by leaping from the car window, as elsewhere related — about eleven P. M. Here we found an empty cattle-train that had just passed us, bound west. As it was very dark and raining heavily, I sent Wesley groping in the dark to the rear of the train to have a look into the caboose. Returning soon, he reported that there was a man sitting

within who looked like Pender, despite which information I
thought it best not to miss the opportunity of getting as far
away from Wheeling as possible, even on the same train with
him; therefore we crept up on the top of a car and let ourselves down through the trap-door used for feeding cattle.
Soon the train moved on, and by eight o'clock the next
morning we were within a few miles of Zanesville, or about
seventy miles from Wheeling. For want of locomotive power
to draw the train up an incline, the cars were stopped in a
deep cutting, and then a brakeman came along the top, got
down at the front end of the one we were in and uncoupled
it, without even glancing through the bars. Had he done so
he could not have failed to see us two shivering fugitives
crouched down in one corner at the other end, trying to
shield ourselves from the sleet and rain which drove through
the sides and ends of the car. During our long night ride
this had wet our clothing through and chilled us to the very
bones. As soon as the cars were uncoupled, the engine
started with the portion of the train ahead of us, and soon
disappeared over the brow of the incline. We then climbed
out through the trap, jumped off and scrambled up the bank
into a field, stopped at a small stream, washed our hands and
faces, and soon after called at a farmer's house, where we
remained several hours, drying our clothes and enjoying the
hospitality freely accorded until sunset, when we walked in to
Zanesville.

Walking along the crowded main street, with eyes wide
open, we suddenly spied Pender standing in front of a store,
watching the passers-by. Instantly turning, we got away,
and proceeding to another part of the town, I ascertained
that the trains stopped on the other side of the Muskingum
River. Being afraid to take the train at the Zanesville station, we started to walk across the railway bridge, and were
obliged to hasten, as the train was about to start. Following
the railway track we arrived at the bridge, which was about
a quarter of a mile long, and stepped along from tie to tie,

fearing the train would be upon us. Being very dark, the sound of the rushing stream below filled my mind with strange thoughts as to the consequence of a single false step — a plunge into the ice-cold water, from which there could be no escape. It was a terrible walk, and at each step I expected that one or the other of us would go through. When about half-way over we heard the train coming, and at the same instant saw, or rather heard, a man crossing by the foot-way which ran along the side, this having escaped our notice. Indescribable were our feelings of relief when, after cautiously climbing across to the foot-path, we found ourselves in safety. Hastening across, we reached the station just in time to get on the train, and arrived at Dresden, the junction with the Pittsburgh, Fort Wayne & Chicago Railway, having expended my last cent in paying our fare. It being ten o'clock, and the train northward three hours late, we lay down on the station-house floor and slept until the rumbling of the approaching train aroused us to the necessity of continuing our flight.

Although we had no money to buy tickets we went aboard, and when the conductor came along I gave him fifty cents in stamps, explaining that I had been down in West Virginia, that I was out of money and had been disappointed in receiving more from home, and that I would send him the balance for our fares as soon as I reached home. But on this occasion my eloquence was wasted. The conductor said : "You can ride as far as the fifty cents pays ; then off you go!" Sure enough, it was not long before the train stopped in the woods, and we were promptly put down on the muddy ground. But we were not tired or hungry — were more than one hundred miles from Wheeling, and felt quite safe. A kind farmer gave us a good breakfast, and we walked on all day long. The heavy boots which I wore had taken the skin off my ankles, and by sundown I could hardly move along. We stopped at a farm-house to ask for relief, but the inmates whom we saw plainly through the windows, would not come to the door in response to our knocks. As I could go no farther, I lay down on the grass, and Wesley went on to the next house, returning soon with a gentleman, who incidentally informed us that he was lately from Appomattox and Richmond. I leaned on the shoulders of the two and thus reached the captain's home.

We were received by his old parents with the utmost hospitality; the mother, after bathing and bandaging my feet, furnished us a good supper and showed us to a delightful, clean, soft bed, from which I arose the next morning a new man. After breakfast, these good Samaritans drove us to the Coshocton railway station. We now watched our chance, getting unobserved into an empty freight-car, and rode about one hundred miles to Norwalk, where this road joined the Lake Shore Line.

Here I went into a saloon opposite the station and asked the proprietor to purchase a silk undershirt I had on. When I had explained to him that I wanted the money to pay my fare to Chicago, he said:

"Wait till the express train comes in, and there will be two express company's cars; stand by, and as soon as the train starts step on the platform between them. The conductor only goes through the passenger cars, therefore you can ride as far as you like undisturbed, only be sure to step off as the train arrives at a station."

We followed his advice, and were soon speeding along at thirty miles an hour toward a place of safety.

It will be remembered I was brought from another State on a requisition charging me with felony. That charge not being substantiated, I should have been sent back to the State from which I had been taken. Being illegally imprisoned I had no scruples in attempting a general "jail delivery," and I especially desired to liberate Peney, who had a life sentence.

The convicts were dressed in striped woolen clothes, therefore Wesley and I had distributed our civilian garments among our fellow conspirators, retaining only enough to cover ourselves. We managed to fit out all but one whom I will call Peters, and he was obliged to escape in the striped suit. Although it was dark, he had no sooner got into the street than the prison clothes were recognized; he was pursued, recaptured, and returned to his old quarters, where he survived but a short time, owing to the cruel treatment. A worse fate might have befallen me — the leader.

The following winter my wife and I were in New Orleans for two or three months, and while walking on the levee one day I met Peney. He looked rather dilapidated, and said he had been steward on a river steamer, but had been out of a job for some time. As he had stood by me like a man in the Wheeling jail affair, before I left New Orleans I gave him in all some four or five hundred dollars, since which time I have seen or heard nothing of him.

While on the southern tour I met a man named McCabe at Mobile. He had been an ex-Confederate soldier — so he claimed — but was in the Wheeling jail when I arrived there. Having but a short time to serve, he would take no part in the plan of escape. This man then informed me as to what occurred after my " departure "; among other things, what I have before stated about Peters. He also gave me the particulars of the recapture of Marks, who, it appears, unwisely remained in West Virginia working at the carpenter's trade. After some time he was recognized by one who informed Jones, and soon he was back in his old quarters to finish his seven years.

Marks had been all his life an honest, hard working man, never having been implicated in crime until Charley Meredith, the gambler, had induced him to take part in the Adams Express robbery.

As this is a typical case of several which have come under my observation, I will ask the reader to stop for a moment and ponder the question: Is it best, when a man breaks jail without doing bodily injury to any person — and goes to work with a determination to gain by his labor an honest livelihood — and has been doing so for a considerable length of time — to recapture him and force him to serve out the remainder of his sentence?

The Swiss never punish any man for attempting to escape; they claim that it is natural for all creatures to try to regain their liberty when deprived of it; and it is the business of the authorities to guard prisoners and prevent them from escaping, and the prisoners' right to escape if they can.

Soon after my escape I went to New York, and calling on Mrs. Bolivar — a lady of very respectable family — I gave her a sufficient sum to pay her expenses to Wheeling. She at once proceeded there and procured a remission of one-half of her husband's sentence; so he was set at liberty four months after I quit that model jail.

During her efforts to obtain her husband's freedom I was in correspondence with her, sending her some money as required, and both came directly on to Baltimore to meet me, according to pre-arrangement. They then proceeded to New York, settled matters there, and removed their household goods to West Virginia.

All through the Wheeling affair " Bovar " had claimed to be a victim, and had made a good many friends; and it was for this reason that he had determined to set up as a " doctor " in West Virginia. However, after a few months' " practice," he was back again in New York, having been obliged to fly on account of some " bad luck " in the exercise of his " profession." Not long after his return to New York his amiable wife joined the silent majority. After some vicissitudes, he fell in with and married a wealthy Kentucky heiress, but by some means his new father-in-law learned something of his antecedents, and, by stratagem, got his daughter home, and threatened to shoot Bolivar if he ever put in an appearance there. Thus stood the matter when I went to England, and as to what was his ultimate fate, I have, at the moment of writing, no knowledge.

BOW STREET POLICE STATION.

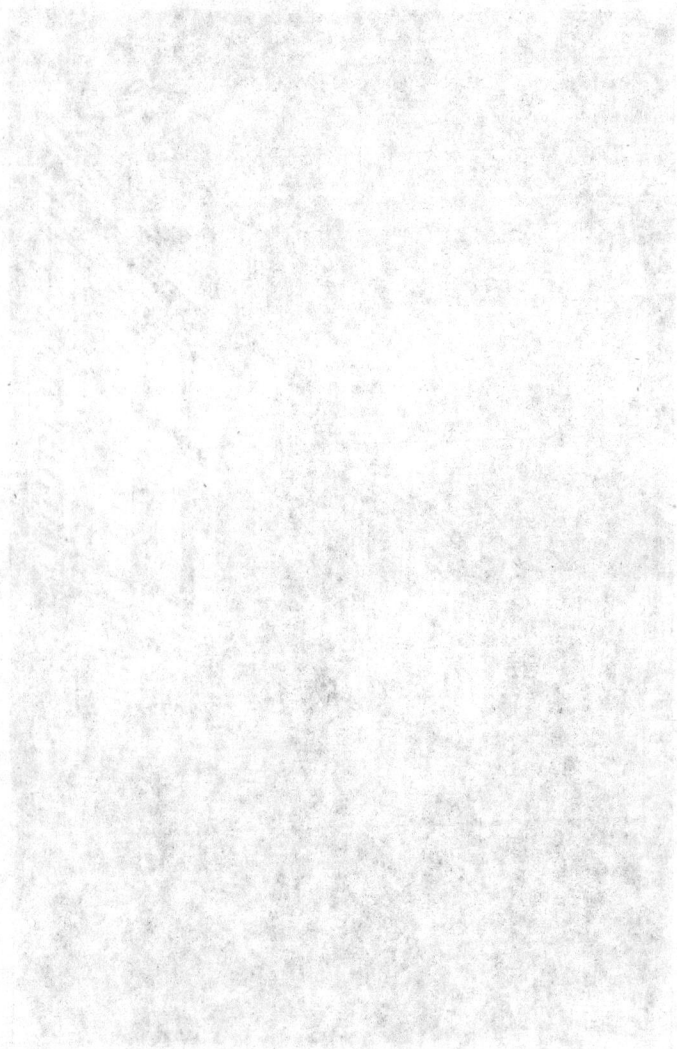

CHAPTER XII.

A HISTORY of my operations in New York would be incomplete without some account of the leading but not dangerous part which on several occasions I took as buyer. For a long time it was a questionable point in my own mind whether I ought to expose the *modus operandi* with which some of the most successful gold forgeries of the period were consummated. I queried: Even if I give false names and dates, dare I make an exposition which will reflect on those who are appointed to guard the public against the attempts of the criminal classes ?

Many other reasons suggested themselves which were well nigh sufficient to deter me from proceeding with this chapter. But I have set out to perform a task, to lay bare the most salient points of a checkered life, in the hope that the recital may prove interesting to all readers, and that many may be led to look upon the serious side of the question. I will begin with the first actual forgery with which I was connected.

It will be remembered that I left Hilton in the Ludlow Street house of detention. By the expenditure of fifty or sixty thousand dollars, and my aid as negotiator, he was set at liberty without trial, although charged with having supplied the Confederate government with blank notes and bonds. In 1867 Hilton introduced me to a Mr. Wilkes, whom I accompanied to the Brandreth House, where we had a long interview. He then accompanied me to a restaurant where he said a friend was awaiting him, and introduced me to one whom I have since discovered to be Walter Sheridan, whose portrait appears in Inspector Byrnes's "Professional Criminals." I have no doubt that Wilkes introduced me to Sheridan that the latter might be able to judge as to what kind of a customer had been picked up as a monkey to pull their chestnuts out of the fire.

After some general conversation Wilkes and myself returned to the Brandreth House, where he revealed to me that he had procured a genuine draft from a San Francisco firm on Messrs. Bowen, McNamee & Co., at that time the largest drygoods firm in America; that on presentation of this draft for payment, the firm stamped on it their acceptance and endorsed it, making it payable at their bank — the ―――― National, on Broadway.

"Now," said Wilkes, "Hilton has made me two books of blank drafts which have the names of St. Louis houses printed in. All you have to do is to go into Wall Street and buy gold, fill in a draft for the amount, come out to me and I will put on the acceptance exactly like the genuine; then you can take it back, pay for the gold with it, let them send it to the bank to get it certified, then go back and take away the gold, provided there is no hitch at the bank. He went on to explain his plan in detail, which will appear as subsequent events are narrated. As the art of forgery was then to me a strange one, I was as much astonished at his revelations as I had been formerly at those of Frank Kibbe's — being incredulous that such an operation could be successfully executed. However, I concluded to try it, and taking a man to act as my servant, I went to the Stevens House on lower Broadway, and engaged a room, to which Wilkes came unobserved. I then took my servant with me to a firm of gold and bullion brokers in Wall Street, Wilkes remaining outside for a purpose which will soon appear. I asked the price of gold? "One eighty (say)," was the reply. "I will take thirty thousand dollars,"

I said — took out a book of blank drafts, filled one in for the amount, remarking, " I will have to send this up to my correspondents for acceptance " — at the same time saying: " Here, James, take this up to Bowen, McNamee & Co., have it accepted, and bring it back to me. Hurry up ! " The servant left, and as previously instructed, went to where Wilkes was waiting, who immediately filled out another draft which had the forged acceptance endorsed across its face, and sent it to me by the servant. I handed it to the broker who looked it over and said :

" This is payable at the ——— National bank, and as we never deliver gold or other securities to strangers unless we get the bank's acceptance, I will send and have it certified."

He gave it to a messenger who started for the door, but as he was passing I joined him, and as we came out I asked him how long he was likely to be gone. This was done in order that Wilkes, who was on the watch, might identify the messenger who had the draft, and be enabled to follow him to the bank to learn if it was accepted without demur. Meanwhile I remained in the office. But what if suspicion should be aroused on presentation of the draft at the bank — inquiry be made at Bowen, McNamee & Co.'s, and the forgery discovered ?

Of course I should at once be arrested at the broker's office. To avoid such a risk, after the messenger had been gone a few minutes, I looked at my watch and remarked : " I have time to meet another engagement, and will return soon." I then went to a place just round the corner, as previously arranged with Wilkes. In about half an hour he came to me very much crestfallen and said :

" I lost the messenger somehow, and did not see him in the bank ; but I think it is all right, for I went in a few minutes since, everything appearing quiet, and I saw nothing unusual."

" Well," said I, " shall I go and risk trying to get the money ?"

"No," he replied, "I don't want you to take any chances; it is better to try again in another place."

I immediately took the servant, and with the exception of using the other draft-book with a different name, I went to an office nearly opposite the former place, and purchased twenty-five thousand in gold, going through all the same manœuvres as before. This time he came back still more crestfallen than before, and said he had again lost sight of the messenger.

As previously stated, such operations were new to me, but in the light of after experience I am able to deduce the probable cause of his failure. He was an old forger, and a great coward, one who would fly at his own shadow. Wall Street and the brokers' offices at this time were thronged with speculators. At the offices where I made the gold purchases, persons were constantly passing in and out, and as there was a throng on the sidewalk, it was necessary in order to be sure of the messenger, that Wilkes should stand on the walk near the door. This he feared to do from the remote possibility that in some way suspicion might be aroused and I be arrested. In case of such an event he believed that I might do as perhaps he would were the case reversed — point out the man at the door as the actual forger. No doubt when I came out with the messenger, others were passing in and out about their business. Wilkes did not wait to see, but fled a short distance, then not being pursued, he recovered from his panic, and made his way to the bank in the hope of there meeting the messenger.

The failure of these well-concerted schemes of robbery, after having executed my part so well, disgusted me. We adjourned to the Stevens House, and burned in the grate of the room I had taken all the papers connected with the case. It had cost Wilkes and Sheridan a thousand dollars to prepare for the job. This and many other failures in the different branches of crime that I have known of, prove that the most skillful and experienced law-breakers often lose the capital invested. I afterwards ascertained that the bills were duly certified and that the brokers held the gold ready for delivery, but as I did not call for it, they sent word to Bowen, McNamee & Co., inquiring why their customer had not called for the money. This resulted of course in a disclosure of the attempted forgery, and the bank officers no doubt congratulated themselves on the lucky escape from loss. I had no more to do with forgers or forgery until some years later, when I met George Engles.

To show that forgers did obtain money, though failing to follow up the messengers, I will here introduce another character—a skillful manipulator who took a prominent part in other transactions to be described.

Despite the resolution I had formed—from the moment I had succumbed to Kibbe's temptation at Baltimore—to have nothing to do with persons who committed crimes which, if detected, would send the doers to state prison (Kibbe's mode of merchandise swindling not then incurring that penalty), the reader who has followed the thread of my story will perceive that one step led to another, until now I experienced no great repugnance at making the acquaintance of a man who I was informed lived by forgery. I saw him for the first time a few months before going to England.

George Engles was by birth a Prussian, blue-eyed, blonde-haired, and slim in stature. Like Kibbe, he was a great coward, but unlike him he was true to his friends. Although the product of his numerous forgeries amounted in the aggregate to hundreds of thousands, he never had any money long. The reason of this was that as soon as he obtained possession of any sum, however large, he was sure to play at faro until his last dollar was gone. He also drank heavily. He was well educated, and had been a good business man. At about twenty-two years of age he had left his German home and settled in the city of New York, where he became a dealer in naval stores. While in this business he married a lady of German parentage, and at the time I became acquainted with the family they had six children. The wife appeared a good woman, and greatly attached to her husband and family. The children were bright, and had no suspicion as to the way their father, at that time, made his money. Some years previously he had failed in business, and never after got a fresh start in an honest way of life. Under the pressure of poverty he had gradually relaxed the honest business principles brought from his fatherland, going on from one petty swindle to another, until, becoming bolder, he tried his hand at larger operations, till he finally turned to forgery, and at the time of which I write he was known as " The Terror of Wall Street." He always remained in the back-ground, prepared the forged papers, checks, etc., leaving to the more foolhardy the risk of presenting them, and the subsequent trial and imprisonment.

With the mutual acquaintance who introduced me to George Engles, I one day visited the home of the latter. We accepted an invitation to stay to dinner, believing that it would prove first-class, for we knew that he had the previous week received a large sum, the proceeds of an extensive forgery.

We were a little staggered at discovering the furniture, carpets, etc., in his rooms to be pretty common and worn out. When dinner was announced, we went below to the usual basement dining-room. His anxious and amiable wife must have been greatly embarrassed in her attempt to entertain guests in such an ill-furnished, dilapidated place. The chairs and table were broken; the cloth riddled with holes; the dishes cracked and mismatched. Everything was clean, and the food provided was well cooked by Mrs. Engles' own hands; but the lack of variety and insufficiency in quantity made us feel as though every mouthful we took was needed by the hungry children.

"And is it possible," I soliloquized, " that a man with whom I divided several thousand dollars three days since, who is so pleasant, good-natured, and generous among his associates, can have become so infatuated with the game of faro as to have dropped the whole amount into the jaws of the " tiger," giving no part of it to relieve the wants of this faithful wife and her innocent children ?"

This was my first and last visit to George Engles's house, for soon after he left with me for England. Some months later he returned alone to America; I remained to pass half a lifetime in misery, taking a view of life from behind the bars, with plenty of time for retrospections.

RETROSPECTIONS.

Some days before the dinner referred to, George Engles came to the house where I lodged. After some preliminaries, he said he was again out of money, and that if I would procure the genuine check of some firm in good credit, one which would be likely to hold a heavy balance in bank, he would have some *fac-simile* checks printed, and draw out all their money. I at once went to Newark, N. J., and going to a hotel I wrote an order for about fifty dollars' worth of sample goods, enclosing a bill of exchange for one hundred dollars, payable to the order of, say Smith & Co., the letter being about as follows:

MESSRS. SMITH & Co., New York:

GENTLEMEN, — Please ship to me, at your earliest convenience, one ten-gallon keg of the best brandy you can sell by the cask for $4.00 per gallon. I am about making a shipment to the South, and if the brandy proves satisfactory, you may receive a larger order. Please deduct the amount from enclosed bank draft, and remit me your check for any balance in my favor, with invoice, and oblige, etc. (signed any name).

The next day I received the keg of brandy, and shipped it to a friend to sell for what he could get. I also received Smith & Co.'s check, and returning to New York, gave it to George Engles, who in two days had the blank checks ready.

For certain reasons I wish to cover up, as far as possible, the place and names where the following operation was carried out. The next morning our party of three went to the vicinity of the Wall Street of a certain city, where we met a man in citizen's clothes. This was a constable who had long been on special duty in the interests of the bankers and brokers, to prevent forgers, thieves, etc., from operating among them. He was introduced to us as "reliable," and I started out to buy gold, which was then about $1.80. This time I went in, and after getting the price, I agreed to take — I forget how much — say $10,000, and said I would be back in ten minutes to pay for the same; I proceeded to the place of rendezvous near by, and George Engles, in the presence of ourselves and the constable, filled out a check bearing the forged signature for the amount. This I took, followed by the constable and two others, who kept me in sight, and handed it in at the broker's office.

The broker gave it to a messenger, who hurried to the bank not far away to get it certified. Those who were on the watch followed him, and one of them went into the bank and saw the check handed to the cashier, who certified and gave it back to the messenger. In the meantime, as soon as the latter had gone toward the bank, I made an excuse to

UNDERGROUND PASSAGE AND STAIRS LEADING TO OLD BAILEY DOCK.

leave the office and hastened to a place near by, as previously agreed upon. As soon as the man who followed the messenger into the bank saw that the check was duly certified, he came out, and upon reaching the steps, lifted his hat in a natural way so as not to attract attention.

This was recognized as a signal that the check had been duly accepted, and that it would be safe for me to return to the broker's office for the money. Accordingly the constable, who happened to be nearest to where I was waiting, came within view of me, lifted his hat, and wiped his forehead with his handkerchief. I " caught on " — if I may be permitted the use of an expression which came into usage while I was in an English prison — and hurried back to the broker's office, arriving there ahead of the messenger, who, when he returned, saw me standing quietly by the counter. The broker took the check and handed me the roll of Custom House gold certificates, which I deliberately counted, then walked out. As soon as I was in the street one of the party brushed by me, and as he passed I slipped the notes into his hand; he went direct to the Custom House, drew the gold for them, and brought it to the place of meeting, where we were by this time all arrived. The reason I instantly got rid of the notes was that had I been arrested the next moment, my confederates would have used the money to effect a compromise to procure my release, if other means failed.

After concerting new places of meeting, I went and made a second purchase in a different part of the street, which was equally successful with the first.

On again meeting at the place of rendezvous, the question came up as to whether we had drawn out all the firm's balance in bank. After an exchange of pros and cons, the constable said :

" We may as well have another go, boys ; for if their balance is all drawn out, they have good credit, and the bank won't dishonor their check. Besides, in case of trouble, I shall be the first officer on hand, and as they all know me to

be 'dead nuts' on forgers, I should be the one called on to
arrest Meigs [the name I was known by]. If that happen,
I will take him through a quiet street towards the police
station. While on the way, as soon as we are in a suitable
place, I will give him the tip, and he must 'pop' me square
in the eyes, so as to put them both in mourning, and then
clear out as though the devil was after him. Of course I'll
go back and be condoled with by my friends, the brokers, for
my damaged eyes. But I say, boys [with a wink at the
bags of gold, and a broad laugh], can't I afford to stand a
good right-hander for my share in that yellow stuff?"

As I was the chief actor in the operation of this day, I
had stood by silent while the discussion was going on, ready
to try again or otherwise, as they should decide. The constable's words decided the point. I went and made a third
purchase, the same series of maneuvers being used as before,
but owing to the throng about the door of the office where I
made the purchase, those on watch outside mistook the messenger, following the wrong man. After discovering their
error, one of them came and gave me the signal to remain
where I was. It will be perceived that we were now in precisely the same dilemma in which Wilkes and I were on a
former occasion, viz., we did not know whether the check
had been certified or not; in consequence of which it was not
safe for me to present myself for the money until that point
should be settled. However, we were prepared for just such
an emergency — to meet and to overcome it.

The constable sauntered in the direction of the office
where I had made the last purchase, stopping in at the
various offices, as he was accustomed to do, inquiring if
there was anything stirring in his line of business, until he
reached the office in which we were for the moment interested. As he entered there he gave a rapid look around, and
saw that all was going on as usual — as he afterward told
us — then said to one of the partners, carelessly:

"Well, is there anything 'crooked' going on, to-day?"

"No; I hear nothing," was the reply.

He came out to where I was waiting, and said:

"All right; go for it."

I went straight to the broker, and said:

"I have been detained at the Custom House. I suppose you have my gold ready for delivery?"

The gold notes were handed over, I counted them, walked out unmolested, and passed them to a confederate, as on the other occasions. Soon we were all at the place where Engles had remained during the day. We there divided the proceeds of the day's spoils. The constable pocketed his share, equal to a year's salary, shook hands all around, and departed highly pleased with his day's "police duty"; the others of us returned to our places of residence in New York, some of them to squander the ill-gotten gains in doubtful enjoyments.

CHAPTER XIII.

GEORGE M'DONALD'S EARLY LIFE—GOES TO HARVARD COLLEGE—HIS PARENTS—
HE LEAVES HOME—MEETS KIBBE, "THE ROGUE"—GETS INTO THE "TOMBS"
I MAKE HIS ACQUAINTANCE—SKETCH OF AUSTIN BIDWELL—A "MALE QUAR-
TET" OFF FOR EUROPE—ARRIVAL IN LONDON—A "DUET" VISIT IRELAND—
"FREAKS" ENDORSED ON BANK OF ENGLAND NOTES—MR. GREEN—HE INTRO-
DUCES "WARREN" TO THE BANK—MR. FRANCIS AND MR. FENWICK, BANK MAN-
AGERS—WARREN OPENS AN ACCOUNT AT THE BANK OF ENGLAND.

IN the early spring of 1872, soon after the events recorded
in the last chapter, I agreed to make a foreign trip with
George Engles, with a view of "raising the wind" out of
European capitalists. I was as yet but a novice in the art of
forgery, and acted as subordinate to Engles who was the actual
forger.

As George McDonald was one of our party, a short sketch
of his early life will be appropriate at this point. Although
our circumstances in life were originally so unlike, yet we
both reached the same goal—a prison.

McDonald belonged to a good family, of Scotch-Irish
descent, on the mother's side in a direct line from the
O'Neils, who were ancient kings of Ireland. He was born in
1846, near Boston, in a beautiful country villa, the property
of his father. This was surrounded by an evergreen hedge,
beyond the limits of which the children were never permitted
to stray, and were kept in charge of nurses and tutors until
sent away to school or college. The mother was a high-
minded, noble-hearted woman, of a religious character, and
devoted to the moral and intellectual education of her children.
The father was unbending and severe in the treatment of all
delinquencies, and required his children to be, like himself,
upright and exact in all the relations of life. Even when

(132)

well grown they were seldom permitted to associate with others of their own age for fear of contamination, and on those rare occasions, great care was taken in the selection of their companions. At an early age George was sent to Harvard college, with the understanding that he was to become a physician.

The foregoing will show that his opportunities were excellent — in marked contrast with the physical and mental privations of my early life. To that comparison I will add a very singular coincidence. After I had parted with Kibbe in Buffalo, as related in a former chapter, McDonald, having left home as the result of some intrigue, and being afraid to face his stern father, started out to seek his fortune. Arriving at Chicago he fell in with Kibbe, much in the same way that I had previously done. Kibbe's plausible way of " putting things " soon undermined his new pupil's sense of honor, with the result that a merchandise swindling business was put in operation, and according to his usual plan " The Rogue " appropriated all the proceeds of the fraud, just as he had previously done by me. And like me, his doubly deluded victim believed he could make a fortune in this wonderful, newly discovered way — one which, to his inexperienced mind, appeared the " open sesame " to easily and safely acquired wealth. Of course it was not long before he was in " trouble."

I first met him in the " Tombs," where he was a fellow-prisoner for a short time in the same cell with an acquaintance of mine. After I had effected the release of the latter, he urged me to go to the " Tombs " to see and to use my " influence " in behalf of his late associate. I agreed to do so, and a few days later the young man McDonald was also set at liberty, he having lost it as the result of an attempt to get rich in the way Kibbe had shown him.

Upon more intimate acquaintance I ascertained that he was of a wealthy family, well able to assist him into an honorable business, and urged him by all means to go home — that there could be but one end to such practices, and that end a prison. I told him that I had been engaged in the perpetration of these merchandise frauds long enough to realize the danger, still, as I had no friends to assist me, I must continue on for *a short time* until I had a small capital to start with. I also added that each time I had almost gained my point, some " trouble " had caused me to expend all my cash in exchange for my own liberty, or that of some of my confederates. People seldom act on good advice, and shame of appearing among his friends also deterred him from acting on mine.

As the time has come when I must introduce my brother Austin on the scene, I will, in this connection, give a brief sketch, showing how he ultimately became in any way connected with us in the Bank of England affair.

He had been brought up in the same religious atmosphere as myself, but, being the youngest child, had escaped some of the burdens, described in former chapters, that weighed down the lives of us who were older. I have elsewhere stated that when I finally joined Kibbe, I supposed that his newly invented mode of getting rich would give me, in a month or two, all the capital that I then considered sufficient to reëstablish myself in a legitimate business. Above all things, I had endeavored to conceal from my family my wanderings from the path of rectitude. But for the reasons already related, I never did succeed in reëstablishing myself, and am still, at fifty-five, working for that end, only in a different way — one which I trust will meet the approval of the many readers of this book.

My brother Austin was a fine, steady young man, and universally regarded as one likely to fill an honorable position in the world.

Now what train of circumstances blasted those prospects? Who led him into the maze, the intricate windings of which at last landed him within a prison's iron gates? It was I, George Bidwell, his brother!

The reader already knows the circumstances which turned

my steps into that maze. While engaged in a merchandise swindling operation, carried on under the guise of a wholesale grocery and commission house, I needed the assistance of another reliable person. As the business had every appearance of genuineness, I believed I could induce Austin to come and assist me until I should be ready for the wind-up — then send him home none the wiser.

Enjoining on my partner the importance of keeping my young brother ignorant of the real nature of our transactions, I accordingly sent for him and set him at work, believing that the swindle then in course of execution would be my very last. Austin proved himself a very efficient assistant. When about ready to close the business, I made an excuse to send him home, and he departed, unsuspicious as to the real state of affairs. Of course this was not my " very last operation," and the time came when I found it convenient to use his services again — and again.

After a time his eyes became opened to the real nature of my business operations, but so gradually that his mind was not shocked as it would have been if suddenly enlightened regarding the dishonest practices.

In the settlement with Kibbe at Buffalo, after I had run him to earth in Canada, as related in a previous chapter, I took in payment a large quantity of goods that had been shipped to Henry Harvey Short & Co. In applying at the depots and wharves for their delivery, I did not dare do the business under an alias, for the reason that in case any of the parties who had shipped them should arrive and question my right to their possession, or should arrest me, I could give references as to myself or Austin, and show that I was doing nothing illegal, so long as no guilty intent on my part could be proven. Therefore, wishing to keep my given name out of it, I rather inconsiderately did the business in the name of Austin Bidwell. In later instances I did the same thing, and I have ascertained, while writing this book, that the police have him down as the actual perpetrator and principal in that

and many frauds with which he either had nothing whatever
to do, or which had been planned by myself and others. He
being so much my junior, I always felt a heavy responsibility
resting on me, and was ever more solicitous for his safety
than for my own, after he learned my mode of life. In consequence of this feeling I kept him in the background as far
as possible, and would not permit him to take risks in any
operation in which I was engaged. I may here state that,
such was my ruling idea in the subsequent Bank of England
affair, I absolutely refused to have anything to do with it
unless Austin should first be safely out of Great Britain —
we two brothers should not at the same time risk our liberty
in the same operation.

The British government have been informed that he was
the principal actor in the operations above referred to, and
many others in America and on the Continent. This I deny
in toto, as *I* am the man who did nearly everything mistakenly
attributed to him; and I furthermore aver that Austin was
never a principal in any fraud in either of those countries.

I now fully realize, and for long years have deeply grieved,
the terrible ruin I unintentionally, yet inexcusably, wrought
on his young life. Naturally wishing to exonerate him, and
to aid in removing any obstacle which may be delaying his
restoration to liberty, and consequent labors to reëstablish
himself as a worthy member of society, I have considered it
imperative on me to give the above facts. I do not claim
him to have been an "innocent," but a thousand times less
guilty throughout than myself; and if given an opportunity to
begin life anew, he will never disappoint the expectations of
those who are instrumental in gaining him that opportunity.

Having enlightened the reader regarding the *dramatis
personæ* in the "tragedy" to follow, I now resume the thread
of my narrative.

Austin having desired to accompany me to England, I
finally concluded to take him along, as an outsider, in case
I should be arrested and exigencies arise whereby his assist-

LONDON POLICEMAN.--- ST. PAUL'S IN DISTANCE.

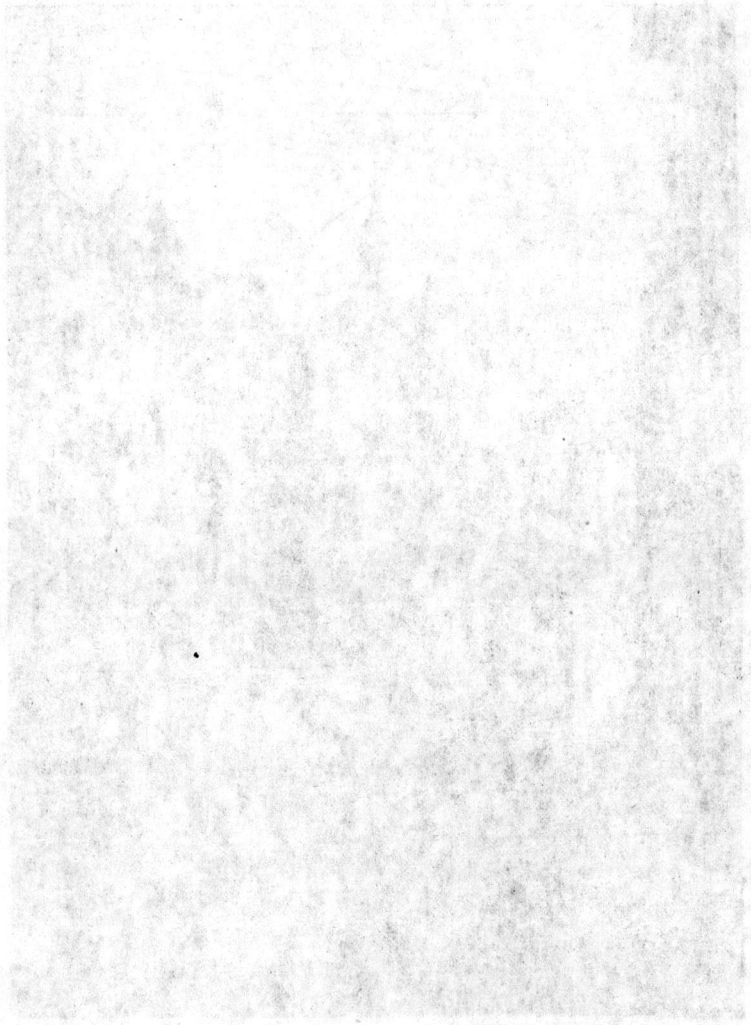

ance might be required. In pursuance of Engles' plan, he, McDonald, Austin, and myself met on board the steamer — McDonald's mother making a considerable journey to see him off, believing her son to be engaged in carrying on a large business in cotton.

Soon after our arrival in London, Mac received an invitation to visit some relatives in the north of Ireland, with whom he was in correspondence, and invited Austin to accompany him, I being absent from London for three days. They were to start immediately, but Austin had £2,000 of my money in his pocket in bank-notes. Not liking to risk taking them along on the journey, it became a question as to how to dispose of them until his return from Ireland. Finally it occurred to him that on the way to the railway station he could call in and deposit it with his tailor, Mr. Edward Hamilton Green of No. 35 Saville Row, he having an appointment to call there to try on a new suit of clothes that morning.

Upon the occasion of the trial, sixteen months later, the number of aliases used by us caused some comment, and in this connection I may as well show how some of them came to be used; though, as a matter of course, when men start out with the intention of taking part in crime they generally drop their right names and use aliases. For example, in my own case, I regret to say that I had become so used to aliases that their employment had become a matter of indifference, though in private matters I generally went in my right name; but frequently I would give another out of mere caprice, or a sudden freak. One of these "freaks" came about as follows: After my arrival in England, it was not long before I had occasion to offer in payment a £5 Bank of England note. The dealer handed it back, and asked me to put my name and address on the back of the note. "But," I replied, "this note is payable to 'bearer,' and requires no endorsement." However, the dealer insisted that he could not accept it unless I should endorse it. As such was not the custom in my own country, it looked to me like a piece of tom-foolery to require

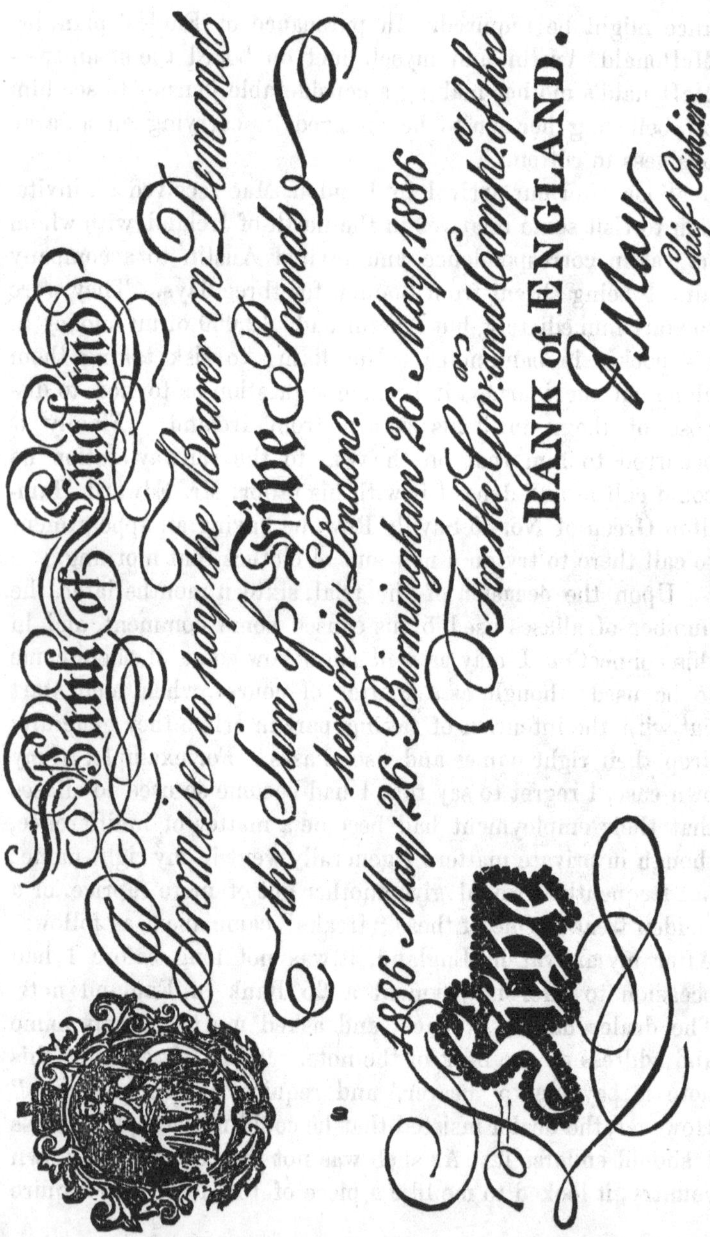

The counterfeit plate.

that notes payable to the bearer should be endorsed. Suddenly I seized a pen and scribbled on "Tom Noodle, Thames Embankment," or some other absurdity, and this was quite satisfactory to the shop-keeper. Occasionally, even when paying cash for an article in gold or silver, the shopman would ask for my name and address, with a result similar to the above. At the trial in the following year, the prosecution desiring to overwhelm us with quantity to make up for the lack of quality and exactitude of evidence, brought forward every shop-keeper to be found, from whom any of us had made purchases, in order to produce a worse impression by the number of aliases; and this sort of thing was carried so far that several witnesses made mistakes in identification, etc.

Austin's acquaintance with Mr. Green began in this wise: Soon after his arrival in England, on the 18th day of April, 1872, he was sauntering along Saville Row, taking a general view of high life at the " West End," when his eye lighted on some cloth in a shop-window. He entered the place and found himself in the presence of Mr. Green. He ordered and paid for a suit, through some freak giving the name of F. A. Warren, No. 21 Enfield Road, where I was lodging. Now there is nothing more certain than that when this occurred there was no intention of using Mr. Green for any purpose beyond his legitimate business; yet the prosecution brought this circumstance in as a link in the alleged long-prepared scheme of fraud.

The 4th of May following, on the way to the railway station, according to the plan mentioned at the beginning of this chapter, they had the cab stop at Mr. Green's. After trying on the clothes, Austin asked him to keep £1,200 until his return from Ireland. "Austin Bidwell said he had more money than he thought it prudent to leave at his lodgings, and that it was about £2,000. I did not like to keep so large a sum, and recommended him to deposit it in some bank; adding that my bankers were close at hand. Austin Bidwell then accompanied me to the Western Branch of the Bank of

England, where I kept an account, and I introduced him to the assistant manager, Mr. Fenwick." The foregoing are Mr. Green's own words at the trial, and he had "forgotten" a good deal which would have shown Austin's disinclination to leave the money elsewhere, giving as the reason that he should return from Ireland in a few days; but behind this was the consciousness that he was known to Mr. Green as Warren, and in case of an introduction to the bank it must necessarily be in that name.

WESTERN BRANCH.

Upon being introduced to Mr. Fenwick, Warren (as I shall call Austin in this connection) asked Mr. Fenwick to give him a simple receipt for the £1,200, which was the sum he wished to leave. Mr. Fenwick advised him to leave his signature and take a check-book, remarking that he would find it very convenient to be enabled to check for money wherever he happened to be. Warren declined accepting the offer, on the ground that he had no use at that time for a bank account, and repeating that he should want the money on his return from Ireland. This was quite true, as I had already matured my plans to go to Rio Janeiro, not having the remotest idea of any opening in England for a " specula-tion." Mr. Fenwick gave further reasons why it would be better to open account with the money than to leave it other-wise, and finally, as McDonald was waiting, he acceded to the proposition, and started for Ireland with him.

I had no knowledge of all this until their return, three or four days later, and I was greatly surprised when I was told about the Warren account with the Bank of England. Indeed, when it was first alluded to I paid no attention, thinking, as I had a good right to do, that they were endeav-oring to " take a rise " out of me. Not till the bank and check books were produced did I give their incredible story any credit. Austin asserted that when going to the bank with Mr. Green, he had no idea that it was to the Bank of England. At all events, after the matter had been communi-cated to me and duly considered, I could not perceive any benefit to be derived from a continuance of the account in a false name, and as before said, I had decided to go to Rio Janeiro, expecting to make use of my capital there, and then go home without returning to England. For this reason, I directed " Warren " to withdraw the money and close the account.

Within a week of his return from Ireland he called at the bank for that purpose. Now mark what passed. It is a rule of the bank of England that every depositor must keep a bal-ance of at least three hundred pounds. Warren informed the manager of his intention to close the account as he was intend-ing to leave England. Upon hearing this the same arguments that were used to induce him to open the account were again brought forward to show him the advantages which would arise in case the account was continued. Warren said that he expected to employ all his money and could not leave the balance required in order to keep the account open. After many pros and cons he concluded to leave the odd money — a balance of thirty-nine pounds — at the same time assuring the manager that there was no probability of his having any occasion to make use of the account. A week later I sailed from Liverpool on board the Steamship *Lucitania* for Rio Janeiro, expecting to go around the coast of South America to San Francisco, and thence by rail to New York, and the bank of England account lay forgotten until the defeat of my South American plan and return to Europe the first of September following.

At the trial the prosecution slurred over this and every other fact which would tend to show that the " Great Bank Forgery " was *not* a long planned scheme. Also, in pursuance of their theory, which they considered absolutely necessary to establish in order to clear the bank-managers from the charge of looseness in conducting business, the witnesses from the bank at the trial, on being pressed on these points, had " forgotten " or could only say to " the best of their belief," and so on. By bringing to bear their more than imperial power, unbounded influence, and the expenditure of $350,000, they succeeded in " proving " that we had been working and preparing the scheme during more than a year before the possibility of such a fraud had ever entered our heads. The success of the prosecution on that point was one of the chief causes which got us life sentences, instead of the ten years or less, usual in cases of forgery. It may be that *I* deserved even so severe a sentence as that, but surely some of the others — well, I refrain, leaving the reader to judge for himself.

To sum up the matter: The bank-books will corroborate my statement regarding the small balance lying a long time without additional deposits. The eagerness shown to have " Warren " open the account in the first instance, and the breaking of a bank of England rule in permitting the account to remain open with one-eighth of the required balance — no business being transacted during three months or more — at the time filled me with surprise, and I can now account for it only on the supposition that the Western Branch had not been long established, and that the manager, or his representative, wished to increase the business as much as possible in order to make a good showing at the head office.

BANK OF ENGLAND SCENE.— VISITOR HOLDING £1,000,000 ($5,000,000) BANK OF ENGLAND NOTES.

CHAPTER XIV.

BORDEAUX, MARSEILLES, AND LYONS "DONATE" $50,000—A BAD QUARTER OF AN HOUR—EGGS AND PEASANT WOMEN—"SWEETS TO THE SWEET"—A MYSTERIOUS STRANGER DISAPPEARS AMONG THE TOMBS—REUNION IN LONDON—COWARDICE OR "PRUDENCE" OF GEORGE ENGLES.

BEFORE leaving New York, Engles had come into possession of several letters of credit issued by the Bank of North Wales, Liverpool, which had been picked from the pocket of an English traveler while getting on a train in Jersey City. These the thief had discovered were worthless to him, and as there are threads of intercommunication running through all the different classes of criminals, it was surmised that though the papers were valueless to an ordinary thief, the opposite might be the case with a forger. We proceeded to make use of them in the subsequent fraudulent operations by which French bankers were victimized. I purchased a circular letter of credit from the London and Westminster Bank, one of the largest banking institutions at that time in Great Britain, the Bank of England excepted, and about the only one which did not require any reference regarding the above purchase. I next procured lithographed letter heads which were *fac-similes* of those in use at the London and Westminster Bank. In the letter of credit was a list of the bank's correspondents throughout the world, so that the traveler might get the notes which were attached to his letter turned into the currency of whatever country he happened to be in. On the lithographed letter-sheets mentioned above were written letters of introduction addressed (say) Messrs. Smith & Co., Bordeaux; Brune & Co., Marseilles; Blank & Co., Lyons; all reading as follows:

(144)

THE RIGHT HONORABLE SIR SIDNEY WATERLOW,
Lord Mayor of London in 1873, in official costume.

[Printed letter heading.]

LONDON AND WESTMINSTER BANK,

LONDON, March 22, 1872.

MESSRS. SMITH & Co., Bordeaux, France:

GENTLEMEN, — A valued customer of ours, Mr. Thomas Hooker, is about to visit your city. Mr. Hooker holds our circular letter of credit, also special letters of credit issued by the Bank of North Wales. We shall take pleasure in honoring any drafts which he may have occasion to draw against these Whatever you may find it convenient to do in forwarding his business affairs, or contributing to his enjoyment, will, as occasion offers, be cordially reciprocated.

I remain, gentlemen, very sincerely,

(say) LEWIS SMITH,

Manager London and Westminster Bank.

I have forgotten the names given, and make use of any others by way of illustration. These letters were mailed in London, envelopes sealed with wax, and stamped in exact imitation of those sent out by the bank. The day they were mailed I went alone to France, having in my possession the genuine circular letter of credit with notes attached, issued by the London and Westminster Bank, and three false letters of credit purporting to be issued by the North Wales Bank, for about three thousand pounds each. All these documents had been written by George Engles.

Crossing the channel from Dover to Calais, the small, black, side-wheel steamer — a pitching, rollicking, little monster — seemed to enjoy all the discomforts of the passengers aboard. In due time I arrived at Paris, and without delay took the train for Bordeaux.

Before leaving London, letters were posted to Thomas Hooker, in care of the firms I intended to victimize in the three cities named. Therefore, on arriving at Bordeaux, I called on Smith & Co., and inquired if there were letters for me. They at once gave me the one mailed to myself, which had come in the same mail with one for their firm purporting to be from the London and Westminster Bank. The receipt of

10

my letter satisfied me that Smith & Co. had received theirs, which must naturally place me very high in their estimation. During my criminal career I never could avoid experiencing a certain qualm, when taking advantage of the confidence placed in me by gentlemen who received me courteously and with marked attention. But the thirst for riches, once implanted, will lead any man to unthought-of depths of infamy. As soon as these gentlemen were aware that I was "Mr. Hooker," they lavished every attention upon me — invited me to dinner, and a drive through the city afterward. I thanked them, and explained that I was obliged to decline, as my agent was waiting for me at Bayonne, where I had purchased some real estate; and having been recommended to their firm, I should feel obliged if they would cash my draft for two thousand pounds, and endorse it on my letter of credit (handing over one on the North Wales Bank). Mr. Smith replied that it was the custom of the French bankers to require twenty-four hours' notice before drawing a check, and asked me if the next day would not answer. "We shall be happy to assist you," said he, "in passing the time pleasantly." This was a new custom to me, but I answered instantly, expressing regret that the nature of my business precluded delay, it being necessary that I should reach Bayonne that night. "I suppose," continued I, "that your bankers will not mind your checking out a small sum without the usual notice. However, if it occasions any embarrassment or inconvenience, I can easily procure the money elsewhere." One of the partners replied that their bank would without doubt honor their check, and the matter should be attended to at once. I sat down for a half hour, conversing on a variety of topics. Of course this was a most trying period to me; the least show of haste or anxiety might have betrayed me to those lynx-eyed, experienced men of business. In the midst of our conversation, an undercurrent of thought kept running through my mind, thus: "Who knows but they have sent a dispatch to the London and

Westminster Bank, merely as a matter of business precaution, and that they are delaying me to get a reply? In that case, I shall have a good opportunity to learn the pure French accent, while passing my days in the Bagnio at Toulon." At last, however, the amount was paid over to me in French bank-notes. I deliberately counted them, and took leave, lighter in mind, and heavier in purse by fifty thousand francs.

I had arranged with Engles (whose merits for a criminal calling in the way of cowardice were described in a former chapter) to go every morning to the Queen's Hotel, London, for letters which I should send addressed to "H. Cowper."

After receiving the money, I enclosed it in a large envelope, addressing it to Cowper, London. I also wrote on the envelope: "Echantillions du papier" (*i. e.*, samples of paper), after which I posted it at the post-office.

As I wished to reduce the risk as much as possible (the train for Marseilles not leaving for three hours), I took a carriage and told the driver to carry me towards the next station on the route to that city. After we were fairly out in the country, I got outside and sat with the driver, discoursing with him about the country we were driving through, arriving in the village about half an hour before the train from Bordeaux was due. I dismissed my driver at a small village cabaret or tavern, walked to the station, got aboard the train, and early the next morning was in Marseilles. I breakfasted at the Hotel d' Europe, and looked over the papers to see if the Bordeaux fraud had been discovered. As I could see no indication of it, about 10 A. M. I took a carriage and went to call on Messrs. Brune & Co.

Here, as before, I found a letter for Mr. Hooker, which assured me that they had received the bogus one addressed to themselves, consequently every thing looked clear for the fresh fraud contemplated.

On making myself known I was, as usual, received with the utmost courtesy, began to talk business, and one of the firm got into my carriage and rode with me to his bank to effect the sale of my draft on London for the sum of £2,500. Arriving at the bank I took a seat in the front office, while Mr. Brune went into the manager's room to introduce the transaction; the clerks eyed me as I thought suspiciously, but doubtless only curiously, because they perceived I was a foreigner. Another thing which I noticed sent a shiver through me. After Mr. Brune had been a few minutes in the manager's room, the bank porter stepped to the outer door, closed and locked it. It being but 12 o'clock, I imagined the precautionary measure must be due to my presence. "The Bordeaux affair is discovered and has been telegraphed all over France," was my first thought; "all is over with me. I am a candidate for a French prison, sure. My poor wife! My poor children! Alas! what a fool have I been!"

These and a thousand other thoughts flashed through my mind during the quarter of an hour preceding Mr. Brune's reappearance with his hands full of bank-notes. I could hardly believe my eyes. I had suppressed all signs of the internal hurricane which raged during those prolonged moments of suspense.

Now the revulsion of feeling was so great that I nearly fainted. However, by prodigious mental effort, I recovered my self-possession and effectually masked all inward convulsions.

Mr. Brune placed in my hands sixty-two thousand francs, in notes of the Bank of France, and we then descended to the carriage and drove to my hotel, where, after mutual expressions of esteem, I, a base swindler, separated forever from a victimized and honest man. I paid my bill at the hotel and at once made preparations to start for Lyons, which was to be the next and last scene of my operations in France.

As my train did not leave for three hours, I got into a carriage at some distance from the hotel and was driven towards the next station, located on the beautiful bay a few miles from Marseilles.

After driving along the shore of the bay for some miles I remember we met two women, dressed in the quaint costume common to that part of the country, each carrying a basket of eggs. I stopped the carriage and endeavored to enter into conversation with the pair, but could not understand a word of their *patois*. I then took a couple of eggs, handed out a silver franc piece, and drove on, leaving two astonished women standing in the road, gazing alternately at the piece of money and at the back of my carriage. Arriving at the station I found it would be an hour and a half to train time, and driving to a hotel on the shore, I ordered dinner to be served in the upper room of a two story tower overlooking the bay, with Marseilles in the distance. After dining I strolled along the beach, looking at some queer fish, not found north of the Mediterranean, their colors vying in brilliancy with the plumage of tropical birds. Returning to the station I took a ticket for Lyons, stopping off at Arles about sunset, as I wished to see the ampitheatre and other relics of the Roman occupation.

I sent a dispatch to Lyons addressed to myself (Hooker), care of Messrs. Blank & Co., as follows:

"T. Hooker: Bring sixty thousand francs to Arles at once, as I have completed the purchase.   C. E. HOOKER.

It will be seen what use I made of this dispatch. I remained in Arles till midnight, then took the train arriving in Lyons at nine the next morning. Repairing to the Hotel-de-Lyons I had breakfast, and on looking over the papers, became satisfied that as yet no discovery had been made. Therefore I resolved to carry out my third and last financial enterprise, and then return to London with all speed.

I called a carriage and drove at once to the establishment of Messrs. Blank & Co. Here I found a letter from London and the dispatch from Arles. I sat near the desk conversing with the head of the firm as these were handed me. I opened the letter and found nothing but a blank sheet of paper, having forgotten that one of them had thus been sent. I saw the merchant's eye on it, and remarked in an explanatory way, " I see, it is written with sympathetic ink," and put it in my pocket. I then opened the dispatch sent from Arles, and after reading, handed it to him saying: " I see that I shall have use for sixty thousand francs, and must ask you to cash a draft on my letter of credit for that amount." He immediately stepped to the safe, took out a bundle of one thousand franc notes, and counting out sixty gave them to me, I, of course, signing a draft on the London and Westminster bank, and having the amount endorsed on my forged letter of credit.

As it was almost certain that the Bordeaux fraud would soon be discovered, I determined, now that my dishonorable work was completed, to attempt an immediate escape from France, by way of Paris and Calais. I did not, therefore, take the train direct from Lyons to Paris, but engaged a carriage and drove back to a junction toward Marseilles. Here I took a train which intersects farther to the northward with another road leading through Lyons to Paris. After going the roundabout route above described, I was back at the Lyons station at 9 P. M., in a train bound for Paris, where I arrived without further incident.

The next morning (Sunday) as I left the railway station, I thought detectives were watching me, but in all probability it was only the imagination of a guilty conscience. I was then wearing a full beard, and as a precautionary measure I that morning had all shaved off save the mustache. Not daring to leave Paris on the through express, which started at three o'clock P. M., nor to purchase a ticket to either Calais or London direct, I went to the station, and took the noon accommodation train which went no farther toward Calais than Arras, a town some thirty miles from Paris. I arrived there about one P. M.

As it would be about three hours before the express train was due I went to a small hotel and ordered dinner. To while away the time I took a stroll through the main street, where were many mothers and nurses with children, nice black-eyed French babies. As I was always a devoted lover of children and other small creatures, I stepped into a shop and bought a package of confectionary, which I distributed among the little ones and their smiling nurses, receiving therefor, almost invariably, the grateful exclamation, " Merci, Monsieur! " I gave some to children eight and ten years old, a crowd of whom soon gathered about me. Perceiving that I was attracting too much attention, it was clear that I must get rid of my young friends as soon as possible, or the police would also be attracted, and their presence might lead to unpleasant results in case the frauds had been discovered and enquiry was being made for an " Englishman." Purchasing a second supply of candies I hastily gave them out, and with a " *Restez ici mes enfants*," I passed through them and continued my walk up the street. Quite a number followed at a respectful distance, and I was cogitating how to double on them when I came to the gateway of the town cemetery, through which I hastily entered. The children remained outside and watched me as I walked up the slope and disappeared. At the rear of the cemetery I observed an old man at work in the adjoining field. I climbed upon the stone wall, which instantly crumbled away, and I was landed on the old Frenchman's domain without leave, amidst a pile of stones. Startled by the racket, he looked up from his digging, and, seeing a stranger uprising from the ruins of the fence, began consigning him to " *le diable*," with a volley of vigorous French expletives delivered in peasant patois. I listened to him much amused for a moment, and then held up a five franc piece. As soon as he beheld it a wondrous change came over him. He eagerly seized the silver and straightway showed me to a lane which led almost directly to the railway station. I purchased a ticket for Calais and took the Sunday afternoon express, arriving in London the next morning, after an absence of but four days. The money procured in Lyons I had with me, but the one hundred thousand francs sent by mail without registry I was uneasy about. I therefore hastened to find my companions to ascertain if the letters had been received at the Queen's hotel.

Engles had been left in London to secure the money-letters at the hotel as fast as they should arrive. But he had been afraid to go there and inquire for them, and when I reached London, I was thunderstruck at his rather too extreme caution. I immediately took a valuable hand-bag filled with linen, etc., went direct to the hotel, registered the name to which I had addressed the letters, asked if there were any letters for me, and they were all handed over forthwith. I had the lady clerk assign me a room, and left my bag. I then walked leisurely away, and have never been back for the bag to this day. The principal reason for leaving Engles in London was to give him an unobstructed opportunity to exchange the foreign bank-notes into English gold before my first bogus draft should arrive, for as soon as the detectives were put on the fraud, they would go at once to all the London Exchanges and broker's offices to watch for any one who offered large sums in French notes. Owing to his pusillanimity I had been obliged, after returning from my trip to France, to undergo the additional hazard of calling at the Queen's hotel. Engles having thus failed to act his part, we were encumbered with a large amount of French paper and a bag of foreign gold which could not be offered safely for exchange in London. I therefore decided that Engles should go to Paris, accompanied by one who had played no part in the fraud, as an assistant, leaving myself, the guiltier one, safe in London. They accordingly left at once, Engles taking the bag of gold, and his companion the notes. The latter afterwards informed me that, during the whole journey from London to Paris, Engles sat with the bag of gold under his coat, ready in case of any imagined emergency to throw it out of the window or overboard while crossing the channel. After their arrival in Paris the assistant was obliged to do the whole business, not only of selling the gold but also the notes.

While he was in different brokers' offices—for he did not dare to offer a large amount in one place—Engles stood at a distance, ready to run away at the slightest indication of danger. However, they arrived safely back in London with the proceeds of my three days' nefarious work in France.

And thus ended—viewed from the forger's standpoint—perhaps as brilliant a "solo" operation as has been recorded in the annals of crime.

CHAPTER XV.

ENGLES remained in London about a week, preparing forged papers for me to use on the trip to South America, which was already decided upon, and then took steamer for New York from Liverpool. On the same day I sailed for Rio Janeiro, accompanied by one known in this adventure as Munson. Since my return from England I have heard some particulars of Engles' life and death since we parted in Liverpool.

In 1879 Engles sent a party to England who took over drafts forged by him with which they procured $40,000 from Seligman & Co., bankers, London. Our party were sentenced for life, as a warning that Engles and Wilkes should not attempt their operations in England. But I have ascertained that during the time I was in prison, not a year elapsed that one or the other did not either go over or send a gang with forged paper, prepared by them in New York.

In 1880, in company with Wilkes, Hamilton, and Burns, Engles went to Italy, where all but himself were arrested, Burns killing himself while in prison.

Hamilton and he were chained to the wall on opposite sides of the room. Wilkes' confession plunged Burns into a

(154)

state of desperation. He seized upon a prayer-book, lay down, and bending the covers back he placed two corners each side of his wind-pipe and pressed so hard that he choked to death.

Hamilton from his side of the room gazed upon this fearful scene, at first too horror-stricken to act, then began screaming and shouting madly for assistance, but none of the Italian jailers were aroused by his frantic efforts until after his friend had accomplished his purpose.

And we were incarcerated for life as a warning to prevent forgers from coming into Europe! I think that I have remarked elsewhere that the imprisonment of one person seldom has any " warning " effect upon others, because no person takes part in a crime committed to obtain money, unless he feels sure that his arrangements are such as to secure his escape — despite all examples to the contrary, each one believes himself the one who will not be caught.

As stated, Engles escaped from Italy and was arrested, but for want of proof the extradition case against him failed, and United States Commissioner Osborne discharged him from custody. He had, however, lain in the Ludlow Street jail over twelve months, during which time the case against him was in progress. In 1884 he made up another party, going to England himself, and obtained a large sum on forged paper.

On every occasion some of the men were arrested and imprisoned for presenting the forged paper. While in prison, at different times, I had word sent to me by prisoners that they were in for presenting forged paper, and that they had come to England with Engles. Two of them were Hebrews of respectable birth, natives of Poland, who had lived in New York for several years. When arrested they were sharp enough not to let it transpire that they were from America, in consequence of which they got off with five years' penal servitude, instead of the fifteen, or life sentences, which would have been given them had it been known that Engles had brought them to England.

In the relation of Engles' European operations, I have somewhat anticipated my story, and will resume it with his arrival in New York in 1872, and his establishment of a faro bank in that city. His peculiar reputation among the "crooks" of America brought to his place many people ambitious to fight the "tiger." He would soon have become a second John Morrissey, had he only been able to restrain his own propensity for drink and gaming; but these habits had now become so firmly fixed that he was no longer master of himself. He had a great many "ropers-in"—those who lounge about the hotels, make acquaintance with merchants and other visitors from the country, and entice them into gambling-houses and other dens. A "roper-in" is a well-dressed, plausible-speaking man, one who has the faculty of conveying to strangers the idea that he is one of themselves; and is paid one-half of all the money he can, "by hook or by crook," induce his dupe to disburse at the various dens visited. Such gaming-houses as the one in question pay these pimps one-half of all the money "won" from their *protégés*, they acting as mentors and advisers to their confiding dupes. In consequence of this mutually profitable arrangement, Engles gained a great deal in the way of "winnings" at his own faro bank, but soon tired of playing, in effect, against himself, for whether losing or winning, there was no risk of ultimate loss. Therefore, he could feel none of that peculiar excitement, kept at fever heat, which had become necessary, and which he had experienced while throwing his ill-gotten gold lavishly into the jaws of some other gambler's "tiger," especially those at that time on exhibition at the splendid establishments of the "Honorable" John Morrissey in New York, and at Saratoga during the fashionable season. At these were lost most of the large sums procured by the extensive gold forgeries in Wall Street and elsewhere. Engles was the only gambler with whom I ever had anything to do, as I considered it especially dangerous to do any "crooked" business with the assistance of either gamesters or drunkards.

It was now the same as it had been with the large sums obtained by forgery, for all the booty raked in at his own establishment was immediately staked and lost elsewhere, regardless of the claims of an affectionate wife and children. His taste for brandy had so grown upon him that he required, more and more, the stimulus afforded by that potent fluid, and was constantly under its influence. His originally strong constitution succumbed at last to the long-continued strain, and he died miserably, after a year's sickness, in 1886, leaving his family impoverished. His wife is carrying on a small business near New York, and endeavoring to bring up her children to become respectable members of society.

The reader's attention is now directed to the steamship *Lucitania*, of the Pacific Mail Line, ploughing the waters of the rough " Bay of Biscay, O." While she is rapidly approaching the coast of France, I will relate what preparations were made in London to carry out the object of our voyage. While " Warren " was settling up his account, though leaving a small balance at the Bank of England as previously described, Engles had busied himself in completing the forged letters of credit that I was to take with me on our voyage. These purported to be drawn and issued by the London and Westminster Bank. In filling them out he had signed only the manager's name, but as I had noticed that in the " circular " letters of credit issued by that bank, both that and the sub-manager's name were signed, I argued that the same should be done in regard to the " special " letters. But Engles insisted that one name was sufficient, because, as he stated, he had seen several genuine letters of credit of the same description, which had been issued by the Bank of North Wales, Liverpool, with the manager's name only. Nothing could induce him to put on both names, although he might have done it in a few minutes, and he being an " old head " in the business I was reluctantly obliged to give way. As will be seen in the sequel, the want of acumen shown in this instance by my usually astute confederate, saved the good bankers of

South America, in all probability, a million of dollars, defeating my project at the outset, and causing us to return to England contrary to our wishes or expectations. It may be curious to note here, as an instance of how slight a thing may change the whole future life of a man, that this decision of Engles not to spend five minutes in putting on another name, led to the discovery of the plan to make use of the Bank of England account, and all that followed. And this, besides the narrow escape (about to be recounted) from passing our lives on the island of Fernando da Noronha, which lies in the Atlantic about three hundred miles off the coast of Brazil. On this island is located the one great convict establishment to which are transported the convicts of the Brazilian Empire. Both on the voyage and return the steamer passed within sight of it, and on each occasion the view excited within me very curious feelings — in going, the thought that, despite my precautions, we might find the end of our journey there — and in returning, the thought of our narrow escape from being there instead of on board the steamer in the enjoyment of all luxuries.

To resume — the good steamship *Lucitania* rapidly neared the mouth of the Garonne, or Gironde, on an estuary of which is situated the old city of Bordeaux. Arriving there, she lay at anchor for some hours, taking in and discharging freight, and receiving emigrants for various parts of South America. When the steamer was about to leave, it was a strange and rather comical sight to witness the farewells and leave-takings from the crowds of friends who had come to see them off. The customary performance appeared to me so peculiar that I will describe it as well as I can after so many years: Two men standing face to face, one clasps the other round the body, the other passive, then leaning back lifts the party clear off the ground once, twice, or thrice, probably according to the degree of relationship or amount of affection; then the operation is reversed, the embraced becoming the embracer. In some cases the ceremonial is repeated the second or third time, neither kissing nor crying being the fashion there.

The next morning we were off the coast of Spain watching the silvery gleam from the ice-clad peaks of the Pyrenees — at least those of us who were not engaged in the more disagreeable employment of discharging their debt to Father Neptune. However, by the time the ship arrived at the small port of Santander the passengers were mostly recovering from the *mal de mer* occasioned by the rough water in the Bay of Biscay. While leaving this tiny land-locked harbor, one of the propeller blades touched the rocky bottom and broke short off, but she continued her voyage with undiminished speed, and within three days was steaming up the Tagus to Lisbon. Here the passengers who wished to avail themselves of the opportunity, had a few hours on shore, then we were off for the long diagonal run across the Atlantic, unbroken save by a call at one of the Canaries.

" The Lady of the *Lucitania*," as she was called, because there was no other lady among the saloon passengers, was the wife of Captain ——— of the British army, who was going out for a few months' hunting on the pampas of Buenos Ayres, and of course accompanied by numerous dogs, with an assortment of guns. There was also a chaplain in the British navy who was going out to join his ship at Valparaiso. A strange character was he; being a big, burly man, about 28 years of age, and the most inveterate champagne-drinker on board, and that is saying a good deal. Whenever he met any of the " jolly " ones of the saloon passengers it was " Come, old fellow, will you toss me for a bottle of phizz ?" as he called his favorite wine, and he had no lack of accepters. The majority in the saloon consisted of a party of fifteen young Englishmen, civil engineers, who were going under the leadership of a Swedish colonel to survey, for the Brazilian government, a railway line across the southern part of Brazil, from the Atlantic to the Pacific. In all there were twenty-five young men, full of frolic and fun, who made matters rather lively about the afterpart of the ship. They went in for every thing from which any fun could be extracted. At the equinoctial line they roped in the "greenhorns," of whom I was one, to look through the field-glasses at the line, and having fastened a hair across the field of view, of course we could all see it plainly. Father Neptune came on board, and those of the crew who had never crossed the Equator were hunted out of their hiding places, dragged on deck, lathered with a whitewash brush dipped in old grease, shaved with a lath-razor, and then tumbled unceremoniously backward into a cask of water.

THE "SUGAR-LOAF" IN THE BAY OF RIO.

During the whole voyage I laughed, and increased in weight twenty pounds. After a prosperous voyage of three weeks we arrived within sight of the famous "Sugar-Loaf," and were duly disembarked at the custom-house,

where I found it indispensable to use a little " palm-grease "
in order to get my baggage through that institution without a
long waiting. The evening succeeding our arrival a banquet
was given at the Hotel d'Europe, which was attended by
most of the saloon passengers, including " The Lady of the
Lucitania."

The next morning Munson called at a banking-house, presented his false letters of introduction, and was well received.
He immediately commenced business — showed them a letter
of credit, and making out a bill of exchange, drawn on the
London and Westminster Bank, he sold it to the banker, and
drew ten thousand pounds in the currency of the country,
leaving the balance on deposit as the nucleus of a bank
account. I had been waiting outside, and saw him come out
with the currency — a package a foot square — under his arm.
At some distance from the bank he gave me the package, and
I took it at once to an exchange office and purchased English
sovereigns for the whole amount — about $50,000. On the
voyage, Munson and myself had acted as strangers to each
other, and now we stayed at different hotels, being careful
not to be seen together, meeting in the parks or other
public places, though in isolated parts of them. Having
bogus letters to other bankers in Rio, this first easy success
satisfied us that we could obtain all the money — say two or
three hundred thousand dollars — that we should think it
prudent to ask for in that city.

After the lapse of two days, Munson again called at the
same bank and was immediately invited into the manager's
room and introduced to " Mr. Solomons," a Hebrew, who proved
to be one of the leading brokers on the Rio Exchange. As
before, I was waiting outside, and owing to the long time
Munson was in the bank, I began to feel uneasy, and surmised that something was going wrong. At last he made
his appearance, and I saw by his flushed face that he had
been under a strain. Upon reaching a suitable place, he
related to me the particulars of the interview. The danger

11

we were in no doubt tended to indelibly impress upon my memory Munson's statement, which was in substance as follows:

"The manager, after introducing me to Mr. Solomons, said that a short time previous a letter had been received from the London and Westminster Bank which stated that from that date all letters of credit issued by them would be signed both by the manager and sub-manager. He then said that the letter on which he had purchased my bill of exchange had but one name. The Hebrew broker sat all this time with his crafty eyes fixed upon me, as though he would read me through, and it required all my nerve to enable me to stand the situation without showing signs of uneasiness. I replied that really I could not say how the omission occurred, but I supposed it must have been accidental, and then told him I would look at my other letters and see if they were the same. Mr. Solomons said it was a very singular circumstance that an assistant bank manager should neglect to sign a special letter of credit, still he must have done so; but for his part he should not feel justified in purchasing bills on such letters. After some further conversation, the manager asked me if I had letters to other parties in Rio. 'Certainly,' said I; 'I have letters to the English Bank, and to Messrs. —— & Co., both of whom have doubtless had advices from their London correspondents regarding me, and I will ascertain at once whether I am to have the object of my long journey hampered by the neglect or oversight of the sub-manager.' I then came away. The fact is, I am feeling very shaky; the Hebrew is a shrewd old codger, and the manager refused to purchase any more exchange on London on the pretext that he had all he could use. This is awful! I had a hot time of it, and no mistake! That Solomons is as sharp as a razor, and as suspicious as a boarding-house mistress. I think he is assured in his own mind that something is wrong. I am afraid it is all up, and I wish we were well out of this country."

"There can be no doubt about it," I replied; "and at this moment they are doubtless consulting as to what measures can be taken to secure the ten thousand pounds paid you until they can get advices from England. The cable is not yet completed, and they must wait the slow movement of the mail, which will take forty days. You informed him that you expected to remain in Brazil three months, and as it is known that no one can get out of the country without getting his passport viséd at police headquarters, they will not arrest you for fear that after all it may be only a mistake, unless you attempt to leave Brazil. A bold step must be taken. Here are the other letters of credit; take this pen and write in the sub-manager's name."

Although Munson was a skillful penman, he had never attempted to forge names himself, Engles having performed that delicate operation during the short time we had been in such business. The ordeal through which Munson had passed had made him nervous; therefore, though not a drinking man, I procured a glass of brandy, which he swallowed. In a few moments he began to write in the names, though with rather a shaky hand. When finished, I compared them with the genuine signature in my possession, and found it very shaky; but we were in for it, and I could see but one way out; therefore I selected the best, handed them to Munson, and said:

"It is not an hour since you left the bank. Take these letters back immediately, and show the manager *both* signatures, remarking at the same time that the second name must have been unintentionally omitted from the one on which you drew the ten thousand pounds. He cannot fathom that you could have forged the sub-manager's name in so short a time. See if it does not prove a 'poser.' Though it may not wholly allay suspicion, it will give me time to make and execute a plan for getting you out of the country. Of that I am certain. Rely on me, keep cool, and above all keep a stiff upper lip, and act up to the character you have assumed. Be sure to offer them more exchange on London, as I wish to ascertain how they take the proposition; and if they decline to purchase, say that you will have to transfer your account to the English Bank of Rio."

Starting on his decisive errand, followed by me as before, he was not long in the bank, but reappeared empty-handed, no one following to "shadow" him. Upon meeting at the designated place, Munson informed me that the manager was evidently agreeably surprised when he was shown the letters with both signatures; nevertheless, he had refused to purchase any more exchange, but had transferred the endorsement from the letter that had but one signature to one with both. All this convinced me that his suspicion was fully aroused. It was therefore clear that our safety depended upon the invention of a plan by which I could get Munson out of Brazil, and at the same time convince the bank manager that he intended to remain. It must be a plan which would throw off any one attempting to watch his movements, and make it appear that he was still in the country until the steamer in which he sailed should have been at least twenty-four hours at sea.

This plan, and how it was successfully executed, will be detailed in the following chapter.

CHAPTER XVI.

WHETHER the law remains the same as it was in 1872, I am unable to state; but at that time every person desiring to leave Brazil must be provided with a passport — if a foreigner, one from his own government — if a native, one from the Brazilian. When ready to start, he must take his passport to police headquarters and have it viséd, then leave it with the ticket-agent where he buys his ticket. This agent, after ascertaining from the chief of police that the intending passenger is not " wanted " by the authorities, transmits the passport to the purser of the steamer, who, in turn, hands it to the owner after the ship is at sea. It will be seen that these regulations render it very difficult for any suspected person to leave Brazil by the regular channels of communication ; and if difficult for a native, how much more so for a stranger, ignorant of the country and its language, the Portuguese. French, Italian, or German, did well enough in the large towns, but the moment a fugitive who did not understand their language got into the country, he would stand a poor chance of getting far away from Rio. There-fore, I was obliged to abandon the project of going south to Buenos Ayres — a journey by land of fifteen hundred miles — or of crossing the continent to the Pacific by way of the Amazon. At last I determined on a bold *coup* to get Munson

(165)

away on a steamer which was to leave on a certain day. Accordingly, I had an American (U. S.) passport filled in with the name Gilmore, by which I was known during the voyage from England, by the agent of the steamship line, and others in Rio. This I took to the police headquarters, and finding the anteroom crowded with people, I supposed I should be obliged to wait my turn; but presently the interpreter came along, and, presumably, judging by my appearance that time was more valuable to me than a little money, he whispered in French: "If you are in a hurry, you will save time by sending in a small 'douceur' to the chief, or you may have to wait all day." I took the hint and slipped into his ready palm a few reys, with which he disappeared into the inner room. In a short time I was ushered in and my passport viséd without my being troubled with an interrogation. Proceeding to the ticket-agent I delivered up the passport, receiving and paying for a saloon passage to Liverpool. He recognized me as one of the party who had arrived a few days previously by the *Lucitania*, and expressed some surprise at my early return, it being the best part of the year for a sojourn in the tropics. I explained that having completed my business, I was in a hurry to get back to my own country. My next move was to walk along the water-front and find where row-boats with oarsmen were to be let. As these were to be had at several points, I selected the most obscure one toward the northern boundary of the city. Here I found a boat, and was rowed out to the steamship *Livingstonia*. I went on board and found the purser, to whom I showed my ticket, and asked him to assign me a state-room by myself. Having paid him the extra price required for the privilege of being the sole occupant, I received the key, took a good look around, that I might find the room again without the necessity of making inquiries, and left for the city, after informing the purser that I should remain on shore until the hour for sailing the next day. Upon meeting Munson I requested him to call at the bank and casually inform the manager that he should start the next morning for S. Romao, a town in the interior of Brazil, to be absent a week. He was then to go to the Hotel d'Europe, pay his bill, at the same time stating that he was to leave Rio by the four o'clock train the next morning. As Munson had two trunks, and other *impedimenta* befitting a man of his pretensions, it was necessary to take a carriage to the station, which was nearly a mile distant. It would be unsafe to go in a carriage belonging to the hotel; therefore, he was to say that a friend would call for him. As it was still two hours to sunset, I suggested that after he had arranged matters, he should saunter out, walk about the streets until dark, then return to the hotel and be ready when I should call for him at three o'clock the next morning.

After these arrangements we separated, I following to ascertain if he was being watched or shadowed by detectives. When he entered the hotel I remained within view of the entrance. It was not long before he reappeared and walked leisurely along the street, with gold-headed cane, and real diamonds flashing in the tropical sunlight. A few seconds later I saw another man come out, cross the street, and go in the same direction. I followed him, and was soon satisfied that he was keeping Munson in view. This sort of double hunt was kept up until dusk, when Munson returned to his hotel, unconscious that a moment later his "shadow" entered the place. Here was a "stunner" and no mistake, though it was no more than I had anticipated as among the possibilities; still, I had indulged in the hope that the bank would rely entirely on the passport system, and take no further steps for a day or two, which was all the time required to carry out my plan. Though Munson had good nerve, it was already somewhat shaken, and surely the situation would have unnerved most men. Therefore, fearing that the certain knowledge of imminent danger might still further confuse him and cause some false move, I determined to keep my discovery to myself. Leaving Munson and his

"shadow" to their own devices at the hotel, I next proceeded
to an obscure part of the town, and stopping at a small but
respectable looking tavern, I engaged a room for the next
day. I also engaged a carriage, with an English-speaking
driver, to be in readiness at three o'clock the next morning
— then returned to my own hotel for a few hours' sleep.
Promptly at the hour I was at the livery stable, where I
found the carriage ready, and was driven to the Hotel
d'Europe. Sending the driver up to the office on the second
floor, Munson soon appeared and informed me that he had
promised to take to the station a man who was stopping at
the hotel. "He is going to S. Romao by the same train,"
continued Munson, "and seems a good fellow, for I had a long
talk with him last night." Upon seeing signs of disapproval
in my face, he explained: "Well, you know, he said he could
not get a carriage at so early an hour in the morning, and I
thought it could do no harm to take him in, and he is waiting
up stairs."

It would be difcult for the reader to imagine the effect of
this surprising communication upon my mind, for it was clear
enough that this was the very person who had been "shadow-
ing" Munson the day before, and had skillfully ingratiated
himself into his new friend's confidence. I could but admire
his unwonted "cheek" in asking a contemplated victim for a
ride to the station. I said to Munson: "What in the world can
you be thinking of? Don't you see you are blocking our
whole plan? Go up and tell him your carriage is loaded
down with luggage, and express your regrets that you cannot accommodate him."

This Munson was obliged to do, though with repugnance,
it being against his nature to do anything that looked "mean."
During this time the baggage was being placed in the carriage,
and as soon as Munson had dismissed his "passenger," who
for some reason, did not show himself to me, we started rapidly for the station. On the way I requested him to avoid
making any new friends until he should find himself well out

at sea. Said I, "It might be fatal to attract the attention of any one, or to let any one see you leave the train. Of course this new acquaintance of yours is only a countryman, but it is not possible to foresee what disaster the least mistake or want of caution might originate. Now listen: if you will be guided entirely by me, you will be safe on the broad Atlantic to-night. You know," I continued, "that these cars are on the English system, divided into compartments. You must go into the station, stand near the ticket-office until your new acquaintance comes; then observe if he buys a first-class; if so, you take a second, and *vice versa*. Pay no attention to him, and let him see you get into your compartment, but keep an eye on his movements. In case he comes to get in where you are, despite the different class of the tickets, tell him the compartment is engaged. Everything depends on how you carry yourself through the next twenty minutes. A single false step, a word too little or too much, will surely prove fatal to us both!"

In accordance with our pre-arranged plan, I stopped the carriage opposite the station, it being still dark. Munson alighted, went straight inside, and in a few minutes saw his "passenger" come puffing in, nearly out of breath. Unquestionably supposing Munson's baggage to be already on board the train, he purchased a ticket, and after seeing his intended victim enter a compartment, got into another himself just as the train began to move. This was the vital moment for which Munson had been waiting, and having previously unlocked with his master car-key the door opposite, he stepped off on that side, hastily crossed to the other platform of the dimly-lighted station, and made his way unnoticed into the street. While this was passing I sat in the carriage, and it was not many minutes before I had the satisfaction of seeing Munson coming back to me. For the benefit of the driver we then had a dialogue somewhat as follows:

"It is too bad! Our friends have not arrived; what shall we do?"

"Well, I suppose we must go back to the hotel and wait for the afternoon train," I answered.

"But I have paid my bill there," said Munson, "and do not care to go back."

"Then," I replied, "meet me at the station, and I will look after the luggage."

In case they recovered the trail, the information obtained from the driver would cause confusion and delay sufficient, I hoped, to enable me to get Munson out of Rio.

I then told the coachman to drive into the city. It was not yet daylight, but after a while I saw a sort of eating-house and tavern combined, and had the carriage halted there. Alighting, I entered, and said to the person in charge that I did not wish to disturb my friends at so early an hour, and would pay him for taking care of my baggage, as I wished to discharge the carriage. This offer was of course accepted, the baggage housed, and the carriage dismissed. In the meantime Munson was waiting for me in an appointed place not far away, where I joined him, and we went to the obscure tavern where the room had been engaged.

So far my plan had been successful. Munson was hidden safely away before dawn, while at the same moment his very clever new friend was some miles distant on a "wild goose chase" into the interior. Arriving back at my hotel soon after daylight, I took a leisurely breakfast, after which I sallied out and engaged two stalwart slave porters, whom I found, according to the custom of their class in Brazil, busily occupied in plaiting straw for hats while waiting for a job. Motioning them to follow me, I led the way to where Munson's baggage was stored. Dividing it between the two, we proceeded to the place I had selected as the safest to get off to the steamer without attracting notice, and had it put into a boat. Paying the porters, I followed and was rowed off to the steamer. The baggage was hoisted on deck, the trunks deposited in the hold, and the smaller articles carried into my state-room: after which I went ashore to await the hour of the decisive movement for which I had made such elaborate preparations. There was no train by which the detective could return to Rio until late in the afternoon; and I felt certain that when he should ascertain that Munson was not upon the train, he would be confident that his intended victim had slipped off at a way station in order to make his escape into the interior. Under this impression he would naturally make inquiries at the likely stations, and even if he sent a dis-patch to the bank, it would doubtless be to the effect that his quarry had left Rio on the early train that morning with himself.

The baggage had taken up my time until ten A. M., and returning to my hotel, I packed into a knapsack as many bags of gold (about £8,000) as I could conveniently carry, called a carriage, and was driven to where Munson had been waiting in great anxiety for several hours. Taking him in, we were not long in reaching the place of embarkation, and were rowed about five miles up the harbor, where the steamer had gone to take in coal. Amid the usual confusion attend-ing the departure of an ocean steamer, we got on board unnoticed, and went direct to the state-room. By the time we were in it the gold had become excessively heavy, and I was glad enough to stow it away in one of the berths. We had not been long in the state-room before we heard the wel-come sound of the bell, warning all who were not about to make the voyage to leave the steamer. I parted from Mun-son, recommending him to remain in his state-room until the ship should be well out into the Atlantic. Getting into the boat again, I was rowed away a short distance, then had the oarsman rest on his oars, and soon had the pleasure of seeing the *Livingstonia* glide past with her prow pointed toward the "Sugar-Loaf." Now, for the first time, I breathed freely, and felt a great weight of responsibility roll from my shoulders. "Munson is safe, and the danger is over," said I to myself, joyfully. Ordering the boatman to row ashore, he turned in that direction, and then I saw a boat coming toward the

steamer, with every oar strained to the utmost — but no attention was paid to it.   The occupants soon gave up the chase,
and through my field-glass I recognized the manager of the
bank and the Hebrew broker, Mr. Solomons, both of whom
had been pointed out to me.   They had probably just received
a dispatch from the detective who had been so cleverly out-
witted and left to journey alone, but having no time to procure an order to delay the ship, had hurried off, hoping to get
on board, confident that the captain would grant every facility
for a search, and, in case of success, assist them to get Munson
on shore again.   Had they succeeded, I should have been
involved, and probably learned the lesson on the island of
Fernando da Noronha that I did later in England.

CHAPTER XVII.

DURING my stay in Rio Janeiro I received from the Swedish Colonel, before alluded to, an invitation to be present at a special presentation of " Ernani " at the grand opera-house in honor of the Imperial family, in accordance with which I became one of the favored audience. This was very small, and appeared to be composed of the *creme de la creme* of Brazilian society, the Imperial box being occupied by the Emperor Dom Pedro, the Empress, their daughter and son-in-law, the latter having made his name famous in Brazilian history by his gallant conduct during the late war between the gigantic Empire of Brazil and the liliputian State of Paraguay. At the Academy of Fine Arts in Rio I noticed a large painting representing him seated on a fiery war-horse plunging about amid shot and shell, the princely rider, with sword waving on high, guiding the storm of battle. The Imperial family formed a marked contrast with the remainder of the audience, being plainly dressed and making no show of diamonds or other jewels.

Now that Munson was safely on the broad Atlantic, with the bulk of the gold in his possession, I felt at ease, though there was still a chance that when it became certain that he had made his escape out of the country, I might be regarded with suspicion and detained. But as I had been extremely careful not to be seen in his company, I felt no great anxiety on that point.

(173)

The great mistake of that period of my life was that I did not abandon every other plan and go at once to Chicago to establish a legitimate business, in accordance with my original intentions.

After securing all the cash we safely could at Rio, Munson taking the leading part, we had intended to go down the coast to Montevideo and Buenos Ayres, and repeat the operation, I doing the leading business in those cities. Going thence by steamer *via* the Strait of Magellan to Valparaiso, we were to continue northward, stopping at the large sea-ports along the Pacific Coast as far as San Francisco, from which place we intended to reach New York by the trans-continental railway, with at least a million dollars in our possession.

It will be seen that this was a gigantic and well-devised scheme, which might easily have proven a complete success — my experience having led me to believe that such expectations were by no means unreasonable — had not Engles's obstinacy thus frustrated our plan. In yielding to him the point that came up in London, as to whether both the manager's and sub-manager's names should appear on the forged letters of credit, I acquiesced in a step which virtually defeated the whole scheme, and changed an easy money-making affair into what just missed turning out a tragedy.

After due consideration, I could see no way of getting out of Brazil otherwise than by a voyage to the Rio de la Plata (river of silver), it being supposed that I had sailed for Europe on board the last European steamer; in consequence I had to keep myself secluded as much as possible, to avoid running against the Pacific Mail Line agent and others.

As it would be some days before I could obtain passage southward, I passed the intervening time in making excursions and sight-seeing, Rio and vicinity being a good place for both. I need not weary the reader with an extended description of the beautiful bay of Rio, closed in on all sides by mountains which rise almost from its shores, with the unique Sugar-Loaf, 900 feet high, like a huge sentinel guarding the entrance to a harbor which vies with the far-famed

SCENE NEAR RIO JANEIRO.

bay of Naples in the natural beauty and grandeur of its situation and surroundings.

The approach from the sea is very attractive. First

appear distant peaks, scarcely distinguishable from the clouds. Approaching, the outlines become more distinct, and other mountains become dimly visible in the distance, while the hills and slopes are covered with luxuriant tropical vegetation. Until the steamer nears the land, it appears as if she is about running against a solid wall; but when quite near, the cleft through the mountains opens up, and as she enters this, a part of the city appears in the distance. On the north side, opposite the Sugar-Loaf, is the fort of Santa Cruz, on which is a lighthouse; other fortifications guard the harbor, and no obstruction prevents ships from entering it in safety day or night. The water in this land-locked harbor is deep enough and its area sufficient to accommodate all the navies of the world.

The Sugar-Loaf seemed so near the city that I thought it would be a good day's sport to climb to the summit, and accordingly hired a boat with two oarsmen to row me down to its foot. After a long row, to my surprise it appeared as far away as ever; and as I could not understand the jabbering of the boatmen, I reluctantly gave the signal to return. A visit to the Horticultural Gardens, with their rows of gigantic palm-trees, and every variety of tropical flowers and plants, was exceedingly enjoyable; but nothing could be finer than a drive along the sides of the mountains behind the city, not more than a half-hour's ride from its center. Here were located the villas of merchants and bankers, almost hidden by the foliage of shrubs and trees, and commanding a view of both city and harbor.

One day, with an acquaintance, I took the early train on the same line where the detective was perhaps still looking for Munson, and alighted at a small hamlet on the border of a stream, about thirty miles from Rio, beyond the mountains. Calling at the only store, we found no one able to speak either French, Spanish, Italian, or German. Happening to look across the street, we saw a sign reading, "Schroeder, Painter." We hurried over, and entering, received in answer to my "Sprecken sie Deutsche?" a "Ja, mein herr."

VIEW OF MONTEVIDEO.

With the painter's aid, as interpreter, we were soon mounted on horse and mule respectively, I taking the latter. My companion intended to be considerably amused at my efforts to make the mule keep up with him; but he counted, on that occasion, without a proper knowledge of the character of that particular mule, which proved the better horse of the two.

We rode for some miles through a country covered with mound-like hills, no sooner coming to the bottom of one than we were ascending another. These hills were covered with coffee bushes, filled with red fruit about the size of cherries, each containing two kernels. The coffee was being picked into large flat baskets by slaves, which when filled they carried away on their heads to the drying ground. The roads were bordered with orange trees loaded with luscious fruit, to which we helped ourselves. After a time we turned into a bridle-path, and rode three or four miles through a dense forest. We emerged upon the outskirts of a coffee plantation, where the slaves were just on their way to dinner; and another half-mile brought us to the planter's residence. Thirty or forty slaves of both sexes and all ages were grouped upon the grass, engaged in eating a black looking stew out of metal dishes, their fingers serving for knives, forks, and spoons. Seeing two horsemen ride out of the forest, they stared in stupid wonder, until one, more intelligent than the others, went in search of the overseer. Presently a white man appeared, and to our question: "Parlez vous Francais?" shook his head. "Sprecken sie Deutsche?" another shake, and the same to "Habla Espagnole?" but, on hearing, "Parlate Italiano?" came the smiling answer, "Si, signor." He proved to be an Italian overseer, in charge of this plantation owned by a merchant in the city, who seldom visited the property. The overseer showed us over the place and explained all the processes of preparing the coffee for market.

In one corner of a large, unpainted wooden building was what he called the infirmary, and a comfortless looking place

12

it was. He said there was no doctor employed and that he dealt out medicine to the slaves himself. After being served with coffee, we departed and returned to Rio by the evening train.

As the south-bound steamer was due the next day, the question which occupied my mind was: "How am *I* to get out of Brazil?" Munson had left me his passport, from which I erased his name and description, and put in my own. The next morning I hired a person to take my passport to police headquarters, grease the official palm, and have it viséd, although the chief was by law obliged to compare each pass-port with its holder. He soon returned with the document in proper shape, and I then purchased a ticket, leaving the passport with the agent. I embarked without trouble, and in four days was laying off Montevideo, at the mouth of the Rio La Plata, waiting for the health-officer. At that time there was no telegraph cable, and everything went slow along the coast of South America.

After keeping the steamer waiting for some hours the health-officer condescended to come aboard, and although there had not been a single case of sickness, to declare us in quar-antine. Accordingly, after discharging the river freight, she ran out to sea thirty or forty miles to the Isle de Flores (flower island), on which the passengers were landed and kept there ten days, paying three dollars per day for board. At the expiration of this tiresome period we were taken on board a small steamer and landed at Montevideo.

In that beautifully situated city of revolutions, the win-dows are barred like those of a prison, and the walls beveled so as to enable the inmates to shoot up and down the streets.

Taking the night steamer, I was landed at Buenos Ayres (good air) the next morning. At that time the place was a mongrel between the oriental, tropical, and a brand-new west-ern town. After a few days I determined to return to Europe. Therefore, my proper name being in my passport, I purchased a ticket for a passage by the steamer *La France* to Marseilles.

Running up the coast of South America we were in a pampero (hurricane) for twenty-four hours; and although the *La France* was one of the largest steamers then afloat, the waves dashed away over her smokestack and tossed her about like an empty cask.

The *La France* ran into the harbor of Rio Janeiro and lay off the city for several hours. When she came to anchor a sidewheel steamer of the line which ran from Rio to New York was at the point of leaving. I hailed a boat and was rowed off to her to ascertain if I could secure passage to New York. When my boat reached the side of the New York steamer, I was informed that nearly all passenger accommodations had been secured for the Brazilian Prince Imperial, and that I could not be permitted to come on board.

What slight circumstances may change the destiny of men for better or for worse,—for a life of poverty and wretchedness or prosperity and happiness,—for a long life or a premature death! Had I been able to proceed direct to New York, and from thence to Chicago, to carry out my long-deferred plan, my whole destiny would have been changed; for the possibility of perpetrating the frauds on the Bank of England was then among things unknown, and afterwards discovered only by accident.

Among my baggage I always carried a galvanic battery, and as there were several hundred Spanish, Portuguese, and Italians in the steerage — none of whom had any experience with electricity, as developed by human agency — we had no end of sport by tempting them to take a silver coin out of a bucket of electrized water, and by playing many games to give them unexpected shocks. These people were ignorant and superstitious and soon came to believe that we were in league with the devil.

In due time I landed at Marseilles, took the train for Paris *via* Lyons, and arrived in Paris where I joined Munson. In the next chapter will be detailed the series of operations which led to the disastrous affair with the Bank of England.

CHAPTER XVIII.

AFTER my return to Paris I met Munson, who related to me the incidents of the voyage from Rio Janeiro, and subsequent events. The following is an epitome of his story:

"For some little time after you left me on board the *Livingstonia*, I remained perfectly quiet in the state-room, until I heard the screw begin to revolve and I felt satisfied that the steamer was at last under way. I then ventured out on deck, and recognized you in the boat. I also, through my glass, saw a boat at a distance pulling hard toward the steamer, and the sight made my heart give a great thump; but as the steamer continued on past the last fort, headed for the ocean, I recovered my equanimity and drew a breath of relief, you may be sure. Then, for the first time, I realized what a terrible strain I had undergone for the week previous to my escape from Rio Janeiro. It was just the tightest bottle I was ever corked up in, and had I known of those regulations about passports, I never should have put my neck so nearly into the Brazilian halter; and when we were passing the lonely island where the convicts are kept, I gazed upon it, happy that I was no longer a candidate for a long residence in that desolate-looking place. On board I found everything correct, and no suspicion existing that I was not the man who had purchased the ticket.

"When we were about two hundred miles out the engine broke down, and for a time I thought she would have to put

(180)

back to Rio. In that case I knew it would be all up with me, and you can imagine the state of my feelings while the suspense lasted. However, after a few hours the break was repaired, and we got under way again.

" The $40,000 in gold, which I kept in my state-room, was a source of much anxiety. I hardly dared to go on deck, or into the saloon at meal-time, through fear that it might be stolen. At last I put the money in possession of the purser, who charged me two per cent., or eight hundred dollars, claiming that it was the regular rate. On the arrival of the steamer at Lisbon, I determined to go on shore, and make my way to Paris overland through Spain, for the reason that I feared dispatches might have been sent from the nearest cable station to England, warning the police to be on the lookout when the steamer should arrive at Liverpool.

"As the gold was too heavy a load to lug about, and likely to attract attention, I went to an English firm of brokers doing business in Lisbon, and purchased Portuguese stocks. Having thus got the money into portable shape, I journeyed by rail and diligence to Paris, where I have since remained."

A few days later I met McDonald. He was eager for " business," and almost the first question he asked was, " What is the programme ? "

" Let us return to the United States," I replied. " We have a good capital now to put into a straight mercantile business. Let us do no more 'crooked' work, which will be certain to get us into trouble sooner or later." For that " one more operation" among all classes and grades of thieves, from the common sneak to the colossal bank defaulter and " boodler," is continued until the small ones get into prison, and the great ones (generally) get out of the country.

We finally concluded to go to Paris and Vienna for a time. When we reached the latter city we were delayed by the sickness of McDonald, who was suffering from a disease like modern " malaria." I nursed him for two or three weeks, and during the time gave him several powerful shocks from my battery, which nearly raised him out of bed, if they did not cure him.

We were living in Vienna—McDonald at the Golden Lamb, and I at the Grand Hotel. While waiting for Mac's recovery I visited the Imperial opera-house almost nightly, and never tired of listening to the music of the magnificent orchestra — then the best in the world — each member being a solo artist or professor, and receiving a large salary or pension from the Emperor. The operas were rendered in the German language, and "Orpheus and Eurydice" was brought out in a manner that left an indelible impression upon my mind, although I had previously witnessed that great creation of Glück's in Paris, London, and New York.

As I passed the entire day with McDonald at his hotel, I must have contracted his malady to some extent, for when he began to get about I was prostrated and confined to my room for a whole week. As I had never experienced serious illness of any kind since childhood, I became so impatient by the end of the week that, notwithstanding the doctor's commands, I declared myself recovered, got up and dressed myself for a walk. On each floor of the Grand Hotel in Vienna there was at this time (1872) an office where a servant or two was in waiting to answer the bells. When I was ready to go out I had occasion to call a servant, and touched the electric button. I distinctly heard the bell in the office ring in response, as I stood, cane in hand, waiting at the open door of my room. Soon I touched and held down the button for a longer time, and again waited in vain. In my then nervous condition I lost both patience and temper, and continued the pressure on the button with the following result: My room was located in a back corridor farthest from the office. When I touched the button I heard the electric bell connected with my room tingling rapidly; soon another joined in — then another — and another — until I had a concert of at least a hundred bells going. Presently servants came rushing through the corridor, and seeing me, one of them explained that my bell had set all the other bells in the house going, and in consequence they could not tell what room the call was from. I could only tell them that if they had answered my first or second call there would have been no concert. Thenceforth my calls were promptly answered so long as I remained at that hotel. Had Mark Twain been at the Grand Hotel that day, I am sure he could have obtained material for an entire humorous chapter.

While on the way to Mac's hotel I used frequently to stop in at a news-office to purchase the daily paper, which I read assiduously to improve my knowledge of the German language. This news-office was conducted by two sisters, who were fair specimens of their sex in a city famed the world over for beautiful women. I used to air my German by asking in that language for the papers I wanted, and generally, to my great satisfaction, found that they understood me. After I had been a regular customer for some time, I ventured to attempt a compliment upon the good looks of one of the sisters, remarking: "Sie sind schon!" A look of surprise and the exclamation "Was?" (what) caused me to repeat in my best German: "Sie sind schon!" The young lady blushed, looking at me earnestly, and seeing that I wore an innocent air and was apparently unconscious of anything but pride in my knowledge of German, cast her eyes thoughtfully downward for a moment, and then suddenly burst out laughing, clapped her hands vigorously and said: "Oh Meinherr! Sie wollen sagen schön!" (You are beautiful). The reader will observe the two dots (diaeresis) over the "o" of the last "schon," without which the pronunciation of the word is quite different, and signifies "already" instead of "beautiful." I had no intention of saying to her, "You are already!"

Of the many incidents connected with this Vienna trip, I distinctly remember two. While on the train between Paris and Frankfort—having no money current in the German States—I could purchase nothing to eat. This was before the new Prussian coinage had displaced the wretched system previously in vogue, by which each petty State manufactured its own circulating medium. In the same compartment with me was a Hungarian gentleman and his wife, on the way from Paris to their home in Prague. This gentleman spoke English fluently, and as soon as he learned that I was an American, both himself and wife became enthusiastic in their efforts to be sociable. Noticing that I did not get out at the halting places for meals, he finally inquired the reason. When I acknowledged the dilemma I was in, he produced a large pocket-book, which he opened and handed to me saying: " Help yourself." From a large amount in Austrian bank-notes I selected one of the smallest denomination, and returned the pocketbook with my thanks. On arrival at Frankfort, I at once procured the amount at the hotel and sent it to the courteous Hungarian.

On another occasion, at the station of a German town, a young married couple came into the same compartment. They appeared to belong to the prosperous portion of the community, and a throng of well-dressed people came to the train to see them off. The bridegroom wore a big, loose German wrapper, something like an ulster, and I observed that the pockets were like bags well filled. Not long after we came to a dining station, where all but the bridal pair and myself had dinner. I naturally supposed that the excitement of the occasion had taken away their appetites, but was thoroughly undeceived when, a little later, the man spread a newspaper over their laps, took from one pocket a loaf of bread at least one and a half feet long, and from another a monstrous bologna sausage. Then, taking out his pocket-knife he cut off a " chunk " of each for his bride and for himself. In a remarkably short period they had eaten fully one-half the provisions, and the remainder was consigned back to the pockets until supper time.

I mention these incidents of travel merely to illustrate the proverbial generosity and honest simplicity of the Slavonic and Germanic character.

CHAPTER XIX.

ONCE more in London with my two companions, the question arose: "What next?" I had determined to abandon a dangerous business; but difficulties arose which caused delay in the execution of my project, until finally I concluded to go to Amsterdam to see if I could find an opening for one more operation which was to be the very last — and such the one opened up by this journey proved to be. Leaving my companions in London, I arrived in the city of dykes and canals, and at once began prospecting among the bankers. But the cautious Hollanders would have nothing to do with strangers at any price, no matter how plausible the pretext. It was in vain that I showed them my circular letter of credit and United States passport. These awe-inspiring documents, which elsewhere had proved a sufficient introduction, had no effect with the good burghers of Amsterdam. They received me very politely, and on my expressing a wish to purchase a bill of exchange on London (or any other city), the reply invariably was: "Have you a letter of introduction to us?" Upon my replying in the negative: "We never transact business of any kind with persons unknown to us," was added in way of explanation. Then handing over the documents above

(185)

mentioned, I said : " Unfortunately I did not procure letters
to any one in this city, not expecting to make any stay, but I
suppose my letter of credit and passport will be a sufficient
introduction for the purchase of a bill to be paid for in cash ? "
" Anyone can procure a circular letter of credit," was the
reply ; " besides it is our invariable rule to decline all dealings
except with those with whom we are acquainted, either personally or by introduction." A few trials with the same
result satisfied me that some other plan must be discovered.
I was nearly at my wits' end as to how to insert the small end
of the wedge which should pry out a good-sized nugget from
the " pocket " of one of these bulky — in body and estate —
but justly cautious Hollanders, who really understood how to
do business safely.

Some time previously I had purchased several bills of
exchange in Frankfort, drawn on merchants in Amsterdam,
but not yet due. I now called on them, and, in each case,
had the bills accepted, at the same time telling them that I
wished to use the money and would feel obliged if they would
pay their bill at once less the discount. The reply was as I
expected, that they based all their merchandise operations on
paying bills only as fast as they became due. The real object
of the request was that I should have some excuse for asking
the address of a broker whom I could employ to purchase
bills, etc. My ruse was successful— for, supposing that one
who held their own paper to a considerable amount must be
all right, upon my request a member of one of the firms on
whom I called gave me the name of a Mr. Pinto, a Hebrew
member of the Amsterdam Stock Exchange. In this way I
soon procured several addresses. With the list I returned to
the " Black Eagle," and after a twelve o'clock dinner I went
in search of Mr. Pinto and found him at his residence — a
front room of which served for an office — in the Juden
Strasse (Jew Street), and a strange place it is on a Saturday
afternoon, the time when I first visited that unfragrant quarter. Informing him of my business and the name of the mer-

chant who gave me his address — which he appeared to think a sufficient introduction — he took the matter in hand, and leaving 20,000 guilders in Dutch bank-notes with him for the purchase of bills on Hamburgh, also the Frankfort bills before named, to be sold on "Change," I departed. Calling the following day I found that he had accomplished the transaction. I then deposited a still larger sum with him, and requested him to purchase some bills in "marks banco." These were duly purchased and delivered, but so far I could see no opening for a "speculation" of my peculiar kind. Having no particular plan of procedure up to this moment, I was only casting about in an experimental way. A day or two later I called, and arranged to have him sell on Change all the bills on Hamburgh. Later he informed me that the rate of exchange on that city was lower and that he had not sold on account of the price. Upon explaining that I had another operation in view that would recoup me for the loss, he immediately went on Change and sold out at a loss of fifty pounds sterling. Among the bills previously purchased was one on Baring Brothers, which I had sent to McDonald in London, and which, as will be seen, proved to be the first step in the "Great Bank Forgery."

Aside from the Barings bill the purchase and sale of all those bills had accomplished nothing but to increase my respect for the cautious, therefore safe modes of transacting business in Holland. In these respects, far ahead of any other country in which I ever had business transactions, the strict uncompromising methods of the Dutch rendered the country a most unfruitful field for all classes of swindlers. I had sold out the bills as above, because there seemed to be no possible way, that I could see, to "beat the Dutch," and I had in consequence resolved to proceed to Frankfort-on-the-Main, with the hope of finding some way to make the Rothschilds contribute a small part of the wealth accumulated at the original starting-place of that remarkable family. My preparations for going to that city being completed, at the moment of departure I received a dispatch from Mac that changed the whole aspect of affairs, and proved that the unpremeditated sending of the Baring bill gave the first impulse to a train of ideas which finally culminated in the fraud on the Bank of England. Let the reader bear in mind that this was in November, less than four months before the first false bills were sent to the Bank of England for discount. The dispatch read as follows:

LONDON, November 2d, 1872.

To GEORGE BIDWELL, Amsterdam:

Have made a great discovery. Come immediately.   MAC.

This dispatch was really the first inception of the fraud; and yet the bank managers, in order to protect themselves from the charge of carelessness, although aware of the existence of the dispatch, made every effort to carry the impression that we had contrived the plan of the fraud in America; had there spent many months in making preparations; and that all of our operations on the Continent, described above and elsewhere, were a part of the original scheme. I have no desire to extenuate or excuse, but this fact, together with the alleged " attempt to escape from Newgate " during the trial, was what really got us the " life sentence."

That dispatch was a great mystery to me, but I quickly decided to obey the summons, first obtaining through Mr. Pinto a number of bills of exchange drawn on first-class London houses. Arriving in London the following night, I received from McDonald a solution of the mystery. I give his explanation, as near as I can remember, in his own words:

" As soon as I received that bill on Baring's I went there to collect the money. Instead of paying the amount by check or in gold or notes, as I expected, the cashier stamped on the face: ' Payable at the London and Westminster Bank,' and endorsed it. Upon taking it there it was cashed without a question. It occurred to me immediately that if we were to get some blank bills of exchange, we could make as many as we liked by imitating the original, and draw the money from the bank with the same ease that I did for the genuine bill."

Such was the "great discovery" that had brought me from Holland, and it might have worked for the small sums that could be drawn in one day, with due regard to safety. That did not suit me, and Mac's financial plan was never put in operation in the form he had conceived; nevertheless it served as an initiatory step in the long journey which we were preparing to undertake.

McDonald had no sooner informed me of the particulars regarding his "great discovery" than it flashed through my mind: "Here is the opportunity to use the long-neglected Bank of England account." I reasoned that as the bank had paid the Barings bill to McDonald without verifying the signature, it must be the custom in England to transfer bills of exchange from hand to hand without sending them to the acceptors to be initialed. If this was true, it followed that the banks discounted paper without making any inquiry as to the genuineness of the signatures, relying entirely on the character of the customer who offered the paper for discount.

Here was an opening, indeed!

When this proved to be a fact, all I had to do was to start a manufactory for making imitation bills, and deposit them in the Bank of England for discount through the medium of the "Warren" account.

This reasoning appeared to be sound; still, I could not believe it to be among the possibilities that any bank, especially an institution like the Bank of England, should do business in so loose a manner. In New York, so long ago as 1854 — the year of my first visit to that emporium — it had been the custom among the bankers and brokers to send all offered paper to the purported drawers or acceptors to have it initialed by them. In consequence of that very necessary precaution, any attempt to perpetrate on a New York bank such a fraud as the one so easily carried out against the Bank of England, would have been nipped in the bud.

The following letter from the London *Times* comes in *apropos* at this point:

LONDON, September 8, 1873.

To THE EDITOR OF "THE TIMES":

SIR, — The revelations which have been made, in connection
with the late Bank of England forgeries, have shown us a weakness in our way of doing business in neglecting to obtain the verification of acceptors and drawers to bills discounted.

Doubtless the presentation and initialing of every bill discounted
by our large London bankers would entail much time and extra
labor, and would in many cases be impossible; but it would be a
comparatively easy matter to send a copy of each bill discounted to
the acceptor and drawer, informing them that such a bill had been
discounted by Messrs. ———, printed forms being kept for the
purpose, leaving a blank place for name, date, and amount.

I am, etc.,   BANK MANAGER.

In turn I explained my plan of using the Warren account
in the Bank of England that had been lying so long comparatively useless. Without delay the bulk of our money was
placed in Warren's hands to deposit in the account, so that
in case we finally concluded to attempt the execution of the
fraud, the large balance would show well on the bank books.
I also sent the following cable dispatch to E. Noyes Hills
("Noyes"), New York:

Come by first steamer. Answer, Langham, London.

In sending for Noyes at this time, my idea was to have
"Warren" introduce him to the bank, and let him open an
account, by means of which the fraud could be carried on,
leaving Austin entirely disconnected with it, save in having
introduced Noyes. I imagined that in such a case no proof
could be adduced that he knew, at the time of introduction,
of Noyes' intention to defraud the bank. On more mature
reflection I saw that such a transfer might thwart the whole
undertaking, by starting inquiries which should bring to light
the very slender foundation on which the Warren account
had been opened with the Bank of England. Besides, that
account had been made more solid by the length of time it
had been opened, and the amount of legitimate business

transactions through it. I therefore proposed an alternative plan which was at once put in execution, as follows :

On the 2d of December, 1873, Austin, who had not yet had the warning of a portending railway accident, opened an account at the Continental Bank in the name of C. J. Horton, depositing £1,300 in bank-notes. As anticipated, seeing their new customer deposit such a sum, no embarrassing questions were asked by the managers, and, doubtless, noting that he had "business" transactions with a depositor in the Bank of England, whose checks were duly honored there, they were led to believe that further inquiry was unnecessary. The next day I had a Warren check deposited to Horton's account, and the operation repeated, varied with checking out small sums, from day to day, in order to give the affair an air of genuine business. I also purchased several bills of exchange, and had Warren take them to the bank manager, Mr. Francis, for discount. Upon returning from the bank, he said there would be no risk in taking £50,000 in false bills and bringing away the gold, thus ending the whole matter at a stroke. But this appearing to me a hazardous undertaking, I adhered to the slower plan, though, as the sequel shows, such a *coup* might have been successful. The backs of the bills were covered with the endorsements of the various firms through whose hands they had passed. These endorsements were copied in *fac-simile* so that the false bills in contemplation should have all the characteristics of the originals.

As bills of exchange will be frequently mentioned, some of my readers may not know exactly what they are, and how used. For example, a manufacturer of silk in Lyons sells goods to the amount of five thousand dollars to a responsible merchant on six months' credit. The merchant gives his note or bill for the whole, or, as is usual, several of five hundred or a thousand each, to the order of himself, or the manufacturer, payable at (say) Rothschilds' in London. He is careful to see that his balance is sufficient or to arrange with the Rothschilds to accept and pay them when due. The manufacturer endorsing pays them out, or puts them in his bank for discount. The bank in turn also endorsing, sells them to a customer who has bills to meet in London. After endorsing, he likewise remits them to his correspondents, who pay his bills with the proceeds of their discount or sale — first, however, sending them to be accepted by the Rothschilds, from which time they are known as "acceptances."

It may be easily seen how I was enabled to plan and execute this mammoth fraud, when I state that the Bank of England cashed acceptances such as I have described without sending them to the Rothschilds to see *whether their signature or acceptance was genuine.* The last seven words give the key to the whole mystery. While in Germany I had purchased every variety of ink on sale at the stationers, so that in case of need I could have not only any written document imitated, but also written with like ink. I had also, out of curiosity, purchased a great variety of blank bills of exchange, printed in French, German, Dutch, Italian, Russian, Turkish, and Arabic. At the time of this purchase, my companions laughed at me for "lugging about a lot of trash" for which I had no possible use. But, now that I was about to tackle the Bank of England, I found them, like Mrs. Partington's coffin-plate, handy to have in a portmanteau. I also continued sending remittances to my Hebrew broker in Amsterdam, Mr. Pinto, requesting him to send me several bills on London. These, together with some already in my possession, gave me the opportunity of getting a great number of the endorsements, stamps, and signatures of leading firms on the Continent and in London.

I went to the printing and stationery establishment of Sir Sidney Waterlow, then Lord Mayor of London, before whom we were afterward under examination at the Mansion House, at intervals for four months (see cut), there I left an order for two books of blank drafts or bills of exchange, and in a few days called at the city office for them. The manager had to

THE BANK OF ENGLAND.   (From the Jubilee No. of *London Graphic*.)

send to the printing-house for them, and in consequence kept me waiting more than an hour, he and the clerk talking with me for some time. Yet those two men within three months swore before their master, the Lord Mayor, on our examination, that McDonald was the man — he having light hair and blue eyes, my hair being black — and Mac and I sitting beside each other in full view of the witnesses.

I only mention this as an instance of mistaken identification, which less than fifty years ago might have hanged Mac, and set me, the real actor, at liberty. In this connection it will be proper to state that, not wishing any one to suffer for my own acts, as soon as the day's examination was over, after returning to my lonely cell in Newgate, I wrote a full account regarding my visit to the Lord Mayor's establishment, giving particulars which proved so conclusive that those important witnesses did not appear at the subsequent trial at the Old Bailey.

I also required some small wood engravings — fac-similes of the various bank and private endorsement stamps. It had been a part of my plan that I was to remain in the background, contriving and giving directions, leaving others to carry them out. The reason for this was that I might be free from anxiety for my personal safety, and would thereby be enabled to act with coolness and judgment in the management of the business, and in disposing of the proceeds of the fraud in case the project should be successful. I also intended that no one of us, except Noyes, should show himself in England in connection with the affair, therefore I sent McDonald, who could pass for a Frenchman, to Paris to get the required blocks engraved. After three or four days' absence he returned to London without them, and gave me the surprising information that there were " no wood engravers in Paris." I afterwards discovered that while there he whiled away the time, and returned to play that tale on my credulity.

Placing implicit belief in that statement, I had a serious argument with myself as to whether I should not throw up the whole matter and go home, rather than do anything which might involve me and leave a possible clue to connect myself with the fraud ; for it would be a very delicate operation to procure the blocks, etc., in London, without arousing suspicion, and I would trust no one else to do it. Suppose that the actions or words of the person sent should excite the suspicion

of the engraver, trifling indications of which might not be noticed, or thought worth reporting to me? The engraver would communicate his suspicions to the police, detectives put on, and we "ambushed" in the midst of our operations. Finally I resolved to order the blocks myself — *there being no wood engravers in Paris* — though with great reluctance, and with the feeling that I was committing a grave error. I therefore made a list of all the wood engravers in London, and spent two or three days driving about in a cab, selecting five out of the forty or fifty with whom I conversed, to do the work, judging them to possess simple, unsuspicious natures. The result proved that I made no mistake in my selections, as the work was quickly done, and no suspicions as to its real object transpired.

It would appear that the qualifications thus worse than wasted, if properly used might have taken me to the top round of the ladder; though I do not mention this in a boasting spirit, but only to show that where I made a failure of getting rich by dishonest means, others would doubtless have been defeated, for "something" always happens.

In the meantime Noyes had received my cablegram and sailed for England. An hour after his arrival in London I met him, and in answer to his inquiries, informed him that I was speculating on the Merchants' Exchange, and expected to wind up my operations shortly. I told him he must ask no more questions, but follow my directions implicitly and promptly; that I should not even let him know where the rest of us lodged, after the first of January. I further informed him that he was to act as clerk for "Horton," and though our operations were a little irregular, that he should be taken care of, kept out of danger, and be well paid for his services; and impressing it on his mind to obey orders like a soldier, I left him.

And yet, this man, who was to be paid with about five per cent. of the proceeds of the crime, received the same life sentence, and is at the present time serving his sixteenth year at hard labor in Portsmouth Prison, England. When arrested, *he would not betray us!* even though the prosecution offered to permit him to turn Queen's evidence, the acceptance of which would have freed him as soon as the trial should be finished. Let his case be a warning not to touch pitch lest ye be drawn into the slimy depths.

In order to secure Noyes against any fatal disaster in case of a premature discovery, I had an advertisement for a situation as clerk, by one who could deposit a cash guarantee, inserted in the Daily Telegraph (London). This Noyes was to show to the landlord of Durant's hotel where he was staying, and arrange a meeting between himself and Horton, taking care that persons should be within hearing while the latter bargained with the former to become his clerk. To cover this source of danger to Noyes more surely, I had them go to David Howell, solicitor — of whom more anon — who drew up an article of agreement between them, for which that delectable limb of the law charged ten pounds sterling. On December 28, 1872, I mailed from Birmingham to the Bank of England genuine bills of exchange, amounting to four thousand three hundred and seven pounds, for discount, in order to ascertain if our "Fraud Machine" was in working order, and as they were discounted without question, this proved to be the case.

Shortly after the events just recorded, I received a letter from my wife which determined me to return home at once, and woe to me that I failed to carry out that determination. Going immediately to the Grosvenor Hotel, where my two principal associates were staying, I informed them of my resolution. After some discussion it was agreed to drop the plan against the Bank, and I reverted to my old idea of going to Chicago to engage in trade.

Upon leaving I told my brother that I was going to pay my bills, and should call later for a check for my share of the money in the bank. Having paid up all my personal debts, I found that I could get off to America by the next day's steamer from Liverpool. Permit me right here to call attention to one of those very slight causes which affect a man's entire future existence, and which made me change my plans, so that, instead of passing happy years amidst family and friends, I came to endure long years of misery in a foreign prison. Thus it happened: While I was absent, McDonald requested my brother Austin to propose to me that I should leave my share of the money behind in the bank and draw for it after my arrival in America. Accordingly, when I returned, that proposition was made to me, and it placed me in a quandary; for I did not like to show apparent distrust by refusing, nor did I like the idea of leaving it behind. Besides such a proposition at that juncture, made me suspect an intention on their part to remain behind with the idea of attempting to carry out the plan of fraud. In my opinion, any attempt to undertake the management of such an operation, involved certain disaster, as neither of them possessed the exact qualifications requisite, especially an exact knowledge of, and experience acquired in, legitimate business. I theorized thus to myself: "This is one of those unique operations which, if anything, will result in a great success or a terrible disaster. I see clearly that the affair can be carried on so that only one person need show himself, and if each does his part thoroughly, it can be done with little or no risk. Still it will not be common prudence for us two brothers to take part in the same criminal operation. If I go into this, he shall go home; and if I should get into trouble, he could look after my family. But that 'if' is what troubles me. To be sure, I can shroud the operation and the operators in so thick a veil of mystery that it would trouble them to get a clue or even to discover the fraud until two months after we should all be out of England." It will be perceived that the whole plan and system of operations stood clearly outlined in my mind. One thing alone gave me cause of distrust, and that was the possibility of carelessness or neglect on the part of my ablest associate; but I thought I could make such strict terms and conditions that no disaster would be likely to happen from that source, *unless I was directly deceived* and kept in the dark regarding his movements, and I believed he had too much good sense to do that. The result will show, by one of the most remarkable examples on record, that the only road to final success is to keep clear of the slightest contact with wrong-doing, no matter how plausible the reasonings.

Certainly, in planning so gigantic a fraud, I believed every point could be so completely covered, that even my name would never be known, for otherwise I should have been hunted through the world. Without this apparent certainty I should have abandoned the idea of a job which turned out so badly that it took me nearly fifteen years to get out of it.

If among my readers there may be one who has become possessed with the idea that he cannot make money enough honestly to satisfy his desires, and is inclined to try the other plan, my counsel is — *don't!* Better to reduce the desires to fit the circumstances, than get into circumstances the end of which may be a prison — in any event, disgrace.

I tried one plan thoroughly, and as sure as *you* do, it will come home and blast your life, as it has blasted mine and the lives of those near and dear to me — and as it has invariably blasted the lives of all who have "tried it on".

Still that "if" stood in my way; however, I finally concluded to defer my journey home for a day or two, that I might have time to consider this new phase in the posture of affairs.

CHAPTER XX.

AFTER some consideration I decided, instead of returning to America, to take the management of the contemplated fraud on the Bank of England; for it appeared as
certain as any human event that, with proper precautions and
skillful handling, the scheme could be carried out without our
real names becoming known, and that no clue need be left by
which any trace of the perpetrators could be discovered.

Even with this prospect, I resolved that my brother
should not take the risk of remaining in England, so that
in case the attempt resulted disastrously, he at least would be
in safety.

I was regarded the only one who could manage the affair
with any hope of success, and I declined to have anything to
do with it unless Austin was first beyond danger.

At this juncture a remarkable circumstance occurred,
which, with his engagement, decided the matter according
to my wish. Thus it happened: About the first of January,
1873, Austin left for Paris. The express train, beyond Calais,
ran off the track, and one man or more was killed in the
same carriage with him. He was jammed in the wreck,
badly wounded with splinters, and so shaken that he was
carried away on a stretcher to the other train. He believed
his escape almost miraculous.

I have referred to Austin's engagement, the nature of
which was as follows: While in London, he had made the

acquaintance of a young lady whom he determined to marry. Matters had come to this stage before I was informed of the affair.

When he disclosed to me his intention of marrying the young lady, I said to him: "Do not think of marrying her before you are settled in business. Go home, and with the money you have, get into some legitimate occupation; then you can marry with a good conscience," etc. But when did a person in love ever act from prudential considerations, and on wholesome advice?

The matter remained thus until after the railway accident before mentioned, and I now found him very willing to go home, cutting off all connection with the contemplated fraud; also to give up the idea of marriage until he had established himself in business. Accordingly I went with him as far as Calais — he to take the steamer at Havre for New York — and returned to London to begin putting the forged bills into the Bank of England, rejoicing in the fact that my brother was then on his way back to America and consequent safety; but, as I discovered some months later, he remained in France.

After we parted at Calais, it occurred to him that it would be a fine plan — one that he thought could do no harm to any one — to turn the trip to America into a "wedding journey." He had money with which he believed he could go into business there, and with unwise reasoning, usual to young men in love, he easily convinced himself that the best thing he could do was to take a wife with him to America. Therefore, he arranged with a friend of the young lady's mother to bring them both to Paris. This was done, and soon after they were married at the American embassy — he settling a considerable sum on his wife, which was placed in the mother's safe-keeping. The mother returned to England, and the newly married pair started on a tour through Spain, taking the steamer at Cadiz for Havana.

The following dispatch, copied from the London *Times*,

will serve to show the beginning of the sequel to his rash but lover-like proceedings:

[*Times*, April 7, 1873.]

PHILADELPHIA, March 25th.

The arrest of Austin Bidwell, another of the persons implicated in the Bank of England forgeries, who was captured at Havana, through the agency of the cables, has probably already been announced in England. A telegram from Havana states that although there is no extradition treaty with England, the authorities intend to give Bidwell up and allow him to be taken to London as soon as the proper proofs are furnished.

As soon as Austin and his wife were brought to London, she deserted him.

I again resume the thread of my narrative. It had occupied about two months in making the preparations described in the last chapter, and I was still so doubtful as to the possibility that the Bank of England would not discover the fraud with the first batch of bills, that I had fully prepared only what represented £4,250. I had preserved the endorsement blocks used in their manufacture, so that in case we were disappointed, and the bank really discounted them, we could rush up a larger number in a few days. It was exactly this doubt which had prevented the accumulation of a sufficient quantity of false bills; for despite the fair look of the thing, it was difficult to believe otherwise than that the bank had what looked like a vulnerable point guarded in some way that had escaped my scrutiny. Besides, I had the Warren account with the Bank of England, and the Horton account at the Continental Bank. With these simple means I now proposed to enter the bomb-proof vaults of the greatest financial fortress of which history gives account.

My brother was safely out of England. All was prepared for the trial test.

" Will the false bills go through? Will the argus eyes of the renowned Bank of England detect the imposture at the first glance?" These and similar questions agitated my mind at this juncture. To settle the question, I took the

£4,250 in false bills and went to Birmingham. There I engaged a room at the Queen's Hotel, and on paper brought with me I wrote in Warren's name, imitating his hand-writing, to Mr. Francis, Manager of the Western Branch of the Bank of England, the following:

BIRMINGHAM, January 21, 1873.

DEAR SIR:

I hand you herewith, as per enclosed memorandum, bills for discount, the proceeds of which please place to my credit on receipt. I remain, dear sir,   Yours very truly,

F. A. WARREN.

On the previous day all the money, except about one hundred pounds, had been drawn out of the London banks, so that in case of a discovery that would be the only additional loss — the previous preparations having cost about as much more. We had also prepared everything for an immediate flight in case it should prove a failure. I waited in Birmingham until the next day, in order to hear from Mr. Francis, or otherwise get a clue as to the fate of the false bills. In case the forgery had been discovered, he would doubtless reply to the letter all the same, and simultaneously put the Birmingham police on the scent, or send a detective from London to watch at the post-office and arrest the person who called for the letter. Suppose I should be thus arrested? Mr. Francis could not recognize me as otherwise connected with his customer, Warren, he never having seen me; but I should have been asked some awkward questions, and why I had called for Warren's letters. That I might have even a lame excuse ready, I wrote a note as follows:

BIRMINGHAM, January 22, 1873.

POSTMASTER:

SIR, — Please deliver any letters for me to the bearer, and oblige   F. A. WARREN.

Calling at the post-office, and seeing no sign that it was specially watched, I handed in the order, and was given a

letter. Had I been arrested, I should have said that I met a
gentleman on the train and fell into conversation with him,
and just before arriving at Birmingham he remarked that he
must continue his journey to Liverpool, and would feel obliged
to me if I would call for his letters and forward them.
I hurried to catch the London train, and as soon as I was
under way I opened the letter, which was to the following
purport:

WESTERN BRANCH OF THE BANK OF ENGLAND,

LONDON, January 22, 1873.

F. A. WARREN, ESQ., P. O. Birmingham:

DEAR SIR, — Your favor of the 21st, enclosing £4,250 in bills
for discount, is received, and proceeds of same passed to your
credit as requested. Hoping you are recovering from the effects
of the fall from your horse, and that I may have the pleasure of
seeing you in London soon, I remain, dear sir,

Yours faithfully,　　　　　　P. M. FRANCIS.

On arrival in London, I gave Noyes "Warren" checks for
£4,000, which he deposited in the Continental Bank to Horton's credit. I next filled in and signed Horton checks for
about £3,000, with which he purchased United States bonds
from Jay Cooke, M'Culloch & Co., at their banking-house in
Lombard Street — the Wall Street of London.

This completed the operation, and as soon as we could
prepare more false bills we were ready for another of exactly
the same kind, only on a larger scale — and thus we kept
repeating until the discovery.

Thinking that the purchase of such large sums of United
States bonds from day to day might attract attention, I
devised another plan, viz.: The forged bills being sent from
Birmingham by mail, discounted and placed to Warren's
credit at the Bank of England, the amount immediately
transferred to the Horton account at the Continental Bank
by means of Warren checks — I had Noyes reduce the latter
account by drawing out Bank of England notes. These were
taken to the bank and exchanged for gold, which was deliv-

ered in sealed bags of £1,000 each, and immediately carried back and exchanged for notes by another person. The object of this double exchange was to break the connection, it being obligatory that a list of the numbers of all notes paid out, and to whom, must be preserved by bankers and other dealers. Even when passed from hand to hand, the person who pays out a note must endorse on the back of it his or her name and address, and this notwithstanding that they are made payable "to bearer" exactly like "greenbacks." And, indeed, the disposal of so much gold without attracting notice was one of my chief anxieties — in fact, I found there was such a thing as having too much of that useful metal. The reader may realize this fact when I state that while the "business" was in operation our "income" was at times more than $50,000 per day.

I cannot refrain from relating, right here, an incident which illustrates the folly of "crowing before one is out of the woods," or "counting chickens before they are hatched."

One evening in January, while the "fraud machine" was in full operation, three stylishly dressed young men met in a private parlor of the St. James Hotel, Piccadilly. Two of them appeared to be in high spirits — perhaps possessed by evil spirits, whom spirits of another kind might conciliate — and one of the party called for a bottle of "Vueve Cliquot" in honor of the occasion, the "golden calf" having been worshiped that day to the jingle of many bags of sovereigns. The elder of the trio was in a pensive mood, and was rallied by his hilarious companions for his taciturnity, which became more marked as their merriment increased. They saw themselves safely back in America, the possessors of fortunes, however wrongfully obtained, yet obtained in a way that would leave behind no ruined widows and orphans to linger out the remainder of their blighted lives in poverty. That was a point which added zest to their enjoyment of the prospect. Being obtained from an institution, into whose impregnable vaults flowed the wealth of the world, was a source of inexpressible satisfaction to those gentlemanly appearing robbers. At last the elder could endure the situation no longer, and addressed the party very much as follows:

"Well, my friends, you believe that nothing can happen to hinder the full realization of your hopes, and that you are as safe as if you were already off for America; but I advise you to moderate your ardor and not be too sanguine — too certain. It is true that everything is so arranged, works so smoothly, and ourselves shrouded in so dense a fog — a London fog — of mystery, that, even in case of a premature discovery, they may not be able to reach us or get a clue to our personality.

"It appears as if the bank managers had heaped a mountain of gold out in the street, and had put up a notice, 'Please do not touch this,' and then had left it unguarded with the guileless confidingness of an Arcadian. Who could ever have imagined they would have left such an open path to their bags of gold? Thousands of Englishmen have gone out to India to 'shake the Banyan tree,' but this beats that 'legal' way of 'making' a fortune out of sight. Despite the smooth surface, I have a foreboding that Aeolus is brooding a storm that may send our gold-laden bark among the rocks, and ourselves with it. Negligence or accident will beat the 'best laid plans,' and we shall have the greatest success or the most terrible disaster possible. Let us do no more crowing until we are out of the woods."

With these words the speaker relapsed into his thoughtful mood, and soon after departed, leaving his goblet of Vueve Cliquot untasted.

It was not long after this that a truly laughable incident occurred. During our stay in London, it was frequently remarked that McDonald bore a strong general resemblance to the Prince of Wales. One afternoon Mac and I were sauntering past the "Horse-Guards," and as soon as the magnificent sentry (placed on horseback in the gateway) saw us, he brought his sword to the salute and kept it there until we were past. Exactly who he took *me* for has ever since been —not a *casus belli*—but a subject of curious cogitations— especially when in prison, writing petitions to the Home Office for my release — whether I should not refer the secretary of State to the sentry, in order to prove satisfactorily that I was a " somebody."

On the 27th day of February my associate and myself had a consultation as to whether we should stop with what we had, or put in one more batch of bills. It was finally decided to put in another, and the very last lot. In thus taking the pitcher once too often to the well, too little account was taken of two all-important points — neglect of business and the possibility of accidents, the latter, of course, usually arising out of the former. Early the next day I posted in Birmingham to the Bank more than $100,000 in false bills, congratulating myself that the affair was so nearly finished, and that the next day I should be off for America. When these bills were mailed the balance in both banks had been reduced to less than a thousand pounds.

Remaining in Birmingham, early the next morning I sent a cabman to the post-office with an order for letters addressed to Warren, and kept a watch on him to see if he was followed from the office. After satisfying myself that he was not being " shadowed," I got from him the letter, which was from Mr. Francis, stating that the bills had been received, discounted, and the proceeds placed to the credit of the Warren account. Of course, this was the last of a number of letters from Mr. Francis, which had been received by me during the progress of the affair, and as each came to hand I could not repress a feeling of regret that by the irony of fate I seemed destined, in the execution of " speculations," to abuse the confidence of some of the best of men. The fact that, as in the present instance, I was taking no advantage of facilities afforded by a position of trust—Mr. Francis never having seen me—was the excuse with which I had always, in such cases, tried to salve my conscience.

The letter in question satisfied me that our false bills had gone through the mill, and would be laid away in the vaults of the bank to be forgotten until they should become due two months later; and thus it would have been, but for an unforeseen occurrence to be related shortly. I hurried to the station, and taking a train arrived in London by the

GARRAWAY'S.

time the banks were open for business. In order to be certain that all was right before sending Noyes into the Continental Bank, I gave him a check for a small amount, which he sent in by a commissioner for collection, with order to bring the money to him at the Cannon Street Hotel. I took care to be in the bank when he arrived, that I might see what passed. The check was paid without demur, and he left the bank, I keeping him in view until he had passed the public house where Noyes was waiting for me. I hastened in and told him to go and get the money from the commissioner, which he did, then come to meet me at Garraway's, our usual place of rendezvous. Inasmuch as many generations of all nations visiting London, have been accustomed to resort to Garraway's coffee-house, for pleasure or business purposes, and as it was closed for the last time on Saturday, August 11, 1876, a picture of this celebrated place may be of interest to the reader.

At the time of the " South-Sea bubble," Dean Swift wrote the following lines regarding the brokers and their victims, the speculators, who were accustomed to congregate at Garraway's :

> There is a gulf where thousands fell,
>   Here all the bold adventurers came,
> A narrow sound, though deep as hell —
>   Change-alley is the dreadful name.
>
> Subscribers here by thousands float,
>   And jostle one another down,
> Each paddling in his leaky boat,
>   And here they fish for gold and drown.
>   *   *   *   *
> Meantime, secure on Garway cliffs,
>   A savage race, by shipwrecks fed,
> Lie waiting for the founder'd skiffs,
>   And strip the bodies of the dead.

Dr. Radcliffe, a celebrated character, was a rash speculator in the South-Sea scheme, and could always be found during business hours planted at a table, to watch the turns of the share market, and to receive his patients, as was the custom in the last century with coffee-houses in general. One day he had invested five thousand guineas in one project, and upon being informed that he had lost it all, replied:

EXAMINATION OF BIDWELL AND HILLS BEFORE THE LORD MAYOR OF LONDON.

"Why, 'tis but going up five thousand pairs of stairs more."
"This answer," says Sydney Smith, "deserves a statue."

Coming down to later times, we find in Dickens's "Pickwick Club," where Sergeant Buzfuz, in the case of Bardell *vs.* Pickwick, quotes the following letter:

GARRAWAY'S, twelve o'clock.

DEAR MRS. B.: — Chops and tomato sauce.

Yours,   PICKWICK.

As some of my readers may be in a Pickwickian state of mind on the food question, I will reserve the account of the discovery of the great fraud, and the arrest of Noyes, for the next chapter.

CHAPTER XXI.

IT appears that when the last lot of bills arrived from
Birmingham they were handed by the manager, as usual,
to a clerk whose duty it was to look over and enter them in
the books. In running them over, he threw out two on
which the date of the acceptance had not been put. Supposing this to have been an oversight of the acceptors, no notice
was taken of the irregularity beyond laying the bills aside,
that the supposed neglect might be rectified. Accordingly, on
the morning of the 1st of March, 1873, the bills were sent to
B. W. Blydenstein (the supposed acceptor), and were at once
declared to be forgeries. Instant measures were taken to
arrest the perpetrators. This occurred just after we had sent
the commissioner with a Horton check as related in the last
chapter.

Upon meeting Noyes at Garraway's I gave him Warren
checks for seventy-five thousand dollars, with which he purchased United States bonds from Messrs. Jay Cooke & Co. I
also gave him about thirty thousand dollars in Warren checks
to deposit to the credit of the Horton account. After having accomplished that business, it only remained for him to
withdraw the money from the Horton account, which would
finish, and we be ready to leave the country with our booty.

A quarter of an hour would end my anxieties!

It had been my intention to send a commissioner to draw
the money, so that in the apparently impossible case of a dis-

covery Noyes would be safe from arrest. Should there be a premature " tumble " and we become aware of it in time, we could easily get him out of the country — he being the only one who was known to the bankers. But having just visited Jay Cooke & Co. and the Continental Bank, he justly felt certain that all was right, and thought it would be best, and quite safe, for him to go and do the business in person instead of sending a commissioner.

We had previously sent commissioners for large sums in bonds, etc.; but in such cases they had acted only as messengers, not knowing the value of the packages they carried. The checks we had sent by them were for small sums, and now to send one to draw $30,000 might cause inquiry at the Continental Bank. For these reasons I concluded to let Noyes have his own way. Had I known what was at that moment passing not a stone's throw from where we sat in Garraway's, my thoughts would have been of quite a different nature. After the discovery, as related, the telegraph was set to work, and detectives procured from the Bow Street police station, which was but a short distance from where we sat discussing our next and last move — the last indeed! They went to the Continental, Horton's bank, and waited to meet Noyes as he came in about one o'clock P. M. to draw the money. He was arrested and taken to Bow Street station, the party passing close by me on the way, of course neither Noyes or I taking any notice of each other. As I had foreseen and provided for this possible contingency, the occurrence did not alarm me, for I knew that *if all my precautions had been lived up to*, no harm beyond temporary inconvenience could come to Noyes, and not the slightest clue be obtained to connect Mac or myself with the fraud. Austin, the only other one known to the bankers, was, as I supposed, safe in the United States; therefore, as I felt secure that no information would be got out of Noyes, all we had to do was to lie quietly in London until the furore of excitement was a little cooled, and then to make our way out of the country at our leisure. Nothwithstanding these seemingly impregnable plans and precautions, and as a striking example of how crime comes to light, it will be interesting to have the causes which nullified the execution of the ideas outlined in the last sentence.

During the operation Mac occupied lodgings in an aristocratic quarter, St. James Place, Piccadilly. There all the bills were made. When the last lot was ready, I made away with and destroyed by burning or otherwise, the articles used in their manufacture.

As soon as Noyes was arrested, I went to Mac's rooms and made a clearance. As I was about to put all the waste papers in the fire Mac said he had some letters to write and asked me to leave a piece of blotting paper. I selected a piece that appeared not to have been used and laid it aside for him — a fatal concession, as will be seen in the account of the trial, showing what telling use was made of it. I was less particular in the clearance because when I represented to him the danger of an American moving from his lodgings at such a juncture, he agreed to remain quietly there. Then judge of my astonishment later in the day, when he said to me at Garraway's: " Well, I've got all my things out of that place, anyway." It was too late to repair so false a step, and he assured me that he had not left a scrap of paper behind. Subsequent events showed that his landlady saw in a paper an account of the forgery and arrest of Noyes, and coupling it with her lodger's precipitate flight — he having previously given no notice of his intention to leave — her suspicions were aroused; she went directly to the rooms and gathered up every loose bit of paper she could find, among which the only thing that proved of special value was the piece of blotting paper, and sent word to the police station.

Mac paid the penalty of this thoughtless act as this piece of blotter proved to be the principal, if not the only direct link, which connected him with the forgery.

I had occasion to part from Mac for an hour, and on my

return at about six P. M., found a note written by him, stating that he had just time to catch the last evening train for Dover. He really went to Liverpool ; but becoming suspicious, doubled on the police, ran to Chester, from there crossed the country by way of Taunton to Southampton, crossed to Havre, from which place he managed to get on board the steamship *Thuringia*, and sailed for New York.

MANSION HOUSE, ILLUMINATED.

This unexpected departure disconcerted my plans completely. The effect it had on my future proceedings will be detailed in the chapters relating to my flight through Ireland, and beyond.

The following regarding the discovery of the fraud, arrest, and examination of Noyes, is compiled from reliable sources.

It was on Saturday, March 1, 1873, that Noyes was arrested and taken to the Mansion House. The ordinary business of the day had concluded at twelve o'clock, but about two o'clock Noyes was brought to the bar on the charge of having been concerned in the forgeries in question.

The Lord Mayor Waterlow had not then taken his seat, and few people were present, except the officers and a few stragglers. On the Lord Mayor taking his seat, he stated that there were reasons for hearing the charge in private, and

he therefore requested, under a power given him by statute, that everyone not connected with the case would retire from court. Upon this the reporters, for whom the intimation seemed specially intended, withdrew in a body. The charge was then proceeded with, and sufficient evidence was produced by the Messrs. Freshfield,

C. K. FRESHFIELD, M. P.,
SOLICITOR TO THE BANK OF ENGLAND IN 1873.

who appeared on the part of the Bank of England, to warrant the Lord Mayor in remanding the prisoner until the next Friday, when the evidence taken at the first hearing was allowed to transpire without reservation of any kind as part of the case for the prosecution, and the prisoner's counsel had opportunities offered him of cross-examining witnesses who had given it. A contemporary account states that since his arrest a week previously he had much altered in appearance for the worse; and throughout the protracted examination of March 7th, he seemed anxious and dejected.

The Lord Mayor took his seat in the justice-room at twelve o'clock, and on that date the prisoner was put to the bar. Mr. Freshfield, the solicitor to the bank, attended to conduct the prosecution on the part of the Governor and Company; the prisoner was defended by Dr. Kenealy, Q. C.

Mr. Alfred D. Rothschild, one of the directors of the bank, occupied a seat on the bench. Mr. Frank May, the deputy cashier of the Bank of England, said that from inquiries he found that some portions of the proceeds of the forged bills had been paid into the Continental Bank in Lombard Street, and in consequence he went to that bank on Saturday to obtain further information. He there saw the prisoner, and gave him into custody.

He asked the manager of the Continental Bank, in the prisoner's presence, if the prisoner was Mr. Horton's clerk, and he replied in the affirmative. The prisoner then said, " Why are you giving me into custody?" Witness told him that he came from the Bank of England and he charged him with fraud.

Mr. Richard Amery, ledger-keeper at the Con-

DR. KENEALY.

tinental Bank, said he knew the prisoner by the name of Edwin Noyes. He also knew a Mr. C. J. Horton, who had an account at the bank. The prisoner was in the habit of bringing cash to be paid to Mr. Horton's credit, and also of presenting Horton's checks to be cashed.

In reply to Dr. Kenealy, the witness, Mr. Amery, said he only knew the prisoner as Horton's clerk, and as either paying in or cashing checks on his account; and Col. Francis stated that he never saw the prisoner until the day upon which he was given into custody. Dr. Kenealy, addressing the bench, said he wanted to know with what offense Mr. Noyes, the prisoner, was charged. Mr. Oke, the chief clerk to the Lord Mayor, replied that he was charged with fraudulently obtaining £4,500 by means of documents alleged to have been forged, and by conspiring with other persons, at present unknown, with intent to defraud the Governor and Company of the Bank of England. A letter was about to be read, upon which Dr. Kenealy objected unless there was evidence to show that it had been brought to the knowledge of Mr. Noyes. Mr. Freshfield said it was an act on the part of a co-conspirator. Dr. Kenealy submitted that the prosecution must first establish a conspiracy. On the occasion when the prisoner was first brought before the court he understood the case against him was heard *in camera.* He protested against such a course being resorted to while trying a man upon a criminal charge. They were not going to have the Inquisition in this country, and he submitted that the trying a prisoner *in camera* was a relic of the Inquisition. The Lord Mayor explained that in the exercise of his discretion, and availing himself of the power given him as a magistrate under Jervis's act, he had decided that the preliminary investigation should be heard in private. The prisoner had then been in custody only a few hours; there was at that time reason to believe that an enormous fraud had been committed, and that the ends of justice might be frustrated if the circumstances were made public at the first hearing. He had exercised his discretion in the matter, the prisoner's counsel had since heard the evidence taken on the first occasion and was now in a position to appreciate and use it. Although the prisoner was not represented by a counsel on the first occasion, the Lord Mayor took good care in the discharge of his duty to see that he was in no way prejudiced by the manner in which the investigation was conducted. He would be ultimately charged with conspiring with one Horton, otherwise Warren. Dr. Kenealy replied, that according to that theory any merchant's clerk in the city of London might any day be subjected to the same treatment that Mr. Noyes had experienced.

He protested against it until a conspiracy had been established between Noyes and Warren. Mr. Noyes, in the transactions in question, had done nothing more than cash genuine checks for his master, and why he should be assumed to have been concerned in a forgery he was at a loss to understand. The Lord Mayor said it was clear by the evidence that he had cashed checks which were the products of those forgeries.

Jonathan Pope, a city policeman, spoke as to the prisoner having been given into his custody on Saturday preceding at the Continental Bank, and to finding upon him at the police station an open check for £100, drawn by Horton on the Continental Bank, two bank-notes for £100 and £10 in gold, a gold watch and chain, a diamond ring, and a number of memoranda.

Detective Sargeant Spittle, who was recalled by Dr. Kenealy, said he had looked over the papers found upon the prisoner, and among them was an agreement entered into in January between him and Horton, by which he became Horton's clerk and manager at a salary of £100 a year. He appeared to have paid £300 to Horton as a premium. He also found a number of letters addressed to the prisoner and referring to an advertisement for a clerk's situation which he had inserted in the daily *Telegraph*. There were likewise among the papers several letters important to the prisoner. In one of these letters referred to by the witness, dated the 28th of January, Horton told the prisoner to give up his room at the Bridge-House Hotel and to take another on the first floor at the Cannon Street Hotel, and advised him to obtain a trusty porter whom he could send with deposits to the banks, and with stocks or bonds to the offices of Messrs. Jay Cooke

& Co. and Messrs. Clews, Habicht & Co. He added that as soon as he got settled in his chambers he would engage another clerk so that he (Noyes) should not have so much running about. Another letter was as follows :

London.

E. Noyes, Esq.:

Dear Sir : — I shall be unable to come to the office to-morrow as I shall be very busy at the West End, and will not be able to come as far as London Bridge, so you can go on with the business just as I told you, and do not fail to collect the money and bring it with you to Broad Street station at three o'clock, and meet me in the first-class waiting room, or down at the ticket office at the foot of the stairs. I will then give you further instructions.

I am yours, etc.,

C. J. Horton.

All the above devices and documents were pre-arranged by me for just the emergency in which Noyes then found himself, and they would have proved ample to protect him, had no others of the party been arrested — our arrest affording the opportunity to prove previous acquaintance.

At this stage Mr. Freshfield applied to the bench to have the prisoner remanded for a week. The evidence he said, went to show that he had been dealing with very large sums of money and acting almost in the character of a principal, certainly in that of an accomplice. Dr. Kenealy submitted there was no evidence whatever against Mr. Noyes, and that the Lord Mayor was bound to dismiss him. There was no proof that Warren and Horton were the same person. It was impossible to come to any other conclusion than that they were distinct. There was evidence that Noyes was a clerk to Horton and that he was never seen in the branch Bank of England at the West End. The only person who spoke of seeing the prisoner was a clerk of the Messrs. McCulloch, and that was at their place of business. What had Mr. Noyes done more than any clerk of a merchant in the city ? It might be assumed that bills proved afterward to be forgeries often passed through the hands of innocent people who had no knowledge of the risk they run. The learned counsel dwelt upon the circumstances as proved by papers found upon him, that Noyes had advertised for a situation as clerk on coming to this country from America, in December last, and that he had no previous acquaintance with Horton. Was it likely that if Horton was about to embark in a gigantic fraud he would take a perfect stranger into his confidence? Dealing with the evidence as it stood, he submitted there was only one transaction between them and that was not of a nature to justify his detention. Mr. Freshfield said Dr. Kenealy must not assume that he agreed with him in that at all. The Lord Mayor said, looking at the evidence as it stood, he could not take any other course than remand the prisoner, having regard to the circumstance that he was found dealing on one day with money amounting to £22,000, the produce of forged bills, and that a letter was found upon him asking him to bring the money to a person whom he would find in the first-class waiting-room at a railway station. He could not come to any other conclusion than that the prisoner must have known the moneys with which he was dealing had been acquired by unlawful means. He remanded him until that day week to his old quarters in Newgate.

CHAPTER XXII.

HUNTED THROUGH IRELAND — $2,500 REWARD FOR MY CAPTURE — DETECTIVES "SPOT" ME AT THE CORK RAILWAY STATION — OBLIGED TO ABANDON TAKING PASSAGE BY THE ILL-FATED ATLANTIC — A GAME OF "HARE AND HOUNDS" — ELUDING A DETECTIVE "TRAP" — ENGLISH MISRULE IN IRELAND — AM TAKEN FOR A PRIEST — A TYPOGRAPHICAL THUNDERBOLT AT LISMORE — AN EARLY MORNING WALK — A RIDE ON AN IRISH JAUNTING-CAR — "ON THE ROAD TO CLONMEL" — SHELTER IN A "SHEBEEN" — HOW THIRSTY SOULS GET THE "CRAYTHUR" IN IRELAND — A GOOD OLD IRISH LADY — PURSUIT, AND REFUGE IN A RUINED COTTAGE AT CAHIR.

WITHOUT the remotest suspicion that my right name was known, or that anything had been discovered to show my connection with the fraud, I resolved to take the steamer *Atlantic* of the White Star Line, at Queenstown, for New York. Knowing that all the railway stations in London were being watched, and that any man buying a ticket for America might have to give an account of himself, I sent a porter to purchase a ticket for Dublin *via* Holyhead. I intended taking the 9 P. M. mail train, and, as a precaution, I waited until the last moment, after the passengers were on board and the waiting-room doors shut. As the mail was being transferred from the wagons to the train, I took the opportunity to walk through the big gate unobserved amid the rush and confusion. The car doors were all locked, but on showing my ticket to a guard (conductor) he let me into a compartment, no doubt supposing that I had obtained admission to the station from the waiting-room and had been loitering about. The same was probably the case with the two or three other men looking out of the waiting-room window at the platform, whom I judged to be detectives. The train rolled out of the station, and soon I was leaving London behind at the rate of fifty miles an hour. After midnight we took the steamer at Holyhead and arrived at Dublin about seven A. M. I should not have felt so comfortable throughout this night's journey had I known that the telegraph was flashing in all directions:

"£500 reward for the capture of George Bidwell, who is supposed to be one of the persons engaged in the great bank forgery. He is an American, about forty years of age, of dark complexion, and is supposed to be in Ireland."

A whole column regarding myself and my transactions was published in the Dublin papers of that morning. Not suspecting they contained "news" regarding me, I neglected purchasing one, and remaining ignorant of my imminent danger, took the train for Cork, where I arrived about four P. M. I had two or three London papers of the previous day in my hand as I left the station. I had never been in Cork until then, and as I passed into the street two detectives, who were watching the passengers, turned and followed me. A few yards from the station one of them stepped up by my side and said:

"Have you ever been here before?"

I slightly turned my head toward him, gave a haughty glance as I replied, "Yes,"—then looked straight ahead and continued my slow gait, paying no further attention to him. He continued walking by my side for a few steps, as if irresolute, then dropped to the rear, rejoining his companion. I did not dare to look around, or make inquiry as to the location of the wharf from which the tug-boat started to convey mail and passengers to the New York steamers, which waited in the outer harbor. Therefore I continued my walk along what appeared to be the main business street, perhaps for a quarter of a mile, then turned into a druggist's and called for some Spanish licorice. This was done to enable me to ascertain if the detectives were still following. In a moment they passed the shop gazing intently in, and saw me leaning carelessly against the counter with my face partially turned to the street. As soon as I had paid for the licorice, I continued my walk in the same direction, but saw nothing of the men, they having evidently stopped in some place to let me get ahead once more. In a short time I approached an inclosure, over the gate of which was a sign that informed me I had come by accident direct to the wharf of the New York steamers. Entering I found the place crowded, and the tug-boat ready to convey the passengers to the steamer *Atlantic*. Before attempting to step aboard the tug I took a covert look around and saw my two detectives standing back in one corner with their eyes fixed upon me all but their heads being concealed behind the crowd waiting to see their friends off for America. Apparently unconscious of their presence, I threw my papers, one by one down among the passengers; and as the deck of the boat was eight or ten feet below, the detectives could not see to whom they were thrown. I stood leaning on the rail a short time gazing at the scene, then left the wharf not even glancing in the direction of the detectives. I felt that any attempt of mine to embark would precipitate their movements, therefore I at once abandoned all ideas of taking passage from Queenstown.

Now mark the irony of fate! That was the last passage ever made by the magnificent steamer *Atlantic!* Some magnetic influence deranged her compass so that she ran twenty miles out of her course, striking on the coast of Nova Scotia, at Meager's Head, Prospect Harbor, broke in two, then rolling into deep water, sank in a few minutes. Out of 1002 persons on board 560 perished, including most of the saloon passengers and all the women and children. The elegant cabins and state-rooms became their tombs — and one might have been mine. But not for me such favoring fate; a moment's struggle ended their sufferings, while I was left to undergo the pangs of a thousand deaths!

I continued my walk up a hill among the private residences of the city, and hailing a cab told the driver to take me back to the station. Eager for a job, he asked to drive

me a mile beyond on the railway. Thinking I might elude
the detectives at the Queenstown station, I acceded and he
made his little Irish horse rush along at a pace which brought
us to the stopping-place just before the train arrived.

I purchased a ticket and hastened into a carriage, where,
lo and behold! sat the two detectives. A few minutes brought
us to Cork again. I was not yet aware they were in possession
of my right name and the knowledge that a reward of five
hundred pounds was offered for my capture, nor that their
hesitation was occasioned by doubts as to my identity, which
the first false step on my part might remove. I did not suppose they were looking especially for me, but for any one in
general whose actions and appearance might indicate that he
was one of the operators in the bank forgery. Under this
erroneous belief, I crossed to the Dublin station, which was a
quarter of a mile from that of the Cork and Queenstown, to
inquire for a dispatch that I expected from London to the
name of Bodell. When I stepped up to the telegraph-counter
and gave the name, the pretty girl in charge looked at me in
a very " speaking" manner, and without making examination
replied, " No." As I turned away, I saw my two detectives
standing at the other side of the room. " Well," I thought
to myself, " this is very strange; I left the Queenstown station ahead of them, and here they are again, all alive." I
walked away into the most thronged streets of the business
part of the city; turning a corner, I glanced backwards and
saw them following at some distance in the rear. As soon
as I had fairly turned the corner, I started at a fast walk,
turning the next before they came in view; and after three or
four such turnings I went into a small temperance hotel and
took lodgings for the night. There was but a single commercial traveler in the sitting-room — a special room set apart
in every English hotel, sacred to the "drummer" fraternity.
In the course of the evening he handed me a small railway
map of Ireland, which, in my subsequent flight through the
country, proved of incalculable service to me.

The next morning I went out and purchased a hand-bag, a Scotch cap, and a cheap, frieze ulster. My night's cogitations had not enabled me to solve the detective problem, but I felt confident that *something* was decidedly wrong. I then hired a covered cab, driving past the post-office to reconnoiter, and saw one of the detectives standing in the door-way. This sight deterred me from going in to ask for a letter. Dismissing my cab, I took another and drove to the place where I had made my purchases, taking them into the cab, and going through a by street which brought me close to my hotel.

From the commercial-room in the second floor front, I looked out and marked the farthest house I could see to the left, on the opposite side. Stepping to the desk, I wrote an order directing the postmaster to deliver any letters to my (Bodell's) address to the bearer. This I gave to a cabman, instructing him to drive to the post-office and bring my mail to the house I had marked, returning myself to the commercial-room to watch. In a few minutes I saw the cabman drive to the house, and seeing no one waiting there, he turned and drove slowly down the street past the hotel, holding up at arm's length a letter to attract my notice — which it did to my two detectives walking along a short distance behind him, on the hotel side of the street, with noses elevated and eyes peering everywhere.

" Well," I thought, " this is getting to be hot, and it is time for me to ' skip' Cork." I was now fully aroused to a sense of my danger. No one happening to be in the commercial-room for the moment, I left my hat on the sofa, and wearing the Scotch cap, slipped downstairs just as they were past the hotel, following them until I came to where the cab was waiting with my luggage. I ordered the driver to take me to a canal-boat wharf, where I dismissed him; then, with bag in hand, I walked across the canal bridge, stopped in a small shop and hired a smaller boy to go for a jaunting-car, and a few minutes later I was rolling to the northward.

On the road I threw some small coins to poor-looking

people, who then, as now, comprised among their numbers the most honest patriots and the truest-hearted sons of Erin. While gazing upon the mud huts and turf cottages which constituted, with but few exceptions, the abiding-places of a poverty-stricken people, I could not help apostrophizing thus: " To what a state of degradation has not English misrule and oppression, long continued, brought the noble Celtic race ? Doubtless over this very road many a humble Irish peasant has been hunted to the death at a time when it was only necessary for his English murderer to offer in defense, before a jury composed of his own countrymen, that he had only killed an Irishman; where life was no more valued by the English of that time than are now the lives of the convicts in the English prisons." How low that valuation is may be judged by the words spoken to me by the chief warder of Dartmoor prison, in 1877: " We think no more of killing a convict than we do of killing a dog; indeed, we value the life of a good dog above that of a convict."

Seeing me throwing the pence to the poor folk, cabby took it into his head that I must be a priest — a good criterion of the estimation in which the benevolence of the Fathers is held by their own people. And I may here remark that all the Catholic priests I have known, occupying the post of chaplain to the convicts of that religion, were without exception faithful and entirely devoted to the duties of their holy calling, speaking fearlessly to the authorities whenever Catholic prisoners were being wrongly treated by the warders. I had no intention of traveling as a priest, and when I told the driver as much he would not believe it, but insisted that I was really a priest traveling incognito; therefore, when we stopped at a small, wayside tavern, about twelve miles from Cork and two to Fermoy, he privately informed the mistress that I was a priest who did not want the fact to become known. Accordingly the good woman treated me with marked attention during my short stay. It was then nearly sunset, and as I did not wish the cabman to get back to Cork until late at

15

night, I kept him eating and drinking until dark, when I paid the bill and started him homeward, uproariously rejoicing. I then started for Fermoy station, about two miles distant, taking the hostler along to carry my bag. When within half a mile of the village I let him return. While passing through the village I went into a shop and purchased a different Scotch cap, the " Glengary."

Arriving at the station, I noticed a man near the ticket-office who appeared to be watching those who were purchasing tickets. This made me change my plan — instead of taking a ticket to Dublin, I bought one for Lismore, the end of the road in the opposite direction. The exclamation, " Well, are you going to stay all night ? " was the first intimation I had of our arrival at that place. I rubbed my sleepy eyes, and saw with dismay that all the passengers were gone, and one of the porters was putting out the lights. At the platform I found a cab, and by nine P. M. I was at the Lismore House.

After eating supper I entered the sitting-room, finding a single occupant whom I took to be a lawyer; and, judging by his conversation and manner, in the light of later events, I do not doubt that he surmised who I was. He was reading a newspaper, which he once or twice offered to me; but not dreaming of the interesting nature of its contents, I declined to take it from him. About ten P. M. the gentleman retired, leaving his paper on the table. I carelessly picked it up, and the first thing that caught my eyes was a displayed heading in large type:

500 pounds reward for the capture of George Bidwell, who is in Ireland. He cannot escape, for all the stations are watched and the seaports guarded. The whole constabulary and detective force of the country are after him (etc.)

A thunderbolt, indeed! For a few minutes I stared at the paper in blank dismay. It was fortunate for my temporary safety that there were no witnesses present. " Well," I thought to myself, " this *is* a predicament! How did they obtain my right name? I thought I had covered up the whole affair so deep in mystery that not a clue to our personality could be obtained; and here in this paper appears the whole business as correctly as if I had told them myself! There has been carelessness or treachery somewhere!"

I sat for an hour alone in this Lismore Hotel, utterly dumbfounded, bewildered, paralyzed. I had experienced some shocks, some "take-downs," in my time, but never one to compare with this. After priding myself in having laid a plan and managed an operation to lighten the plethoric money-bags of the most gigantic financial institution in all the world — one that never has less than $60,000,000 in its impregnable vaults — an institution which boasted that its system of transacting business had become so perfect that it was secure from the attempts of the designing, yet had permitted me and my assistants to carry off its bags of gold *ad libitum,* — here I was in such a fix, and everything supposed to have been so carefully hidden, so deeply buried, that nothing less than superhuman genius could unearth it, had come to the surface as by the touch of a magic wand in the hands of a prestidigitateur.

Arousing myself from a state of mental stupefaction hitherto unknown, I began to realize the necessity of immediate action if I wished to avoid falling into the merciless jaws of the British Lion. I put the paper into the fire, and retired to the room allotted to me. For the first time I fully realized how far I had departed from the principles inculcated by my father and mother. For the first time I saw myself on the verge of the yawning gulf toward which I had been almost imperceptibly gliding ever since the day of my fatal meeting with Frank Kibbe in Baltimore.

Before daylight in the morning I had decided upon the first step, and as the lawyer had asked me if I intended to remain over Sunday, I resolved to be as far away as possible before he was out of bed. While it was yet dark in the house, I left my bag in the bedroom and crept gently down the stairs to the basement, where the porter-hostler was sleeping in a box of rags. I suppose the poor wretch had not long finished his multifarious duties, for I could arouse him only to a state of semi-consciousness, and could get no information from him. I then went up to the front door, carefully turned the key and stepped out on the piazza which ran along the front of the hotel. Another shock was in store for me. A man posted on the other side of the street was watching the hotel!

It was now quite light, and I sauntered carelessly up the street, apparently taking no notice of the man over the way, and endeavoring to show by my actions that I was out for an airing before breakfast.

As I turned the next corner and glanced back, I saw him following. I noticed a place where jaunting-cars were to be let, but passed on, at each turn glancing back to see my follower the same distance in the rear. I now took a circuit around by the hotel, but instead of going in, I hastened and turned the next corner beyond — he, when reaching the corner near the hotel, not seeing me, doubtless thought I had gone in, and planted himself in his old position. I thought Lismore to be getting rather hot, and hastening to the livery stable, found the hostler just getting up. He informed me that all the horses were engaged for the day (Sunday, March 9, 1873) except one, the fastest they had, but as this was engaged for a long journey on Tuesday, they were letting him have a rest. I said: "But, my good fellow, I must have a horse, and at once, with you to drive, and there will be a half sovereign for a good Irishman, such as I see before me." My "blarney" began to do its work. Scratching his head, he finally said: "Well, I will waken up my master, and you can talk with him." So he rapped at a window, and soon a night-capped head appeared, and after some parley the master consented to let me his equipage. In a few minutes from the time I had lost sight of my follower we were rattling out of the town of Lismore at the full speed of a blooded Irish horse. I had left my bag behind, taking only the Scotch caps and

CHATHAM.—CONVICTS AT LABOR.

ulster with me from the hotel. I found, by reference to the small map and railway guide, that Clonmel was less than thirty miles distant, and connected with Dublin by a branch line. When I engaged the jaunting-car, I had told the owner that it was uncertain what part of the day I should require it, and after we were about five miles from Lismore I said to the driver:

"You say that you are going to Clonmel on Tuesday for a passenger. Well, now, as I must go there before I leave this part of the country, you may as well continue in that direction, and I can return with you on Tuesday."

This pleased him, and we drove on till about noon, when we stopped at a country grocery about five miles from Clonmel. As we drove up to the door, the words of an old Irish song went jingling through my brain:

> "At the sign of the bell,
>   On the road to Clonmel,
>   Pat Flagherty kept a neat shebeen."

The rain poured down in torrents. I gave my driver a lunch of bread and cheese, which — of course there — included whisky. I also gave him a sovereign, telling him to pay his master for the horse-hire and keep the change for himself; then started him back brim full of delight and the "craythur," receiving his parting salute:

"Yer 'onor is a jintleman, and no mistake."

I arranged with the store-keeper to let a boy take me in his car to Clonmel.

"The Green Isle!" Well, I found out that day what keeps the grass green in Ireland. My Irish frieze and every thread on me were water-logged, yet the Irish lad, my driver, took the "buckets-full" as a matter of course. Amidst this deluge of rain, we arrived in Clonmel and stopped at a "shebeen," kept by the boy's uncle — driving into the back yard through a gate in a board-fence fifteen feet high, which shut it in from the street.

I went into a room in the rear of the sale-room. the door

of which stood open so that I could see all that passed within; and, as I stood drying my clothes by the turf fire, I saw how thirsty souls on the " ould sod," evaded the Sunday liquor law. The proprietor stood in the shop in a position whence he could covertly keep an eye on the policeman patrolling the street, and as soon as he was out of sight, a signal was given, the back-yard gate thrown open, when a dozen men rushed in, and the gate closed. Coming hilariously through the dwelling into the shop, these were soon busily drinking their " potheen," laughing and boasting about how cunningly they had " done the cowardly informer of a policeman."

It was now two o'clock P. M.; the rain had ceased, and starting out, I walked along a main street until I saw a sign, " Cabs to let." I went into the house and was shown into an inner room, where the proprietress sat crooning over a turf fire. She motioned me to a seat beside her, and when I told her I wished for a conveyance to take me to Cahir, a place eight miles distant, she asked me several questions, among others, how long I wished to be gone, and if I were not an American. To all of which, I replied to the following effect: That I was going to visit some friends who were officers stationed in the fort at Cahir; and as to her mistaking me for an American, the ancestors of the " Yankees " went from about Norfolk county, England, to America, of course taking the accent with them, and I being from the former place (Norfolk) of course had the same accent.

This explanation appeared to satisfy the old lady, and she became quite confidential; and, anxious to remove from my mind any trace of offense at her unusual questioning, she drew closer to me and said:

" I can see that you are all right; but, the fact is, that the captain of police sent an order that I should notify him at once, in case any stranger wished to hire a vehicle, especially if I thought him an American. But I do not care for the curs; they are nothing but a parcel of spies and informers in the pay of the English government; so even if you were the one they are looking for, they will wait a long time for me to inform them, and you shall have my best horse and a good driver."

I heartily thanked the good old Irish lady — for I have found true ladies and gentlemen among the poor and humble as well as the wealthy, especially in Ireland — and in a few minutes I was bowling gaily along toward Cahir.

This is a small, ancient, walled garrison town, the nearest railway station being at Clonmel. This miniature city has been the scene of many a heart-stirring event in the distant past. Here Cromwell was for a time held at bay, and his fanatical hordes made their Celtic opponents pay in blood for their patriotic and desperate defense of their homes and firesides.

Driving through the town gate, I saw in the main street a grocery store with a blind down, and telling the driver to halt there, I paid him and sent him back. I then went into the grocery, and after taking a lunch of bread and cheese, continued my walk up the street. I saw a hotel just ahead, but not wishing to attract attention to my movements, I crossed to the opposite side, and while doing so, glanced back and saw a car come through the same town gate I had just entered, and dash furiously up the street, pulling up at the walk a few yards behind me. Just as they sprang out, I turned to the left into a narrow lane in which I saw a gateway to the fort, just within the entrance of which a sentry was pacing, there being opposite several roofless cottages. The soldier's back being turned, quick as thought I sprang unseen within one of these, and in a moment I heard some men run around the corner and interrogate the soldier, who stoutly declared that no one had entered. The men then demanded to see the captain, were admitted, and after a short time I heard them come out and depart. I stood in that ruin two mortal hours until dusk, then walked out unseen by the sentry, and turning to the left, came into a narrow street lined with small dwelling houses.

CHAPTER XXIII.

CROSSING the narrow street in Cahir, referred to at the close of the last chapter, I went in hap-hazard at the first door, without knocking, and saw a family eating their humble supper. As I walked in I addressed the family at the table thus:

"Good evening. Pardon my intrusion, and do not disturb yourselves; but by all means finish your supper."

"Good evening, sir," was the reply from the man, whom I will call Maloy. "We are glad to see you; will you sit by and have pot-luck with us?"

"No, thank you," I answered. "I am an American — and it is my custom when traveling in any country to make unceremonious calls like this, in order to see the people as they really are at home."

After supper was over I related to Maloy and his family several stories and incidents concerning the Fenians and their doings in America, which of course interested them greatly. When it was fairly dark I arose to go, and Maloy went outside with me. He had previously informed me that he was employed by the government in the civil service. I will not state in what capacity, for although so many years have

(232)

elapsed, the true-hearted Irishman may still be earning his bread in the same humble employment, and the knowledge that he assisted one whom he supposed to be a Fenian leader in 1873 might even now cost him dearly. If what he did was discovered at the time, and he suffered in consequence — should he be still alive, or if not, his wife or children — it would give me great pleasure to hear from the family, and to render them such aid as is now in my power. I am sure they cannot have forgotten me. When we were outside the door I said:

" The fact is, Maloy, I am a Fenian leader, and the police are after me! I have been dodging them for two days, and they are looking for me now in Cahir! I have important papers for prominent Fenians in various parts of Ireland, and it would delay our plans if I am obliged to destroy them. But I fear I must do so at once, unless you can help me. I would almost sooner forfeit my life than to lose these papers, and I shall fight to my last breath rather than let them fall into the hands of the police, for it might be the ruin of several good men! My plan is to double back to Clonmel, and I want your assistance to get me out of Cahir!"

" O, sir," he replied " it is too bad you did not let me know a little sooner, for the mail-car is gone; it starts at six o'clock."

Just as he finished speaking, a car came rumbling past, and he exclaimed joyfully:

" We are in luck! There goes the mail-car to the post-office! Come with me!"

We hastened through a narrow, dark lane to the gate — the same I had entered from Clonmel — walked through and at a hundred yards beyond waited for the mail-car, which soon came along. Maloy being well acquainted with the driver, hailed him, saying that a friend of his wanted a ride to Clonmel.

After shaking hands warmly with Maloy, I climbed upon the car, and the next instant I was whirling along — into fresh dangers — in that unique vehicle, an Irish jaunting-car.

Arriving near Clonmel I saw a tavern, and ascertaining from the driver that it was near the railway station, I left the car and entered the place, only to find that the best, and in fact the sole food to be had for supper was eggs. Having been on the move since dawn, after a sleepless night, and almost without food, I hesitate to divulge how many eggs I disposed of that evening, for the statement might tend to throw distrust on the general veracity of my narrative. Having dried my wet clothes and put myself into a presentable condition, I went to the railway station to take the eleven P. M. train to Dublin. Seating myself on a bench outside, I handed some money to a porter and sent him for a ticket, which he obtained. There were but a few waiting about, so I stepped into the small waiting-room and sat down near three other men. The one nearest, whom I at once put down for a local policeman in private clothes, turned and spoke to me. I replied with civility to his questions until finally he said: "But, are you not an American?" I replied to his startling question in such a manner that he appeared satisfied.

"You must excuse me, sir, for questioning you," he explained, "but there has been a great forgery in London, and it is said some of the parties are in Ireland, and I am anxious to get a claim on the 500 pounds that is offered for each one of them." I told him that instead of being offended, I was greatly pleased to see the zeal he exhibited in the execution of his duties, and expressed the hope that he might be successful in securing at least one of the forgers, which would give him not only the 500 pounds, but undoubtedly promotion. I got on the train all right, resolving that I would not speak another word of English while in Ireland, and forthwith turned into a Russian, who could speak "une veree leetel Froncais," confident that I should not be in danger of exposure by encounter with any one who could speak the Russian language. I threw away the ordinary Scotch cap I had been wearing, and put on the Glengary. When I arrived at the Maryborough junction, the train on the main line from Cork was late, and I walked up and down on the platform, well-knowing that the detectives would scrutinize more closely those who appeared to shrink from observation; therefore I affected the bearing of a Russian prince as nearly as I knew how.

I got on the train unmolested, and arrived in Dublin at one A. M.

There appeared to be some special watching of those leaving the train, but I passed out unchallenged and took a cab. Not knowing the name of any hotel, I told the driver I would direct the route as we passed along, and he drove away at a great pace. Very soon I noticed another cab following at an equal speed. I had mine turn a corner, but the one behind came thundering after; and though I bade my driver to turn at nearly every corner, still I could not shake off my supposed pursuer until, after apparently being followed about two miles, the stern-chaser turned off in another direction, much to my relief. We soon approached the Cathedral Hotel, where I alighted about two A. M., rang up the porter, and was shown to a room.

At seven o'clock in the morning I sent for my bill, left the hotel, went direct to the "Jew" quarter, and purchased a valise and some second-hand clothes. Noticing the old Jewess's looks of curiosity at seeing one of my appearance making such purchases, I remarked: "A Fenian friend has got himself into a scrape, and the police are after him; so I am going to get him out of the country, and wish to let him have some things that do not have too new a look." At hearing those (in Ireland) magic words, "Fenian," "police," she became all smiles, let me fill the valise with old garments at my own price, and at parting said: "God bless you! May you have good luck, and get him off safe to America!"

I then went to a more pretentious locality, where I procured a silk hat draped with mourning crape, put the Glengary in my pocket, and became a Frenchman. At this moment I discovered that I had left in my room at the hotel

a large silk neck-wrapper on which were embroidered the
initials " G. B." I immediately stepped into a shop and left
my new purchases, resuming the Scotch cap, and started for
the hotel (where I had given no name) to secure the dangerous article left behind. Coming in sight of the hotel, I saw
a man stationed opposite, leaning on a cane, who appeared to
be watching the house. As I approached nearer he kept his
eyes covertly fixed upon me; therefore, instead of entering
the hotel, I walked past it and turned the next corner, glancing backward as I did so, and, to my dismay, saw the man
following me. I now adopted the same plan of action that
succeeded so well at Cork, and in a half-hour I had shaken
him off and returned to the place where I had left my new
silk hat and valise. Doffing the hat, with valise in hand, l
was soon seated in an Irish jaunting-car, on my way to a
station about ten miles out on the railway to Belfast.

   Upon reflection, I was satisfied that the chambermaid had
found the silk wrapper and taken it to the hotel office. There
the initials, together with the knowledge of my arrival at so
unusual an hour, without baggage, and my early departure,
had aroused the suspicion that I was the George Bidwell of
the newspapers, and the police had been notified at once. At
about eleven A. M. I arrived at the station, and going into a
store, paid my Dublin cabman, and called for a lunch. About
five minutes before the train was due from Dublin, I walked
into the empty station, presented myself at the ticket-office,
and said, " Parlez vous Français, Monsieur?" and received
the reply, " No." I then said, in a mongrel of French and
English, that I wished for a ticket to Drogheda — not daring
to purchase one through to Belfast. Supposing me to be a
French gentleman, he was very polite and ordered the porter
to take my baggage to the platform. There I found myself
the solitary waiting passenger. As the train approached, I
saw a pair of heads projecting from the carriage windows,
eagerly scanning the platform. Two men jumped off, and
hastening to the station-master, began to talk to him in an

excited manner, all the time glancing toward me. As I passed near the group to get on the train, I heard the agent say: "He is a Frenchman." No doubt he informed them that I had purchased a ticket to a way-station only — a fact that would naturally allay suspicion. At the next stopping-place they actually arrested a man, but went no further.

I afterward ascertained that twelve men were arrested on that and the preceding day, among the number being a fraudulent debtor trying to escape to America by the same steamer —the *Atlantic*.

The following extracts from contemporary newspapers will give the reader some idea as to what a "hot" place Ireland was for me:

[By cable to the New York *Herald*.]

LONDON, March 18, 1873.

Three shabbily dressed men, who from their accent are believed to be Americans, were arrested in Cork, Ireland, this morning, while attempting to deposit $12,000 in that city.

They are supposed to be the parties who recently committed the frauds on the Bank of England.

[From the London *Times* of same date.]

To EDITOR OF "TIMES":

SIR, — The case of Dr. Hessel has been so lately before the public, and so much has been written both in the English and German papers against the English police, that probably a little evidence upon the procedure of the German (or, I ought probably to say, the Bavarian) may not be uninteresting at the present moment. Myself and son, a sub-lieutenant, R. N., made a great effort to reach the grotesque old city of Nuremburg on Saturday last, 8th March, arriving there about seven P. M We were asked to put our names in the stranger's book, as usual, which we did, and retired to bed. Imagine our surprise, on rising on Sunday morning, at receiving a visit from one of the chief police officers requesting us to "legitimize ourselves." I asked him his object for making this demand, when he replied that a man named "Horton" was wanted by the English police.

In vain I showed him an old passport and letters addressed to me, showing that my name was Hutton; he informed me that I could not leave my room, and placed two policemen at the door. At one o'clock I remembered an influential inhabitant of the town who knew me, and I sent for him. He at once went to head-quarters and gave bond for me to a large amount, and at six o'clock in the evening myself and son were released. You will remember that in the case of Dr. Hessel four persons swore to his identity before he was deprived of his liberty. In my case a similar name to that required was sufficient to deprive me of mine.

I have since received, thanks to the strenuous and prompt action of the British Minister at Munich, a very ample apology in writing for the blunder that had been committed. It is signed by the Burgermeister of the city, and as the intelligence of this worthy seems to be equaled by his simplicity, he sends me a safe pass to protect me in my further travels, in case Hutton should again be considered the same as Horton. I remain, sir,

Your obedient servant,

CHAS. W. C. HUTTON,
Ex-Sheriff, London and Middlesex.

FRANKFORT-ON-THE-MAINE, March 15, 1873.

I now return to my narrative. In the second-class compartment where I sat were two burly, loud-talking, well-informed farm proprietors, one of whom had imbibed a little too freely of the native distillation. The sober one had just finished reading a column article on the " Great Bank Forgery " to his lively companion, who at length turned and addressed me. I answered him politely in broken French, and he then went on to give his opinion of the bank affair, as nearly as I can remember, as follows:

" You, being a Frenchman, don't understand about our great bank; but I tell you those Yankees did a mighty thing when they attacked that powerful institution. The one they have got penned up here in Ireland can't possibly escape; indeed, according to the newspapers, he is already in the hands of the police. I am almost sorry to hear it, for in getting the best of that bank so cleverly the rascal deserves to get off; and see, here is a description of him."

I looked at the paper and saw that it was a fair general outline of my appearance, even to my ulster which I had with me in the valise, and the Scotch cap which was in my pocket. Before we reached Drogheda I had explained to one of my new friends, in broken French, that, owing to my ignorance of the English language, I had purchased a wrong ticket, and being liable to make a similar mistake, should feel obliged if he would take the trouble to procure me a ticket at that station. He readily assented, and by this means I procured it without exposing myself. The hunt for me was becoming so extremely hot that I dared not show myself again at a ticket-office; and if I should be found on a train ticketless, that fact might lead to closer scrutiny — the rule in that country being that every passenger must be provided with a ticket before entering a car, under the penalty of fine or imprisonment.

The train arrived in Belfast at nine P. M., and I at once took a cab to the Glasgow steamer. It was very dark, and I went on board unobserved, two hours before the time of departure. Going down into the saloon cabin, I saw the purser sitting near the entrance, to whom I said: "Parlez vous Français?" He shook his head. I then asked in jargon for "une billet a Glasgow." Surmising what I wished, he gave me a ticket, putting on it the number of my berth.

Expecting to be followed, I had taken that instant precaution of impressing on the purser's mind that I was a Frenchman. I passed into the wash-room, just opposite where the purser sat, washed myself, and brushed my hair. Just at this moment I heard steps descending the cabin stairway, then the words:

"Purser, a cab just brought a man from the Dublin train. Where is he?" "Oh, you mean the Frenchman," replied the purser; "he's in the wash-room."

While this was passing I had put on my silk hat and taken up my valise, and was standing before the glass (*à la Français*), taking a final view of my *toilette*, and snapping off some imaginary dust and lint, as two detectives stepped in, and after looking me well over, went out, and I saw them no more. That proved to be the last ordeal through which I passed in the hunt through Ireland. After being convinced that they had left the steamer, I went to my berth, and being thoroughly exhausted, I fell asleep in an instant, not awaking until the steamer was entering the harbor of Glasgow.

After my arrest a month later in Scotland, during the transfer to London, and afterward at Newgate, while awaiting trial four months, the detectives told me that they were in Cork three hours after I had left, and one of them related their adventures substantially as follows:

We arrived in Cork Saturday afternoon, and were not long in finding the temperance hotel where you stayed on Friday night, and the hat you left behind. After a long hunt we ascertained that a jaunting-car had left the stand some hours previously, and was still absent.

We had a good laugh at those blunder-heads, the Cork officers, letting you slip through their fingers, and then showed them how we do things. After some delay, we traced the cab across the bridge to the shop where you got the boy to go for it. The shop-woman was quite voluble about you, saying she knew all the time that you were an American by the accent, and described the bag and ulster which we had ascertained were in your possession. Of course we were now satisfied that we were on the right scent, but could get no further trace, or the direction taken by the cab. We therefore sent dispatches to all the telegraph stations within fifty miles to put the police on the watch, and sent messengers to the outlying places; but somehow you slipped through our meshes, and nothing turned up until the carman returned at about eleven P. M., as drunk as a soldier on furlough. After putting him under a water-tap until he was half drowned, we got him sober enough to tell where he had left you; but he swore you were a priest, and his evident sincerity caused us all to roar with laughter. This angered him, and he said: "Ye may twist me head an dhroun me intirely, but I wull niver spake another wurrud about the jintelman at all, at all," and sure enough, we could get nothing more out of him.

CASTS OF THE HEADS OF NOTORIOUS CRIMINALS.

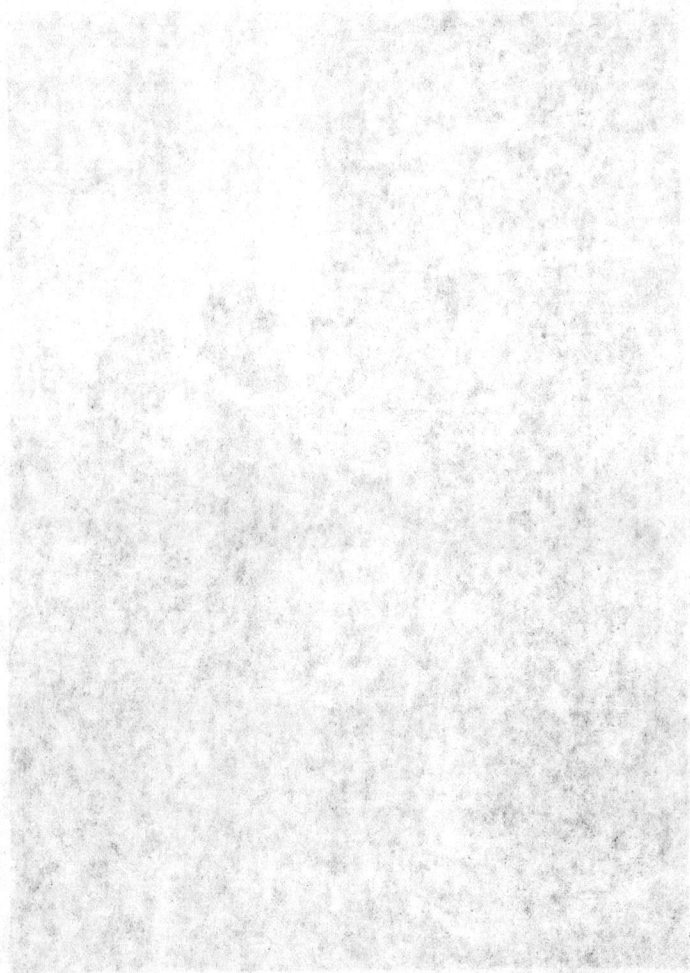

We had a carriage ready, and, jumping in, we were at the way-side inn by midnight, and terrified the old woman half out of her wits in arousing her out of bed. After a while she gathered them sufficiently to show us that you had six hours the start of us. The boy who carried your bag could give us no points, but we concluded you intended taking the branch line at Fermoy for Dublin. We drove right on, arriving at the Fermoy station at one A. M.; but getting no trace, we telegraphed to all the stations along the line to Dublin, and there as well, to be on the lookout. Who would ever have thought of your taking the opposite direction, penning your-self in at the end of a branch line, at a small, inland town like Lismore? Why, you were, as we discovered the next morning, at that moment sleeping quietly at the Lismore Hotel, and only about ten miles from where we were working so industriously for that £500! Well, you "done" us fine, that time!

After you so cleverly threw us off the trail, we could get no trace until Sunday morning, when we received a dispatch from Lismore, stating that a man had come on the last train, stayed at the hotel, and left at daylight without paying his bill; also, that he had left a bag in his room, which contained some collars marked "G. B." "Hello!" said I, as soon as I read the dispatch, "we never suspected Lismore; he has been there all night, and is off, again!" We telegraphed to Clonmel, Waterford, and other places; then left for Lismore, where we arrived, paid your bill, and took the bag with us. Surmising that you might make for Clonmel, we looked for and found the place where you got the car, but no news as to what direction you had taken. It would have made you laugh, as it did us, to see the old livery-man stamp about and tear his hair when he found how easily he could have made the £500 — if he had "only known."

Starting on the way to Clonmel, we soon had news which satisfied us we were once more on the right track. Shortly after we met, sure enough, the cab you had sent back from the country store. Arriving there we took the boy, who had just returned from driv-ing you to Clonmel, with us, and feeling sure that we should soon come up with you, we made our horses spin toward that town. Arriving there, we saw the Inspector, who informed us that he had sent a constable in pursuit of a man who had hired a car to go to

Cahir. [This must have been one of the men in the car whom I escaped by dodging into the ruined cottage.— AUTHOR.] It being then sundown, we drove to Cahir, with all speed, arriving there just after dark, passing the Clonmel mail car inside the gate ; but it contained no one but the driver. [It appears that the Bow detectives arrived just as I was going with Maloy through the lane, as previously described]

We soon found the constable sent from Clonmel, who said you had disappeared into the fort, where a friend must have concealed you, and that you must be there still. He then took us to the fort, which was closed for the night. As soon as my eyes lighted on the ruined cottages, I asked him if he had searched them, and received an answer in the negative. " Why," said he, " they are, as you see, all open to the day, without roof, doors, or windows, and no one would think of hiding in them." " You are a fool," I replied ; " Give me your lamp, and come in with me." After a look around, and seeing how easily any person could stand in a corner out of sight, I remarked to him, emphatically, that he was the biggest specimen of a goose I had ever seen in my line. "I think," said I, " you had better go home and play pin. Here is where he dodged you, and now he is off again, with an hour or more start ! " We worked until after midnight, and gave Cahir such a " turning over " that the inhabitants won't soon forget, but could not get hold of the least trace, except at one place [Maloy's], where a woman said a stranger came in at supper time, who said he was an American seeing the people in their homes. We cross-questioned the man, but could get nothing out of him more than that you had departed.

At last we gave it up, went to the hotel to get some sleep, which we needed badly, and the next day went to Dublin, heard about the finding of your neckwrapper at the Cathedral Hotel, and knocked about Ireland for some time. During this time we arrested several persons, but soon discovered none of them were the right party, and we never obtained a genuine trace until you gave yourself away later in Edinburgh.

Readers who may discover any trace of exultation in my relation of the cool and skillful manner in which I eluded the detectives, will bear in mind that the story is told from the

standpoint of my then state of feeling. It is only fair for me
to say that, at the moment, while in the thick of it, I did feel
a certain exultation and full confidence in my ability to keep
out of the way for all time. But my name had become known,
which, with other disclosures, showed that I had been a victim
of misplaced confidence ; and, though I might have gone anywhere with impunity, while they were still hunting me
in Ireland, I lay dormant in Edinburgh rather than to be *hunted
through the world.*

Chapter XXIV.

ON arrival of the steamer at Glasgow, about three A. M., it was a question whether I ought not to go directly back to London, and, while it was believed I was still in Ireland, make a rush across the Channel, through France to Marseilles, then by steamer to Rio Janeiro. On arrival there it would be easy to take one of the coast line steamships for New York. But, feeling that my escape from Ireland had cut off all trace of me, I concluded to take the train to Edinburgh and lie by for a while. Arriving there I stayed one night at a small temperance hotel, assuming the character of a German, and the next day I took a room at 22 Cumberland Street — a lodging house for medical students. Here I remained from the 10th of March until the 3d of April, sometimes passing the day in wandering about this interesting ancient city. A stroll through the old Edinburgh streets, and the old Market Cross, furnished material for reflection on the vicissitudes of life as illustrated in the pictures of the past, which filled my mind as I gazed upon these relics of generations in whose footsteps I was now treading.

It had all along been a great mystery to me as to how the detectives had so easily unveiled the actors, and so quickly ascertained the connection of McDonald and myself with the forgery. But now having access to the newspapers, shock after shock nearly overwhelmed me as I saw how I had been

(244)

duped to take part in a crime without the slightest chance of keeping it enveloped in the darkness in which I firmly believed it was wrapped. But enough on that point. The object of this book is not to inculpate—still less to exonerate myself

OLD EDINBURGH STREET.

from the justifiable charge of having been a fool. The following is compiled from the numerous accounts detailing my arrest and return to London.

It appears that about the 10th of March, a person named Coutant arrived in Edinburgh (it is supposed from Ireland) and took up his residence in Cumberland Street. From the 11th to the 20th, he made it a daily practice to call at a news agent's shop in Dundas Street, for the purpose of purchasing the Edinburgh and London

papers. After pondering the matter over in his mind, it occurred
to the news agent that his visitor was exceedingly like the description given in the newspapers of Bidwell, one of the Bank of England forgers. He at last became so confirmed in this idea that he
mentioned his suspicion to a gentleman who was in the habit of
visiting his shop. This gentleman who is in the employment of
Messrs. Gibson-Craig, Dalziel & Brodies, agents for the Bank of
England in Edinburgh, as a clerk, informed the partners of the
suspicion of the bookseller. The firm on hearing their clerk's
statement, sent for detective M'Kelvie and instructed him to make
inquiries regarding Coutant. On Wednesday morning he determined to visit the shopkeeper in Dundas Street, and a plain-clothed
constable named McNab, on the application of the agents, was sent
to assist him if his inquiries were successful. On interrogating the
shopkeeper he was directed to the house on Cumberland Street, in
which Coutant resided. On proceeding to the place indicated,
M'Kelvie inquired of the landlady, who said that a gentleman from
Hamburg or Rotterdam had been residing with her for a few
weeks, and had ordered her to keep him very quiet, as he was in
rather bad health. M'Kelvie then rejoined McNab whom he had
left at the bottom of the stairs. About twenty minutes to one
o'clock, a person answering the description of Bidwell emerged,
and M'Kelvie observed the landlady nodding to him, as much as to
say " That is the man." Coutant, after looking up and down the
street, re-entered, which movement still further excited the suspicions of the detectives. M'Kelvie here remarked to his friend, that
the action of Coutant scarcely seemed like that of an honest man.
After waiting till a few minutes past one o'clock, Coutant again
came out to the street and walked up Drummond Place to the top
of Scotland Street, where he posted a letter in a pillar letter-box.
Coutant, or Bidwell, now became conscious that he was being followed, and that, evidently, there was something wrong. He
accordingly began to dodge about a number of streets and lanes in
the locality, and finally took to his heels. The detectives followed,
and now began a most exciting chase. The fugitive, with great
agility, scaled one after another a number of garden walls, lying
between Bellevue-Crescent and Scotland Street. Being pressed
closely by M'Kelvie, who was just at his heels, he deliberately
entered the back door of a house, ran along the passage, and made

his exit into the area in Scotland Street. He then ran up the stairs, scaled the railings, and made off down the street, along Royal Crescent, and up Duncan Street. M'Kelvie still kept well up, the constable having fallen considerably in the rear. Seeing that his efforts to escape were now becoming hopeless, Coutant turned around and with a stick which he had managed to carry along with him, made several strokes at M'Kelvie. The detective warded off the blows and succeeded in gripping his man. M'Kelvie then called a coal porter, who was in the vicinity, and with his assistance, he conducted Bidwell to Pitt Street, where a cab was got. He was then conveyed to Messrs. Gibson-Craig, Dalziel & Brodie's office in Thistle Street, and information of the capture was sent to the police authorities.

In the custody of the two officers Bidwell was removed to the central office in High Street and locked up. The police proceeded shortly after the apprehension, to his lodgings and took possession of his luggage. On opening the portmanteaus, a number of valuable diamonds, a large quantity of jewelry, and several letters bearing the name of George Bidwell were found.

On Wednesday, at the police court, before Bailie Wilson, Bidwell was placed at the bar, on the charge of being concerned in the forgeries. Mr. Morhah, the clerk of the court, read a petition, setting forth that on or about the 7th of March, the Procurator Fiscal received information from Inspector Bailey, of the city of London police, charging George Bidwell with the crime of forgery.

Mr. Morhah asked for a warrant authorizing his detention. Bailie Wilson granted the necessary warrant. The prisoner was then removed, and was shortly afterward conveyed in a cab to the Waverly Station. There he was handed over to the care of the two detective officers from London, who left with him about eleven o'clock, a compartment of a first-class carriage having been engaged for them.

A crowd assembled at the station to see the prisoner. He was very lame, having evidently sustained severe injuries while being pursued the previous day. He did not sleep during Wednesday night, but occupied his time in reading. He had in his possession ten diamonds, which a jeweler in Edinburgh valued at about £150 each.

Detective Sergeants Spittle and Smith, of the city police,

who had been sent specially to Edinburgh to bring him, arrived at the Euston Square terminus, about half-past nine, and Bidwell was conveyed thence in a cab, under a strong escort, to the Bow-lane Police Station. On alighting from the cab he appeared lame, and walked with some little difficulty into

MARKET CROSS, EDINBURGH.

the station. He looked sickly and careworn. Major Bowman, assistant commissioner of city police, arrived at the police station while the prisoner was answering some formal questions put to him by the inspector on duty, Mr. Knight. Being asked his name, he smiled slightly and hesitated. Upon that he was asked if he declined to give it. He still hesitated, and the inspector explained to him that he was not bound to give his name. What they wanted to know was whether he was disposed to give it or not. At length, smiling slightly, he replied, that he would rather not give it then. Being asked his address, he gave one in Edinburgh, which appeared to be only audible to the inspector, but it was understood to be in Cumberland Street. The inspector followed up the reply by inquiring his business or profession. To that again he at first hesitated, and then said, "Mercantile." Being asked if he meant that he was a merchant, he replied, after a short pause, in the affirmative, adding that he was out of business. The officers, in whose care he was, showed him much kindness, and as he was about to retire for the night, allowed him the use of some rugs from among his luggage. He was then escorted to one of the ordinary cells of the Bow Station, in which to spend the night, and had a proper guard placed over him.

After the lapse of fifteen years, I can read with a good deal of equanimity, the account of my arrest, in which M'Kelvie figures as the most important character — he, at the time, indulging in much self-glorification.

On arriving in London, I was taken to the Bow-street Police Station and put into a cell, to pass a sleepless night, and about ten the next morning, made my first appearance in the Mansion House before Mayor Sir Sidney Waterlow. After some preliminary sparring between the lawyers, I was consigned to Newgate, to ruminate upon my gradual descent into that hades.

Chapter XXV.

EXTRADITION OF AUSTIN BIDWELL FROM CUBA AND GEORGE McDONALD FROM NEW YORK — AUSTIN ARRESTED IN HAVANA — A "NEW YORK HERALD" EDITORIAL — SYMPATHY WITH "FILLIBUSTERS" — CABLE DISPATCHES TO "THE HERALD" AND "THE LONDON TIMES" — GENERAL SICKLES'S INTERVIEW WITH SENOR CASTELAR AT MADRID — BIDWELL ESCAPES — RECAPTURE — HE IS SURRENDERED TO THE BRITISH GOVERNMENT — ARRIVAL IN ENGLAND — McDONALD ARRIVES IN NEW YORK — DETECTIVES IRVING AND FARLEY TRICK SHERIFF JUDSON JARVIS — BOARD THE "THURINGIA" AT QUARANTINE — CURIOUS "SEARCH" OF McDONALD — SHERIFFS JARVIS AND CURRY TOO LATE — NO BONDS RECOVERED — SEIZE WATCHES AND DIAMONDS — McDONALD AT LUDLOW STREET JAIL — EXTRADITION PROCEEDINGS — STARTLING ARREST OF SUPERINTENDENT KELSO AND DETECTIVES IRVING AND FARLEY — McDONALD'S RIDE DOWN BROADWAY — IN FORT COLUMBUS — SURRENDERED TO THE BRITISH GOVERNMENT — EXIT ON STEAMSHIP "MINNESOTA" — THE "DOMINION'S SELFISH PROTECTION OF BANK DEFAULTERS, BOODLERS," ETC.

I T will be remembered that in Chapter XX was detailed the imprudent marriage of my brother, and his arrest at Havana while on his wedding journey.

I now resume the story, giving in this chapter some account, from contemporary sources, of his extradition from Cuba and his arrival in London.

[Editorial *N. Y. Herald*, March 29, 1873]

CUBAN AFFAIRS — BIDWELL'S IMPRISONMENT.

The special telegraph advices which we publish to-day in reference to the imprisonment at Havana of Bidwell, one of the parties accused of the recent forgeries on the Bank of England, are very interesting, touching the jurisdiction of the Island authorities in this matter. It appears that Bidwell was arrested at the request of the British government, on the supposition that he was a British subject; but it is represented that he is a citizen of the United States of America, a native of Michigan, and that his arrest in Cuba is not justified by any extradition treaty with England nor by any other authority, except that of the Captain-General, whose will over the Island is the supreme law. If it can be established that Bidwell is a citizen of the United States, his case certainly calls for the intervention of Mr. Secretary Fish. The prisoner, it seems, desires a transfer to New York, which is perfectly natural; *but we suspect that the international difficulties* suggested, touching his detention in Cuba, will not materially improve his chances of escape.

Not long before the arrest of my brother in Cuba, the steamer *Virginia*, an American vessel, was captured by a Spanish cruiser. On the charge of being " fillibusters," the crew and all persons found on board were shot. Among these were several Americans. The United States government sent for the *Virginia* and demanded reparation for her capture, and indemnity for the lives of the Americans. This was the cause of serious international complications, which threatened to end in war. It was this state of affairs referred to in the italics of the *Herald* editorial above quoted, which caused his final surrender.

There is no longer any doubt that the punctilious Spaniards would never have surrendered Austin Bidwell to the demand of the British government, had it not been for their posture of hostility toward the United States. There was considerable ground for this feeling in the sympathy shown in some parts of the United States for, and assistance rendered to, the Cuban insurgents.

It will be perceived, by the following dispatch, that Austin was supposed to be a British subject.

[Telegrams to the *New York Herald* of 29th, referred to in above editorial.]

HAVANA, March 26, 1873.

The man Bidwell was, it appears, arrested on the charge of complicity with the forgeries on the Bank of England, at the request of the British government, communicated to the Captain-General of Cuba by the Spanish Ministers in London and Washington, who supposed him to be a British subject. Bidwell is, on the contrary, an American, a native of Michigan. His arrest is not justified by any treaty of extradition between Spain, England, or the United States. Such proceedings could be carried out in no other country than Cuba, where the Captain-General does not always act in accordance with law. Distinguished lawyers and judges of this city, in conversation with the *Herald* correspondent, denounce the act as being utterly illegal, and without precedent, except in the case of Argeumes, in the year 1864.

COMMON LAW AND TREATY SET AT DEFIANCE.

The gentlemen also declare that it is a violation of the laws of Spain and of the treaty stipulations with the United States, and in contempt of the guarantees of the law of 1870 relative to foreigners. The same lawyers and judges assert that it would be better that a delinquent should escape than that so bad a precedent as the act of delivery of Bidwell would make should be established.

THE PRISONER'S TREATMENT AND FEARS.

Bidwell has been now seven days incommunicated — not permitted to see a lawyer or his wife. The *Herald* correspondent has been refused permission to see him.

The British Vice-Consul obtained, by compulsion, the sum of $5,000 from Mrs. Bidwell, in United States five-twenties. Complaints having been made, the Captain-General ordered that the sum should be deposited.

Bidwell is afraid that there exist no guarantees for a due and proper administration of justice here. He has expressed his desire to be sent to New York.

[Cable dispatches from Havana to the *London Times.*]

NEW YORK, April 4, 1873.

Great efforts are being made by the lawyers to obtain the release of Bidwell, and an action for illegal arrest is threatened.

HAVANA, April 4th.

The American Consul here demands from the Cuban authorities the release of the prisoner Bidwell, *alias* Warren, on the ground that he is an American citizen.

MADRID, April 8th.

Gen. Sickles has formally notified Senor Castelar that the American government will consent to the surrender to the British government of Bidwell, now in custody in Havana, upon a charge of being concerned in the forgeries upon the Bank of England.

HAVANA, April 10th.

The British Consul continues to counteract the efforts that are being made to prevent the extradition of Bidwell.

Generals Portello and Renegassi have been relieved of their posts, and are ordered to return to Spain. (For opposing Austin Bidwell's extradition).

[By cable from Havana to *N. Y. Herald*, April 13, 1873.]

Bidwell, the alleged Bank of England forger, escaped yesterday by jumping over the balcony. He was partly dressed. He is supposed to be hiding in this city. Bidwell's Havana friends, seeing the impossibility of counteracting by legal means the efforts of the British Consul to secure his extradition, undoubtedly planned the affair.

HAVANA, April 14th.

Bidwell has been recaptured on the seashore twenty miles above Havana. He was severely bruised in the hands and legs while escaping from prison. He had leaped from under the soldiers' bayonets, from the Arsenal second story into the crowded street, and got clear out of Havana without assistance.

[By cable to the *London Times*.]

HAVANA, April 17, 1873.

While Inspectors Hayden and Green, and a clerk of the Bank of England, were on their passage from New York to Havana, a notorious thief, named Wilson, opened the detectives' trunks and extracted some money. His object is said to have been to secure the documents relating to the extradition of Bidwell. Wilson has been arrested on a charge of burglary. The English detectives and the British Consul have completely baffled the efforts to obtain the release of Bidwell.

[From the *London Times*, May 28, 1873.]

Among the passengers who landed at Plymouth yesterday afternoon, from the Royal Mail Company's steamship *Moselle*, were Austin Bidwell, *alias* Warren, in charge of detectives Sergeants Michael Hayden and William Green, of the city police, and Mr. Curton, private detective (of Mr. Pinkerton's staff, from Chicago). They were joined at Plymouth by detective Sergeant John Moss of the city police, who had come down from London the previous night to meet the steamer. It being known at Plymouth that Bidwell was expected from Havana in the *Moselle*, a large number of persons assembled on Milbay pier, to await the return of the steam-tender with the mail, in order to get a sight of the prisoner, and so great was the crowd that it was with some difficulty that Bidwell and his escort managed to reach a cab and were driven to the Duke of Cornwall Hotel, adjoining the railway station. They left by the 7.45 P. M. mail train for London. A large crowd was present to see them off. Mr. Good, from the western branch of the Bank of England, who went to Jamaica to identify the prisoner, also came home in the *Moselle*, and went on in the steamer to Southampton, *en route* for London. Bidwell will be taken before the Lord Mayor at the Justice-room of the Mansion House this morning.

I have it from what I consider the best authority, that among the secret stipulations of the treaty for settling the steamer *Virginia* affair — in which Great Britain had a hand — was one in effect binding the United States government to consent that Austin might be delivered to the British authorities by the Spanish government.

I would call the especial attention of our neighbors of the " Dominion " to the foregoing. On this occasion it was an American — to whom the laws of his own country properly refused protection, after the committal of a crime abroad — who was extradited from Cuba, despite the fact that there was no extradition treaty between Spain and England. It makes a difference whose bull is gored.

Long previous to 1873, a British dependency (or independency?) has been a safe refuge for bank-defaulters, boodlers, etc., from the United States — and this because of the dishonest money they squander or invest in the " Dominion." Short-sighted policy! Will not reflection convince our neighbors that seeing criminal " exiles " strutting about their towns in stolen plumes, living in high style, and squandering their illicit gains in divers ways, is a direct incentive to their young men to " go and do likewise " ? Such a blind policy is sure to entail its own retribution, with compound interest, and even now we have a Canadian colony of the same kidney protected by the starry flag.

In Chapter XXI I gave a sketch of McDonald's flight and embarkation at Havre for New York. As soon as the *Thuringia* was fairly on her voyage he felt comparatively safe, believing that even if the fact transpired that he was one of my party, it would be impossible to extradite him from New York.

But before the steamer arrived Mr. Kelso, then superintendent of the New York City police, received a cablegram from Inspector Bailey of the City of London police, with full particulars, and at once detailed Detectives Irving and Farley to meet the steamer and arrest McDonald.

At the same time the law firm of Blatchford, Seward & Da Costa, agents for the Bank of England, received the same information, also that McDonald had a large sum in bonds and other valuables. They at once procured a writ of attachment from the Supreme Court which they confided to Sheriff Brennan for execution.

Commissioner Gutman appointed Detective Irving United States Deputy Marshal to serve the warrant against McDonald. The action of the plaintiff's attorneys made the police officers responsible for the person of McDonald on the criminal charge, and held Sheriff Brennan responsible for the seizure and attachment of all the valuables and property found upon him. It became important, therefore, that the police and sheriff's officers should act jointly, and arrangements were made for both police detectives and sheriff's deputies to go together down the bay to meet the incoming steamer. Therefore, Detectives Farley and Irving, Deputy Sheriff Judson Jarvis, and special Deputy Lawrence Curry, went down the bay on Tuesday, March 18th, on board the police boat *Seneca*, and prepared to board her from the quarantine boat. The detectives and Deputy Sheriff Jarvis had gone ashore for this purpose, leaving special Deputy Curry on board the police boat, which was in charge of a sergeant.

The detectives before going aboard the quarantine boat urged Deputy Sheriff Judson Jarvis to remain on shore until they sent for him, alleging that they feared the forger might divine the object of their visit, and make away with the bonds which it was certain he had on his person. Their real object was to see him alone first, as they knew he would confide *his valuables to them for safe-keeping.* Ponder on the import of those italics. This the deputy declined to do, and went aboard the quarantine boat with them, but on attempting to board the *Thuringia* at the same time with the detectives, Mr. Jarvis was prevented by Dr. Moshier, deputy Health Officer in charge, although insisting on his right as a sheriff serving an order of the Supreme Court. The detectives with whom the deputy sheriff was acting in concert, of course, made no attempt to explain to the Health Officer, but hurrying below got from Mac, with whom they were well-acquainted, all the bonds in his possession, while Deputy Sheriff Jarvis was thus prevented from executing the order of the Supreme Court.

Meantime special Deputy Curry, on board the police boat, becoming suspicious from the long delay that something was wrong on board the *Thuringia*, requested the sergeant to run down alongside the steamer, and a rope being thrown him, he immediately climbed on board. Finding that his superior had been detained on the health boat, he immediately ran to the other side, and assuming authority, ordered the boat forward, and Deputy Sheriff Jarvis sprang up the side of the vessel, and both officers at once went below. The *search* of McDonald, of course, had been concluded, when the sheriffs entered the state-room and made the attachment of what little property was found. This consisted of about $10,000 in gold, that being too heavy for the detectives to carry away, and it would have been dangerous to attempt to make way with the watches and diamonds, Mac having displayed them on the voyage,— two gold watches, one diamond ring weighing ten karats and worth probably $10,000, two diamonds weighing four and one-sixteenth karats, and one diamond weigh-

NEWGATE.—PREPARING FOR AN EXECUTION.

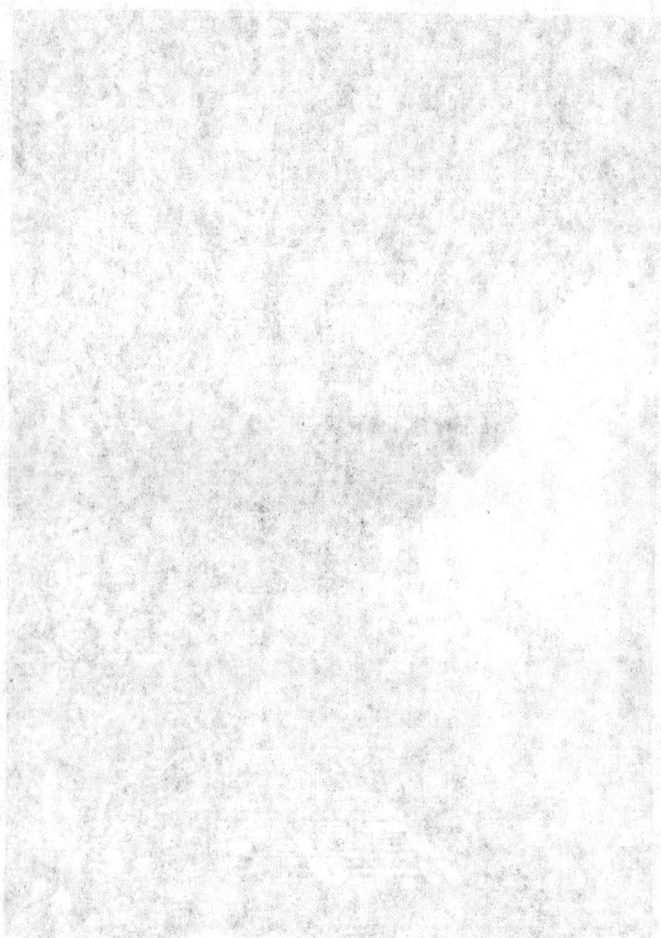

ing four and one-half karats. Not a single bond of any description was found by the sheriff, and only a few gold coins were left on Mac's person. On being searched a second time McDonald laughed and said, "I'm clean; you can't prove anything on me; you can't send me back to England on any such charge."

In order to throw dust in the eyes of the sheriff, the detectives pretended to become suspicious of others on board, and at their suggestion, the custom-house officers searched the person of one named Philip D'Artigue who had come aboard at Havre, and who had been frequently in conversation with Mac during the voyage. It was rumored on board that he had 300,000 francs on his person when he started, but no bonds of any description or money were found on him. Other passengers were searched but none of the bonds were found, and McDonald was taken to the Ludlow Street house-of-detention.

After depositing the captured property in safe keeping, Deputy Sheriff Jarvis reported the seizure that had been made to Messrs. Blatchford, Seward & Da Costa. Those lawyers were astonished at the result of the search, which disappointed their well-grounded expectations. Inquiry was made by them into the circumstances of the deputy sheriff's detention, and they asked his opinion of the proceedings, but this he declined to give.

Finally, after consultation among themselves, they directed the deputy sheriff to serve the same warrant of attachment he had served upon Mac, upon Detectives Irving and Farley; also on Superintendent Kelso. After some hesitation and inquiry of his own counsel, the deputy sheriff found it was incumbent upon him to take this extraordinary and unusual proceeding. He therefore repaired, about six o'clock P. M., to the office of the superintendent, and immediately served an attachment on him and on Detectives Farley and Irving. The service of the writ on Superintendent Kelso was a great surprise to him. This service rendered all three subject to examination about the bonds.

17

During the extradition proceedings before United States Commissioner Gutman, Superintendent Kelso purged himself and his subordinates, Detectives Farley and Irving (who skillfully evaded examination on the ground that their superior, Superintendent Kelso, was responsible for their acts and must answer for them, they reporting detective services only to him), from the implied charge of having appropriated bonds, etc., by making oath that he had nothing "except a revolver taken from the possession of the said George McDonald."

I am not able to say that the superintendent was in the confidence of his subordinates, in the case in question; but I do know, on the best authority, that the two detectives did take a considerable amount of United States bonds from Mac on board the steamer, and that the whole object of their maneuvering to prevent the deputy sheriffs, Judson Jarvis and Lawrence Curry, from getting on board the steamer at the same time with themselves, was for the express purpose of affording them that opportunity. I could give some startling particulars in regard to this and cognate matters — but let it pass.

Mr. E. M. Archibald, British Consul, made a demand on the part of his government for the surrender of McDonald, and had orders to aid the Bank of England agents, Messrs. Blatchford, Seward & Da Costa, in procuring his extradition. Mr. J. R. Fellows, the present District Attorney of New York City, Charles W. Brooke, and Mr. J. R. Dos Passos acted as counsel for McDonald.

The legal proceedings lasted from the 20th of March to the 5th of June, 1873. The array of counsel on both sides made it a forensic contest between giants, in which all past history was invoked for precedents, pro and con. These two extradition cases caused international complications, in which ambassadors and consuls took an active part. I have the McDonald case complete in all its details, but not the space to record the full legal proceedings.

After United States Commissioner Gutman had finally

decided to surrender him to the demand of the British government, appeal was made to the United States Circuit Court, Judge Woodruff, then to the Supreme Court, Judge Barrett, before whom McDonald was brought by writs of *habeas corpus;* but the commissioner's decision was sustained, McDonald was sent to Fort Columbus for safe keeping, while counsel were vainly arguing on new writs of *habeas corpus* and *certiorari*, and before any conclusion could be reached, he was hurried away by his custodians. He had scarcely time to bid good-bye to his counsel, when he was handcuffed to a United States officer, and with him crowded into a carriage in Chambers Street, guarded by Chief Deputy Marshal Kennedy and Deputies Robinson and Crowley, and driven rapidly down Broadway to the Battery, so that the large crowd who gathered to witness his departure from the metropolis had very little time to feast their eyes.

McDonald was lively and chatty during the ride, smoked his Havana, and looked through the windows of the barouche as freely as if his hands were unshackled. He was transferred from the battery to Governor's Island by a tugboat, and subsequently handed over by the deputy marshals to the charge of Major J. P. Roy, who had him escorted to Fort Columbus, and saw him placed in one of the casemates, under the vigilance and charge of two guardsman and the surveillance of Deputy Marshal Robinson, and the English detective, Mr. Webb. Lieutenant J. W. Bean had him furnished with necessary requirements, and the deputy marshal and English detective with sleeping apartments near by.

The following morning, United States Marshal Fiske, with Deputies Crowley and Purvis, Mr. Peter Williams, solicitor of the Bank of England, Sergeant Edward Hancock, a London detective, Deputy Marshal Colfax, and others, boarded the steam-tug *P. C. Schultze* at the Battery, and steamed across to Governor's Island. At half-past ten o'clock, Captain J. W. Bean, on post at the fort, received through Major J. P. Roy the following order from United States Marshal Fiske:

MAJOR J. P. ROY, *United States Army, Commanding Fort Columbus :*
   SIR, — You will please deliver to Deputy United States Marshal
John Robinson, the prisoner George McDonald, now in custody,
and oblige,   OLIVER FISKE, *United States Marshal.*

On receipt of the above official notice Captain Bean prepared to deliver up the prisoner to the charge of United States
Marshal Fiske and his party, who had by this time arrived at
Fort Columbus, and were waiting at the doors of the casemate.
The sentries paced the iron balconies with uninterrupted
attention to duty, apparently unconcerned about the exigency
on hand.

McDonald immediately recognized his visitors and understood the object of their visit, greeting them cordially as
they entered the gloomy corridor. He looked, as usual, in
good spirits, with some slight furrows of trouble and care
upon his forehead, and a sort of distressing and affected mood
of indifference in his deportment.

Captain J. W. Bean read to him the order of United
States Marshal Fiske to Major J. P. Roy, and then delivered
him over to United States Marshal Fiske's charge, with whom
he descended the steps from the balcony of the fort, and
marched, with a deputy at either side, through the tiled path-
ways and groved and shaded avenues, to the wharf at the
other end of the island, where the *Schultze* was awaiting his
arrival. A large crowd of spectators, soldiers, and civilians
lined the wharf, lingering anxiously to see McDonald "off."
But Mac walked very leisurely, smoked, laughed, and appeared
in a state of unaccountable good humor. He reached the
Schultze barge, however, in due time, shook hands with the
deputies, marshals, sergeants, and detectives, and then went
on board, and entered into conversation of some trivial kind
with Messrs. Williams, Hancock, and Webb.

It was nearly eleven o'clock when the *Schultze* steamed
away from Governor's Island wharf and whistled and rattled
down the bay to await the arrival of the *Minnesota*, which lay
at anchor during the forenoon near pier 46, North River, and

did not sail until some minutes after twelve o'clock. The *Schultze* meantime waited, steaming around the lower bay until the *Minnesota* arrived. It was after half-past one o'clock. The sun was burning hot, and the browned and florid complexion of all showed its effects. The steam-tug neared the bulky and huge vessel, and McDonald was finally taken on board by United States Marshal Fiske and Deputy Marshals Robinson, Crowley, and Colfax, and given into the custody of the English detectives, Sergeants Webb and Hancock, who in return gave the usual receipt to Marshal Fiske.

For the present, I leave Mac on the Atlantic, sailing swiftly eastward, to meet his terrible doom.

A fitting finale to these remarkable extradition cases will be the following adventure, in which one of the English detectives figured rather ingloriously.

The three Bow-Street officers, Inspectors Hayden, Hancock, and Webb, expressed a desire to detectives Irving and Farley to be shown the sights of New York. Accordingly, these, acting in an unofficial capacity, accompanied their English visitors upon a night's round of the most notorious resorts. Previous to starting, however, the English officers were advised to leave their watches and other valuables at the hotel, lest they should be stolen during the excursion. But Hayden, who was to sail for Havana a few days later to arrest Bidwell, scorned the idea, and set out for his night's amusement.

Towards morning he became sleepy, and taking a nap, he subsequently discovered that he had been robbed, not only of his watch and pocketbook, but also of the papers for the extradition of Bidwell, which he had foolishly carried in his pocket. Of course, he was greatly dismayed at the loss of these important documents, but they were returned to him by Superintendent Kelso, who had received them from Capt. Leary of the City Hall precinct. They had been surreptitiously left at the station-house on the day following the robbery. The watch and pocketbook were not recovered.

Chapter XXVI.

FIRST NIGHT IN NEWGATE — GOVERNOR JONAS — EXERCISE AT NEWGATE — DR. KENEALY — MR. GEORGE LEWIS — DAVID HOWELL, A "PATTERN" SOLICITOR — A FATAL CONCESSION ON MY PART — DON'T "SWOP HORSES WHILE CROSSING A STREAM" — HOWELL "FEES" BARRISTERS FOR US — HIS "MANAGEMENT" OF OUR CASE — HOWELL "HOLDS" MY DIAMOND STUDS — 108 WITNESSES — VISITORS AT NEWGATE — HOWELL'S "BENEVOLENT" CALLS — MISTAKEN IDENTIFICATION — LONDON ALDERMEN — ANOTHER PHASE OF "LIFE IN NEWGATE," FROM "THE LONDON TIMES" — CAGED ANIMALS — ALFRED DE ROTHSCHILD AND ONE OF HIS "FAMILIARS" — VISIT FROM THE RUSSIAN PRINCE IMPERIAL, THE PRESENT CZAR — LORD MAYOR WATERLOW AGAIN — THE PRINCE'S RETINUE — I CONTEMPLATE RETURNING HIS CALL AT ST. PETERSBURGH.

TO be sure, I was not to be hanged, as was the man at that moment sitting on the bench in the "condemned cell" in the same ward. But that first night in Newgate! A sleepless one, indeed — given up to retrospections and vain regrets. I at last had reached that dread abode of which I had read so much; that place, the scene of so many horrors in the dim and misty past, whose history, extending over a period of eight hundred years — one long record of crime — had rendered the very name infamous. While lying restless on the pallet, with closed eyes, my mind wandered in a chaos until I almost fancied myself the victim of an oppressive nightmare. Opening them upon the cheerless surroundings, as seen by the gas-light shining dimly through the glass plate imbedded in the wall, dissipated the illusion, and the whole horror of my position surged anew through my seething brain. Toward morning, dropping off into fitful slumbers, I dreamed of happier days, only to awake each time with a start, to realize more fully the degradation I had brought upon myself.

The next morning the governor (warden he would be called in the States) of Newgate, Mr. Jonas, since dead, came

into my cell and said that if I did not wish to live on the jail
fare, I could have food brought in from a restaurant, to the
amount of half a crown per day — thirty cents' worth — at

CONDEMNED TO BE HANGED.

my own cost. I thought this rather a small allowance, but
Mr. Jonas explained that the jail regulations permitted no
more.

Governor Jonas also informed me that in anticipation of
my arrival he had put a cot bed in the cell for me to sleep
on, instead of the sailor's hammock, which hangs from the
side walls, and which, afterwards, I found so difficult a con-
trivance to sleep in, and so easy to fall out of. Soon after I
was taken to the doctor, who asked me if there was anything
he could do for me; but I declined his services, with thanks.
In the afternoon I was taken into the inner court, (see illustration, page 33), for an hour's exercise, and a motley crew
they were, walking round and round the court. While there,
detectives came in every day to see if they could detect

among the "new chums" any old offenders, and seldom failed to call out several, as shown in the following cut.

Not knowing any solicitor in London, I sent for George Lewis, whose name I had seen in the newspapers in connection with criminal trials. The next day Noyes and myself were again before the Lord Mayor at the Mansion House, and after some sparring between Dr. Kenealy and Mr. G. Lewis on our behalf, and Mr. Freshfield on the part of the Bank, we were once more remanded to our cells in Newgate.

A DETECTIVE IDENTIFYING OLD OFFENDERS AT NEWGATE.

As some of my readers may not understand the distinction between solicitors and barristers, it may be well to explain that the solicitor takes the case and transacts all the business connected with it. A barrister is the lawyer who is employed by the solicitor to argue and conduct the case in court. He does not come in direct contact with the prisoner, but gets his instructions from the solicitor — all this being different from the system pursued in our own country.

When Noyes found himself so unexpectedly in the grasp of the British Lion, not knowing any other solicitor, he sent for Howell, the man who had charged him so exorbitant a fee for the articles of agreement between himself and " Horton." It was precisely this that prevented me from sending for him, on the principle that " a straw shows which way the wind blows," and it would have been well if on this and other occasions I had " stuck to my text."

Although, very properly, talking was by the Newgate rules prohibited, still, like many other prison "prohibitions," this was evaded. Noyes being with me in the same court-yard at exercise, asked me to give up Mr. Lewis and employ Howell, so that we could communicate safely with each other through him. To this I demurred, because my one interview with the former gentleman, together with his admirable conduct upon the occasion of our first examination at the Mansion House, had convinced me that he was not only a skillful but also a straightforward lawyer. However, Noyes arranged with Howell to have me called into the consulting-room. On entering, I saw before me an under-sized, spare man, with a sandy complexion, red hair, small, covetous eyes, and the general air of a Shylock ; and when he spoke, it was in a squeaky voice. After some preliminaries, he began to insinuate various things against Mr. Lewis, speaking of him as that " sheeney " (Jew), etc. Of course the strain of the previous days had somewhat affected my judgment, and to oblige Noyes I finally agreed to transfer my case into his hands. And a fatal concession it was.

I have often wondered since, what possessed me to " swop horses while crossing the stream," especially as I had that famous saying of " Honest old Abe " in mind at the moment. Mr. Lewis would have guarded against the occurrences which caused us to get the life sentences.

At this juncture another brother, John Bidwell, an honest man, arrived in England, and brought with him some bonds — United States seven-thirties — to use in our defense. Not being posted in money matters, he placed $4,000 in Howell's hands for him to sell, and use the proceeds in engaging barristers of the highest standing for our defense.

On one of Howell's daily visits to Newgate to see us, he sounded me as to the price I thought he ought to receive for the bonds. Upon my asking him what he could sell them for, he said he had credited them at a price which was thirty per cent. under the market rate. I soon undeceived him as to his idea of our ignorance on that point, by informing him of the fact that John had sold, by my direction, since the $4,000 was put into his hands, another lot of bonds for the full market price. This incident is only an introduction to others regarding this "pattern" solicitor, the reading of which will, I think, please and amuse Mr. Freshfield, the Bank of England solicitor, and the barristers whom Mr. Howell engaged to defend us.

After he had received the $4,000, and £300 Mr. Lewis had paid into his hands, he applied in open court for an allowance for our defense, to be paid out of funds taken away from us, on the ground that he had received nothing from us, and consequently could not pay the barristers. Accordingly the judge ordered that £100 for each one of us four should be refunded. We had directed Solicitor Howell to secure the services of barristers who stood high in their profession, such as Mr. Powell, Q. C. (Queen's Counsel), Mr. Besley, Mr. McIntire, Q. C., Mr. Moody, Mr. Ribton, and Mr. Hollings; and to pay the Q. Cs. each £100 or £150 fees, and the others in proportion. During the trial I ascertained that Howell had, instead of payment, enlisted their sympathies, and on the ground that he had only the £300 allowed by the court to the three of us whom he represented — McDonald having wisely secured the services of an honorable solicitor, St. John Wentner — induced them to work almost for nothing.

We being foreigners, and the case an important one, the barristers stepped over the usual bounds and took suggestions directly from us, an example of which may be seen in the illustration, page 49, in which McDonald is speaking with his barrister, Mr. Straight. They are very good likenesses of the lawyer and client in 1873.

Before being arrested, I had sent Mr. George Lewis £300, to use in the defense of Noyes. To show the difference between Mr. Lewis and Howell — who spoke disparagingly of him and took the meanest course to get my case out of his hands, as previously mentioned — when Mr. Lewis ascertained that Noyes had already sent for Howell, he paid over to the latter the £300, instead of showing my note to Noyes, which would have secured the case and the £300 to himself. It will be seen by the above that at the time Solicitor Howell applied for an allowance of money, he had above £1,000 in his hands, which, with the £300 allowed by the court, made £1,300, the greater part of which he applied to his own use and benefit, paying out but a small part of it in the preparation of a proper defense. He managed the case on our side, according to my observations, exactly as Mr. Freshfield would have desired in order to carry out the latter's theory, exonerating the Bank managers from a charge of neglect, etc., as elsewhere explained.

A copy of the book of depositions taken before the Lord Mayor was given to me by Solicitor Howell, with the request that I would memorandum on the broad margin left for the purpose, any criticisms of the evidence I might wish to make for the guidance of the lawyers. Accordingly I worked at it from the close of the examination, the 2d of July, during a month, and showed where the witnesses against me had contradicted themselves — engravers swearing they had engraved letters which appeared on the false bills, that I could have proved another had actually done, etc. — so that their evidence must have been thrown out. Yet Solicitor Howell suppressed all this. I also gave him an order for a set of diamond studs, valued at $1,000, to hold for me, and he has "held" them ever since. A few moments previous to the sentence I ascertained that he had received them, and was then wearing them in his shirt-front. They were set in black enamel, and doubtless our barristers whom he defrauded out of their just fees may have since observed what a sparkling light in the profession he had suddenly become. These and other circumstances convinced me, before the eight days trial at the Old Bailey was half over, that Solicitor Howell was playing into the hands of the prosecution, and, to prevent discovery of his malappropriation of money and valuables to the amount of $10,000, connived to get us put out of the way for life — especially me, whom he feared had penetrated his designs.

All this was so clear that on the seventh day of the trial I determined to get up in open court and expose the whole matter, but on taking counsel with one of the barristers he dissuaded me from my purpose. I hope that he used the information I then gave him to extract from Solicitor Howell just fees for himself and his brother barristers.

It was Solicitor Howell who gave Governor Jonas information, exaggerating something I said to him, thus causing the great scare during the trial about an alleged plan of escape.

During the five horrible months I was awaiting trial, it was a great relief to be called out of my cell into the consulting-room every day to pass five or ten minutes with Solicitor Howell, and for a long time my opinion of his character as first formed was modified by such a proof of his considerate kindness. But after he had made about one hundred visits I ascertained that he was charging ten dollars each visit, though I had on several occasions endeavored to ascertain whether he was charging for them, but was put off with a laugh and the remark: " O, I have business in the jail."

It was a relief to be called out of my cell, no matter for what purpose. Upon several occasions I was turned out into the yard with a dozen other prisoners, as shown in illustration, page 65, in order that a person or persons should be compelled to point out from among a number the one against whom he was to testify, or whom he accused of some offense. Of course the above way is a fair one to accused and accuser, and is the usual plan in England; but in my own case, on more than one occasion, some one of the one hundred and eight witnesses were brought to identify me while I stood in the dock at the Mansion House, many of whom professed to having seen us but once or twice several weeks or months previously.

Another great relief from the monotony of my cell was the advent of a visitor. In the illustration, page 81, are seen the prisoners with their faces pressed against the wire grating — the meshes being about one-quarter inch square — talking to their friends who have come to visit them, the space between the two wire gratings being four feet. An officer stands at one end or paces back and forth in this space to prevent any small article or written communication from being passed across by use of a slender cane or wire, etc. But I found that there, as elsewhere, a judicious application of " backsheesh " would enable me to pass to my relative such private instructions as I did not wish other eyes to see. I took pleasure in evading such an unjust restriction, preventing prisoners who had not even been examined, indicted, tried, or convicted — in many cases only held on suspicion — from communicating freely with their friends. Prisoners are not permitted to see the newspapers, and are kept wholly in the dark as to what is going on in the world, just the same as if they were already convicts.

In our own country all this is different. A prisoner confined in jail awaiting trial is permitted all proper indulgences, such as visits without listeners, food, fruit, newspapers, etc. Even in the Tombs, the New York city prison — that well-named sink of iniquity — visitors are admitted to stand at the cell door, as seen in the illustration, and talk to their heart's content. The bars leave spaces of four or five inches square so that the visitor can at least squeeze the fingers of the incarcerated friend. To show the difference : Being rather dyspeptic I felt the need of some fruit, and when Governor Jonas made his round one day I asked him to let some fruit be purchased for me, with some of my money then in his possession. He informed me that it was not in his power to grant my request, and referred me to the visiting magistrate — I think Alderman Sir Robert Carden, whose likeness is shown in the court scene, page 97 — saying that he would bring him to me when he came to the prison. A day or two later my cell door was thrown open and in stepped the governor accompanied by the alderman. I stated my want, and after some conversation, he wound up by saying: "I can see that you are a gentleman, and I will talk to the governor about it, but such a thing has not hitherto been permitted."

Whatever may have been the nature of his subsequent conversation with Mr. Jonas, I got no fruit, and I think I have remarked elsewhere that from the moment of my arrest to my discharge, nearly fifteen years later, the only "fruit" I ever had consisted of potatoes and cabbage. Think of that, ye gourmands, and beware!

The following extract from the *London Times* of July 2, 1873, illustrates another phase of life in Newgate:

(Extract from the last day's examination before the Lord Mayor.)

THE PRISONERS, GEORGE AND AUSTIN BIDWELL, EDWIN NOYES, AND GEORGE McDONALD, AT THE MANSION HOUSE.

The prisoner George Bidwell said he had an application to make to his Lordship (Mayor Waterlow). He had now been three months in Newgate, undergoing the most rigorous solitary confinement, and on twenty-three occasions he had been pilloried in that dock. His position was greatly saddened by the fact that one who was so near and dear to him as his brother was should have been placed at his side on the same charge, and under circumstances which he desired to say were caused by himself alone. His brother was many years his junior, and owing to family misfortunes, he and several others had been placed, when quite young, under his charge (G. B's). He found, according to the rules of Newgate, two persons were sometimes permitted to occupy the same cell during some part of the day, and he asked that the privilege be granted to him and his brother. He appealed to his Lordship that this last boon — this last gleam of sunshine which they might ever be permitted to enjoy, — might be granted, — remembering that, in case of conviction. they would be forever separated from each other. It would be impossible for him to long survive the imprisonment which would follow a conviction. Austin also made the same request.

VISITOR TRYING ON THE HANGMAN'S IRON PINIONING BELT AT NEWGATE.

The Lord Mayor said it rested not with him. but with the visiting justices, who were this month Aldermen Sir William Rose and Lusk.

The prisoner Noyes applied that a small ring given him by his sister before he left America should be returned to him. He had not applied before because he expected to be free. The Lord Mayor ordered it to be returned to him."

In accordance with the Lord Mayor's statement I had applied to the alderman above named, but my application failed —they avoiding a direct refusal by an "I'll see about it," which I afterward found to be the hackneyed phrase regarding most applications. From July 2d, until August 18th, we were kept rigorously secluded, and though we were to be tried together, could have no opportunity for concerting a mutual defense. Had we been permitted to be together a few hours more or less every day, I could have prevented Austin from being taken in by the warders' imaginary plan of escape from Newgate. We were not even permitted to exercise in the same court-yard together.

I was "favored"—people are curious to see caged animals of all descriptions—with numerous calls, not of the exact kind depicted in the accompanying cut, where the gentleman is trying on the hangman's irons for the "amusement" of the ladies, but from some of the "great guns" of the universe; men, but for whose aid the world would cease to revolve, judging by the way some people cringe to their superiors in wealth—perhaps inferiors in all other qualifications.

One day, soon after my arrival in Newgate, a warder unlocked my cell door, and informed me that I was wanted in the consulting-room. Upon entering, I saw two men of the most opposite appearance—evidently a god and a demon. Alfred de Rothschild was a well-built man, above the medium height, with auburn hair, blue eyes, and a rather pleasing expression of countenance, save that he looked as though he had been up late nights. He had the air of a gentleman, and I found him possessed of the manners and language characteristic of one, whatever his worldly circumstances. He was seated near one end of the desk which ran across the room

A CORRIDOR OF THE TOMBS. NEW YORK.

opposite the door. Seated at the opposite end was an under-sized man with a face on him such as I had never seen. He was evidently one of the "familiars" or followers — the usually unseen "shadows" and protectors — with whom money and other kings have, in all times, been obliged to surround themselves. His face was of an exaggerated He-brew type, his nose an eagle's beak, the eyes prominent, large, black, and lustrous, with very arching brows — the whole expressive of a diabolical cunning which could only belong to a Faust and a Mephistopheles combined. His one rapid penetrating glance at me as I entered the door, evi-dently satisfied him that it would be safe to let me ap-proach and speak with his master face to face. At the moment, not taking in the object of his presence, without halting I took a chair by the side of Mr. de Rothschild. The wardens stood outside, covertly peering in through the sash which formed the walls of the room, curious to fathom the design of a visit from so great a money-king. The pre-cise object of his visit I do not remember, but I took ad-vantage of the occasion to see whether anything could be done to relieve Noyes and my brother Austin from the probable consequences of their connection with McDonald and myself.

During the interview, I said : " Mr. Rothschild, I believe most other men placed in the same circumstances, would have done much as I have. I was brought up honestly, and the greater part of my life I have been an honest man. I have plunged myself into a gulf of misery and degradation, but mark my words, I shall live to redeem my character, and, if force of will counts for anything, I shall not die until that end is accomplished."

I have worked, suffered, and *lived* through fifteen years, the resolve then expressed being a beacon light — a light which for long years, though shining brightly, appeared very dim from its vast distance away, and at times it seemed to my wavering eyes to flicker and become extinguished, leav-

18

ing me in the darkness of despair. Having been protected from birth against every rough wind, Mr. Alfred de Rothschild could see nothing in me worth saving, and the future will decide if he was right.

O ye mighty of the earth! who are yourselves living in luxury — even all who are going through life untroubled by unending struggles for existence — continue unobserving, thoughtless, and blind to the great ocean of misery ever ebbing and flowing beneath the placid surface of society, until the billows of socialism or anarchy suddenly overwhelm all in a common ruin!

A few days later the Lord Mayor Waterlow entered my cell alone. I had already been before him several times at the Mansion House. I do not remember what induced him to make the visit in question, unless to see for himself how I was standing the terrible ordeal, or to judge if I was the desperado I had been represented. At all events, his manner was very affable, and he appeared much interested in the conversation until, as we were standing face to face, I put my hand to my breast pocket to get a letter or paper to illustrate something I had been saying. Seeing the movement of my hand, he suddenly stepped sidewise, out of the cell door. Why he did so flashed through my mind instantly, and I was so shocked that I should be taken for an assassin that I could not continue the conversation.

Whether he went and reported me as having an intention to assassinate him, I know not; but the circumstance led me to think, "If that is their idea of my personal character, what kind of a chance do I stand for an unprejudiced trial?" In the subsequent trial Justice Archibald ruled against us in every objection made by our counselors, and granted every objection or request of the prosecution. But that Imperial Power, the Bank of England, was against us.

On another day the Lord Mayor was doing the honors of the city to the Russian Prince Imperial, the present Emperor. He brought him to my cell accompanied by a retinue of aristocrats, of course the class for whom the world and all it contains was created — I mean its pleasures and the *dolce far niente*, not its pains and labors.

I presume the Lord Mayor wished him to see me as an example of one of the products of modern financial civilization. The retinue remained gazing through the door at me, while the Prince stepped inside preceded by the Lord Mayor Waterlow, who put the "animal" through his paces, no doubt much to the Prince's edification.

The Prince was condescendingly gracious enough to ask me some questions in perfect English, but really, though a wretched prisoner, I could get up no feeling of gratification at his notice beyond what I should have felt at the notice of any gentleman of education and refinement, and such an one the Prince surely was. I think I am entitled to call him an old friend, and to visit him at my earliest convenience in St. Petersburg.

CHAPTER XXVII.

ON the 2d of July, 1873, occurred the last of the twenty-three preliminary examinations before the Lord Mayor Waterlow. It was, all together, an ordeal which I trust no young man who reads this book will ever be called upon to endure. Pilloried in the dock day after day, exposed to the gaze of unsympathetic and curious crowds of people, who coldly speculated as to the result of the trial, and endeavored to penetrate, by dint of staring, through the cloak of impassibility with which the prisoner attempts to hide his real feelings. When the Lord Mayor at last announced that we were to be held for trial, the knowledge that I should remain undisturbed for the month or more before it could take place seemed like a respite.

I had made up my mind to plead guilty, believing that by doing so I should give the others a chance of escape, as their advocates could throw the *onus* on me. I had ascertained that we should be taken to plead to the indictments before Judge Chambers, and was assured by the experienced prison warders that if I pleaded guilty he would not give me more than seven years. But such a course on my part would have spoiled the "big case" which the Bank agents had spent so much time and money in getting up in order to let our fate be a warning to all who dared think of meddling with British money-bags. I believe, and always shall until assured to the contrary by Mr. Freshfield, that these latter had a potent

(276)

"influence" in causing Solicitor Howell to oppose my plan of pleading guilty, but as what he could say had no effect on my decision, he doubtless instructed my barrister, Mr. Besley, in whom I placed confidence, to advise me not to carry out my intention. Accordingly on Tuesday, the 12th of August, we were taken before Judge Chambers, and when I in my turn stood up to plead, Mr. Besley stepped up to the dock and said to me, in a low tone of voice:

"I hope you are not going to plead guilty?"

Such a remark from such a source, at that moment, staggered me; the clerk of the court was waiting my reply, and I blurted out the fatal words, "Not guilty" — words which cost me the possibility, nay, the probability, that I should never again see the outside of prison walls. Does it stand to reason that a gentleman like Mr. Besley would have caused me to do such a thing unless Solicitor Howell had instructed him to that effect, when even I could see that it was a foregone conclusion that I was to be convicted? I only mention these things to show that however cleverly a man may arrange his rascalities, "something" will happen by which in the end he meets his just deserts.

As a proof of this, in my own case, I will now give an account of the trial, which I have procured from an authentic source, and which will doubtless prove of interest to many outside of the legal profession.

I shall intersperse some criticisms and explanations — not, however, in the way of exculpations, but to show where prosecutors and witnesses made mistakes in facts, identifications, etc. I first introduce the account of the trial by the following editorial from the London *Times* of August 13, 1873:

THE BANK FORGERIES.

Monday next has been fixed for the trial of George Bidwell, Austin Bidwell, George McDonald, and Edwin Noyes, the four Americans who stand charged with the gigantic forgeries on the Government and Company of the Bank of England. The prisoners

will be arraigned before Mr. Justice Archibald, at the Central
Criminal Court, and the trial will probably last the whole week.
Meanwhile, the voluminous and circumstantial depositions taken
before the Lord Mayor at the Justice Room of the Mansion House
by Mr. Oke, the Chief Clerk, have been printed for the convenience of the presiding judge and of the counsel on both sides.
They extend over 242 folio pages, including the oral and docu-
mentary evidence, and make of themselves a thick volume, together
with an elaborate index for ready reference. Within living memory there has been no such case for length and importance heard
before any Lord Mayor of London in its preliminary stage, nor
one which excited a greater amount of public interest from first to
last. The Overend-Gurney prosecution is the only one in late
years which at all approaches it in those respects, but in that the
printed depositions only extended over 164 folio pages, or much
less than those in the Bank Case, in which as many as 108 witnesses gave evidence before the Lord Mayor, and the preliminary
examinations — twenty-three in number from first to last — lasted
from the first of March until the 2d of July, exclusive of the time
spent in remands.

Those remands, of necessity, were unavoidable, having regard
to the complex character of the forgeries and to the circumstance
that two of the chief conspirators fled the country on the eve of
the discovery, a circumstance which led to much tedious delay,
first in capturing them and then in applying extradition treaties
to their cases, and bringing the prisoners to England. Edwin
Noyes, who was first arrested in this country, has been in custody
continually since the first of March last, upwards of five months,
and the remaining three for periods varying from the 3d of April.
In the case of two prisoners, Austin Bidwell and George McDonald (apprehended in Havana and the United States respectively),
the tedious delay, consequent upon the extradition proceedings, was
further aggravated by long sea voyages to this country, where the
prisoners were at length given up to justice by their respective
governments. Upon Noyes, in particular, the protracted confinement preceding trial appears to have told considerably. During
the last examinations before the Lord Mayor, he seemed exceedingly careworn and anxious. There, from first to last, it may be
observed he always behaved in a manner entitling him to respect,

apart from the crime of which he is charged, his demeanor being altogether free from unseemly levity. As a rule, too, during the preliminary examinations George and Austin Bidwell conducted themselves well before the Court.

Once during one of the concluding remands, Noyes, for some moments and for the first time, became fairly unmanned. Towards the end of a long day, while a letter of his written to his brother, and in which kindly references were made to his father and mother, was being read by Mr. Chabot, the expert in handwriting, he burst into tears which he tried in vain to conceal, and sobbed like a child at the recital of a passage in which he rejoiced at the prospect of keeping the homestead together for the family. It may be mentioned as an incident in the case, that a witness named James M'Kelvie, a private detective in Edinburgh, who was mainly instrumental in arresting the prisoner George Bidwell in that city, has died since he gave his evidence before the Lord Mayor. The circumstance, however, is not likely to affect the issue.

Much satisfaction has been felt and expressed by all interested in the integrity of commercial transactions, at the prompt and cordial co-operation of the Governments of the United States and Spain with our own Government, in the steps necessary to bring to justice the persons suspected of complicity in the great fraud recently effected upon the Bank of England. Our own foreign office, under the direction of Mr. Hammond, Lord Enfield, and Lord Tenterden, took up the subject with an energy which contrasts strongly with the apathy popularly attributed to it, and at once telegraphed to Sir E. Thornton at Washington, and to Mr. Layard at Madrid, urging them to use their utmost influence to induce Mr. Fish, American Minister in Madrid, and Señor Castello, Spanish Minister, to arrest the delinquents, while their appeals were as strongly seconded from this side by Gen. Schenck and Señor Moret, Spanish Minister at Washington.

CHAPTER XXVIII.

O N the opening of the August sessions of the Central Criminal Court, this morning at eleven o'clock, the four Americans, George Bidwell, forty years of age, merchant — George McDonald, twenty-eight years of age, described as a clerk — Austin Bidwell, twenty-five years of age, described as merchant's clerk — and Edwin Noyes Hills, twenty-eight years of age, called a clerk — were put upon their trial before Mr. Justice Archibald, for the forgeries on the Governor and Company of the Bank of England. The court was much crowded from the beginning, and continued so throughout the day. Alderman Sir Robert Carden, representing the Lord Mayor, Mr. Alderman Finis, Mr. Alderman Besley, Mr. Alderman Lawrence, M. P., Mr. Alderman Whetham, and Mr. Alderman Ellis, as commissioners of the court, occupied seats upon the bench, as did also Alderman Sheriff White.

Sheriff Sir Frederick Perkins, Mr. Under-Sheriff Hewitt, and Mr. Under-Sheriff Crosley, Mr. R. B. Green, Mr. R. W. Crawford, M. P., Governor of the Bank, Mr. Lyall, Deputy Governor, and Mr. Alfred de Rothschild, were present. The

NOTE—I have caused certain portions of the following eight chapters, which contain an account of the trial, to be printed in italics, and it is to these, in general, that my interspersed comments refer.— G. B.

(280)

BANK OF ENGLAND PARLOR.

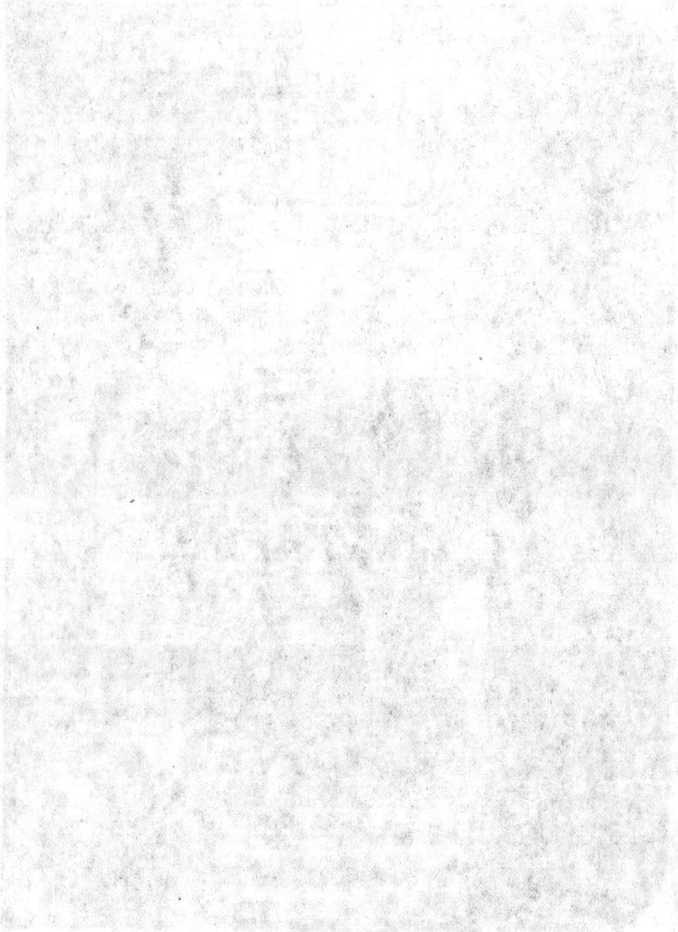

members of the bar mustered in force, and the reserved seats were chiefly occupied by ladies. Mr. Hardinge Giffard, Q. C., Mr. Watkin Williams, Q. C., Mr. Poland, Mr. H. D. Green, Mr. J. H. Crawford (instructed by Messrs. Freshfield, the solicitors of the Bank) appeared as counsel for the prosecution.

The prisoner George Bidwell was defended by Mr. Powell, Q. C., and Mr. Besley ; Austin Bidwell, by Mr. McIntyre, Q. C., and Mr. Moody (all instructed by Mr. Howell, solicitor) ; George McDonald, by Mr. Metcalf, Q. C., and Mr. Straight (instructed by Messrs. Wontner, solicitors), and Edwin Noyes by Mr. Ribton and Mr. Hollings (instructed by Mr. Howell).

Mr. Powell, Q. C., addressing the judge, said he was instructed on the part of his client, George Bidwell, to apply to the court for a future postponement of the trial. There were no fewer than sixteen indictments against the

R. W. CRAWFORD, M.P., GOVERNOR.

prisoners, charging them with offenses of the gravest magnitude. The evidence was most voluminous and very complicated, and the preliminary inquiry before the Lord Mayor lasted from the 1st of March, when Noyes was arrested, until the 2d of July, when they were all committed for trial. On the 7th of August the prisoners were served with a notice by the Bank solicitor, to the effect that no fewer than ninety-three additional witnesses, whose names they gave, and " divers other persons " might possibly be called upon the part of the prosecution. Except in one or two cases, the prisoners were kept in the dark as to the nature of the evidence the new witnesses would give, and it was therefore impossible, without some investigation, to be prepared with a reply to it. Those

witnesses, it was stated, generally would be called to speak of banking or bill transactions with one or other of the prisoners abroad, or to produce letters written by them, and he need hardly say that these matters might, and doubtless would have an important bearing on the case. The prisoners had not had time to inquire into the evidence about to be given, or to instruct counsel with reference to it, and he submitted that it was only fair to them, under the circumstances, that a further adjournment should be granted.

GEORGE LYALL, DEPUTY GOVERNOR.

Assuming that the new witnesses would simply corroborate others already examined, the necessity for inquiry on the part of the prisoners was still very urgent, inasmuch as the production of such a mass of additional evidence was almost an admission that the depositions already taken failed in certain particulars or points that might be of importance to them. Looking at the fact that many of the witnesses lived on the Continent, and that only ten days' notice had been given to the prisoners by the prosecution, he urged that it would be taking the accused, who were foreigners, at a very great disadvantage if the trial was hurried on at that moment, and that there would be a serious risk, and that justice would not be done them. He added that the application was not made with any view to unnecessary delay.

Mr. McIntyre, Q. C., supported the application on behalf of Austin Bidwell, observing that if the prosecution had, prior the last adjournment, formed an intention to call the new witnesses, they should, in fairness to the prisoners, have given them notice six weeks since. If, on the other hand, the existence of ninety-three witnesses had been discovered, or any necessity for calling them had transpired since that adjournment, the prisoners were certainly entitled, on every principle of justice, to an opportunity of defending themselves on the new points about to be raised. It was unfair to the prisoners to expect them to meet allegations which were not gone into before the committing magistrate, and of the substance of which they were as yet unaware.

Mr. Metcalf, Q. C., made a similar appeal on the part of George McDonald, urging that the case for the prosecution had been doubled in extent since it left the Mansion House, that many new heads of evidence were about to be opened, and that it had been impossible, during the nine or ten days since the notice had been served, to make any inquiry as to the statements the witnesses would be called upon to give.

Mr. Ribton, on behalf of Noyes, said applications for postponement were very frequently made in that court, and were hardly ever opposed or rejected, especially when they came from persons in the dock. As for his own client (Noyes) his case differed materially from that of the others, and it was very unfair to be informed, at the last moment, that it was proposed to show the previous acquaintanceship of all the prisoners in America, seeing that the accused men had no opportunity of inquiring into the character of the persons who were about to give such evidence. He should have thought that the Bank authorities, acting, as it might be supposed they did, solely in public interest, and possessing inexhaustible resources, would have been ready to consent to such a reasonable application.

Mr. Giffard, Q. C., for the prosecution, strongly resisted the applications. He pointed out that, although the case had lasted upwards of four months at the police court, the delay, if any, had arisen from the fact that Austin Bidwell had to be brought to this country from Havana, and McDonald from New York. The charge was in itself a very simple one, but the tracing of the various bills was somewhat complicated.

There was no legal obligation on the part of the prosecution to give the accused notice of fresh evidence, but such notice was invariably given out of mere fairness. It was quite impossible for any one at a preliminary inquiry to say what new witnesses might be forthcoming between the date of the committal and the trial, so it had been found in this instance. Of the new witnesses referred to, forty were bank clerks and others, who would, if necessary, give more formal proof on matters already investigated, and some of the rest would speak to the purchase by the prisoners of genuine bills at various places on the Continent, which were afterwards used as models for forged bills.

There had been great difficulty in getting some of the witnesses from America and the Continent, and if the trial were again postponed there would certainly be a failure of justice. The application by the prisoners was simply made with a view to delay, and in the hope that some of the material witnesses would be wanting on a future occasion. He submitted with confidence that no cause for the delay had been shown.

Mr. Justice Archibald, having taken time to consider his answer, said he had carefully weighed all that had been urged on the part of the prisoners, and he had come to the decision to refuse the application, having a very clear opinion that no injustice to the prisoners would ensue if the trial proceeded without delay.

A jury having been empaneled and sworn, Mr. Avery, the clerk of arraigns, addressing them, said the prisoners were severally indicted for forging and uttering on the 17th of January last, a bill of exchange for £1,000, purporting to be drawn by H. C. Streeter of Valparaiso, and accepted by the London and Westminster Bank, with the intent to defraud the Governor and Company of the Bank of England. In other counts he said they were charged in like manner with other forgeries, variously stated.

Mr. Giffard then proceeded to open the case for the prosecution. The prisoners he said were indicted for forging and uttering a bill of exchange for £1,000, but that in reality formed but a very small part of the scheme, or fraud, which it would be his duty to lay before the jury.

The charge against them was in substance that of uttering ninety-four bills of exchange, all of which were forged, and the effect of which was to obtain from the Bank of England very large sums of money. The jury would therefore at once perceive that they had to try a charge of fraud for which they might seek in vain a parallel in the criminal annals of the country. Such an enterprise, as might well be imagined, involved very considerable difficulties, but that all those difficulties were long contemplated the jury in the end would probably have no doubt, and as little doubt that they were surmounted with such consummate art as to produce a feeling of regret that the prisoners had not employed their talents to legitimate purposes in the ordinary business of life. Moreover, that scheme of fraud, but for one of those accidents which had come to be embodied in various shapes in the common proverbs of the country, was all but successful in the result. The jury would, therefore, perceive the class of men they had to try, how deeply they had laid their plot, and with what consummate skill they carried it into execution. The prisoners George Bidwell, Austin Bidwell, and George McDonald, as would be proved, came to this country in the spring of last year *to set on foot an original scheme of fraud. The first difficulty with which they had to contend was to procure an introduction to the Bank of England or to some first-rate bank, and at which they might discount bills. Austin Bidwell had been accustomed to deal* with a respectable firm of tailors named Green, in Saville Row, and one day in May, 1872, having made a purchase from them, he stated that he was about to depart for Ireland, and that he had a large sum of money in his possession, of which he wished them to take charge in his absence. Mr. Green declined the responsibility, and suggested that he (Bidwell) should place the sum *on deposit at the Western Branch of the Bank of England,* where his

firm banked. The suggestion was adopted, and he and
Bidwell walked together to the bank, where they saw Mr.
Fenwick, the sub-manager. Bidwell gave the name of Frederick Albert Warren, and having deposited the money, *he
innocently inquired if, supposing he had any further sum to
pay in, he need trouble Mr. Green who had introduced him, to
come with him for that purpose. He was told that their
account was henceforth his own and that he could pay in the
money direct.* The amount paid in upon that day was £1,200,
and the prisoner subsequently deposited a further sum of
£1,000. After that the account was allowed to rest until
September, when the prisoner called at the bank, and requested
Col. Francis, the manager, to sell for him £8,000 worth of
Portuguese three per cent. bonds. This was assented to,
and the prisoner drew £2,000 on account. During that
interview with the manager the prisoner stated, casually,
that he was an American contractor, or agent, charged with
the introduction on an extensive scale of Pullman's sleeping-
cars into this country, and upon the Continent, that he was
about to build them at Birmingham, and that he hoped to
have some of them running for the impending exhibition
at Vienna. *The prisoner's account at the bank went on
smoothly and regularly* and no particular attention was paid
to it by the authorities. (See page 139 *et seq.*)

It would be found that having obtained the all-important
introduction to the Bank, and having overcome the preliminary
difficulties, the next point with the persons concocting this
gigantic fraud was to know what to forge. *During September
and October, therefore, they were actively engaged in various
capitals and cities of Europe in making inquiries as to the
solvency and status of various large commercial houses, and
the amount of respect their bills were likely to command in
London, and to acquaint themselves generally with the ordinary
course of transactions there and in this country,* so that they
might be perfectly armed at every step of their way. [I did
the whole of that work.—G. B.] About this time two of the

prisoners became ill, and on the 5th of October Austin Bidwell wrote a letter to McDonald containing this passage : " G. (meaning his brother) has just telegraphed if we shall not wait until you are completely restored, and in answering it I trust that you will not be governed by any thought that we want you to go on at once. Far from it ; the first consideration is your health, and if necessary we will postpone business until Christmas, and if you require rest for ten days or more, for heaven's sake take it ; it might be highly dangerous for you to stir about. Then, we have a good capital, and when ready can largely increase it on short order. Above all things, if your health requires it let us wait, for business cannot be injured by delay ; it is only a matter of resting for that time."

[In establishing his theory that the fraud was a long-contemplated one, Mr. Giffard made an effective usage of the letter from my brother ; but it will be seen by reference to page 186 that the first inception of the " scheme " was not till on or about the 1st of November, nearly a month later than the date of my brother's letter. The telegram referred to as from G. is one I sent from Amsterdam while prospecting in search of an opening for a " speculation " somewhere on the Continent.—G. B.]

Mr. Giffard continued : The scheme had in consequence to be postponed, and the prisoners did not in fact commence active operations until Christmas. Between November and January George Bidwell, under the name of Gilbert, procured a large number of bills, which not only formed the model of the various forged ones, but, being paid into the Bank of England and duly honored, served to establish the mercantile credit of Warren there. It would be found also that either McDonald or Austin Bidwell, giving the name of Warren, went to Rotterdam and applied to a Mr. DeWael, a merchant there, for a draft on the London and Westminster Bank.

He was told that there was only one person at Rotterdam entitled to draw on that bank, and that he charged highly for it. Warren replied that he did not mind the expense, but that he must have the bill on that particular bank, and he accordingly left £622 with Mr. DeWael to purchase a draft, giving as his address in London the Golden Cross Hotel. [Another case of mistaken identification. I transacted that business with Mr. DeWael.—G. B.] Bills to the amount of between £4,000 and £5,000 were obtained by the prisoners during these three months, their evident object being to get first-class paper and induce the bank to discount their bills. On the 29th of November Austin Bidwell went to Col. Francis, and producing two genuine bills for £500, each accepted by Messrs. Suse & Sibeth, an eminent firm in London, asked him if he would discount paper of that sort. [Bills purchased for me by Mr. Pinto in Amsterdam. See Pinto's evidence.—G. B.] The manager promised to make inquiries, and finding they were first-class bills he discounted them. The prisoners having thus, with consummate skill and at one stroke, obtained credit with the Bank of England and the models for the forged bills which were to come, next provided for the distribution of the plunder and their means of escape. It was manifestly impossible that the money could be withdrawn in gold alone, and the prisoners no doubt felt that to receive it in bank notes was the most dangerous course they could adopt.

The difficulty was surmounted by the opening by Austin Bidwell [By my direction.—G. B.], in the name of Charles Johnson Horton, of an account at the Continental Bank in Lombard Street, into which he could pay the money received at the Western Branch and then draw it out again in a different shape. The account was opened on the 2d of December [After McDonald's "great discovery." See page 188.—G. B.], which day also introduced the jury to the fourth prisoner, Edwin Noyes. He was in New York at the time, and the prisoner, George Bidwell, telegraphed to him in effect to come over to this country on the next steamer without fail.

The jury would probably find in the end that a fourth per-

TRYING THE FORGERS.

son had become absolutely necessary to the successful execution of the scheme.

George Bidwell and McDonald had by that time become deeply concerned in it, and were thenceforward to be kept in the background. It was necessary, therefore, that some person who up to that time had been a stranger to the transaction should be introduced, and Noyes was selected for the purpose. On the 17th of December he arrived in England, and apparently without any luggage. *In the previous August McDonald had been in communication with him by telegraph*, and the jury would see eventually whether Noyes was the stranger he affected to be. He arrived in London on the 17th of December, and on the 18th or 19th he was dressed up for the part he had to play, and various precautions were taken to conceal his identity. It was absolutely astonishing to note in the progress of the fraud *the number of aliases* [see page 135] the prisoners, with the exception of Noyes, had occasion to assume. The jury would have occasion, as the trial proceeded, to note the intimacy which existed between Noyes and the other prisoners, and would find that up to the 11th of January, from his first coming to this country, he was in the closest relations with them. On Christmas day there was a dinner party at which all the four prisoners were present. That was the state of things up to the end of January. During December neither of the prisoners, George Bidwell nor McDonald, had been idle. Austin Bidwell was the person to open the account at the Western Branch of the Bank of England, and *part of the plot* was that he should be out of the country before the first forged bill was uttered. [See page 198.] The other prisoners, as to whom the Bank could have no information, were not only the persons who procured the models for the forged bills, but who actually forged them.

The jury would find George Bidwell going to various engravers for that purpose. He [Mr. Giffard] would not describe each individual transaction of that kind; it would

19

suffice to say that whenever the prisoners obtained a genuine
bill, they had the means in their own hands of counterfeiting
it, by having recourse to engravers, and that by various expe-
dients suspicion was disarmed. One of the forged bills purported to be accepted at the London and Westminster Bank,
and a stamp was fabricated so as to imitate that by which the
genuine acceptance of the bank was accustomed to be made.

It was necessary to protect the man Noyes, who was acting as Horton's clerk, and it was therefore clearly impossible
that he could have any connection with Warren's account at
the Bank of England. An extremely cunning device was
then arranged. Austin Bidwell explained to Col. Francis
that his workshops were being constructed at Birmingham,
and that his presence there was necessary; and he stated that
his bills, instead of being presented personally as hitherto,
would be sent through the post in registered letters. *The
first letter was dated the* 30th *of December* [two months after
the first inception of the fraud. See Chapter XIX.— G. B.],
and contained ten genuine bills for £4,307 3s. 6d., all of
which were discounted and subsequently honored. On the
5th of January an advertisement was inserted in the newspapers, by Noyes, to the effect that a gentleman of active
business habits, and with a small capital of £300, required
a situation as clerk or partner, and answers were to be
addressed to him at Durant's Hotel, where he was then staying. A great many answers were received, and McDonald
called at the hotel personally. [Another mistake in identification, as it was not McDonald who called at the hotel.—
G. B.] After he left, Noyes told the waiter that he was his
future master, and that he had deposited £300 with him as a
guarantee for his good conduct. On the 11th of January a
formal agreement was entered into between Charles Johnson
Horton of London Bridge, a Pullman car manufacturer, and
Edwin Noyes of Durant's Hotel, merchant's clerk, whereby
Noyes agreed to serve the former as clerk and manager, at
a salary of £150, the latter depositing a sum of £300 as

security for the due performance of his duties and honesty, said sum to be returned without interest on his leaving. The agreement was witnessed by Mr. Howell, a solicitor in Cheapside, who was now defending the prisoners, and it was found in Noyes's possession on his arrest. It was evidently intended to shield him when the fraud was discovered, and when all the other parties had made their escape. Up to this time very good bills had been sent up to the Bank for discount, but before the forgeries commenced a grand *coup* was determined upon. Accordingly Austin Bidwell, early in January, obtained a considerable quantity of foreign money and left London for Paris. On his way there he was considerably injured by an accident on the Great Northern Railway of France, but he turned the accident to account by introducing himself to Messrs. Rothschild, who had a close financial connection with the Railway Company. He induced them, against their ordinary practice, to sell him a bill of £4,500, and with this he returned immediately to London. [I purchased all this foreign money in London, and sent Austin to purchase a bill from Rothschild, the railway accident having nothing to do with it, beyond influencing the bankers to accede to his request.— G. B.] He had an interview with Col. Francis, and in the course of it he complained in some degree that his bills were being unnecessarily watched, inasmuch as all which he had presented were of the highest possible character. [Complained that his bills were being unnecessarily watched! If that statement is well founded, it should have been quite sufficient to arouse suspicion and cause inquiry— but no forger would be so stupid.— G. B.] He then threw down the bill of Messrs. Rothschild, saying he supposed that would be good enough for the Bank. It not being advisable for him to confess that he had left Birmingham and obtained the bill in Paris, he stated that the injuries from which he was suffering had been caused by a fall from his horse. He also stated that his workshops at Birmingham were full of new sleeping-cars, and that he expected his transactions to be very large in the course of the ensuing month.

The scheme involved not only the protection of the conspirators but the safety of the plunder, and accordingly it was, beyond all doubt, arranged that he should be on his way out of the country before the first forged bill reached the Western Branch of the Bank of England. It had been suggested at the preliminary examination before the Lord Mayor that because Austin Bidwell was out of the country he was not amenable for this offense. That was neither sound law nor common sense. There was a very old legal maxim that a man who did an act by another, did it by himself. The prisoner, Austin Bidwell, might have done what he did either at Rome or Kamtschatka, but he would be equally responsible, notwithstanding.

[The Northern Railway accident, while on his journey to Paris, and his engagement, caused Austin to give up connection with the partially prepared fraud, and he was absent on his "wedding journey." See Chapter XX for particulars. But Mr. Giffard's assertion is "good law and common sense," and should be a warning to any who contemplate perpetrating crime by proxy.—G. B.]

On the 22d of January, 1873, in a letter signed by Warren, dated on the 21st, came the first batch of forged bills to the Western Branch. That was the first experiment, and if it passed muster the scheme was successful. Austin Bidwell would then appear to have fled, and Noyes could set up the defense that he had merely acted as his clerk. The scheme was successful; *the bills had been engraved by skilled artisans* and had passed muster; the thing was done; and having got the first forged bills discounted, the next step was to operate on the account previously opened to get the plunder, and to escape. But having obtained so much money, how were they to deal with it?

Notes could be traced. The scheme contrived was as artful as the rest of the fraud. Anybody presenting banknotes at the Bank of England had a right to demand gold in exchange, but it might not be so generally known that the converse proceeding was equally easy, viz., that a person tendering gold at the Bank of England could receive its equivalent in notes. The device adopted in this case was this :

One of the prisoners went to the bank with notes and obtained gold for them. Another of them went on the same day and obtained notes for the gold ; so that unless it could be shown that the two prisoners so acting were associated in a common design the connection between the fraud and the property actually obtained by it was broken. That process was repeated to such an extent that between the 21st of January and the 28th of February, the notes changed into gold by Noyes amounted to no less than £23,650, and the gold exchanged for other notes by McDonald to £16,950. There was thus a large balance in favor of the amount in gold, but both it and the notes were afterwards expended in the purchase of United States bonds. Austin Bidwell left this country in the middle of January, and was married to an English lady in Paris. And he seemed to have gone about France and Germany selling the bonds which had been bought in London and buying others with a view further to destroy all trace of the proceeds of the fraud. [If he did so it was without my knowledge. — G. B.] About this time, also, Noyes sent out £1,000 to some relations in America, and it was, therefore, idle to pretend that he was merely the innocent clerk of the other men.

The business up to this point was eminently successful, and the diligence of the prisoners in the previous December was not without its reward.

From the 28th of January every bill which was sent to the bank was a forgery and had been fabricated on the model of the genuine bills, Messrs. Rothschild included, which had previously been discounted.

The first batch amounted to £4,250 and was discounted on the 21st of January, and then came the following in quick succession. On the 4th of February, £11,072 ; 10th of February, £4,642; 13th of February, £14,696; 20th of February, £14,686; 24th of February, £19,253; and 28th of February, £24,265.   The prisoner gave no address at Birmingham, but he explained that as he was staying with a friend a short distance out of town he should like his letters addressed to the post-office there, and that was accordingly done. On the 1st of February, McDonald deposited £1,200, part of the proceeds of the forgeries, with Messrs. J. S. Morgan & Co., the American bankers, and drew it out again on the twenty-first of that month. One of the bank-notes in which the sum was paid had been traced into the possession of George Bidwell, and another was found upon Noyes at the time of his arrest.   In this transaction, therefore, the four prisoners were concerned. The first forged bill would become due on the 25th of March, and it was so arranged that during the whole of the time the forged bills were pouring into the bank the genuine bills previously discounted were becoming due and being paid.

While the prisoners were making their arrangements to escape, the forgeries were discovered in the most accidental way.   Two bills for £1,000 each, purported to be accepted by Mr. W. Blydenstein of Great St. Helens, had been made payable at sight, but curiously enough the date had been omitted, and the bank authorities suspecting nothing wrong, sent a clerk on to Mr. Blydenstein's office to get the omission supplied.   The moment the bills were seen the forgery was discovered, and the scheme of the prisoners was at an end. The bank found that Warren had been operating upon Horton's account at the Continental Bank, and by a mere accident the chief cashier of the bank happened to be making inquiries there when the prisoner Noyes entered.   He was at once pointed out and given into custody, and it was found that on the same day he had purchased £26,000 worth of American bonds, and had cashed a check of Horton's for £5,000.   What was his conduct when arrested? He knew that both McDonald and George Bidwell were within the grasp of the law, but he made no disclosure, and he merely gave an address at Durant's Hotel, where he had not slept for a fort-night. He thus allowed his confederates time to collect the plunder, then lying at his and their lodgings, and to send it to other countries, the result being that some part of it was still unrecovered. A day or two later Bidwell and McDonald went to a hotel at St. Leonard's, and ordering a large fire to be prepared, they, as the prosecution alleged, destroyed all the plant used in the course of this scheme. [This is an error, it having been destroyed at Mac's lodgings in London, as previously stated. — G. B.] On the same occasion they sent to New York £50,000 worth of American bonds in a trunk addressed to Major George Matthews, which has since been seized by the police. In the rooms occupied by McDon-ald in St. James Street, blotting-paper was found bearing impressions of the writing in some letters addressed to Austin Bidwell at New York, and of the stamps and endorse-ments of the forged bills, and a London directory was also discovered from which a list of engravers was cut. Mr. Giffard then went in detail into the circumstances of the pris-oner George Bidwell's escape into Ireland, of his ultimate arrest in Edinburgh, and read a passage in a letter addressed by him to George McDonald, as follows:

Your friend has had a series of most extraordinary adventures since you saw him. A hell's chase and no mistake. His nerve has stood him through two taps on the shoulder, and four encoun-ters with detectives. He has been a Fenian, a priest, a professor, a Frenchman, a German, a Russian who could speak only "veree leetle Engles, mais un peu de Français et Allemand," and a deaf and dumb man with a slate and pencil,— all in the space of a week.

The learned counsel also described the prisoner's unsuc-cessful efforts to get rid of some of the witnesses in the case, and his attempts to make sure that the property reached America safely. He also stated that George Bidwell had assumed sixteen different *aliases*.

That he said was the case for the prosecution, and the jury would say by their verdict when they heard the evidence whether it was possible to entertain the smallest doubt that each and all of the prisoners combined together in carrying out their gigantic scheme, and having as they thought destroyed all traces of the proceeds, sought to betake themselves to another country, and there enjoy their ill-gotten gains.

It being now five o'clock, and Mr. Giffard having finished his opening statement, after speaking upwards of three hours, the trial was adjourned until next morning, and the jury were escorted by a sworn officer of the court to the Cannon Street Terminus Hotel, to pass the night without separating.

About one o'clock each day the court adjourned for luncheon. The illustrations will give an idea of what kind of a time the lawyers were having, while we poor wretches were put beneath into a large vaulted cell in the basement of the Old Bailey. Some food was brought in from a restaurant, but none of us were in circumstances to feel jolly over our dinner. Neither of us could avoid the thought that a very slight turn in the tide of affairs, at some period of his life, might have made him one of the laughing lunchers above, instead of a *miserable* below stairs.

BENEATH OLD BAILEY COURT ROOM.—COURT ADJOURNED FOR LUNCH.

Chapter XXIX.

A T the opening of the court at ten o'clock, the trial begun
the day before continued to excite much interest.

The first witness for the prosecution was Mr. Edward
Hamilton Green, a master tailor and army clothier at 35
Saville Row. He said, replying to Mr. Watkin Williams, Q.
C., that he recognized Austin Bidwell and George McDonald.
They called on him in April, 1872, with another person, and
ordered some clothes, signing their names in a book. Austin
Bidwell signed the name of F. A. Warren, and gave an address
at 21 Enfield Road, Hagerston. McDonald signed Edward R.
Swift, and gave the same address. The third person, named
Sebert, did not sign. Witness made them a quantity of clothes.
On the 4th of May, the two prisoners, Austin Bidwell and
McDonald, called again in a cab with Sebert, and tried on the
clothes which witness had made for them. The two prisoners said they were about to visit Ireland, and were in a hurry
to catch a train. Austin Bidwell said that he had more
money than he thought prudent to leave at his lodgings, and
that it amounted to about two thousand pounds, and he asked
witness to take charge of it. Witness recommended him to
some bank, adding that his bankers were close at hand, and he
accompanied him to the Western Branch of the Bank of England, where witness keeps an account, and where they saw Mr.

Fenwick, the assistant manager. Witness introduced Austin Bidwell to him, and said he had a sum of money which he wished to deposit. Austin Bidwell had gone with witness alone. [The italicized words do not bear out Mr. Giffard's statement in his opening speech, that Mr. Green suggested to Warren that he should " deposit the sum in the Western Branch." Reference to Chapter XIII will show that the opening of this account was a pure accident, and had nothing to do with a fraud yet unthought of.— G. B.]

A bank signature book was brought, and in that the prisoner wrote his name and address. Mr. Fenwick asked how he wished to be described, and he said as an agent. He then handed the money to Mr. Fenwick, who thereupon gave him a check-book. *The prisoner said more money would be remitted to the Bank in a week or two.* [The preceding words in italics have no foundation whatever in fact, but it was necessary that the witnesses, Messrs. Fenwick and Green, should both " remember " that particular, or the theory of the prosecution could not be sustained. I, by no means, impugn the good faith of either gentleman, but every lawyer knows how easily witnesses, by subtle suggestions or acute questioning regarding events some months past, can be brought to fancy that they really remember a thing that would not be inconsistent with the circumstances of the interview in question. Detectives are adepts in getting up that sort of " evidence." — G. B.]

He returned with witness to Saville Row, and the three parties then went away together in a cab. Witness had since seen them several times. The clothes they ordered were sent to the address given in Enfield Road, Hagerston. [Where I was lodging.— G. B.]

By Mr. McIntyre in cross-examination :— The prisoner Austin Bidwell wrote his name and address as F. A. Warren, 21 Enfield Road, Hagerston, in witness's book. On the 4th of May there was more than one person with him when he came, and when they returned from the bank, there was more than one waiting for him.

He wanted to leave the money with witness, but witness declined the responsibility and offered to introduce him to his own banker. He had seen Austin Bidwell more than once before the 4th of May. Replying to Mr. Giffard, Q. C., witness said the date of the first supply of clothes was the 18th of April.

Mr. Edward Elliott Green, son and partner of the previous witness, was called, and corroborated his father's evidence in material points, and spoke to having seen Warren nearly twenty times at his father's place of business in Saville Row. The third person who called gave no name and address.

ENTRANCE TO BULLION VAULTS, BANK OF ENGLAND.

Mr. Robert Bloomfield Fenwick, sub-agent to the Bank of England at the Western Branch, Burlington Gardens, was examined after Mr. Green. He said Mr. Edward Hamilton Green, the last witness but one, was a customer of theirs. On the 4th of May, Mr. Green came to the bank with a stranger, whom witness now recognized as Austin Bidwell, and who was introduced to him as Mr. Warren. Witness was told he was an American gentleman who had a considerable sum of money, which he wished to deposit. The prisoner himself gave the name of Warren, and he wrote his name and address in the signature book. He first wrote F. A. Warren, and on the witness asking him to write his name in full, he wrote Frederick Albert Warren, and gave his address, the Golden Cross Hotel, Charing Cross. On being asked how witness was to describe him, he replied that he was there more on business for others than for himself. He at length described himself as a commission agent, and he opened an account with £1,200. Witness then gave him a check-book, and a credit slip was made out at the time in his presence.

Witness said a pass-book should be prepared for him, and he believed he afterwards called for it. *He said he should have more money to pay in* [See Green's evidence before and my criticism.— G. B.], and he asked if it should come through Mr. Green. Witness said it was not necessary. On the 7th of January last witness saw the prisoner, Austin Bidwell, again in the agent's room of the bank, Col. Francis, the agent, being present. After some conversation, the prisoner then threw down on the agent's table a bill of Messrs. Rothschild for £4,500 saying: "There, I suppose that is good enough paper for you."

He at first talked about sleeping-cars, and said he hoped to soon see English tourists going to the Vienna Exhibition in them. He also said he had the choice of three different factories in Birmingham, and he added that he was going there at once, and hoped to commence business by the 1st of February. He mentioned a patent brake and also a signal light for the front of railway engines. On the bill being put down, he asked to have it discounted, and Col. Francis acceded to his request.

That was a genuine bill and it was afterwards paid. His account continued at the bank until the 1st of March, and his pass-book was sent to him. It then contained checks which had been received and paid. It was a practice at the bank for customers to sign the signature-book when they received a check-book. Witness produced two of the signatures of the prisoner, Austin Bidwell, in the name of F. A. Warren which the prisoner wrote in the bank-book. The credit slips produced and which had been received between May and August, 1872, were all in Warren's handwriting. Being cross-examined, the witness said he made no inquiries at the Golden Cross Hotel which the prisoner had given as his address. He

BANK OF ENGLAND BULLION VAULTS.

signed two or three times in all. *To the best of his belief he did not remember the prisoner speaking to him at any time about closing his account. His balance was low about the end of May,* 1872. [See page 140.] Including the genuine bill for £4,000 presented for discount and discounted, his balance on the 17th of January was about £3,500, after crediting him with the discount he had drawn.

Col. Peregrine Madgwick Francis, examined by Mr. Poland, said :

I am the agent at the Western Branch of the Bank of England in Burlington Gardens. I entered upon my duties on the 3d of June, 1872, and was absent on leave from the

27th of July to the 27th of August. Up to that time I had not seen the customer F. A. Warren, but I saw him on the 3d of September. I now recognize him as the prisoner Austin Bidwell.

On that day he brought some Portuguese bonds and asked me to take charge of them. They were of the nominal value of £8,000. Mr. Fenwick introduced him to me as Mr. Warren, and he sat down in my room.

I had some conversation with him. He said, in general, that he had come over to England to introduce sundry American inventions, first and foremost of which were the sleeping-cars, and some others. I asked him some particulars about an improved brake, but he excused himself from replying, on the ground that it was a secret. He said he hoped the sleeping-cars would be in use by the time of the opening of the Vienna exhibition, and that he expected soon to introduce a company into England for their manufacture. I understood him to say he was then working with a view to their introduction on a foreign line.

He said he was going to work at Birmingham. That was the substance of the conversation. I knew he was an American, and that the cars were American sleeping-cars. I filled him up a form for the Portuguese bonds, amounting to £8,000, and he signed it in my presence. It was a voucher to receive and hold them on his own account. Next day I saw him again, when he brought £4,000, nominal value, more of the same securities, and said he wished to have the whole of them sold, and he fixed a limit, forty-one and three-fourths per cent., as the price. I undertook to sell them for him. I wrote out the usual request, and he signed it in my presence.

On the 9th of September I saw him again, and he asked me for an advance of £2,000 on the bonds. I made him that advance until the time of the sale, and he signed a paper in ordinary form in my presence, relating to the transaction. The bonds were sold for £5,025, which sum then went to his credit, on the 14th of September. I saw him again on the

26th of November, when he brought in two bills on Messrs. Suse & Sibeth, for £500 each, and asked me if I could discount them for him. They were dated the 31st of October, 1872, and were three-months bills. They were drawn by Isidoro Hess, of Ferrara, and payable at Messrs. Martins in London. He asked if I would discount them for him, and I replied that I must inquire about them first. I took them to the city and got permission to discount them for him. I saw him afterwards, and they were discounted on the 29th of November. He said he might ask us to discount a few more of the same character. The amount of the two bills discounted were placed to his credit, less the discount. I saw him again on the 23d of December, and he then told me he was going to Birmingham and would send us a few bills of the same stamp as those we had taken. He said he was going there about his workshops. Nothing further passed on that occasion, and he left. On the 30th of December I received this letter:

BIRMINGHAM, December 28, 1872.

COL. P. M. FRANCIS, Bank of England (W. B.), London:

SIR, — Enclosed I hand you bills for discount, as per accompanying memorandum. Will you please place the proceeds of the same to credit of my account, and oblige

Yours faithfully, F. A. WARREN.

I have been delaying sending these bills for discount in expectation of a lower bank rate. However, as I have to-day given checks overdrawing my account, you will oblige me by placing them to my credit. I am yours, etc., F. A. W.

The letter contained a memorandum and ten bills for £4,307. They were all genuine bills, and were all paid at maturity. I discounted them, and the amount, less the discount, was placed to the credit of Warren's account. After that I did not see him again until about the 6th of January. At the end of December the balance standing to his credit was £3,604 13s. and 3d. I saw him again in my own room on the 17th of January, when he spoke to me about discounting a bill for £4,500. He brought it out with rather a flourish and put it down on my table in an off-hand way, saying, "I suppose that will be good enough paper for you."

It was a bill on Messrs. Rothschild for £4,500. I looked at it and discounted it for him. Up to that time, including that bill, I had discounted genuine bills for him to the amount of £9,807 3*s*. and 6*d*.

In the list of bills I discounted in December, there was an acceptance by Mr. Gilman for £300. The next time I saw him I said we had made inquiries about the bill, and that we did not want to have a larger amount from that acceptor. The bill, however, was a very good one, and we had no objection to Mr. Gilman. Austin Bidwell, on the 17th of January, looked exceedingly ill, and said he had been thrown from his horse.

That was the last time I saw him until he was in custody at the Mansion House. On the 22d of January I received the registered letter produced from Warren, and three bills enclosed with a memorandum. The amount was for £4,250, and the bills were endorsed by him. The letter was as follows:

BIRMINGHAM, January 21, 1873.

DEAR SIR, — I hand you herewith, as per enclosed memorandum, bills for discount, the proceeds of which please place to my credit.

I remain, dear sir, 　　　Yours very truly,

F. A. WARREN.

To COL. P. M. FRANCIS,

　Manager Western Branch of the Bank of England.

[Above and following letters were written by me, Warren not being in England. — G. B.]

Mr. Giffard, interposing, said: We propose to read the first bill now, as that is a subject of indictment. Mr. Avery, the clerk of arraigns, said the bill was one for £1,000, purporting to be drawn by H. C. Streeter, and accepted, payable three months after date, by the London and Westminster Bank. The acceptance was in the names of Mr. H. F. Billinghurst, the sub-country manager, and Mr. W. H. Nichols, signing on behalf of the secretary. Col. Francis, resuming, said: Those three acceptances are similar to some of the general acceptances given on the 30th of December. They were all discounted, and the account credited with the amount. They became due on the 31st of March, the 3d of April, and the 13th of April. They were presented in due course, and returned as forged.

On the 25th of January I received the registered letter and memorandum produced from Birmingham, with the eight bills mentioned in the memorandum. The letter was as follows:

BIRMINGHAM, January 24, 1873.

COL. P. M. FRANCIS, Manager Western Branch Bank of England:

DEAR SIR, — Enclosed I hand you bills for discount, as per enclosed memorandum, and which please have placed to my credit on receipt. The reduction in Bank rate came quite opportunely for my wants. I am, dear sir,

Yours very truly,   F. A. WARREN.

I do not think the signature to the letter is Warren's. It is an imitation of it, but I took it at the time to be in his handwriting. I also took the endorsements to the bills to be in his handwriting. There were eight bills, and they were discounted by me and placed to Warren's credit.

Mr. McIntyre, interposing, objected to the admissibility of this evidence, on the ground that it was not proved to be in Warren's handwriting. Mr. Justice Archibald overruled the objection, saying it would be a matter on which to address the jury when the proper time arrived. Mr. McIntyre submitted there was no evidence of authority. The judge said he would take a note of the objection. Witness, resuming, said: The amount of the bills in question was £9,350, and that sum was placed to the credit of the account, on the 25th. Of the eight bills, two purported to be accepted by Messrs. N. M. de Rothschild & Sons, two by Mr. B. W. Blydenstein, one by the Anglo-Austrian Bank, one by Suse & Sibeth, one by the London and Westminster Bank, and one by the Inter-

20

national Bank of Hamburg and London; and they were all similar in appearance to bills of the same parties which the bank had discounted previously. On the 4th of February I received the following letter from Warren:

BIRMINGHAM, February 3, 1873.

DEAR SIR, — I did not duly acknowledge your esteemed favor of the 24th of January, as I daily expected to come to the city, but do not find myself yet able for the journey, still suffering greatly from my fall, or rather its effects; but I hope to see you before long.

Please direct as last, as I am staying with a friend a short distance out of town. Letters will reach me directed to this office.

I enclose you bills as per memorandum, of which please place the value to my credit, on receipt. I remain, dear sir,

Yours faithfully,   F. A. WARREN.

Enclosed were eleven bills, amounting in all to £11,072 18s. and 6d. They were discounted, the discount deducted, and the balance placed to the credit of Warren's account. The signature of F. A. Warren to the letter was very bad indeed, and is an imitation of his signature, not so like his own as many of the others. There is an indecision about the endorsements. The acceptors of the bills were Messrs. Rothschild, the Bank of Belgium and Holland, the Anglo-Austrian Bank, the International Bank of Hamburg and London, Mr. B. W. Blydenstein, and Messrs. Baring Bros. One bill for £2,500 in the batch appears to have been altered from £25 to £2,500. The acceptance is genuine, but it was refused payment, in respect of the excess. All the others were returned as forgeries. I acknowledged the receipt of the bills by a letter addressed to F. A. Warren, P. O. Birmingham. On the 10th of February I received the registered letter produced, dated the 8th of February, with a memorandum including two bills amounting, together, to £4,642 19s. and 4d. The letter was as follows:

BIRMINGHAM, February 8, 1878.

DEAR SIR, — Your favor of the 4th, acknowledging receipt of bills mailed the 3d inst., came duly to hand. Enclosed I hand you bills and memorandum, proceeds of which place to my credit on receipt, and accept assurances, etc. I am, dear sir,

Yours faithfully, F. A. WARREN.

The two bills which purported to be accepted by Messrs. Rothschild and the International Bank of Hamburg were discounted, and his account credited with the amount. They were afterwards returned as forged. On the 13th of February I received another registered letter, dated the 12th, from Birmingham, with a memorandum and a batch of bills fourteen in number, amounting to £14,696 16s. and 2d. Those were discounted and the amount placed to the credit of his account. The letter was as follows:

BIRMINGHAM, February 12, 1873.

DEAR SIR, — Enclosed I hand you bills for discount as per memorandum herewith. Please have proceeds placed to credit of my account on receipt. I remain, dear sir, yours faithfully,

F. A. WARREN.

To COL. P. M. FRANCIS, Manager, etc.

There is a P. S. as follows:

MY DEAR SIR, — The mail was so near closing when I wrote my last, that I did not have the time to make a proper acknowledgment of your good wishes in my behalf, as expressed in the P. S. of yours of the 14th inst., and now I take occasion to return you my sincere thanks, and to inform you that I am gradually, but slowly, recovering, and am succeeding thus far in matters of business to my wish. I remain, dear sir, yours faithfully,

F. A. W.

The acceptors were Messrs. Rothschild, the Anglo-Austrian Bank, the International Bank of Hamburg, Messrs. Suse & Sibeth, the Bank of Belgium and Holland, Messrs. Brown, Shipley & Co., Messrs. Baring Brothers, the London and Westminster Bank, and the Agra Bank. Those bills were presented in due course and returned as forgeries. On the 21st of February I received a registered letter, dated the 20th, from Birmingham, inclosing sixteen bills, amounting in all to £14,686 15s. and 4d. The acceptors were Messrs. Mitchell,

Yeames & Co., the Russian Bank of Foreign Trade, the Union Bank, Mr. Blydenstein, Messrs. Rothschild, the Anglo-Austrian Bank, the London and Westminster Bank, and Messrs. Baring Brothers.

The letter was as follows :

BIRMINGHAM, February 20, 1873.

DEAR SIR, — Enclosed I hand you bills with memorandum for discount, proceeds of which please place to the credit of my account, on receipt.

I remain, dear sir, yours faithfully,

F. A. WARREN.

To COL. P. M. FRANCIS, Manager :

P. S.   MY DEAR SIR, — I am happy to inform you that my doctor reports me as doing finely, with the prospect, should no drawback occur, of resuming my active life again in a few days. Under these circumstances, I hope soon to have the pleasure of seeing you, and, in the meantime, I remain, dear sir,

Yours faithfully,

F. A. WARREN.

They were discounted and the amount credited with them. They were subsequently presented and returned as forgeries. On the 25th of February I received a registered letter couched in similar terms, dated Birmingham, February 24th, inclosing bills, sixteen in number, amounting to £19,253 10s. and 3d., which were presented in due course and returned as forgeries. I had discounted them and placed the amount to his credit.

Among the alleged acceptors were the London and Westminster Bank, Messrs. Baring Brothers, the Bank of Belgium and Holland, Mr. Blydenstein, the International Bank of Hamburg, Messrs. Suse & Sibeth, Messrs. Schroeder & Co., and the Union Bank.

I also produce a registered letter I received on the 27th of February from Birmingham, containing a memorandum and I think twenty-four bills, amounting in all to £26,265. The letter is as follows :

BIRMINGHAM, February 27, 1873.

COL. P. M. FRANCIS, Manager :

DEAR SIR, — Enclosed I hand you memorandum with bills for discount, proceeds of which please place to the credit of my account on receipt. I have yours of 25th, acknowledging receipt of bills sent on 24th.   I remain, dear sir, yours faithfully,

F. A. WARREN.

P. S. MY DEAR SIR: — I take this opportunity of thanking you for the trouble you have taken on my behalf in making special application to the Bank Committee about the Anglo-Austrian and Russian Bank bills.

I have some of each to the amount of about £6,000, and shall either get two endorsements on them, or return them to my friends. Accept, dear sir, the assurance of my esteem, while I remain yours faithfully,   F. A. WARREN.

Of those bills I discounted all but two, and the account was credited with £24,265. Those two bills were for £1,000 each, and payable three months after sight. The date of the sighting was omitted. They were sent to the office of Mr. B. W. Blydenstein, the alleged acceptor, on the 28th, to be sighted, upon which they were returned as forgeries.

The remaining portion of that batch of bills was presented in due course and returned as forgeries. [The witness then produced various paid checks of Warren's, including several for considerable sums drawn in favor of C. J. Horton.]

The gross amount paid in from the opening of the account to the end of December was £17,504 19s. and 4d. That included money paid in and bills which I had discounted. Excluding bills which I had discounted amounting to £5,300 in round numbers, the sum paid in to his credit amounting to £12,200 odd was paid in cash or in securities representing cash. Up to January 21st all the bills which were discounted were genuine. The bill for £4,500, discounted on the 18th of January, was also genuine and paid.

Cross-examined by Mr. McIntyre, Q. C.: I have been a bank manager for thirteen years. I was first the sub-agent of the Bank of England at Leeds, then agent at Hull, and subsequently agent at the Western Branch. Before that I was an officer in the army. I succeeded Mr. Pym at the Western Branch. We have there the address of every customer. My attention was first called to the account of Mr. Warren at the close of August on my return from leave. I am not aware that I went through his account at that time, it being an ordinary drawing account. The only address of Warren was the Golden Cross Hotel, and his only description that of a commission agent. The account began with the payment in of £1,200, and I found when I *returned at the end of August that the greater part of it had been drawn out, leaving a balance of about £39.* [That corroborates my account on page 138 *et seq.*] On the 26th and 27th of August Warren paid in £200 altogether. On the 3d of December the balance was £219. When he brought the £8,000 in Portuguese bonds I did not inquire his address, nor did I know his address in Birmingham. The only address I had there of him was the post-office. I made inquiries at the head office of the Bank of England about his bills.

His account then showed a balance of £1,658 in his favor. The bills of Suse & Sibeth were payable in the city. I certainly did not make inquiries as to those bills; it would not have been usual. Upon information obtained I discounted the bills. All the bills I received from Warren until the 21st of January last were genuine and paid at maturity. Up to that period I wrote him at Birmingham and only to the post-office there. The Bank of England has a branch there. The letter of the 28th of December was the first I received from Warren. Between the 28th of December and the 21st of January I had no letters from him; looking now at the bodies of the letters of those dates they seem somewhat different. That did not strike me at the time. There was a general similarity in all the letters after the 21st of January. I believed up to that time that all the letters were in his handwriting. I will not say now that the body of the letter of the 21st of January is in the handwriting of Warren. It may be.

I think the signature is Warren's. I afterwards learned that Warren was not in this country when those letters were written. That may possibly have induced me to change my opinion, but not in the first instance. Very likely that induced me to make inquiries on the subject. There were three bills inclosed in the letter of the 21st of January. Looking at the indorsement of these three bills now I believe them to be in Warren's handwriting. They have all the little peculiarities of his signature and *appear to be written freely.* [I wrote them myself. — G. B.] One I have had pointed out to me, but not by Mr. Chabot, the expert. I never saw Warren at the branch bank after this 17th January, and then he looked very ill. Being asked by Mr. McIntyre in conclusion if he had discounted bills for a man who had only given as an address, the post-office at Birmingham, the witness replied that was so, but said he communicated with headquarters on the subject of the bills tendered for discount. He went on to say he had produced in court that day all the letters purporting to come from Warren. Being examined by Mr. Giffard, Q. C., the witness said on the 17th of January Warren told him that he hoped to have his workshops in full operation by the first of February. That was the occasion on which he brought the bill of Messrs. Rothschild. He had no doubt as to the genuineness of the bills at that time.

Mr. Henry Farncombe Billinghurst was next called. He said he is the sub-country manager of the London and Westminster Bank. Being shown the bill purporting to be drawn by H. C. Streeter, of Valparaiso, upon and accepted by the bank, he said it was a forgery, so far as acceptance and witness's signature were concerned, the signature being a bad imitation of his. The stamp he said, was an imitation of that used by the London and Westminster Bank. Shown a batch of bills bearing similar acceptances and stamps, he said they were all forgeries, none of the supposed drawers having an account with that bank.

Mr. Alfred Charles de Rothschild was called and examined

by Mr. Crawford. He said he was a member of the firm of N. M. de Rothschild & Sons. Being shown eight bills purporting to be those of his firm, he said the acceptance was not in the handwriting of any member of it. The stamp across the bill, he said, was an imitation of the stamp they used for acceptances, and was not genuine. Shown a genuine bill of their firm for £4,500, he said it was in the handwriting of Sir Anthony de Rothschild.

Being cross-examined by Mr. McIntyre, witness said that the bill was drawn by their house in London on their Paris house. He added that the acceptance of the forged bill was exactly that which the firm used.

By Mr. Giffard: The signature to the forged bills produced purported to be that of Sir Anthony de Rothschild, but in every case it was a forgery. There was a certain amount of imitation of the signatures, and some might think it good, but he did not.

Mr. John Rudolph Lorent, manager of the Bank of Belgium and Holland — Mr. Herman Gwinner, manager of the International Bank of Hamburg and London — Mr. Charles John Sibeth, of the firm of Messrs. Suse & Sibeth, 35 Lime Street — Mr. Francis Hamilton, of the firm of Messrs. Brown, Shipley & Co. — Mr. Chas. Lloyd Norman, of the firm of Messrs. Baring Brothers — Mr. Mayern, clerk in the Russian Bank of Foreign Trade — Mr. J. T. Byng, assistant manager of the Union Bank — Mr. W. H. Trumpler, of the firm of B. W. Blydenstein & Co. — and Mr. W. H. Nichols, of the London and Westminster Bank — were also called, and gave similar evidence as to bills purporting to bear their acceptances. This concluded that class of evidence, and the Court adjourned at four o'clock for the day. Two of the jury were unwell, but the charge being one of felony, the members were not allowed to separate during the progress of the trial, and were taken, as on the previous evening, to the Terminus Hotel, Cannon Street, escorted by an officer of the Court, to spend the night.

CHAPTER XXX.

THE TRIAL CONTINUED — THIRD DAY, WEDNESDAY, AUGUST 20TH — GERMAN BARONS AND BANKERS ON THE STAND — OPERATIONS IN FRANKFORT-ON-THE-MAIN — BANK OF ENGLAND CLERKS NARRATE THEIR EXPERIENCES AND DISBURSEMENTS — THE MANAGER OF THE CONTINENTAL BANK IN THE WITNESS-BOX — BANK OF ENGLAND NOTES EXCHANGED FOR GOLD, AND VICE VERSA.

THE trial was continued, at 10 o'clock.

M. August Fleischmann, examined by Mr. Watkin Williams, Q. C., was called. Speaking through an interpreter, Mr. T. Gregory Smith, of the Bank of England, witness said he was a clerk to Messrs. Koch, Lautoin & Co., of Frankfort, bankers. He recognized the prisoner, Austin Bidwell. He saw him on the first of February last in their office at Frankfort. The prisoner transacted some business with witness. He bought some bonds of them, giving no name. Witness produced a note of that purchase, prepared by one of the partners, and which was handed to the prisoner at the time. It was in English, and referred to the purchase of $36,856 in United States bonds, for which he paid in Frankfort bank notes.

By Mr. McIntyre, in cross-examination: The prisoner was a perfect stranger to him. Witness was going in and out of the room during the transaction. He had not seen him since until the trial.

Baron Hugo von Bethmann, a partner in the firm of Bethmann, Freres & Co., of Frankfort, said he knew the prisoner, Austin Bidwell. He first saw him on the 13th of January. He called with some United States bonds and asked them to sell them for him. They agreed to do so. He was known there before as a customer by that name. The bonds

(313)

amounted to $10,000, and witness gave the numbers of them in detail. They sold them for him. The value of them in English would be little more than £2,000, and a bill of £500 was given to the prisoner in part payment for them.

Mr. Giffard, Q. C., addressing the Court, said that was the bill referred to by the witness, Mr. Duncan, on the previous evening, as having been received at the post-office, New York, in the envelope he produced.

The witness, Baron Bethmann, went on to say that the rest was paid in paper money of the Frankfort Bank. On the first of February the prisoner called again and asked witness to sell $10,000 more for him, adding that their price had become higher than it was a short time before, and he thought that a good time for selling them. It was a fact that the price had become higher. They sold the second lot of bonds for him. There were nine bonds of $1,000 each, and two of $500, all new. The value of them in all was about £2,000.

By Mr. McIntyre, Q. C., in cross-examination: American bonds were extensively sold in Frankfort, and his firm were selling them largely at that time. The cashier of witness's firm, and not witness himself, paid the prisoner for the bonds.

By Mr. Giffard, Q. C.: He had no doubt whatever that the bill in question was the one given to the prisoner, Austin Bidwell.

Mr. Meyer Schwartzchild, a banker and money dealer at Frankfort, examined by Mr. Poland, said he believed he recognized the two prisoners, George and Austin Bidwell, the former by the name of H. E. Gilbert. He saw George Bidwell at Frankfort first on the 13th or 14th of October last in reference to some American bonds which he had ordered witness to sell. The prisoner, Austin Bidwell, gave him an order to buy some bonds of Mrs. W. Hall. This was in January. Witness bought some American six per cent. bonds for Austin Bidwell in two or three lots, the value of them being about $5,000 all together. There were two or three transactions. The prisoner paid for them in Dutch and Frankfort notes.

At that time he did not know the prisoner, Austin Bidwell, by any name. He was a stranger to him.

M. Joseph Antoine Buchhein said he was a clerk in the Frankfort bank up to the first of July last. He knew the prisoner Austin Bidwell, and had seen him at the bank. That was on the first of February last. The prisoner then wished to buy two bills on London. Witness showed him one and drew another for him on London. He asked to have one of the bills endorsed to Paine & Co. of London, and witness so endorsed it. The amount of it was £19 4s. which the prisoner paid him. Being cross-examined, witness said the prisoner Austin Bidwell was a stranger to him previous to that occasion.

Mr. Isadore Wolff, a clerk to Messrs. Morepurgo & Weisweiler of Frankfort was called, and recognized Austin Bidwell as a person who had been seen in their office.

[All the foregoing evidence in relation to Austin Bidwell's purchases and sales of bonds on the Continent in January and February, must be cases of mistaken identity; although I do not, at this writing, know sufficient regarding his movements, after I parted with him at Calais on January 18th, to say positively — but it is my belief that before the 1st of February he was on his way to Cuba. — G. B.]

Mr. Frederick Robert Rumsey, a clerk in the Western Branch of the Bank of England, proved from his counterbook that on the 29th of November last, he paid over the counter a check of F. A. Warren for £800 in seven £100 notes, and two for £50 each. That was in one check.

Mr. J. A. C. Good, also a clerk in the Western Branch of the Bank of England, proved that on the 2d of December he paid in exchange for a check of Warren for £1,250, twelve bank-notes for £100 each, and £50 in gold.

Mr. John Thomas Stanton, manager of the Continental Bank, 79 Lombard Street, which is also known as Messrs. Hartland & Co., said he knew the prisoners Noyes and Austin Bidwell — the latter as C. J. Horton. On the 2d of Decem-

ber last he first saw Austin Bidwell. He then called at the
bank and opened an account with them. He said that he
had previously had an account with Messrs. Bowles Bros.,
and that he had been fortunate enough to have drawn from
them £7,500 just before their suspension. Having asked
witness what interest would be allowed, it was arranged that
he should open a current account with the Continental Bank.
He opened that account in the name of Charles Johnson
Horton, and signed the signature-book of the bank in that
name, giving as his address the Charing Cross Hotel. Witness understood that he was an American gentleman. The
account was opened by his paying in £1,300 in Bank of England notes, and he filled up a credit slip for that amount.
Witness produced the notes, with the exception of £100
which was changed for the prisoner. [These were the notes
referred to by the last two witnesses.] That was the first
time witness had seen him. Next day the prisoner called
again and paid in £235 10s., in two checks—one of Messrs.
Baring for £50, and the other for £185 10s. in the name of
F. A. Warren, on the Bank of England. Those were credited
to his account. On the 5th of December he paid in a check
for £95 2s., with which his account was credited. On the
same day a check was drawn out by him, signed "C. J. Horton." [Check was for the amount of £1,000.] It was paid
in bank-notes. On the 27th of December witness cashed a
check for him for £100 by £90 in notes and £10 in gold.
On the 30th of December a check of F. A. Warren on the
Bank of England for £1,550 was paid in and credited to his
account. On the 31st of December there was standing to the
credit of Horton's account £1,645 11s. 11d. On the same
day he paid to Horton the sum of £85 in bank-notes in payment of a check of his. On the 9th of January £3,000 was
paid into the account in bank-notes, the credit-slip accompanying the payment being initialed "C. J. H." On the 11th
of January £500 was paid into the same account by Horton,
and the account was credited with the amount. On the same

day £3,933 2s. 10d. was drawn out by, witness presumed, a check of Horton's, for which they gave him French notes for 28,000 francs, and two drafts on Paris — one for 50,000 francs and the other for 22,000 francs — both drawn on Messrs. Meyer Fils. On the 16th of January £1,250 was cashed over the counter in answer to a check of Horton's. On the 11th a new check-book was supplied to Horton, containing forty-eight checks. On the 16th of January £75 was drawn out by a check of his. On the 18th of January £3,304 16s. 9d. was paid into the account in two checks on the Western Branch of the Bank of England — one for £1,600, and the other for £1,704 16s. 9d. It was not stated upon whom the checks were drawn. On the 21st of January a check of Horton's for £2,000 was cashed, in ten bank-notes of £100 each, and two of £500 each. That was an open check paid over the counter. On the same day a check of Horton's for £807 15s. in favor of Messrs. Jay Cooke, M'Culloch & Co. was paid. On the 22d of January a sum of £3,716 13s. 7d., in two checks — one for £2,300, and the other for £1,416 13s. 7d. — on the Western Branch of the Bank of England, was paid in. On the same day a check of Horton's for £400 was cashed over the counter by two notes of £50 and three of £100. On the 24th of January £2,200 on a check of Horton's was paid, and later in the day a check of his for £45. The larger sum was paid by a check of his on the Union Bank of London, and the smaller check in bank-notes — one of £5, and two of £20.

On the 25th of January, £3,400 was paid in by a check of Warren's on the Western Branch of the Bank of England for that amount. Witness knew the prisoner Noyes. He was introduced to him at their bank by Austin Bidwell, as his clerk. That was about the 18th of January. He said that Noyes was his confidential clerk and that they were to treat him exactly as they treated himself. Witness asked whether Noyes was to be allowed to sign checks. The answer was " By no means," or to that effect. Witness understood that Horton was then going to Birmingham. He did not think he saw Horton after that.

Witness afterwards did business with Noyes in the way of cashing checks and paying in money. On the 25th of January or the day after, he received a letter from Noyes, saying he was to hand the bearer the German money bought for him by C. J. Horton that day. Witness believed that Horton had bought some German money that day which they had not previously had in the bank. It amounted to 2,000 thalers odd, and was given to the bearer, who signed a receipt for it in the name of E. Noyes. Witness, however, sent a clerk from the bank with the messenger to room No. 6, Terminus Hotel, London Bridge, Horton's address. On the 25th of January, a check of Horton's for £1,000 was paid in bank-notes, five of £100, and the rest in foreign money, florins and thalers, amounting to £502 odd. On the 27th of January, a check of Horton's for £451 15s. was paid in favor of Jay Cooke & Co. Next day a check of Horton's for £3,000 was presented and paid over the counter in seventeen £100 notes, five £50 notes, and £1,049 17s. 9d. in Dutch coin. On the 3d of February, £1,000 was paid in to Horton's account, the credit-slip for for which was signed " E. Noyes," in the prisoner's handwriting. That was by a check on the Western Branch of the Bank of England. On February 4th, £3,891 14s. was paid in to the credit of Horton's account by E. Noyes. It consisted of a single check on the Western Branch of the Bank of England. On the same day, a check of Horton's for £1,320 was paid over the counter in six £100 notes, one of £50, one of £10, one of £5, and £654 1s. 9d. in Dutch florins. On February 7th, a check of £3,500 of Horton's was paid over the counter in notes, six of £500 each, and five of £100 each. On February 10th, a check of Horton's for £200 was paid over the counter in notes. On February 13th, £6,250 was paid in to the credit of Horton's account in two checks, one for £4,250, and the other for £2,000, on the Western Branch of the Bank of England, in the name of " F. A. Warren " the credit-slip being signed " E. Noyes." On the same day a check of Horton's for £65 was paid in notes. That sum witness declined to send by a messenger whom Noyes had despatched for it with a letter addressed from the Terminus Hotel, London Bridge. Noyes afterwards called for the money himself, and requested that, in the future, witness would trust the messengers he sent. On February 14th, witness received a letter from Noyes, containing a check of Horton's for £50, which witness cashed at his request, and sent by the bearer to room 6, Terminus Hotel, London Bridge. On February 15th, a check for £332 10s. was paid into the credit of Horton's account. On the same day, he paid a check of Horton's for £4,000 in fourteen bank-notes, two of £1,000, two of £500, and ten of £100. On February 17th, £1,200 was paid in to the credit of Horton's account, in a check of " F. A. Warren " on the Bank of England. On the same day, he cashed a check of Horton's for £2,800 in bank-notes, one for £1,000, two for £500, one for £200, five for £100, and two for £50. On the 20th, he paid a check of Horton's for £1,000 in one note, and that was enclosed in a letter, at the request of Noyes, addressed to Horton at the Cannon Street Hotel, and sent by a messenger. On February 21st, a check of Warren's for £4,500 was paid in to Horton's credit, the slip for which was in Noyes' handwriting. On February 25th, £4,500 was paid partly in bank-notes on a check of Horton's made payable to himself, viz.: four notes of £1,000 each, one of £100, being, said Mr. Poland, one of a batch contained in the envelope produced yesterday by the witness, Mr. Duncan. On February 26th, £2,277 10s. was paid in to the credit of Horton's account, credit-slip for which was signed by Noyes — in two checks, one being a check of Warren's for £2,100, and the other a check of Jay Cooke, M'Culloch & Co.'s for £177 10s. On the 27th of February a check of Horton's for £100 payable to " self or order " was sent, as directed in a letter from Noyes, to C. J. Horton, Room 8, Cannon Street Hotel. Next day a check of Warren's for £6,000 was paid in by Noyes and was payable to Thomas Carter or order. On that occasion Noyes ordered a very large sum of foreign money to be got ready for him by the next day, principally in French notes and the rest in thaler notes. Witness believed the amount of foreign money he ordered was larger than £2,000. On the same occasion, Noyes received cash for a check of Horton's dated the 28th of February, for £2,000 in two bank notes of £1,000 each. On March 1st, Noyes called again, and produced a credit-slip signed by himself for £2,500, handing in at the same time a check of Warren's for £2,500 on the Bank of England payable to C. J. Horton. By that time witness had got a portion of foreign money for him, but it was arranged that he should call for it again later in the day. He called again a little before one and then produced for payment a check of Horton's payable to self or order for £5,000. He had to wait a short time while the check was being collected. Mr. May, a gentleman connected with the Bank of England, came into the bank while Noyes was waiting. Upon that witness pointed him out to Mr. May, who had brought in a policeman with him, into whose custody Noyes was then given. Witness had not at that time paid the £5,000 check presented by Noyes.

The witness underwent cross-examination by Mr. McIntyre, Q. C., and Mr. Ribton, but without his evidence in chief in any material respect being impaired. He said, however, on every occasion for a considerable time, he dealt with Noyes, believing him to be Horton's clerk, but after Horton said he (Noyes) was to be treated with as much respect as himself, witness thought Noyes was to be treated as somewhat of a principal. Horton, however, gave witness emphatically to understand that Noyes was not to sign checks.

Mr. Edward Brent, a clerk in the issue department of the Bank of England, said he knew the prisoner Noyes as a person who used to come from time to time to the bank to exchange notes into gold. On every occasion he asked the prisoner whether the gold was for home use or for exportation, and in most cases Noyes said it was for home use; in the other cases, at a later period, he said it was for Paris. He gave as his address 28 Manchester Square, Durant's Hotel. The total value of the notes he so exchanged was £13,285.

Mr. Frederick Pearse, a clerk in the issue department of the Bank of England, handed in an estimate of the quantity of notes which had been exchanged for gold at the bank.

WEIGHING OFFICE, BANK OF ENGLAND.

Mr. H. W. Hughes, a clerk in the weighing-room of the Bank of England, said he knew the prisoner, McDonald. On the 18th of January he saw that prisoner talking to the principal of the weighing department. The prisoner had brought £6,300 in gold which he wanted to exchange into notes.

Witness found there were twenty-three sovereigns too many, and he told him so. He replied that he was not aware of it. The prisoner gave his name as George McDonald and told him how to spell it, saying he had great difficulty in getting people to spell it correctly. On February 23d, the prisoner called again to exchange £650 in gold for notes. Witness took him to the proper department to have exchange effected. On another occasion he brought £9,000 sovereigns of which *fifteen were light and those very slightly so.* [See my remarks in Chapter XXXIII about exchanging those sovereigns. — G. B.] On February 25th, he came again bringing 1,000 sovereigns. On that occasion the prisoner was kept waiting somewhat longer than usual, and was very fidgety. He rang the bell once or twice and wanted to know the reason of the detention. He had been detained half or three-quarters of an hour.

Mr. Joseph Reese Adams, principal of the issue department, said he recognized the prisoner, McDonald. He saw him on the 28th of January at the bank and asked him where he got the gold. The reply was either that it came from Lisbon, or that he brought it from Lisbon. Being asked if he got the gold from Knowles & Foster, of Lisbon, to whom the bank shipped largely, he said he did not. The weight of sovereigns was twenty-one pounds troy-weight to the 1,000.

At this point, the court having sat nearly seven hours, the case was adjourned until the following day at ten o'clock. The jury, as before, were conveyed in charge of the ushers of the court to the Terminus Hotel, Cannon Street.

CHAPTER XXXI.

THE TRIAL CONTINUED — FOURTH DAY, THURSDAY, AUGUST 21ST — DUTCH BANK-
ERS WHO WOULD NOT BE "BEAT" TESTIFY — A HEBREW BROKER OF AM-
STERDAM ON THE STAND — OPERATIONS IN GERMAN BILLS OF EXCHANGE —
ACCIDENT ON THE NORTHERN RAILWAY OF FRANCE — INTERVIEW BETWEEN
BARON ALFONSE DE ROTHSCHILD AND AUSTIN BIDWELL IN PARIS — A £4,500
BILL — HEAVY TRANSACTIONS IN UNITED STATES BONDS ON THE CONTINENT.

UPON the opening of the Court at 10 A. M., it was
crowded as usual with ladies and gentlemen, including
many members of the nobility. Greater interest than ever, if
possible, was evinced, and amidst expressions of sympathy for
the prisoners, it was a subject of general remark that such
men could have made their way to the top round of the social
and business ladder had their abilities been used in a proper
manner.

Mr. Simon Louis Pinto, examined by Mr. Watkin Williams, Q. C., said he was a bill broker at Amsterdam. He
now recognized the prisoner, George Bidwell, by the name of
H. E. Gilbert. He knew some gentlemen named Citroen &
Zonen, gold workers at Amsterdam. Early in 1872 [It was
in October. — G. B.] he learned that a stranger would probably call upon him. Gilbert, otherwise George Bidwell, called
on him with a commissioner from the hotel. He said he had
brought some bills from Frankfort and wished to discount
them. Witness declined to discount them. The prisoner
then inquired whether he could obtain in Amsterdam any long
bills on Germany. Witness said that it was very difficult to
do that, such bills being very dear there. He told him there
had been some bills on Hamburg the day before, and possibly
he might obtain them. The conversation was in broken Eng-

lish and German — witness's son assisting to interpret it. He asked witness to buy some of the bills on Hamburg for him, to the amount of about 20,000 guilders, and only to buy them from good houses — bankers. The prisoner said he was connected with railway works. Witness bought some bills for him, for which the prisoner paid him in Dutch bank-notes. He then gave witness a further order to buy other bills to the same or a larger amount in "marks banco." A day or two after he bought the bills the currency [meaning the rate of exchange] on Hamburg was changed, and Bidwell called and ordered him to sell the bills, saying he had made a mistake and wished to get rid of them. He added he would put up with the loss. Witness found the loss would be so great that he declined to re-sell them without further orders. The prisoner said he had made such large profits in Hamburg by bill transactions that he could well afford to stand the loss, and that he intended to buy something else by which he could recoup himself. The loss was about £50 sterling. Witness sold them for him, upon which the prisoner gave him another order to buy with the moneys some fresh bills on London, and wrote the particulars upon paper. £3,000 was to be by a bill on London at three months, and £1,000 by a bill payable at sight. The prisoner left after giving the order. Witness bought five bills for him, one being a bill for £1,000 on Allard & Co., another by Philip Sohne on the Bank of Belgium and Holland for £1,000, two acceptances by Messrs. Suse & Sibeth for £500 each, and a bill of the Bank of Amsterdam on the Bank of Belgium and Holland, London, for £1,000. Witness delivered those bills to George Bidwell, and there was a balance to pay, which Bidwell handed him in Dutch bank-notes. He saw Bidwell from four to six times. He afterwards, on the 2d of November, received a letter from him before he left Amsterdam. The letter, which was without date and signed H. E. Gilbert, was to the effect that he would not buy more before the next day, and meanwhile witness might sell two bills which he enclosed if he could do so with ease. Witness afterwards received other letters from him from London, one dated 20th of November, and containing 860 guilders in Dutch bank-notes. In consequence of instructions in that letter witness made a purchase for him, and the prisoner replied expressing himself satisfied with the transaction. He received a subsequent letter, dated the 30th of November, from the prisoner, George Bidwell, enclosing 2,105 guilders, and directing him to make a further purchase for him in a bill on Blydenstein & Co., which witness did. On the 3d of January witness received a letter from him dated the 3d, enclosing 1,490 florins, for which he was to send him a three months bill on the Amsterdam Bank. Witness made the purchase for him, sent it by post, and received an acknowledgment by return. On the 25th of January he received another letter from the prisoner enclosing 6,000 guilders, and directing him to make another purchase for him. With that witness bought for him a bill on Messrs. Barings for £500, drawn by A. Guerstin on the Anglo-Austrian Bank, at three months date, and endorsed by witness. Witness procured the bill, and enclosed it to him, with a small bill for £4 10s., drawn by Messrs. Samuel Montagu & Co., on London. Witness afterward received from him 650 florins, with which he was directed to purchase another bill. Witness replied that he would not do business with so small an amount, upon which Gilbert wrote to him on the 13th of February, enclosing 410 florins more. Witness replied to him in effect that with even the two sums together of 650 and 410 florins he could not purchase a three months' bill. The witness afterwards sent him in a letter a bill for £87 10s., and had not since heard from him.

Being cross-examined by Mr. Powell, the witness said that he first communicated with the authorities for the prosecution on the subject about three months ago, through Mr. Phillips, an advocate, who wrote down what he had to say about it. He came to England last Friday. Besides the name of Blydenstein, witness said he suggested to the prisoner the

Amsterdam Bank, and probably others. He now gave the
dates of his interviews with him in Amsterdam, and said his
transactions with him were all of an ordinary kind, and such
as he might have conducted as a broker with other persons.

Mr. Johann de Wael, a banker at Rotterdam, in partnership with his father, deposed that he knew the prisoner,
McDonald, and saw him first on the 15th of November last, at
his office in Rotterdam. [Another false identification. It
was I, not McDonald.—G. B.] He asked if witness could
purchase for him one or more bills on the London and Westminster Bank for about £600. Witness told him they would
be difficult to be had, but he would try to get them for him.
The prisoner produced 7,435 guilders, which was equivalent
to about £623 3s. He gave witness an address at a hotel in
London, to which to send the bills if he got them. Witness
gave him a draft on London, on Messrs. Blydenstein, for
£617 13s., and told him to call on them. He purchased for
the prisoner a bill on the London and Westminster Bank
for £300, drawn by P. S. Lucardie & Sons; and another for
£300, of Collins & Maingay, drawn upon J. C. Gillman. The
prisoner, McDonald, instructed witness that the bills were to
be drawn to the order of F. A. Warren. The bills were sent
in a registered letter to Warren, at the address he gave; and
witness had an answer from him, acknowledging their receipt
and enclosing witness's card which he had previously given
to McDonald. He afterwards purchased for him a bill for
£158 13s. and 5d., by Lucardie & Sons, on the London and
Westminster Bank, and enclosed it in a letter addressed to
one W. J. Spaulding, care of Messrs. Clews, Habicht & Co.,
London. He had not asked for an acknowledgment, and did
not receive one. Being cross-examined by Mr. Metcalf, witness said a Mr. Phillips called upon him about the evidence
he was able to give, and showed him two photographs. He
afterwards saw all the four prisoners at the Mansion House,
including McDonald. That was after he had seen the photographs. He could not recollect exactly, when at the Mansion

House, which of the three prisoners, Austin Bidwell, George McDonald, and George Bidwell, was the man who dealt with him, but it was one of the three. He was now sure that McDonald was the man. [McDonald was not the man — it was I. — G. B.]

Mr. Matthias Harttman, agent at Hamburg to Messrs. Behrenberg, Gossler & Co., proved that on the 2d of December he received a letter signed W. J. Spaulding, containing 1,400 thaler bank-notes, on the receipt of which he sent Mr. Spaulding, at Clews, Habicht & Co.'s, two bills, amounting together to 20,000 guilders.

Mr. Edward Wilson Yates, merchant and banker at Liverpool, said he knew the prisoner, McDonald, and saw him on the 6th of December, 1872, in his own private room. He said he had two or three thousand pounds to invest, and would like to have one or two banker's bills to that amount, adding that he wanted first-class paper. Witness showed him some, and he selected one of Messrs. Brown, Shipley & Co. for £1,000, which he said he would take. He took it, and paid for it in Bank of England notes.

By Mr. Metcalf. He saw the prisoner afterwards in the dock of the Mansion House. That was after he had seen four photographs at Liverpool. He picked out McDonald immediately on seeing him at the Mansion House.

Mr. William Anderson, clerk to Messrs. Richardson, Spence & Co., Water Street, Liverpool, American merchants, said he knew the prisoner McDonald. He saw him first at their office in Liverpool, about the beginning of December. He called to know if they had any first-class bills to sell. Being asked for what purpose he wanted them, he said he had received a large sum of money in England, and wished to make temporary use of it. The answer was that they had no bills to sell. Being asked by witness why he came there, he said he had seen their names on letters of credit, as they were agents for many American houses. Witness said he would be more likely to get in London what he wanted than in

Liverpool. The prisoner asked if witness knew where he could apply, and witness suggested to him to apply at Messrs. Samuels's (now Messrs. Yates's) Bank, and sent Mr. Coupland, a clerk in the bank, to show him their establishment.

By Mr. Metcalf, in cross-examination. Witness afterwards saw McDonald in the dock at the Mansion House. He had previously seen at Liverpool photographs of the four alleged bank forgers. He said in the presence of Coupland, McDonald was the man. Coupland had not then given his evidence.

By Mr. Giffard. He had no doubt that McDonald was the man. Mr. Edward Coupland, a clerk to Messrs. Richardson, Spence & Co., bankers, Liverpool, spoke to McDonald being the man he had shown to Messrs. Samuels's bank in that city in December last.

Mr. Ernest Chas. de Lorelli, a clerk in the English office of Messrs. Rothschild in Paris, recognized the prisoner, Austin Bidwell, as having seen him on the 14th of January last, at their office there, in the name of Warren. He went up to Mr. Gatliff, the head officer of the bank, and asked for a bill at three months on London, for £4,500. Mr. Gatliff declined, as being contrary to their custom. The prisoner said he had been in an accident on the Northern Railway near Calais, and left shortly afterwards. He then had pieces of plaster on his forehead, and looked very unwell. About two hours afterwards he returned, upon which Mr. Gatliff had some conversation with Baron Alphonse de Rothschild, who came in and spoke to the prisoner, who again gave an account of the accident and said he had been much shaken. Baron Alphonse was a director of the Northern Railway of France. The Baron said he was sorry for him, and would do what he wanted in reference to the bill. The bill for £4,500 produced was then prepared, and in the first instance the prisoner handed in 99,000 francs in Bank of France notes, which was not quite enough to pay for the bill. The value of the bill was 113,000 francs, and they sent the clerk to the prisoner's hotel, upon which he paid the balance and received the bill.

Mr. Giffard explained to the court that this was a genuine acceptance of Messrs. Rothschild, which the prisoner, Austin Bidwell, afterwards paid in to Col. Francis, the manager of the Western Branch of the Bank of England.

Mr. Frederick Heinreich, another clerk to Messrs. Rothschild at Paris, was called to prove that, acting on instructions, he took the bill in question, for £4,500, to the Grand Hotel there, and handed it over to the prisoner, Austin Bidwell. He had previously seen him at the bank.

Mr. E. Lewis Osgood, clerk to Messrs. Drexel, Haries & Co., Paris, spoke to having seen McDonald on the 29th of January, when that prisoner applied to them for a letter of credit, and deposited 50,000 francs. Witness was instructed to prepare a check for £1,000 to the order of McDonald. He drew the check and took it to Mr. Haries's room for signature. Mr. Haries then said Mr. McDonald preferred a bill of exchange to a check, and a bill of exchange for £1,000, drawn by Messrs. Simpson & Co. on Messrs. Baring to the order of Messrs. Freres, Bruderer & Co., was substituted for the check. McDonald paid them for the bill after that, and still some money remained to his credit.

Mr. Olivier Bixio, joint manager of the general American Agency Co., in Paris, identified McDonald and Austin Bidwell. He saw both of them on the 29th of January in Paris. Austin Bidwell called there to fetch some American bonds which he had left on the previous day, and which he had offered for sale to them. They declined buying them, and they were returned to him. Austin Bidwell then proposed buying a draft on London for £1,000 at three months. Witness went to the bourse the same day and purchased for him a bill for £1,000 which was afterwards handed to him on his paying the price of it. It was a bill of Sapunzzi, of Constantinople, on Koronaki of Trieste.

Mr. William Butler Duncan, of the firm of Messrs. Duncan, Sherman & Co., merchants and bankers of New York, produced a letter addressed to George McDonald, care of his firm, which was seized and opened by the sheriff of New York. It contained three Bank of England notes, one for £5, and two for £100 each. He also produced thirteen bills of exchange for £4,000 in all which had been sent to his firm for collection, among them being one for £1,000 dated Bahia, Dec. 4, 1872, payable at ninety days sight at Messrs. Barings, drawn by Simpson, to the order of Messrs. Freres & Bruderer, and indorsed by them, Drexel, Haries & Co., and by the latter to George McDonald.

At this stage, it being five o'clock, the case was adjourned until next day.

Chapter XXXII.

THE TRIAL CONTINUED — FIFTH DAY, FRIDAY, AUGUST 22D — A WAITER AND
"CABBIES" TESTIFY — "QUITE LIGHT EVEN IN BIRMINGHAM" — A LADY HOTEL-
MANAGER'S TESTIMONY — MUCH CORRESPONDENCE — A MYSTERIOUS BOX — $220,-
000, LIKE FALSTAFF, HIDDEN AMONG "SOILED LINEN" — MR. DA COSTA OF NEW
YORK, DETAILS "THE RAPE OF THE LOCK" — ANOTHER HOTEL WAITER SPEAKS —
THE SHERIFF TAKES THE JURY FOR AN AIRING IN A COACH-AND-FOUR.

THE trial begun on Monday was continued, and as before
excited much interest and the court was crowded during the investigation.

Josiah Winspear was the first witness called. He said he
was a waiter at the Queen's Hotel, Birmingham, and knew

ACCOUNTANTS' BANK NOTE OFFICE, BANK OF ENGLAND.

the prisoner, George Bidwell. He had seen him twice there,
the last time being about the middle of February. He occupied a private room in the hotel. On the second visit witness

(331)

found the door locked on one occasion. Being cross-examined the witness said there was sometimes nearly a hundred guests at the hotel. He had not noticed anything peculiar in the manner of the prisoner George Bidwell while there. The prisoner wore a light overcoat and carried a satchel. He had the appearance of a foreigner. The next time he saw him he was in the dock at the Mansion House.

Alfred Morley, a cab proprietor and driver, Birmingham, said he recognized the prisoner, George Bidwell. He saw him on or about the 20th of February when he drove him in his cab from the Queen's Hotel, Birmingham, to the post-office. There he gave witness the address of a letter which he was to inquire about, and a florin to buy a shilling stamp. There was one letter waiting for him at the post-office, which he gave to the prisoner and he then drove him back to the Queen's Hotel. Witness noticed that he spoke with a foreign accent, and took him to be a "Yankee." About two hours afterwards witness saw him get out of a cab driven by a man named Barker, and witness spoke to Barker afterwards about the circumstances. He saw the prisoner come out of the hotel on the occasion in question.

John Barker, another Birmingham cab driver, deposed on or about the 20th of February he drove the prisoner George Bidwell, in his cab, and saw the prisoner Noyes. He drove George Bidwell from the Queen's Hotel to the post-office. There the prisoner told witness to get off his box, which he did. He gave witness a large letter and told him to register it. The letter was stamped and he said if there was anything more to pay for it he was to pay it. Witness registered the letter and brought out the receipt to him. Prisoner folded it up, and tore it into very small pieces. Nothing extra had to be paid for the postage. Witness then drove him back to the Queen's Hotel where he got out. He did not pay witness but said he would send his fare out. He joined the prisoner Noyes opposite the railway station. They talked together a few minutes, and then Bidwell went into the hotel and Noyes to the railway station. Presently afterwards the "boots" brought out the fare and gave it to the witness.

Cross-examined by Mr. Powell. That was about twenty minutes to four o'clock, and it was quite light even in Birmingham. (Laughter.) The next time he saw George Bidwell and Noyes was at the Mansion House. He and the witness Morley were together on that occasion. Witness went into the court to see if he could identify any one. He heard Morley give part of his evidence there. They afterwards traveled together in the same carriage to Birmingham. Witness had not then given his evidence. He had been shown a sketch, not a photograph, by a gentleman from London about three weeks before he went to the Mansion House. That might have been a detective officer, but he did not know that he was. The prisoner Bidwell tore the receipt up while in the cab and threw the pieces out into the street. Witness never saw him again until he saw him at the Mansion House.

By Mr. Hollings. The Queen's Hotel, Birmingham, is under the same roof as the station. Noyes joined Bidwell in the yard when Bidwell returned from the post-office. That was the first time the witness had seen Noyes, and he then saw him for about two minutes. He indentified Noyes at the Mansion House before George Bidwell was in custody.

By Mr. Powell. The letter registered was for America.

[In the previous chapter I remarked that "detectives were adepts in getting up" certain kinds of evidence. The witnesses Winspear, Morley, and Barker, are good illustrations of that remark. When they saw me in Birmingham, I was clean shaven, save a pointed mustache, a la Napoleon, and had they not been manipulated by the detectives and had me pointed out as the man they had come to identify, they never could have recognized me, in two or three months after a casual meeting; because when they saw me in the dock my face was covered with a thick, black, uniform, month's growth, of stubby beard. In me a change from a mustache to a full beard effects such a transformation that only friends, or those who have seen me often could recognize me. To show the nature of what he really knew, the letter Barker mailed was to the Bank of England and not to America — the detective had overlooked "refreshing" his memory on that point.— G. B.]

Miss Kate Mary English, manager of Nelson's Portland Hotel since August last, said she knew all the prisoners and had seen them at the hotel. On the 26th of August last, George Bidwell came there and took a room, staying a week. During that week she saw the prisoners, Austin Bidwell and McDonald. They came in those names. George Bidwell said his brother Austin was staying at a larger hotel, and that on a previous occasion he had stayed at the Langham, and had come from a journey in Ireland and was going to Eastbourne. He left on the 29th and returned on the 1st of September. He remained at the hotel two days, and then left saying he was going abroad, and he gave her directions about his letters, and those of his brother and McDonald. On going to the Continent he left a letter for "Mr. Hills," directing witness to give it to him. While he was away letters arrived. After he had gone she received a letter from George Bidwell as to where she was to send his letters in Paris. After that she sent to an address he gave in Paris all letters that arrived at the hotel for him. On the 14th of September she received a letter (produced) from George Bidwell, dated from Trouville, France, directing her where to send any letter that might arrive addressed to Mr. Hills. On the 23d of September she received a letter from George Bidwell, dated Paris, September 20th, directing her as to the further disposal of letters that might arrive addressed to him or to his brother Austin. She afterwards forwarded about a dozen letters to him, and a telegram to an address he had given. The letters had come principally from America. She sent them on towards the end of October, and George McDonald called a few days afterwards at the hotel and thanked her, paying her in the meantime for the postage, and giving her directions as to future letters that might arrive, adding that Mr. George Bidwell, whom he said was traveling on the Continent, would be in London soon. Towards the middle or end of November, George Bidwell himself called at the hotel, and asked for letters, and inquired whether " Mr. Hills " had called, adding that he had been expecting him. He was aware that McDonald had called and paid for the postage. In December "Hills" (Noyes) was at the hotel, and giving as his name E. N. Hills, inquired for letters. She had never seen him before, and asked if he was Mr. Bidwell's friend. He replied that he was, and she gave him a letter which Bidwell had left there for him. He also asked if she would receive letters for him if called for. She replied that he being a friend of Mr. Bidwell she would do so. He called once after that to ask for letters. On the 6th of March witness saw George Bidwell. He took breakfast at the hotel, and asked her to take care of some small things for him until he called for them. A cabman afterwards called with a letter from George Bidwell, directing that the things he had left should be given to the bearer, which was done.

Mr. Alfred Henry Remond, manager at the head office of the North Atlantic Express Co., said he knew McDonald. On the 5th of March he called on witness to have a box (which he produced) sent to a Major Matthews in New York. It purported to be forwarded by Charles Lossing, London, to Major George Matthews, New York, and the contents were described as wearing apparel not in use, and the box was directed to be kept in New York until called for.

Mr. Willard Brigham Farwell, general superintendent of the North Atlantic Express Co., who have an office on Broadway, New York, produced the way-bill relating to the box in question, and said the box arrived there on the 20th of March. He found the box after a search on one of the drays of the company. A woman had come that same day to inquire for the box, producing a letter signed George Matthews, upon which witness stopped the delivery of the box.

The box was afterwards opened in the presence of witness, who found in it three bundles of bonds, representing in all $220,920. He also found in it some visiting cards bearing the name George Bidwell, two watches, some wearing apparel, and dies for stamping. Some of the bonds were wrapped in a nightshirt, and others in some soiled linen. The box was opened in the presence of several witnesses whom witness named. Witness eventually handed all the contents over to the receiver, who gave witness a receipt for them.

Mr. Charles M. Da Costa was next called. He deposed that he was a member of the law firm of Blatchford, Seward, Griswold & Da Costa, of New York, who he said had acted as solicitors there to the Bank of England during these proceedings. He was present at the opening of the trunk produced, and afterwards had delivered to him the bonds produced, and other property, by Mr. Jarvis, the receiver appointed by the Supreme Court of New York. The property having been claimed, as the direct proceeds of the forgeries, it was immediately turned over to Mr. Peter Williams, of the firm of Messrs. Freshfield, solicitors to the bank. It included American bonds worth in English money about £45,000, which were tightly folded up in three parcels, just as they were now, at the bottom of the trunk among some soiled linen. The trunk also contained some watches and dies, with the monogram " G. B." engraved on them, also a little bag of foreign coins, a large collection of shells, an elegant new dressing-gown, and clothes of different kinds. Witness also obtained from the post-office at New York, through Mr. Jarvis, the receiver, the two packages produced, one addressed G. C. Brownell, Esq., Brevoort House, Fifth Avenue, New York, and the other addressed Austin Bidwell, Esq., New York, U. S. A., care of New York Safety Deposit Co., No. 140 Broadway. They had been detained there by Mr. Jarvis, the receiver in the suit, and handed over to witness's firm eventually. The envelope of the second letter bore English stamps, and the New York postmark of March 13, 1873. It was a

TRANSFERRED FROM DARTMOOR TO WORKING PRISON.

registered letter, and bore the London postmark of the 25th of February last, and also the Cannon Street postmark. It contained bonds for $17,500 or $17,600, equivalent to about £3,700 in English money, and the seals on the envelopes corresponded with one of the dies found in the trunk. The other package, addressed G. C. Brownell, Esq., bore the New York postmark of March 20, 1873, and also contained $17,500. It likewise bore a similar seal to that of the other. Witness also procured from the receiver a letter (produced) addressed George M. McDonald, Esq., Post-office, New York City, U. S. A. It was dated the 11th of March last, and bore the Edinburgh postmark of that date, and that of New York of March 24th. It also bore part of the impression of a seal with the monogram "G. B." Witness also produced other letters similar in various respects, found in the trunk, and with that his evidence concluded.

James Richardson, a waiter at Durant's Hotel, identified the prisoners, Noyes and McDonald. On the 27th of December, he said, Noyes came there at night and engaged a bedroom, giving afterwards the name Edwin Noyes, and on the next day he had his room changed, saying he would stay about a month. At first he brought no luggage, but next day did about half-past ten at night. He stayed about a fortnight, and between fifty and sixty letters afterward came for him. *McDonald visited him at the hotel* on one occasion, and they left together in a hansom cab. [Another case of mistaken identification. It was "Warren."— G. B.] Noyes returned to the hotel the same night. He told witness afterwards that he had been very successful in his business with McDonald; that he had advertised for a situation as clerk, which he had obtained, and had paid £300 as security. Witness remarked that it was a risk to pay away so much money to a stranger, to which he replied, "Not with such gentlemen as these. I think I am all right."

At this point, the court having sat upwards of seven hours, the case was again adjourned until Saturday morning.

CHAPTER XXXIII.

A T the usual hour, 10 o'clock, the case for the prosecution
was continued, the court being organized the same,
except that George Bidwell was defended by Mr. Besley. The
Old Bailey court-room was crowded with spectators of both
sexes.

Henry Thomas Hagger, salesman until recently to Messrs.
Kino, tailors, Regent Street, said on or about December 19th
last the prisoner Noyes called at their warehouse, giving the
name of Brooks, and ordered some clothes, for which he afterward paid £3 10s. He subsequently had other clothes for
which he paid £56 8s., and he gave as his address "Nelson's
Hotel, Great Portland Street." Witness also knew the
prisoners, George McDonald and Austin Bidwell, as customers on one occasion in September. McDonald gave
him an address at Chiselhurst. He first saw Austin Bidwell
about the beginning of November when he called and gave an
order for clothes. They made clothes for him to the amount
of £23.

William Mills, shopman to Messrs. E. Bax & Co., hatters,
Strand, proved that on November 26th last the prisoner

(338)

George Bidwell called at their place and bought a hat. On December 19th he and the prisoner Noyes called, and George Bidwell introduced Noyes by the name of Brooks. On January 24th George Bidwell called again.

Thomas Henry Jessy, manager to the same firm at their shop in Duncannon Street, said that he knew Austin Bidwell, George Bidwell, and George McDonald. On August 20th last he saw Austin and George there, when they brought a stick to be mounted and to have the words " G. M. from George and Austin " engraved upon it. After that had been done Austin called for the stick and took it away. The mounting cost £7 10s. George McDonald gave his address at the Alexandra Hotel.

Wm. Henry Boddemeade, salesman to Messrs. Pepe & Plant, hosiers in Waterloo Place, recognized the prisoner Noyes, by the name " E. F. Williams," which he gave on one occasion on ordering a linen shirt. Afterwards tried it on and ordered seven others. They were to be made at one guinea each; gave as his address " E. F. Williams, Nelson's Portland Hotel, Great Portland Street." He paid for them and took them away. Witness had since seen some of his shirts in the possession of the police officers.

Caroline Beard, a chambermaid at the Grosvenor Hotel, recognized the prisoners, Noyes, Austin Bidwell, and George McDonald. She knew Austin as Captain Bradshaw. He came about the beginning of December and left on the 27th of that month. George McDonald, who gave the name of Mapleson, stayed four or five weeks. Austin had previously told her he had a friend coming, and they would make one bedroom do. When McDonald came he and the other occupied the same room. They afterwards said they had another friend coming and she asked them if he would want another room. The reply was that he would. That was about the middle of December. Noyes, in the name of Brooks, came afterward, but only stayed two or three nights. She last saw Austin Bidwell on December 27th.

Miss Agnes B. Green said she kept a private hotel at Number 7, St. James Place, and she knew the prisoner McDonald as Captain McDonald. He took rooms there and stayed from the 6th of February till the 3d of March. He occupied the sitting-room and bedroom adjoining on the ground floor. [All the forged bills were prepared in these rooms.— G. B.] Her landlord was Mr. Walter Coulson, the surgeon. She knew George Bidwell. She saw him several times at the hotel. She used to go to Captain McDonald's rooms. On March 2d McDonald left and took his luggage with him. She saw him on the day he left. He said he was going to Paris. Next day she went into the bedroom, which had not been occupied in the meantime. She found there several news-papers and some blotting paper (four pieces) with some ink impressions upon them. [The blotting paper was produced.] She read something about the case on Monday, March 3d, in the *Daily Telegram*, after McDonald had left, and in conse-quence she communicated with the police, and afterwards gave up the blotting paper to William Smith, a city police officer, and also the city directory (produced) which McDonald had left behind him.

From that, said Mr. Poland, one of the counsel for the prosecution, addressing the court, some pages with the names of engravers upon them had been cut, including those of Thomas Straker of Ivy-lane, Newgate Street, and others. He added that the page with the name of the governor, directors, and officers of the Bank of England had been also abstracted, as also the names of certain merchants and bankers. Mr. Read, the Deputy Clerk of Arraigns, read from the blotting paper the various marks upon it. Among those marks were " accepted payable at," " London and Westminster Bank," " the Bank of Belgium and Holland," "Ten thousand," " St. Petersburgh," " A. Biron," " Schroeder & Co.," " C. E. Dal-ton," " F. A. W.," and many others less distinct.

Witness, resuming, said that she remembered on one occa-sion her manager bringing her a £100 note to endorse. Being cross-examined, witness said she eventually gave information to the city police through her manager at their office in the Old Jewry. She did that in consequence of reading an account of the forgeries. She sent information, she said, because her manager had told her the whole of their conduct was very extraordinary.

Franz Anton Herold, manager of Miss Green's private hotel, said that he remembered McDonald coming there, and giving as an introduction the name of Dr. Coulson. He engaged a bedroom and sitting-room on the ground floor. The window of the bedroom looked into St. James Street. He had seen the prisoner George Bidwell there. He first came on February 7th. Witness knew him by the name George, from Mr. McDonald so calling him. On the day McDonald arrived, he said he should like to have fires as large as they could be made, assigning as a reason, that he came from a very hot climate, and felt chilly. Witness carried out his instructions about the fires, but the prisoner still complained that they were not large enough. On February 10th, George Bidwell was there, and witness got for him the Continental Railway Guide. The same day, McDonald, in Bidwell's presence, asked witness to get a wooden box made for him, saying he wanted to send to India a machine and a cloak to wrap it in. Witness had a box made for the express purpose, and gave it to McDonald. A few days after he had been at the hotel, McDonald ordered him to tell the servants when they came to his door to knock loudly, and not to enter until he said " Come in." He stayed at the hotel until March 3d.

George Bidwell came nearly every day, sometimes as early as half-past seven or eight o'clock in the morning. He generally rang the front door-bell, and McDonald himself used to come out in his shirt sleeves and open the door, his bedroom being next the entrance hall. Witness had heard George Bidwell knock at McDonald's window with a stick or umbrella, and McDonald coming out, was about to open the door, but witness opened it instead. George Bidwell used to remain the greater part of the forenoon, and to go out and in during the day. They were always writing in the bedroom, and used candles and gas almost day and night. They lighted all the gas burners there were in the room. The sitting-room was at the back, and each of the two rooms had a separate entrance and a communicating door. The gas globes in the room were all cracked from the pressure of gas, and the ceiling above the burners was very black. The blinds used generally to be down in the daytime as well as at night. He remembered McDonald asking him for a piece of glass, and witness gave him the piece produced which he found in the room after he left. On going into the room, he used to notice papers like bills of exchange on the table. He remembered once McDonald receiving two telegrams. He last saw Bidwell on March 1st. McDonald left on March 3d, sending his baggage off in two cabs, and walking away himself. He left no address, but said he was going to Paris, but would return that same night. Witness said upon that, "You are a very quick traveler," (Laughter.) He gave some directions to witness about a dispatch box before he went away. After he had gone, witness found in the bedroom and sitting-room several foreign newspapers. On first coming to the hotel, he gave witness £170 in gold to get changed for Bank of England notes. Witness did so.

Replying to Mr. Metcalf and Mr. Besley, in cross-examination, the witness said McDonald was almost always writing in the bedroom, and with the blinds down. Witness sometimes went in to ask for orders without being rung for. His suspicions had been excited before Bidwell went away. Referring to the sheet of glass produced, witness said he took it out of a picture frame in his own room. He never saw the glass used for any purpose. He had seen George Bidwell write in the bedroom, and Bidwell and McDonald were generally together either in the sitting-room or the bedroom.

Thomas Brown Barnard, salesman to Messrs. Newton &

Co., tailors, Hanover Square, said he knew George Bidwell as Horace Arthur. He called there on May 1st, last year, and ordered £43 worth of clothes. Being asked for a reference, he paid £10 on account. He called and tried the clothes on, and afterwards paid for them. Witness did not see him again until December 6th, when he gave an order for more clothes. On December 12th, he called again accompanied by McDonald, whom witness knew by the name of Mapleson. The firm also made clothes for Noyes, who was known as Mr. E. F. Williams, to the amount of £21 15s., for which he paid on the 4th of January. He saw George Bidwell about December 1st, who then gave an order for a dressing-gown as a present. Towards the end of January, George Bidwell gave an order for a hunting suit, which he directed to be sent to the Rugby railway station. On that day, he paid £50 on account. The hunting-suit was sent to Rugby on Feburary 18th, and witness afterwards learned from him that he had received it. On March 4th, witness received a letter in pencil from him " H. Arthur," in consequence, he altered a coat as requested. Next day he called at their shop in a very agitated state and paid his account, taking away with him the clothes they had made for him, some of which, in the possession of the police, witness had since recognized.

Mrs. Ann Thomas said she lived at 21 Enfield Road, Hagerston, in April last, and knew Austin Bidwell, George Bidwell, and McDonald. She saw George Bidwell first. He took apartments at her house in April, in 1872, engaging to leave at any time. He gave the name " Mr. Anthony," and was accompanied by another person. While George Bidwell lodged there, Austin Bidwell and McDonald visited him every day. A parcel came for a Mr. Warren, which she took up to him. It was kept.

Upon the counsel for the prosecution attempting to elicit an unfavorable opinion as to the judgment she had formed regarding George Bidwell from his general conduct while in her house, witness said, with warmth: " No; I thought him a perfect gentleman!" Her spirited reply caused much amusement in court.

Bidwell remained with her a little more than a week. When he left she missed a latch-key, which she afterwards received back in a letter, dated from the Terminus Hotel, London Bridge, in which the writer expressed his obligations for her kindness and attention to him and his friends during their stay, adding that everything in her house was neat, and the cooking had been superb. (Laughter.) After George Bidwell left, Austin Bidwell called and took away some things. In March last she received a letter from "Mr. Anthony" (otherwise George Bidwell), from Edinburgh, dated the 14th, in which he stated that it was his intention to return to his old lodgings in a day or two. [This was just after the hunt through Ireland.—G. B.] Witness had no room at that time, but she engaged a bed and a sitting-room for him at an opposite neighbor's, and wrote to him in Edinburgh to that effect.

Mr. George C. Oke, chief clerk to the Lord Mayor at the Mansion House, produced the original deposition taken by him at the justice's room, of a witness named James M'Kelvie, an Edinburgh detective, who had died since the committal of the prisoners for trial.

M'Kelvie said: "I am a private detective officer, residing at 120 Nicholson Street, Edinburgh. I received certain information from Gibson, Craig & Co. of Edinburgh, writers to the *Signet*, and in consequence of this I watched the house No. 22 Cumberland Street, Edinburgh, on Wednesday last, April 2d, from about twenty-five minutes past ten o'clock in the morning. It is a private house. The prisoner came out of the house to the door, looked around, went back again and remained in about twenty minutes, and then came out, and from his appearance I suspected that he was George Bidwell. I watched him and saw where he went. He posted a letter in a pillar-box, and then he went to a stationer's shop, and then to a baker's shop. When standing at the door he looked 'round and came out and went 'round the corner, and in about twenty yards he set off to run as hard as he could. I ran after him. He ran into a blacksmith shop, from which he turned back and passed me. I took no notice of him as he did so. He walked on a little, and then started to run again. He then ran down Drummond Place and Scotland Street. He went through Scotland Street lane, swung himself over the church railings, and jumped over several stone walls, one after the other. I followed him, and he went through a private house, into Scotland Street again. I got 'round to the street by another way, and was there as soon as he. I ran him to Duncan Street, Stockbridge, in which he came to a standstill and could not run any farther. *He made several thrusts at me with a stick which he had in his hand. I took out of my pocket a small baton and held it out as if it were a pistol, and told him to stand and be a gentleman, and give me his hand ; to be a brother, and not a coward.*" [Pure fancy and self-glorification. — G. B.] "I got hold of his hand and held him. I called him ' brother,' because I fancied he gave me a Masonic sign. I got assistance, and drove him in a cab to Messrs. Gibson, Craig & Co.'s office, and said, ' You are George Bidwell ! You are wanted for the forgery on the Bank of England ! He spoke some foreign language, and I do not know what he said. I understood him to say that he was not a Fenian. I said, ' I know that ; I am not looking for any Fenians.' When I got him to the office I asked him whether he could give any account of himself, and why he ran over those private grounds and stone walls, and he would not give me any answer. A few minutes later he said that he was subject to giddiness in the head, and took to those fits of running away. [Great laughter in court.] I asked him what I might call him, and he said, ' You may call me James, if you like.' He would give no answer to any question, after that. He spoke in very broken English, like a Frenchman. I gave him a book to read. He said that either his father or mother belonged to France, and the other to Germany. He also said that he had been to Paris. I told him that there was an old friend of his doing five years there just now. [More laughter.] I bound up his leg, which was cut and bleeding. He was then handed over to the police in Edinburgh, and I had nothing more to do with him. The stationer's shop into which I saw him go was kept by Mr. Anderson. I did not search him or the lodgings. I only watched the lodgings."

Mr. John Robert Gray, assistant to Messrs. Hawes & Son, 14 Cranbourne Street, jewelers, said that in December last he sold a watch to a person giving the name of George Bidwell, and the address 7 Upper Gloucester Place. The same person called again on January 29th, when witness sold him a brilliant ring for 100 guineas. He paid with a bank-note for £100 and £5 in gold. He also sold him a carbuncle and diamond set for 50 guineas. He paid that sum in gold. The same day witness paid the £100 note into his masters' account at the City Bank. He afterwards saw the jewelry that he had sold to George Bidwell at the Mansion House, and he identified it.

Mr. Walter Weston Goss, cashier at the Bond Street branch of the City Bank, deposed that Messrs. Hawes & Son, jewelers, kept an account there, and on January 29th a £100 bank-note was paid into the credit of their account. [This was one of the notes paid to McDonald at the bank on January 28th, in exchange for gold.]

William Gardner said he was in the service of his father, a commission and diamond merchant at Edinburgh. In February last he was living at Barnesbury, and in consequence of a letter he went to 17 St. James Place on the evening of the 27th. He asked for Mr. McDonald, and was taken to a room on the ground floor, where he saw the prisoner of that name. He showed him some diamonds. After looking at them, the prisoner desired him to call again the next morning. Witness did so, and the prisoner purchased one large and three small diamonds, for £300. He gave

him in payment three £100 bank-notes. Witness made out
a bill and handed him a receipt for the money. On that
occasion McDonald showed him a dressing-bag which he said
had been given to him. Witness returned to the house in
the afternoon, at McDonald's request, and saw the prisoner
George Bidwell in company with McDonald. Bidwell looked
at some diamonds, but declined to purchase them.

Mr. Benjamin Nathan, a diamond merchant in St. James
Terrace, Lambeth Road, said that on August 24th last he was
at Messrs. Welby's shop in Garrick Street, and saw there the
prisoner George Bidwell. He sold some diamonds to him for
£63. He gave the name of Charles Warren, and the address
Charing Cross Hotel. He subsequently made appointments
to meet him at that and other hotels. On March 6th last he
saw him again at Messrs. Welby's. They went to Bibra's
Hotel in St. Martin's Lane, where he sold him four diamond
lockets, two pearl pins, one turquoise and pearl pin in the
shape of a parrot, a small keyless watch, a gold necklet, with
three hooks to hold lockets, and a vinaigrette. [He sold me
the pearls for genuine; they were bogus.— G. B.] The bill
came to £114, which the prisoner paid him. The prisoner
became somewhat excited on that occasion.

Mr. John Henry Welby, wholesale diamond merchant in
Garrick Street, Covent Garden, saw and recognized the prisoners, George McDonald and George Bidwell. They were
both at his place of business in February last. They had
come previously, but no business was done. On March 6th
he remembered seeing George Bidwell and the witness, Mr.
Nathan, in his shop. The prisoner, whom he knew by the
name of Warren, selected some diamonds of the value of
£280. He paid for them in Dutch bank-notes.

Mr. Edward Francis Gedge, an underwriter at the Royal
Exchange Assurance Office, said he knew the prisoner McDonald. On February 24th last, he called there and asked to
have some American bonds in a packet addressed to New
York insured. Witness filled up a slip containing the num-

bers of the bonds, which the prisoner had called over to him
from the bonds themselves. The policy was made out in the
name of E. N. Hills, and the sum insured was £2,100. He
signed the slip " For E. N. Hills, Geo. McDonald." The
policy was never called for. He subsequently instructed him
to insure other bonds of the value of £3,600, in the name of
"Austin Bidwell, New York." The prisoner on that occasion
brought a slip with the numbers of the bonds already written.

Mr. George Peter Richardson, a clerk in the Royal
Exchange Insurance Office, said he saw McDonald on February 25th, when he came about the second policy mentioned
by Mr. Gedge. The prisoner requested the witness to take
charge of the two policies, as he was going abroad for some
time with Mr. Hills.

Mr. Robert C. M. Bowles, said in April last he was a
banker in the Strand. He had never seen the prisoner Austin
Bidwell. He denied that the prisoner had withdrawn £7,500
from his bank, as he had represented to the manager of the
Continental Bank. No one named Bidwell, Horton, or Warren, ever banked with him.

Mr. Henry Harris, the country manager to Messrs. Baum
& Son, money changers, 58 Lombard Street, deposed that he
knew the prisoner George Bidwell by the name of Nicholl or
Nicholls. He first saw him on November 30th last, when he
exchanged £400 in Bank of England notes into foreign money
for him. On January 21st he saw him again, and sold him
£1,220 worth of French gold and notes, for which he paid in
bank-notes. On January 24th he saw a person who gave the
name and address as it now appeared in their books, " Voges,
28 George Street, Manchester Square," for whom he exchanged
£500 in bank-notes into Dutch money. On February 8th he
saw George Bidwell again. On that occasion he brought
£250 in English gold, and the witness gave him Austrian
and Dutch money in exchange. On the 10th he came again,
and brought £170 in bank-notes which he exchanged for foreign money. On February 28th he saw him again, when he

brought £200 in bank-notes. He said he wanted to exchange them for light English gold, remarking that he desired to pay back in his own coin a friend who had a day or two previously given him light gold. Witness took him to Messrs. Barclays' and got the notes exchanged for him.

[The sovereigns were delivered from the bank in sealed bags containing 1,000, and on some occasions, I merely broke the seal and removed the slip showing the date when it was put up,

MACHINE FOR WEIGHING GOLD.

tied the bags up again, and sent them directly back to re-exchange for notes — yet there would be several shillings to pay for loss on light sovereigns. After being in circulation, most sovereigns become "light"—when run through the very delicate weighing machines in use at the Bank of England. But how about those I returned without removing them from the bags? Knowing that all who bring gold to the bank are expecting a deduction for light weights, is such an instance as above some clerk's "perquisite"? Afterwards, I purchased the light gold, the witness Harris mentions, to mix in with that taken from the bank, so that when it was re-weighed, it would convey the impression to the weigh-master that it had been for some time in circulation. In his opening speech Mr. Giffard was correct in stating that this was done to break the connection so that the Bank of England notes could not be traced to us.— G. B.]

Mr. Harold Anthony Smith, clerk to Messrs. Baring Bros., said on January 29th last, he received an application for a letter of credit for £1,000 on New York. The person applying for it gave the name of E. N. Hales. The applicant being asked his address, replied "Brighton." Witness inquired if that was sufficient, and he said it was. The letter was paid for in ten bank-notes for £100 each. (These notes had been paid to McDonald on the 28th, in exchange for gold.) Mr. James Searle, Junior, said he was a stock-broker at Bartholomew House in partnership with Mr. Watson. He knew the prisoner McDonald. He came to their office on February 21st, and asked if they were members of the stock exchange and stock and share brokers. He replied they were, and he inquired in turn his name and who had introduced him to them. He replied he had just arrived from abroad, and was staying at Chiselhurst, and he could give no introduction. Witness told him it was not their custom to do business with any one without an introduction. He answered that he did not know it was necessary, and that he intended to purchase £10,000 worth of American bonds, and that he would pay for them immediately in bank-notes or gold. Witness still declined to do business with him without an introduction, and he left. Next day the prisoner brought to them a letter of credit on Messrs. J. S. Morgan & Co., and they, knowing that Messrs. Morgan did not grant such letters until after inquiry, consented to take that as sufficient introduction. They purchased for him £10,000 worth of American bonds which he duly paid for. On the 1st of March, he came again, and said he had £20,000 to invest. He did not make any purchase on that occasion.

Mr. Alfred Joseph Baker, clerk to Messrs. Jay Cooke, M'Culloch & Co., American bankers, Lombard Street, deposed that he knew the prisoner Austin Bidwell under the name of F. A. Warren, and first saw him some time in May, 1872. He next saw him in August, with reference to the purchase of some Portuguese stock. He first saw the prisoner Noyes on January 9th, and afterwards on twelve different occasions, when he purchased American bonds on behalf of C. J. Horton. Being cross-examined by Mr. McIntyre, Q. C., and Mr. Ribton, he said Austin Bidwell made several purchases of bonds in May, August, and September, 1872. American bonds were purchased to a very large amount in the city. Last year witness's house alone put upon the market $75,000,000 of United States bonds. Witness at first understood that Noyes himself was Mr. Horton. But the prisoner afterwards told him his own name was Noyes and that he was a clerk of Horton's. On one occasion he said his master was about to take an office in the Poultry. There was nothing at all unusual in the transactions with the prisoners. In re-examination by Mr. Giffard, he said on the 28th of February, the day before Noyes was arrested, the prisoner ordered the firm to purchase $25,000 in United States bonds, and such purchase was effected, but the bonds were never delivered.

Mr. Alfred Lidington, chief cashier to Messrs. Clews, Habicht & Co., American bankers, Old Broad Street, said he knew the prisoner George Bidwell by the name of W. J. Spaulding. He bought some bonds of them in January last, and paid with six £100 notes. (These were notes received by McDonald at the bank in exchange for gold.) A few days afterwards he called again and paid a small balance due to the firm. He afterwards bought three bills of exchange, and asked witness if they were good acceptances. Witness promised to inquire, and he left them. He subsequently brought eight or ten other bills for discount. (These were the bills produced by the American witness, Mr. Duncan.) Witness inquired if he had not a banking account, and he replied "Not at present." Witness asked him to sign his name and address in their signature book, and he wrote "W. J. Spaulding, Brighton." Witness said that Brighton was a large place, and that they must have some other address. Prisoner said that it was quite sufficient, and any letter or telegram so addressed would reach him. The firm eventually declined to discount the bill.

Mr. Albert Jordan, another clerk to Messrs. Clews, Habicht & Co., said he was present when the bonds referred to were delivered to George Bidwell. He identified from the package addressed to "G. C. Brownell, N. Y.," some of the bonds so sold to the prisoner. Replying to Mr. Ribton, he said that he remembered seeing Noyes on the 5th of February, when he told him he was clerk to Mr. Horton. He afterwards received a letter from him signed "for C. J. Horton, E. Noyes." He gave as a reference the Continental Bank, and witness accompanied him there. He was there identified as Horton's clerk. Noyes told him Horton was an American merchant then staying at the Terminus Hotel, London Bridge.

Mr. Henry West said he was clerk to Messrs. J. S. Morgan & Co., American merchants. He knew the prisoner George McDonald. He called at Messrs. Morgans on the first of February and wanted to open an account with them with a sum of £1,280. Witness said it was usual, before doing business, to receive some reference, and the prisoner then produced a letter of credit from their Paris correspondents. They consented for the time to receive the £1,280 on deposit, and promised to make further inquiries. On February 20th witness handed him back the money by a check on the London Joint Stock Bank. He gave them a receipt.

Mr. Thomas Straker, an engraver and printer at 16 Ivy-lane, Paternoster Row, said he knew the prisoner George Bidwell by the name of Brooks. He called upon him about December 18th, and he said he had been recommended to him by Messrs. Nelson. He brought two copper plates with blank

DEPUTY GOVERNOR CALLING THE ROLL AT WOKING PRISON.

bill forms on them, and asked witness if he did copper-plate work. Witness replied that he did, and prisoner inquired what he would make him 500 impressions for. He said fifteen shillings. One of the plates had the figure " 1 " upon it, and the other had the word " first," and the prisoner desired that this arrangement should be reversed. Witness said that he could easily do that, but that he could not execute the work before Christmas. The prisoner urged him to do it before that date, and promised to give him five shillings extra if he did. Some of the forms were ready before Christmas-day, and were delivered to the prisoner. Afterwards he printed some forms with the word " second " and with the figure " 2 " upon them. He saw the prisoner early in January, when he ordered him to print a few copies. He next gave him orders to engrave some names of places on separate slips of copper, namely, Cairo, Bombay, Hong Kong, Valparaiso, Yokohama, and Alexandria. Some of them were afterwards inserted in bill forms. He also engraved for him the names of the Union Bank of London, and the London and Westminster Bank, and printed them in the body of the bills. On one occasion he brought him four plates with ornamental scrolls upon them, and the prisoner selected other scrolls from his pattern-book. He put impressions of some of those scrolls upon the bill forms. He also engraved for the prisoner two plates of bill forms, and made impressions of them. In the center of the scrolls he printed the names respectively of H. C. Streeter, T. Perkins, D. R. Howell, and Juan Perez, which were inserted in the bills. Witness made a mistake in spelling the name "Juan Perez," upon which the prisoner was very cross, and the work had to be done over again. The last time he saw him was on the 22d and 23d of February. On an average he used to see him twice a week. He told witness he was getting up samples of bills of exchange. On the last occasion he took away all the bill forms and plates, with the exception of four scroll blocks, which he left behind by accident. He asked witness to show him how to erase the bills from the

23

plates, and witness did so, remarking after the operation that he could not produce another impression of that same bill if he paid him £100 for doing so. No suspicion was excited at any time. He did about one hundred copies. Witness was shown twenty-three of the forged bills, upon which he identified impressions of the various stamps he made for the prisoner. He also said they were all written on blank forms supplied by him. The bills were as follows: one for £2,500, dated Hamburg, December 26th, drawn by Oppenheim & Co., and purporting to be accepted by the London and Westminster Bank; one for £143 9s. 6d., and two for £1,000 each, dated Cairo, December 30th, drawn by T. Perkins, and accepted at the Bank of Belgium and Holland; three for £1,000 each, dated Valparaiso, December 18th, drawn by H. C. Streeter, and accepted by the London and Westminster Bank; three for £1,000 each, dated Yokohama, December 18th, drawn by D. R. Howell, and accepted by the London and Westminster Bank; one for £2,000, another for £1,500, and a third for £1,000, dated Valparaiso, November 18th, drawn by H. C. Streeter, and accepted by the London and Westminster Bank; seven for £1,000 each, dated Bombay, January 16th, drawn by Juan Perez, and accepted by the Union Bank of London; and three for £1,000 each, dated Valparaiso, December 28th, drawn by H. C. Streeter, and accepted by the London and Westminster Bank. When the bills left his hands they were all blank, and were just as Messrs. Waterlow or any other firm might show their customers as specimens.

At this stage the trial was adjourned until Monday morning, at ten o'clock, Mr. Justice Archibald observing that he was sorry the jury had to be detained over a Sunday. The foreman expressed a hope that they might be allowed to attend divine service together, and the judge said there was no objection to that if it could be arranged. The jury were then taken as before to the City Terminus Hotel in Cannon Street.

CHAPTER XXXIV.

THE case for the prosecution was resumed on Monday
morning. The interest of the public continued un-
abated, and there was no standing-room unoccupied.

William Mitchell, a die-sinker and stamp-cutter in Bell
Alley, Moorgate Street, was called. He said he remembered
the prisoner, George Bidwell, coming to his shop in November
last, and giving an order for an endorsement-stamp. On the
bill produced for £1,000 there was an impression from the
die which he cut for the prisoner. Being cross-examined by
the prisoner, George Bidwell, in the temporary absence of his
counsel, the witness gave reasons for believing the stamp on
the bill was that from the die he cut for him, and that Bidwell was the man who brought him the order. The man had
then no whiskers, but he had a mustache. The words were
cut in very ordinary block letters, and there were similar
letters in type. He had very little doubt that the words in
question could be printed in ordinary type, but it was impossible to fit up words of the same dimensions, having regard
to the relative distances, in the same way witness's stamp was
fitted up. Supposing the stamp had been lost, another could

have been made, but the engraver would have required something to guide him as to the relative distances of the letters.

Mr. George Boole Chaloner, one of the late firm of Nelson & Co., of Oxford Arms-Passage, Paternoster Row, said he knew the prisoner, George Bidwell. He first saw him on the 9th of December last. The prisoner then called and gave

BANK-NOTE STORE-ROOM, BANK OF ENGLAND

him, without any name, an order for an electro-plate to be copied from a paper he produced. Witness was ordered to set it up in tpye, from which an electro-plate was to be made. The prisoner gave no name or address, but paid two shillings on account. Nothing further passed on that occasion. Witness afterwards executed the order, mounted the plate on a piece of wood, and then took a proof from it. In correcting the proof he made an alteration of a single letter. A few days afterwards the prisoner, George Bidwell, called for the stamp, and witness gave it to him, with some printing-ink, for which he asked, and some brass rules from which lines could be printed. Witness did not then know the prisoner's name or address. He saw him again on January 28th, when he brought witness four forms of bills of exchange, which he wished to be imitated as nearly as possible with type which he selected. This was executed, and fifty copies of it were printed, the bill forms being left with witness meanwhile. One of them was headed " Calais," and that was executed. The prisoner had corrected the proof of that one, after which a few impressions were taken. He selected six scrolls from a specimen-book, and took four of them away. The prisoner called at various times until nearly the end of February. In December witness had a conversation with him about lithography. The prisoner produced some lithograph forms of bills, and asked witness if he knew any lithographer in the neighborhood. Witness, in reply, mentioned the name of Straker of Ivy Lane. On January 28th the prisoner paid a sovereign on account, and gave the name J. R. Nelson, adding that he was staying at Brighton. Witness being now shown a batch of forged bills, said he found on them all an impression of the German endorsement-stamp he had cut for George Bidwell. (Mr. Poland said that included the bill mentioned in the indictment.) The device in the corner of one of the forged bills produced, witness said was printed from an impression of the bill forms he had set up for the prisoner. It was a bill for £900, drawn at Amsterdam, in January last. Being cross-examined by the prisoner, George Bidwell, witness said his place of business was not far from Straker's, in Ivy Lane, and that he (Bidwell) was the man who gave the name of Nelson. Witness did not see him at Straker's. He next saw him (Bidwell) at the Mansion House, as he was being put to the bar of the justice-room. The impressions on the forged bills were so like those of the plate ones made for the prisoner that even a mistake was imitated, if it was an imitation. They appeared to be impressions from the type which witness set up. The mistake was in German, and witness, not being acquainted with German, did not perceive it at the time. The form was set up in type, the like of which could have been procured from any other printing-office.

William Cheshire, an engraver in Paternoster Row, said he knew the prisoner, George Bidwell, and saw him at his shop between December and February. He came in December, and gave an order for some lettering for the names of various Continental towns, and wished them done in fancy type, including Amsterdam, Lubeck, Bremen, Hamburg, Berlin, and others. A drawing was prepared with that view, and submitted to George Bidwell. Witness afterwards executed it, and Bidwell called and took the blocks away, paying for them, and giving the name "Bohn." Witness did other work for the prisoner, and now produced twenty-five impressions from the stamps he cut for him. In cross-examination witness said any other engraver could have executed similar work with perhaps few small differences. Replying to questions by George Bidwell, he said he first saw him (Bidwell) after his arrest at a cell in the Mansion House. The prisoner was first brought from his cell and shown him, he being asked to take off his cap, and no other prisoner being present. Witness said he recognized him in a moment, though he looked ill, and his appearance was changed. That was about four months after having first seen him. He had not the smallest doubt the prisoner, George Bidwell, was the man.

Mr. James Dalton was next called. He was quite deaf and partly dumb, and had in consequence to be examined through an interpreter by the aid of the finger alphabet. He was an engraver and wood-cutter at 21 Paternoster Row, of the firm of Carter & Dalton. During last November he first saw the prisoner, George Bidwell. On the 4th of December the prisoner called and showed him two pieces of paper with scrolls on them. On December 7th he gave witness an order to print the words "London and Westminster Bank," and for some Dutch lettering. On the 9th he had an order from him for the words "Hamburg Banking Co.," and "Paid"; and he identified a forged bill, part of which he said was printed from one of his blocks. On the 6th of January he received an order for an acceptance block in the name of "Smith, Payne & Smiths," and he identified a proof taken from the block which he had executed for George Bidwell. From time to time, he said, George Bidwell gave him pieces of paper from which he was to print. The prisoner, when he called, communicated with the witness by writing on slips of paper, and the witness produced some of the original writing from which he had to engrave. The prisoner took some pains, on his visits, to make witness understand the German lettering. He gave one order on December 7th, which witness handed to another person to execute, because it was in Dutch lettering. Witness put in an authentic list of the work he did, from which it appeared that each of the forged bills had upon it some of the work he had done for the prisoner. Witness, in cross-examination, said he could fix the dates on which the work was done by him for the prisoner. The order, "London and Westminster Bank," he said was given on the 7th December. He pointed out peculiarities in the forged bills by which he identified work he had executed for the prisoner, and explained that it ought to have been done in brass instead of wood, in which he was asked to do it, for in brass, he said, the lettering would have been sharper and more defined. He said he cut a great many dates and numbers, running through a month, but they were all separate. Witness went into other details in answer to questions, but they were mostly technical and uninteresting. Replying to Mr. Giffard, witness recognized the order in writing he gave to Mr. Evans, another engraver, to be executed for him. It was of a technical nature.

Mr. George Henry Evans, a wood engraver at Newport

Farringdon Street, was called, and recognized the written order Mr. Dalton gave him for some work on December 7th, and he produced a proof impression from one of the blocks he cut for him. Being shown some of the forged bills, he said he recognized the impression of an endorsement made from the engraving he cut.

Mr. George E. Russell proved that in September last, he was in the employ of Messrs. Wyon, engravers. He remembered the prisoner George Bidwell coming to them at the latter end of August, and giving an order for some address cards in name " George Bidwell." He afterward brought a seal to be engraved with a monogram and a coat-of-arms. He had asked witness to look into an heraldic work for the name " Bidwell." Witness found several persons of that name, and the prisoner selected the arms of one which he instructed him to engrave on the seal, and also to make a painting on vellum. He gave two addresses, one being No. 1 Langham Street, and the other, Hotel de l'Europe, Havre. Witness afterward received a letter from him abroad, dated December 13th, from the Grand hotel de Paris, Trouville, requesting him to send the seal there. The seal was engraved with the monogram on the one side, and the coat of arms on the other, and he sent them to him in a registered letter, receiving afterwards, a written acknowledgment from him.

Jonathan Pope, a city police constable, proved that on the first of March, the prisoner Noyes was given into his custody at the Continental Bank in Lombard Street, and that he found on him at the police station a check for £100 on that bank (drawn by C. J. Horton, payable to self or order, and endorsed by Horton), £110 in bank-notes, and a case containing papers which he afterwards handed to Sergeant Spittle. The prisoner was transacting business at the time at the counter of the bank, and his first exclamation was that witness had no right to take him without a warrant.

John Spittle, a city detective sergeant, proved that he told the prisoner Noyes, on the day of his arrest, that he had given an address at Durant's Hotel, although he had left that hotel three weeks ago. The prisoner afterwards said that he had no settled address. He added, if he had an opportunity, that he might find Horton. He was eventually charged and examined before the Lord Mayor, when he explained that the reason for giving his address Durant's Hotel was that Horton had told him to go back there. Witness then spoke of having, with Sergeant Smith, brought the prisoner George Bidwell to London from Edinburgh, after he had been arrested there by the deceased witness M'Kelvie. On being asked if he were a naturalized American, he begged to be excused answering the question, and it was not pressed. At the police station in London, on being asked his name, he said he would rather not give it at that time. He gave an address in Cumberland Street, Edinburgh, but without any number. Witness produced copies of the daily *Telegraph*, from the 6th to the 11th of January last, containing an advertisement of Noyes for a situation of trust or partnership, " in a light business, and requiring a capital of not more than £300." Witness in cross-examination by Mr. Ribton, produced a bundle of letters addressed to the prisoner Noyes in reply to that advertisement. In re-examination, he produced several envelopes and letters which he had found on Noyes, some of them addressed, Terminus Hotel, London, Room No. 6, some addressed Durant's Hotel, Manchester Square.

Mrs. Ann Laverock, of 22 Cumberland Street, London, recognized the prisoner George Bidwell as a person to whom she let lodgings on the 11th of March last, he giving the name of Coutant. He brought a portmanteau, and said he had come from Rotterdam, and had been seasick on crossing. She asked if he were a Frenchman. He answered in the negative, but said that his parents were French. He staid in her house till the 2d of April.

David Ferguson, a detective police officer in Edinburgh, proved that he searched George Bidwell's lodgings there after his arrest, and found, among other things, a letter which he handed over to the police authorities. He also found on his person a quantity of jewelry, diamonds, and a sum of money.

Michael Hayden, a city detective sergeant, deposed that he went to Havana about the 13th of April, and saw the prisoner Austin Bidwell there. He was subsequently given into the charge of witness and Sergeant Green, and brought to England. He found on him six American bonds for $1,000 each, two for $500 each, one for $100, and some money and jewelry. Before he went to Havana, witness searched McDonald's luggage, and found a letter to him from Austin Bidwell.

Mr. Sam. Wilson Robinson, said that he lived in Glasgow, and in the course of May, 1872, he took a voyage to South America, in the steamer *Lucitania*. The prisoner George Bidwell was among his fellow passengers.

Mr. Charles Chabot, the expert, said that he had examined several documents proved to be in the handwriting of Austin Bidwell, including his name in the signature books of the Western Branch of the Bank of England, and the Continental Bank, various credit slips, and several letters to Col. Francis. Taking into his hand the forged bill upon which the present indictment is framed, and other bills, he said the indorsements " F. A. Warren " upon them were in the same handwriting. The letters found in McDonald's luggage and signed "Austin" were also written by him. The signatures to the checks " F. A. Warren " and " C. J. Horton " were undoubtedly in his handwriting. [A fine "expert"! I wrote all those signatures of Warren and Horton myself, except one. — G. B.] He had also looked at some insurance slips, and a receipt for a check given by Messrs. Morgan & Co., which had been proved to be in McDonald's handwriting. He believed the body of the bill for £1,000 (the subject of indictment), and the signature to it, " H. C. Streeter," and the letter to Mr. de Wael, a banker in Holland, signed "F. A. Warren," and dated November 30, 1872, were written by McDonald. He had likewise seen a large number of letters written by George Bidwell, admitted to be in his handwriting.

The signature " H. J. Spaulding," to one of the bills, was without doubt written by the same person, as was also the filling up of two forged bills on the Bank of Belgium and Holland. The letters to Col. Francis, dated from Birmingham, between the 24th of January and the 27th of February last, purporting to come from F. A. Warren, and containing most of the forged bills, were all written by George Bidwell. The same observation applied to the body of the checks on the Western Branch of the Bank of England, while the indorsements to those checks were for the most part in the handwriting of George McDonald. He had also examined various letters to different persons in America, and he believed that they were all written by George Bidwell. Looking at the credit-slips in the Continental Bank, signed by Noyes on behalf of C. J. Horton, the agreement proved to have been executed by him, and a letter signed " Ed.", enclosing a draft for £1,000 to a relative in America, he expressed his conviction that they were all in the handwriting of Noyes, as were also the bodies of the various checks on the Continental Bank. The telegram from " Spaulding, Langham Hotel," to " Edward Hills, Clarendon Hotel, New York," was in George Bidwell's handwriting, and that from George McDonald to " E. N. Hills, St. Denis Hotel, New York," was in that of McDonald's. Replying to McIntyre, the witness said he had had no assistance from other experts in making that investigation. He believed all the signatures to the checks of the Western Branch of the Bank of England had been written by Warren (A. B.) at one sitting. He had seen altogether about one hundred and forty bills all bearing the indorsement " F. A. Warren." Some of those indorsements were in Austin Bidwell's handwriting, but the great majority of them were not. The signatures " C. J. Horton " to the checks on the Continental Bank were all in the handwriting of Austin Bidwell, and were, he should say, written at one time. [I wrote them myself.— G. B.]

Mr. Chas. Anthony Pye, a clerk in the Western Branch, proved that on the 17th of January last, he cashed a check for

£1,500, signed by "F. A. Warren," across the counter, giving in exchange ten notes for £100 each, and one for £500. (Some of these notes were afterwards changed into foreign money at Messrs. Baum's by George Bidwell.)

Peter Steinmayer, a waiter at the Cannon Street Hotel, deposed that he recognized the prisoner Noyes, who occupied a room there from January 30th to February 28th. He knew him by the name of Horton. He used to come three or four times a week in the middle of the day, and stay on each occasion about half an hour. No books were kept in the room, and there was no sign of any business being transacted. Mr. Giffard, Q. C., said that would be the case for the prosecution. At this point, the court having sat seven hours, the trial was adjourned until next day. The jury as before, was taken to the City Terminus Hotel.

Chapter XXXV.

THIS was the most interesting day in a trial of unprece-
dented interest. The court-room of the Old Bailey
was packed, and, as on other occasions, the lobbies were
filled and a crowd in the street waiting in the hope of eventually obtaining admission. Many of the nobility and gentry
were present.

Mr. Giffard, Q. C., put in several letters written by the
prisoners, and they were read by Mr. Read, the deputy clerk
of arraigns. The first was written by Noyes to a brother in
America, enclosing a letter of credit for £1,000 obtained by
him on January 29th from Messrs. Baring Brothers:

LONDON, January 29, 1873.

DEAR BROTHER J——, — I have this day registered a letter to
you containing £1,000 sterling, which you will collect to the best
advantage. The bankers will charge from one-eighth to one-quarter
per cent. for collection. There is a premium on London Exchange.
Before collecting it post yourself as to exchange, so that they will
not charge you exorbitant rates. On it you will get two premiums
— that on London, and the difference between the value of gold and

(365)

greenbacks. I think it will amount to about $5,500 ; I cannot tell exactly, but do the best you can. After you collect it carry $1,400 over to C—— to pay S—— $750; he will also pay that bond of $600 that father owes H—— K—— for that woodland. The bond is indorsed by J—— McL——, so you will see that K—— will sicken at the prospect of getting a hold of our homestead. The bond in Pratt Street let remain until my return. Take $250 yourself, to buy your wife a $150 sewing machine and other things as a present from me. Do not let anyone else know but that you bought them yourself. Also, deduct your expenses to go to Spring-field and out home. Also, hand Robert C—— $50 if he should want it as a loan. Take a receipt for it, to be paid to father when conven-ient, if I am not at home. The balance you may place to my account in the First National Bank of Hartford, subject to be drawn by my sister in case of accident to me, or death, or a longer absence than six months. Make it draw interest. If they will not give interest, put it into the Etna Bank. H—— will introduce you. I am trying to persuade a friend of mine, an English gentleman, to go to America and enter business. If I succeed it will perhaps throw us together. It is not certain when I shall return to Amer-ica. These Englishmen are such sticklers for country it is hard to start them. I confess that I am beginning to like to stay in Eu-rope. [Poor fellow! He is staying abroad longer than he likes.— G. B.] More anon. Yours ever, ED.

The following letters were written by George Bidwell shortly after his escape from Ireland, while in hiding at Edinburgh :

EDINBURGH, March 13, 1873.

DEAR M., — Your friend has had a series of the most extraor-dinary adventures since you saw him; a hell's chase, and no mis-take. His nerve has stood him through two taps on shoulder and several encounters with detectives. He has been a Fenian, a priest, a professor, a Frenchman, a German, a Russian, who could speak only a "veree leetle Englese, mais un peu de Français et Allemand," and a deaf and dumb man with a slate and pencil — all in the space of a week.

March 18.

It made me nearly sick to read what I enclose. [Alluding to what I saw in the papers, showing how our real names had transpired, through my plans in the way of precautions not having been executed as I all along supposed.—G. B.] It is all right as long as I keep inland, but the moment I touch the borders there is the devil to pay. I ran through an awful gauntlet last week in Ireland. Who would have dreamed they could have got on track so soon as that! There was a job put up from Hastings, and I had a hard rub at Cx [meaning Charing Cross]. I am delaying, as every day changes my appearance. Of course it is impossible to say what move or when l shall make one, but my present opinion is that I shall be in London when this reaches you. The telegraph, and I suspect the post also, is an open book for these parties. I suppose they have procured special permit. Therefore, do not on any account use the telegraph.

Mr. Albert Gearing, proprietor of the Terminus Hotel, London Bridge, who was called at the request of Mr. Ribton, proved that the prisoner, Austin Bidwell, in the name of C. J. Horton, hired on the 11th of January last a sitting-room in his hotel, and that he subsequently introduced the prisoner Noyes as his clerk. The room was kept until February 21st.

That was the case for the prosecution. A formal objection was taken by Mr. Metcalf, Q. C., on the part of McDonald, that it had not been proved, in conformity with the Extradition Act, that the crime with which he was now charged was that for which his surrender was obtained in America, but it was overruled by the judge.

Mr. Giffard, Q. C., then summed up the evidence adduced on the part of the prosecution. He said he was entitled, under recent statute, to elicit from his learned friends on the other side, whether they intended to call witnesses or not, and they having informed him that they were not about to present any further evidence to the jury, it became his duty to close, with a few remarks, the case which he had presented to their decision. It was clear as a matter of law that if the particular bill which they were now discussing was forged and uttered in pursuance of a common design and scheme participated in by all the prisoners, all of them were equally guilty, though only one of them actually traced the signature

upon it. The question, therefore, for the jury was whether
all or any of the prisoners had participated in a design to forge
and utter that among a great many other bills. Although
the unity of design comprised, as he urged, the whole of the
prisoners, yet the evidence applicable to each was, however,
identical, for they were all tainted with the same guilty
design. A scheme of this character and magnitude was happily very rare, if not quite unknown, in this country; for it
was incredible that persons like the prisoners should have
sought to taint the whole currency of commerce in this country by a portentous crime of this nature. The bank authorities had been twitted for being so easily led into a net of that
kind, but let the jury consider what were the circumstances in
which Colonel Francis, the manager of the Western Branch,
was placed. His customer was a person who pretended to be
conducting large commercial transactions in this country and
all over the Continent, and his bills were of the highest possible character, and were discounted and paid with facility.
If there had been ever any genuine business transacted by
the prisoner, Austin Bidwell, let him call witness to prove it;
but in the absence of such proof, he denounced that business
as one for the mere manufacture of forged bills, and a device
to dispose of proceeds. Genuine bills to the amount of between £8,000 and £9,000 were first of all discounted by the
Bank of England, and these bills, it had been proved, were
purchased on the Continent by one or other of the prisoners.
They not only established the credit of Warren at the bank,
but they served as the models for the forged bills which were
subsequently sent in. In the forged bill in question, the form
upon which it was written, and the various stamps on its surface, were purchased by George Bidwell. It was filled in and
signed by McDonald, and it bore the endorsement of Austin
Bidwell [Austin was out of England, and did not put on the
endorsement. — G. B.], to whose credit the amount of the
discount was placed. It was therefore shown in this one
instance alone that three of the prisoners had been concerned

PREPARING FOR EXAMINATION BY MEDICAL OFFICER.

in forging and uttering the bill. £65,000 (about $325,000) had been expended by Noyes in the purchase of American bonds, and £10,000 by McDonald, and the rest of the money had gone in other directions — the whole of it having first been withdrawn from the Western Branch, then paid into Horton's account at the Continental Bank, and subsequently changed from gold into notes, and *vice versa.* The examination of the witnesses had proved that Austin Bidwell had left England about the 18th of January, but though absent he was nevertheless engaged in the fraud, for he was found purchasing bills on the Continent, which served as models for other forged bills. [No bills purchased by him after January 18th served as models for forged bills. I supposing him to be on his way home, made it necessary that his continued presence on the Continent should be concealed from me. It was his engagement which caused him to remain in Europe. — G. B.] As to George Bidwell, it was proved beyond question that he had procured various stamps and plates from five different engravers, and that all those stamps appeared on the whole of the forged acceptances, and that he had written from Birmingham the letters to Col. Francis enclosing bills, many of which bore his endorsement. McDonald had been also shown to have filled in the bill forms, and forged the names of the drawers and acceptors. Mr. Giffard then referred to the case of the prisoner Noyes, urging that, so far from being an innocent clerk, as was alleged, he was one of the most active participators in the fraud, and that, like the others, he shared in the proceeds. In conclusion, he advised the jury to receive with great caution any statement which the prisoners, or any one of them, might make as to the innocence or guilt of the rest, observing that it would not be under oath, and that the person making it would not be exposed to any cross-examination, and could not be interrogated by the court. [David Howell, our solicitor, informed the prosecution of the subject on which McDonald and myself were intending to address the court and jury, thus enabling Mr. Giffard to forestall and

24

frustrate any effects our subsequent statement of facts might
have had in favor of my brother and Noyes.—G. B.] He
asked the jury to say by their verdict that all the prisoners
had been engaged in one common design to commit a crime,
the magnitude of which was almost unexampled in the history
of this country.

Mr. Metcalf, Q. C., addressing the court, said he had
attended very carefully to the whole case on the part of
McDonald, together with the summing up for the prosecution,
and he did not think it would be attended with any good
effect for him to address the jury. More than that, McDonald himself desired to make a statement with the consent of
the Bench. Mr. Besley made a similar announcement on the
part of the prisoner George Bidwell. The prisoner George
McDonald then proceeded to address the jury, and the whole
audience listened with deep attention. He said:

The statement I have to make to you, gentlemen of the jury,
was alluded to towards the end of Mr. Giffard's speech, and from
what he said, I perceive he has been informed or conceived
some idea himself as to what it was my intention to say.
He tells you that any statement which I can make to you is
not evidence, and can be received by you only with great caution. I do not attempt to deny that, but nevertheless, I think
that my statement will be supported by the testimony which
the prosecution has elicited, and that it will merit at least a
very careful consideration at your hands. I can easily con-
cede that it would be very difficult in my case to make any
difference whatever, but as I believe that no person is in a
position to give a more accurate or faithful account of this
whole business than I am, I propose to show you, that in the
case of one person at least, if I cannot show it by direct evidence, it is certainly worthy of considerable attention— I
mean the very great probability of Austin Bidwell's entire
innocence in the actual fraud. My only reason for making
this statement is that the truth may be known in regard to
him, for I am well aware that every word I am saying to

you now cuts from under my feet any hope that I may have entertained for myself. It seems to be the idea of the prosecution — an idea which they have endeavored by every means in their power to bring you to believe — Mr. Justice Archibald, interposing said : " As I understand you to say that what you are now saying cuts away the ground of any defense from under your own feet, I can only allow you to address the court and jury on your own behalf, and not on behalf of any other person. I do not know to whom you are alluding, but each of the prisoners are represented by counsel, and if you propose to address the jury on behalf of any other person beside yourself, I cannot allow you."

McDonald : I have not the audacity, my lord, to appear as counsel for any other of the prisoners. What I intend to say, is simply a statement of facts.

The Judge : You can urge anything on your own behalf.

McDonald : It is on my own behalf, but it is perfectly impossible to make the statement I am about to make without referring to the others. I was saying that the idea of the prosecution, which they have endeavored to inforce on your conviction, is that the original intention with which Austin Bidwell, George Bidwell, and myself, came over to this country was to perpetrate this fraud on the Bank of England. I think if that idea could be entertained it would argue for us a knowledge and a prescience something more than men of ordinary ability and attainments could pretend to. It would suppose that we were perfectly acquainted with the mode of doing business in England, that we knew some person or other who had an account with the Bank of England, that we could by some well-devised plan get sufficiently into the confidence of that person to obtain from him an introduction to the Bank of England, and that all the other minor details, which have been so fully explained in the course of this investigation, would all work together for our benefit, would all turn out precisely as we desired, and that in fact, nothing at all would interfere to prevent the carrying out of the fraud. When we first came to England, it was certainly with no such intention. Mr. Green, of Saville Row, has told you that the opening of the account with the Western Branch of the Bank of England was an entire accident, and so it was. That was done on May 4th, and on May 28th we three left England. We left England without the slightest intention of returning. Circumstances occurred to induce us to change our plans, and we came back two months later. There is no doubt but that the intention was to close the account with the Bank of England, because it was of no use. But when we came back to England it was of considerable use and advantage to us to cash any bills that might come to us.

We went from England to the Continent, and our intention, while there, was to do certain business between Vienna and Frankfort-on-the-Main. Circumstances arose while we were at Vienna to prevent that business. In the meantime I was taken very seriously ill, and returned to England for the benefit of medical advice. George Bidwell was in Amsterdam, and he sent me a bill drawn on Baring Bros., which I got cashed myself, by which I saw that the manner of doing business was entirely different than in America.

As soon as I saw how business was transacted, I sent a telegram from the station next adjoining the Alexandria Hotel, to George Bidwell, in Amsterdam, and I stated in that telegram that I had made a great discovery. That telegram, I dare say, could be found, but as it would tend to show that the fraud could not have been contemplated so early in the transaction, it has not been brought forward. In America, when bills are presented at a bank for discount, or when acceptances are presented, it is the custom to send them round to the persons accepting, to be what is technically called "initialed," in order that their validity and genuineness may be certified. I found that was not the case here, and the result of the discovery is, that I am standing before you to-day.

Mr. Pinto, from Amsterdam, has told you that George

Bidwell purchased bills drawn from Amsterdam upon Hamburg, which bills a day or two afterwards were sold again, and others drawn upon London purchased with the proceeds, and the bills so obtained were afterwards discounted by F. A. Warren. The matter went on in that way for some time, until the 11th or 12th of January Austin Bidwell went over to Paris to buy the bill on Messrs. Rothschild which has been so much commented upon — that for £4,500. During this voyage or journey to Paris, he met with a very severe railroad accident, in which one man certainly was killed outright, and I think two or three more, and Austin Bidwell had probably as narrow an escape from being smashed to pieces as any man ever did. On arriving in London he was in such a condition that it was almost impossible for him to move. He was taken to a hotel and visited by a physician, Doctor Coulson, who told him he was in very great danger of being paralyzed for life. On January 17th, when Austin Bidwell took that bill to the bank, I went with him as far as the door, and afterwards helped him back to my quarters. I think on the following day the doctor saw him, and Austin Bidwell then told him it was his intention to leave England immediately. The doctor informed him that if he intended to travel he must do so at once. The evidence goes to show that up to this time every preparation had been made for the contemplated fraud. January 18th was Saturday, and after the doctor's interview with Austin Bidwell, who was then in my room, he told me that it was his intention to utterly withdraw from anything connected with this or any other similar matter. You can easily conceive that up to this time a great deal of money had been thrown away in continually transferring the papers. The idea of losing that money and having no return for it was very displeasing, but as Austin Bidwell was determined to leave, and did, I could only let him go. On Dr. Coulson's advice, Austin Bidwell decided to travel at once, and he left with me two checks, one drawn on the Western Branch of the Bank of England, and the other on

Harcourts & Co. (Continental Bank), to obtain the balance of this account and invest the proceeds in United States bonds, which were to be forwarded to him in Paris. These two checks were cashed, and the proceeds left in my hands. The first forged bill was sent from Birmingham on January 21st. Mr. Chabot has told you that in his opinion the endorsement "F. A. Warren" on the bills was in his own handwriting. It was not. No one knows that better than I do. My hand was the one that put the endorsements on the forged bills of exchange.

Mr. Chabot, the expert, also says the checks on which the moneys were drawn from the two banks were in Austin Bidwell's handwriting, and were all signed at one sitting. Several of them were signed at one sitting — I give that credit to Mr. Chabot — but not by Austin Bidwell. I can refer you in particular to the check which went to the Western Branch of the Bank of England, in which the name of Horton was misspelled. It is admitted that Austin Bidwell was then on the way to Havana. Mr. Chabot does not state positively that these checks were signed by Horton; the Continental Bank was perfectly well satisfied that they were signed by Horton, and I think the expert in that bank was quite as well able to judge as Mr. Chabot whether the signatures were genuine.

Referring again to the accident on the Northern Railway of France — when Austin Bidwell arrived at my quarters in London, his first statement to me was this: "Mac, I have had as miraculous an escape from instant death as perhaps any man has ever experienced." He went on to elaborate his sentiments during the accident, and wound up by saying that so deep an impression had been made on his mind, in those few moments of peril, that he should certainly have nothing more to do with whatever might affect his personal convenience, liberty, and happiness in this world, but also place in jeopardy — according to the view from which he looked at it — his eternal happiness. I think, gentlemen of

the jury, that this is not a far-fetched statement, but is probably one that will commend itself to your attention as being
worthy of a great deal of consideration, namely, that a man
of his age could not have so absolutely and entirely forgotten
the sentiments implanted in youth as to be indifferent to such
a warning. For myself I am willing to confess that, probably from not having gone through such an ordeal myself,
I gave the matter but little attention for the moment; in
fact, I laughed at it and at him; but all I could say did not
change his mind, and on the following morning he left
England.

He left everything in confusion, as far as this business
is concerned, and in a state of unreadiness. When the first
bills were sent into the bank, the intention only was to recoup
the loss on the money transactions, and then clear out. But
when the facility with which they were received and discounted was considered, it was determined to carry the thing
farther, and to do so it was necessary to get up bills, have
printing done, and stamps made, and there was very little time
to do it in. Mr. Giffard, in his address, asked what was the
object of the account. The object was very plain. I do not
propose to insult your understandings, gentlemen, by saying
that a fraud was not contemplated at one time, but you may
perhaps be inclined to believe that such a statement as I am
now making is made only with one motive. Does it redound
to my advantage? does it help to clear me at all? or do I
state to you anything that is intrinsically improbable? I
think not. I have no doubt Mr. Giffard has had a great deal
of experience in this sort of business, and I dare say he will
believe me when I say men engaged in an illegitimate transaction do not place very much confidence in each other. And
if there were an intention, in spite of the withdrawal of one
party, still to carry out the original scheme, it is not likely
that party, after having entirely withdrawn, should be intrusted with any confidence concerning the scheme. He asks
who were benefited by it; and if he sifts the matter, I think

it could be very easily explained. He said it would be very difficult to prove any such statement as I am now making, which is but the simple truth.

Since Mr. Chabot first took upon himself the profession of an expert, business of this kind, like every other, has made very great strides. It has become, as one of the newspapers said, an art.

The Judge: What business do you mean?

I mean fraud, and a very wretched, unhappy, miserable, and contemptible art — it may be to a certain extent called an art, nevertheless. Mr. Chabot would induce you to believe that these checks were left signed by Austin Bidwell. I am unwilling to allow that statement to be left as it was by Mr. Chabot on your minds, when you come to meditate on your verdict. My only object is to make as much reparation as can be done to Austin Bidwell, who, in spite of Mr. Giffard's statement as to its improbability, has been deceived and imposed upon, and has had his confidence violated. If I am successful in pressing that view of the case upon you, I shall have obtained all I can ask for. If I am not I can only regret it, but I ask when you go to consider your verdict, to bear in mind the statement I have made, to consider whether there is anything intrinsically improbable in it, and to say whether it is at all likely that I would stand up here and through any other motive than the one I have mentioned, make observations which must necessarily be prejudicial to myself. That is all, gentlemen, I have to say to you.

[Although I sat by McDonald's side when he made the above statement, I had forgotten what he said about the date of the first conception of the fraud and the opening of the Warren account at the Bank of England. What I have said in relation to those events in Chapter XIII, and elsewhere, was written before I had seen his statement in print. It will be seen that our accounts agree. — G. B.]

The prisoner, George Bidwell, addressing the jury, said there was much he could have urged in his defense by way of comment on the evidence; but, nothwithstanding that, feeling from his sense of guilt in having aided in carrying out the forgeries, it had been his intention to throw himself on the mercy of the court. With that view he had prepared a statement; but after what Mr. McDonald had said, it would be mere repetition in him to attempt it. He confirmed that statement, which he said was the truth and nothing but the truth, adding that Noyes was never trusted by them, and only did what he was told to do. Mr. Justice Archibald, interposing, told the prisoner, George Bidwell, he must confine himself to his own defense, seeing that Noyes was defended by counsel. George Bidwell said he only wished to lay the facts before the court. Mr. Justice Archibald said he could have pleaded guilty, in which case he might have been called as a witness and given his evidence on oath. George Bidwell replied that he had not been aware of that. Mr. Justice Archibald said he might have been informed of it.

Mr. McIntyre, Q. C., speaking in behalf of Austin Bidwell, said he had to contend that the prosecution had failed to substantiate the charge preferred against his client. He knew perfectly well that the magnitude of a crime or the seriousness of the consequences of a verdict of guilty would never deter an English jury from doing their duty; but he was also sure that they would require in a case of that kind the clearest and most indisputable evidence, and failing to obtain it, however suspicious the surrounding circumstances might be, they would acquit the prisoner. He urged that the evidence was utterly inconsistent with the guilt of Austin Bidwell. A great mass of evidence had been placed before them, showing the antecedent connection of the prisoners, and a vast number of other circumstances, but he challenged them to find any proof that, with the bill in question, Austin Bidwell forged or uttered it, or was even aware of the forgery. They could not convict him unless they actually believed that he was concerned in the fabrication of the bill, or that it was carried out with his cognizance and connivance. It had been clearly proved that some time in 1872 the brothers Bidwell and McDonald were living in an obscure neighborhood in London, and that on paying a casual visit to Mr. Green, their tailor, in Saville Row, Austin Bidwell producing a large sum of money requested him to take it and keep it until his return from a short journey. Mr. Green hesitated, and upon his suggestion he introduced the prisoner, unfortunately for him, to the authorities at the Western Branch, who at once agreed to open an account with him. He contended that at that moment there was no fraudulent design upon the bank, and that to the end of the year, and even for some time in January the transactions in respect to that account were perfectly honest.

The prisoner left this country on January 18th, three days before the first batch of forged bills arrived from Birmingham, and from that time his personal connection with the account ceased. Mr. McIntyre complained that the bank authorities had not thought fit to make any inquiries at the address which the prisoner gave in London, and that although possessing a branch at Birmingham they never instituted any investigation as to the solvency or to the position of their customer, who represented himself to be living there and from whom they were receiving almost daily large batches of bills.

It is also inconceivable that they should without suspicion have dealt so largely with a person who only gave his address at the post-office in that town. The prosecution had failed to prove that Austin Bidwell was ever at Birmingham in his life. It had been admitted by Col. Francis that he at first believed all the letters containing the bills to be in Warren's handwriting, and the bills to bear his indorsement, but it has since been proved by Mr. Chabot that nearly all those letters and indorsements were written by George and not by Austin Bidwell. He urged that such was the case in the bill in question, and he asked the jury to believe that Austin had never seen either of them, he being out of England at the time. It was quite clear that Austin Bidwell possessed money of his own, for before any of the forged bills were discounted, £17,000 had passed through the bank in respect of his account. It was thus that he accounted for the possession of the bonds and money found at Havana, and for the circumstances that his brother and McDonald sent him other bonds on his journey thither. It might be that he was willing to join in the venture to some extent, but it was clear that after his accident he changed his mind and had nothing more to do with the matter. All the stamps and blocks were purchased after he left, and not one of the forged bills was presented while he was in the country. In conclusion Mr. McIntyre made an earnest appeal to the jury to acquit his client.

Mr. Ribton followed on behalf of Noyes, observing that his case differed entirely from that of any other, and that there was not a tittle of evidence which would warrant the jury in convicting him. On December 17th Noyes arrived in Liverpool from America and went to London, where he inserted an advertisement in a newspaper applying for a situation as a clerk or partner. The result was that he was taken into the service of the prisoner, Austin Bidwell, who had assumed the name of Horton, and he deposited with him as security the sum of £300. A formal agreement was entered into on January 11th between the parties, and on the same day Horton took an office at the London Bridge Hotel, and introduced Noyes as his clerk. From that time to the date of his arrest he discharged the duties of his position, and these duties had special reference to the paying in or cashing of checks on his master's account at the Continental Bank, and the purchase of American securities.

The jury would recollect that the fraud of the other prisoners commenced in May last, when the account at the Bank of England was opened—that between May and November they were engaged upon the Continent, in purchasing genuine bills as models, and that the account of Horton at the Continental Bank commenced on the 2d of December. All these transactions happened, therefore, before Noyes arrived in

England, and he had no knowledge of them. He was evidently acquainted with the other prisoners, as it was proved that he associated with them directly upon his arrival in London, but he was entirely ignorant of any fraud that was in contemplation, and so he remained down to the time of his arrest. Not a single fact has been proved which would lead to the belief that he was concerned in the forgery, but throughout the whole transaction he had been the innocent dupe of the other men. He admitted that his client had assumed other names than his own but none of them had been used to promote the fraudulent scheme. There was no evidence to show that Noyes had any knowledge of Warren's account at the Western Branch or that he ever saw any of the forged bills, and there was good ground for believing he was kept in darkness on all these points. The jury might regard him if they chose as an adventurer who was anxious to make money, but there was not a scintilla of evidence to show that he had ever been connected with the forgery. It was perfectly clear that Noyes had been selected to perform the part of an innocent assistant.

Mr. Justice Archibald in summing up said the prisoners were indicted for forging and uttering a bill of exchange for £1,000 with intent to defraud. That was the offense charged against them, but in the course taken by the prosecution they had laid before the jury evidence to show that the prisoners were all concerned in a fraudulent scheme for the purpose of defrauding the Bank of England. He did not propose to minutely go over the evidence adduced in the case, because it would doubtless be fresh in the minds of the jury, and especially after the statements of the prisoners George Bidwell and McDonald who had virtually admitted their guilt. McDonald had openly confessed his participation in the fraud, and George Bidwell had adopted his statement though without confessing his guilt. As regards George Bidwell, there was no doubt that he was guilty of forging the bill in question and many others. The learned judge then reviewed the evidence with great care, with a view to ascertain for the guidance of the jury how far the remaining prisoners Austin Bidwell and Hills had been concerned in the fraud. He observed that Austin Bidwell had left England in January, yet if he made arrangements for the forgery to be continued in his name he was just as guilty as though he had written and signed the bill himself.

The jury retired to consider their verdict shortly after seven o'clock, and on returning into court after the lapse of about quarter of an hour, they gave in a verdict of guilty against all of the four prisoners.

On being asked if they had anything to say why sentence should not be passed upon them, Austin Bidwell replied that he had nothing to say for himself, but that he would take advantage of the only opportunity he would have to repair a wrong he had done to a gentleman then in court, and for which he was extremely sorry. He alluded to Col. Francis, manager of the Western Branch, hoping that as years rolled on he would forget the wrong. That gentleman had been the subject of considerable criticism, but speaking from his knowledge of the case, he would say any other man in London would have been deceived in the same manner.

George McDonald observed that he had nothing to say of the verdict as far as he was concerned, but that Noyes was ignorant of the forgery, and Austin Bidwell at the time out of England.

George Bidwell said he did not ask any consideration for himself, but he begged that his brother, who was a young man and but recently married, might be dealt with mercifully. Referring to the prisoner Noyes, he said that he had been kept in ignorance of the real state of the affairs.

Noyes, addressing the court, said he was innocent of the proceedings of the other prisoners, and was kept in the dark as to who the man Warren was. He concluded by making an earnest appeal to the judge to temper justice with mercy.

Mr. Justice Archibald, after a pause, proceeded to pass

sentence. Addressing each of the four prisoners by name, he said : You have severally been convicted of the offense, and, although the indictment only charged you with forging one bill of exchange, it has been necessary in the evidence adduced, for the prosecution to bring before the court and jury testimony which shows you were each implicated in a crime which, perhaps, for the audacity of its conception, the magnitude of the fraud perpetrated, and the misdirected skill and ingenuity with which it was attempted to be carried into effect, is without a parallel. I can see no palliating or mitigating circumstances in your offense. You were not pressed by want; on the contrary you appear to have embarked in this nefarious scheme a very considerable amount of money. You were persons of education, so far as intellectual training goes, without any corresponding development of the moral sense. Some of you can speak several foreign languages, and all of you are acquainted with the banking and commercial business. The success of the enterprise was only rendered possible by the fact that in these times, with the immense commercial operations going on in various directions, it is necessary to extend to those who are engaged in or contemplate such operations, and who give reason to believe they are men of business and of apparent respectability, the utmost confidence. It is not the least atrocious part of your crime that you have given a severe blow to that confidence which has so long been maintained and protected in this country. You, who do not ask for mercy, and who are not restrained by respect for law or honesty, must be met with a terrible retribution, and it should be well known that those who commit crimes, which only persons of education sometimes commit, will be sure to meet with a very heavy punishment. I cannot see any reason to make a distinction in the sentence I am about to pass. In regard to that sentence, if I could conceive any case of forgery worse than this, I should have endeavored to take into consideration whether some punishment less than the maximum might have been sufficient; but, *as I cannot conceive a worse case,** I cannot perceive a reason for mitigating the sentence. That sentence is, that each and all of you be kept in penal servitude for life, and, in addition to that, I order that each of you shall pay one quarter of the costs of the prosecution.

The convicts were then removed from the bar, and thus terminated the remarkable trial.

---

* Justice Archibald ' cannot conceive a worse case" of forgery ! After our crime has been expiated by fifteen years of the worst kind of slavery — while not wishing to palliate anything in the way of crime, or even anything that violates the *Cardinal Principle of life*, "treating others as we should wish to be treated "— I can do no less than call attention to the unfairness and blind prejudice exhibited by him on numerous occasions during the trial. And this is well illustrated by the preceding paragraph. If the honorable Judge is still alive, let him answer the following question: Considered in its moral bearings, and, judging from the relative degree of misery caused, which is the worst act : To obtain money by fraud from a corporation like the Bank of England, to which millions are but a drop in the bucket, or to get away the investments and savings of thousands, including the jointures of widows and the inheritances of orphans, leaving them to drag out lives amid deprivation and want — and worse? To give but one of dozens of instances which have happened in this very England during our imprisonment: The managers of the Glasgow Bank perpetrated all the enormities shadowed forth above. The evidence was conclusive, and the proofs indisputable, but they were not Americans, had influen tial friends, and therefore got off with sentences varying from twelve months to two years. They were soon again at liberty to perpetrate fresh frauds, leaving those of their victims who are not dead to struggle to this day for existence — some of their fair daughters to end wretched lives as *nymphs du pavé*, and I have seen some of the sons in prison.—G. B.

CHAPTER XXXVI.

[From the *London Times* of August 23d, 1873.]

SOME further information has transpired in relation to the
alleged conspiracy to corrupt some of the warders of Newgate, with a view to procure the release of the prisoners, now on
their trial, to which reference was made in the *Times* of Saturday.
There can be now no doubt that this daring enterprise was seriously contemplated, and but for the energy of some of the city
magistrates, and notably of Alderman and Sheriff Sir Thomas
White, had all but succeeded. It would seem that on the eve of
the trial, John Bidwell, a brother of the prisoners, Austin and
George Bidwell, reputed to be a man of substance in the United
States, arrived in this country for the ostensible and legitimate
purpose of assisting his kinsmen with the means for conducting
their defense, and that about the same time a cousin of the prisoner McDonald came on a similar errand. Their movements at
first excited no suspicion, and John Bidwell at least, if not also the
cousin of McDonald, was accommodated with a seat in the body
of the court for several days, though that perhaps was only known
to the sheriff and under sheriffs and the prisoners themselves. All
went well through the first three days of the trial, the movements
of the two visitors exciting no suspicion, but on Thursday last

Alderman Sir Thomas White, upon information he had received, gave strict orders to the police in attendance that one at least, if not two, of the doors in the immediate neighborhood of the dock, and leading from the floor of the court to an outer corridor, communicating in two directions with the open street, should be closed. This arrangement was thenceforward carried into effect, and has since been maintained from day to day. It should be stated here

BURNING RETURNED BANK NOTES.

that from the commencement of the trial all the avenues to the court have been strictly guarded by the city police, but only or chiefly with the view of preventing overcrowding, and the general public have been admitted from day to day so far as was consistent with comfort. On Friday morning, an intimation having been made to Sir Thomas White, the senior Sheriff of London, that there was reason to believe attempts were being made to corrupt some of the warders of Newgate, he lost no time in communicating with his brother magistrates in attendance, Mr. Alderman Finnis, Mr. Alderman Lawrence, and Mr. Alderman Besley, and they at once instituted an inquiry within the gaol, the result being to convince them that the information they had received was sub-

25

stantially true. One of the suspected warders was searched, and upon him were found three letters which he had received from a convicted prisoner in the gaol to post, that being contrary to the rules of the prison and an infringement of the Gaol Act, which provides that letters from prisoners shall pass through the hands of the governor. The warder in question was thereupon suspended, and moreover for that offense was sent before a magistrate at Guildhall by whom he was remanded for a week. The magistrate sitting in Newgate continuing their inquiry ascertained beyond doubt, as we are assured on reliable authority, that two others of the prison warders received £100 each from friends of the prisoners or of some of them, and they have reason to believe that an attempt was to have been made on the night of Friday last to effect their escape. The result for the present is that three of the warders have been suspended, namely, Loch, Smidt, and Norris, the last named of whom is now in Halloway Prison. On Loch being searched £50 odd in sovereigns was found upon him, and he sought to account for the possession of so large a sum by stating that his brother at Brighton had placed it in his hands to pay bills which he owed. Before the discovery, Smidt, one of the three suspended warders is said to have told a detective with whom he is well acquainted, that he was going to Tasmania, and would carry his best friend in his pocket in the shape of £100. This careless avowal caused the detective to watch John Bidwell, whom he followed from Newgate on his departure after making a visit to one of his brothers there confined. One of the above named warders left the prison about the same time, and, according to prearrangement, met Bidwell, and both got on top of an omnibus [the London busses have two seats, back to back, outside]. An assistant of the detective managed to mount the same bus and sat with his back to the two, whom he so successfully "shadowed," and heard sufficient to satisfy himself that the brother had paid out a considerable sum of money to the warders, in pursuance of a plan to assist the four Americans to escape. Some of the incriminated warders had been seen drinking in the evenings with friends of the prisoners, or sympathizers, and from that time their movements were closely watched. One night last week John Bidwell, the brother of the two prisoners of that name, was traced

to the house of one of the three warders in the east end of London, which another of the three was afterward seen to enter.
Thence John Bidwell was traced to his lodgings in a suburb,
where he stayed over night unmolested, he having not then, as
was supposed, committed any offense cognizable by the police, and
he has not since been seen in or about the court. It is a remarkable fact connected with the affair that all the three suspended
warders would have been on duty in the prison during the night
of which there is reason to believe the attempt to release the
prisoners was to have been made. Since the discovery of the
plot extra and most stringent precautions have been taken by
Major Bowman, the chief superintendent of city police, to guard
the prison and the court-house. Six policemen well armed are
now on duty within the gaol at night, in place of the three suspended warders ; a vigilant watch, moreover, is kept outside, and
all around it day and night, and instead of the ordinary warders
who guard the dock while prisoners are on their trial, armed policemen have been posted. After the discovery it was in contemplation for the moment to exclude the public from the gallery of the
court over the dock as an additional precaution, but on reflection
that intention was abandoned. The duty of making the arrangements for guarding the approaches to the court and maintaining
order now devolves on Major Bowman, the chief superintendent of
police, and Sheriff Sir Thomas White has been heard to express his
high sense of the Major's zeal and discretion on the occasion.

" A tempest in a teapot," indeed ! Such an uproar as was
caused by the transaction referred to in the *Times,* and proceeding from so small a cause, would be laughable to one who,
like myself, knew the exact circumstances, but for its tragic
result.

I have elsewhere mentioned that this was the chief cause
why we were not let off with a milder sentence than for life.
I now give the exact circumstances.

It will be remembered that a relative — the one referred
to in the *Times* — John Bidwell, had arrived in London,
having come from the United States, like a faithful brother, to
render such aid as was in his power. Some of the warders

at Newgate saw him coming in daily to visit his brothers —
or rather talk with them across the grating, as shown in the
illustration, page 81. His occupation being that of a farmer, they could not fail to perceive that he was of an honest,
confiding nature, and believing he had money, they concluded
to try for some of it. Accordingly, first one, then another, told
McDonald that they could let him escape, and he communicated the " good news " to his friend Austin.

They both bit at the bait, and had one of the warders
speak to me about the proposed escape. As I was rather
backward about encouraging such a thing, another and
another warder came. They proposed to let us out at night
when on night duty, or even in the daytime should a favorable opportunity present itself. They also proposed to go
with us, vacating a responsible post of trust, thus incurring
the penalty of penal servitude should they ever be caught.
And all this for what consideration? £100 — about $500!
It was too cheap! They saw that I was cold on the project,
and tried by various devices to get me interested. One of
them while on duty carved out of soap a key, using his cell
key for a pattern, and every little while would come to my
cell, open the trap in the door and show me how he was getting on. He said they were going to get a casting from the
soap pattern as they had to give up their keys when they
went home at six or seven P. M. I really began to think
they were in earnest, but said to myself: " Even so — but
what possible chance have we to get out of England, when we
could not save ourselves at a time when we were unknown,
now that our pictures adorn the pages of all the illustrated
papers, and after thousands have seen us."

One day, about a fortnight before the trial began, my brother John, while visiting me at the yard grating, informed
me that Austin had mentioned the plan to him, and wished
him to go into it. I told him it was only a speculation on
the part of those warders, recapitulated the above, and told
him that they could not accomplish it even if sincere; that in

the past ages every possible plan, device, and trick for escaping had been resorted to, and guarded against, so that such offers could mean nothing but an intended swindle.

Still, under the circumstances, I did not feel authorized in attempting to put a veto on the matter, for the others would always feel that I had caused them to throw away a chance of escape. I therefore strongly advised him to go into it only on condition that the money should be deposited in the hands of a third party, to be sent to them or paid over to their order after the job was done. As they would be certain to get the money if successful, refusal of that condition would be tantamount to an acknowledgment that they were only trying to " beat " him out of the money.

Neither of us knew at the time that every cell door was double-locked at ten P. M., so that only with the master key, which was kept by the governor, could a cell be unlocked. I was quite satisfied that the warders would not accede to such a proposition and that the money would be saved. My brother departed, promising not to pay it except as I had advised.

Solicitor Howell came in on one of his daily benevolent ($10) visits, and in order to make sure that John should not be taken in, I informed him, under the seal of confidence, all about the affair, requesting him to advise John to have nothing to do with it. He also promised to do nothing that could arouse suspicion against the warders. Before solicitor Howell saw John, the latter had met the warders, as recounted in the article copied from the *London Times,* and was cajoled into paying one hundred sovereigns each to three of them. The next day John came in and told me what he had done. In one of his visits just before the trial, solicitor Howell questioned me about the matter, and I informed him about the three hundred sovereigns. At the same time I expressed to him my apprehensions of trouble arising that might prejudice our case at the coming trial. He showed visible signs of anger and vexation that three hundred sovereigns had slipped through his fingers, but promised to manage the matter so that it should do no harm — that in accordance with my wish he would see them privately, get back the money, and return it to my brother John. I saw clearly enough that he did not relish the idea of returning the money, for ever since my brother John's arrival in England, he had exhausted every trick and wile to extract from him all the money he had brought with him to England, and was well aware that the sum paid to the warders was nearly all he had left.

I am able, by the light of after events, together with what I extracted from him during the trial, to lay bare the plan evolved by this astute solicitor, by which he accomplished his aim of retaining undisturbed possession of what he already had in his hands, and to secure for himself the three hundred sovereigns. He went to Mr. Jonas, the governor, and divulged the whole matter, stipulating that Mr. Jonas should manage it so that no suspicion should fall on himself, and that no measures should be taken to arrest my brother John, whom he himself could easily frighten out of the country at the proper moment. In accordance with this arrangement Mr. Jonas had a watch set on the warders to see if anything could be discovered that would warrant action independent of solicitor Howell's revelations. A young man, whose name I have forgotten, call him Jones, was in Newgate awaiting trial on the charge of having for some time extracted stamps and postal orders from letters sent to his master. This young man was selected as the proper instrument to use in worming his way into the confidence of us four Americans. In order not to excite suspicion as to his object, he would be brought to one or the other of our cells and set at work shaving, hair-trimming, or scrubbing and cleaning, the cell door standing open and one of the oldest and most reliable warders — called "Old Smith" — in charge. "Old Smith," of whom see a back view in cut "Visitors at Newgate," page 81, was a character, and, so far as I saw, not a bad, though an astute old man. Observing the undue familiarity of some other warders with us, he had on two or three occasions observed to me regarding them: "Those young fellows will get themselves into trouble if they don't look sharp." Governor Jonas had complete confidence in "Old Smith" and accordingly had put him on this duty; and I think that while on duty he would have obeyed orders if directed to obtain evidence which would hang his own brother. Accordingly, leaving young "Jones" in my cell, or that of one of the others, he would walk away down the corridor giving that "tool" opportunities for conversation, of which prisoners eagerly avail themselves as a break in the monotony of their lives. At the time I suspected some design in all this, was on my guard, and did not know until years afterward the result of the intrigue. It may be well to explain that while awaiting trial we were allowed pens, ink, and paper.

At Dartmoor prison, in 1875, this same Jones was cleaner in my ward, and told me the whole affair, and his relation remains vividly impressed on my memory. Said he, "One day, while we were at Newgate, I was in McDonald's cell, and he handed me a letter to take to you the first time I should be let into your cell. After I returned to my own, I read the letter and saw that it was about some plan of escape, and thinking to benefit myself I gave it to Jonas. And I got well paid! Seven years penal servitude! But for the moment it did help me, for when my case was called, Mr. Jonas spoke a good word for me, and I got off with a month in Newgate. When my master discovered by what means I had obtained the mitigation of my sentence, he was so mad that when the month had expired he had me tried on another indictment, and, being convicted, am now doing seven years."

Jones expressed much regret at having served McDonald so shabby a trick, etc. This gave Governor Jonas the opportunity for which he had been waiting, as he could now proceed openly, without being obliged to bring Solicitor Howell's name into the matter.

I now come to the period referred to in the *Times* article

—the fourth day of the trial. It was also rumored that about two hundred sporting men had crossed from New York to hear the trial, although none of our party had ever belonged to that fraternity. Neither ourselves or friends had any communication with any of them in London, yet it was believed that they were cognizant of and participants in the "plot." A numerous body of policemen were detailed, who patrolled, with loaded revolvers, around Newgate and the Old Bailey day and night. Upon our return from the court on the evening of the fourth day, we were accompanied by a body-guard of policemen through the underground way leading to the "passage and stairs," at the foot of which we waited our turn to enter the dock, as depicted in the illustration. Arriving in the ward in which my cell was located, I saw several others with revolver and truncheon in belts. The newspaper columns were rife with particulars, strange to us, about this "daring attempt to escape from Newgate."

On August 28th Warder Norris was again brought before the magistrate at Guildhall, on the charge of having attempted to carry out of Newgate the three letters written by a prisoner. For this he was fined ten pounds sterling, and in default of payment, three months' imprisonment at hard labor. Besides the fine, he was expelled the service, with forfeiture of the pay then due him. He asked for a partial remission, on the ground that he had a wife and six children to support out of his salary of twenty-eight shillings a week, which was now stopped and they left penniless. His request was not granted, and he was sent to prison, leaving his wife and children on the town.

It will be perceived that the affair of the letters was a side issue of the plan of escape, and these events caused important alteration in the management of Newgate.

On September 9th a committee composed of magistrates of the city, the Lord Mayor acting as chairman, was engaged a considerable time at Guildhall, in investigating the circumstances under which the attempt was made to corrupt three of the wardens of Newgate, with a view to facilitate or to connive at our escape from prison while the trial was pending at the Central Criminal Court, Old Bailey. The inquiry, for various reasons, was private and was adjourned, and a report undoubtedly made by the committee to the full Court of Aldermen, so that all the circumstances connected with the transaction transpired.

But at the period when these pages were written, I had been unable to discover any official account of the result of the investigation. While in prison at Dartmoor, I heard that Norris was sentenced to eighteen months' imprisonment, and that the other two were dismissed the service. Of course this looks, on the bare facts, as though they got off very lightly for such a breach of duty. Norris had a wife and six children to support and educate in London on a salary of twenty-eight shillings ($6.75) per week. I have elsewhere entered into this subject of salaries more fully, and the reader will readily see how hard it must be for a warder situated like Norris to resist the temptation of obtaining money in almost any manner consistent with supposed safety.

Amidst all this hubbub, which was very opportune to suit the views of Justice Archibald — to whom it gave a welcome excuse — without permitting a moment's delay after the jury had rendered their verdict, he sentenced us all indiscriminately to penal servitude for life.

I have read in a London paper of contemporary date that "the whole of the prisoners were ready to plead guilty unconditionally," provided that an arrangement could be made by which we should receive a sentence of ten or, at most, fifteen years' penal servitude; but the authorities "peremptorily refused, and said the law must take its course." That statement is incorrect, for Austin and Noyes refused under any circumstances to plead guilty. McDonald and myself were willing to do so if it would be of any benefit to them. Our watches and other personal property, clothing, etc., were ordered by the judge to be sold toward repaying the bank the costs of the prosecution (about $350,000).

To show the opinions of some of England's greatest men, and at least one of America's, I have the honor to submit copies of letters, etc., appended to a petition for Austin Bidwell's release. Notwithstanding the influence of such eminent names, the petition was refused, because of what was said by the American press about my own release — some of the newspapers asserting that I would unfailingly plunge back into crime. Of course if that should prove to be the truth, the authorities would be justified in preventing him from joining me in a criminal career. But I trust the time is not distant when they will be disabused of that belief.

JOHN BRIGHT.

18 Clifford Street, W. (London).

DEAR MR. MATTHEWS, — May I venture to ask you to consider the case to which this letter or memorial refers, and to express my opinion that to consent to the petition would be an act not only of mercy but of wisdom.

A life sentence on a young man of 25 years of age for an offense against property, seems to me very harsh and inconsistent with the better feeling prevailing in our time.

Pray forgive me for thus addressing you. An act of mercy will not lessen the confidence of the public in your eminent office.

Yours very sincerely,

JOHN BRIGHT.

To Right Hon. H. MATTHEWS, *Home Office.*

July 12th, 1887.

I heartily support the request of Mr. Bright.

J. CHAMBERLAIN (M. P.).

Aug. 1st, 1887.

It does appear as if a life sentence at 25 was as severe as could have been had the case been the worst possible to men.

Surely a careful revision is not too much to ask. I earnestly join my request to that of Mr. Bright.

(The Reverend) CHARLES H. SPURGEON.

Aug. 4th, 1887.

I agree with the above.

RANDOLPH T. CHURCHILL (M. P.).

Aug. 4th, 1887.

I strongly support Mr. Bright's request.

JOHN MORLEY (M. P.).

I heartily support Mr. Bright's request.

(The Marquis of) LYMINGTON.

I hope the case will be reconsidered.

(The Marquis of) HARTINGTON.

Aug. 6th, 1887.

I think there is here a very strong case for the consideration of the Home Secretary.

CHARLES RUSSELL (Queen's Coun.).

LEGATION OF THE UNITED STATES,

LONDON, August 9th, 1887.

I earnestly concur in the foregoing petition . . . and ask the favorable consideration of the Home Secretary upon the grounds of justice as well as of mercy.

The prisoner has now been 14 years in penal servitude, counting from the time of his arrest fourteen and one-half years.

As I understand the allowance for good conduct upon time

sentences, the imprisonment he has suffered would be nearly equivalent to that of a sentence for 20 if that allowance was made, and I
am informed that his conduct during the whole time has been such
as to entitle him to the allowance.

I respectfully suggest that for an offense against property only,
not involving any attempt upon human life, committed by a very
young man, the punishment he has already suffered is great, and it
would seem unnecessary cruelty to prolong it.

The connections of the prisoner in the United States are very
respectable, and they are very anxious that a further chance in life
be afforded him, and hopeful that it will be well employed. . . .

The lady who, with great devotion and self sacrifice, has come
from Western America, and has remained a number of months on
this errand of mercy, is warmly commended to me by letters from
persons of high personal and official standing. . . . .

Should a pardon be granted, the relatives of the prisoner will
take him immediately to America, and will engage that he shall
not return to England.

It will be in the memory of the Home Secretary that the elder
associate of the prisoner in the crime . . . has already been
pardoned.

E. J. Phelps (Ambassador).

In January, 1888, a petition was forwarded in Austin Bidwell's behalf signed by Harriet Beecher Stowe, Charles Dudley
Warner, and Samuel L. Clemens (Mark Twain), the reply to
which, received by Mr. Warner, is presented on next page.

On the morning of the fifth day of the trial, solicitor
Howell handed me, while in the dock, a note from my brother
John, saying that he was " just leaving for Paris, not daring
to remain in London, solicitor Howell having ascertained that
the police were after him for the bribery of Newgate warders."

First, this solicitor had now attained his purpose, viz.: No
friend of ours was left in England to scan his account, and
what use he had made of the money placed in his hands for
our defense, and to make him settle fairly through fear of
exposure.

In the reply to this Letter you are requested
to quote the following Number

20568 0
―――
13

Home Office
Whitehall
26th January 1888.

Sir,

The Secretary of State having carefully
considered the application submitted to him by
yourself and others, citizens of Hartford County,
Connecticut U.S.A., in favour of Austin Byron
Bidwell, now undergoing a sentence of penal
servitude for Forgery in this country, I am
directed to express to you his regret that
he is unable to discover any sufficient ground
to justify him, consistently with his public
duty in advising Her Majesty to interfere
in this case.

I am,
Sir,
Your obedient servant,

Godfrey Lushington

To
Mr C.D. Warner
Hartford
Connecticut
U.S.A.

Secondly, he had stirred up a hubbub that ensured me, at least, being put out of the way by means of a long imprisonment. Do I do the man injustice? The bank solicitor, Mr. Freshfield, and in general, the legal fraternity who were obliged to know him, will believe what I say, as he was considered a "beat" in the profession. As has been seen, it was only by accident that he got into so important a case, and it was easy to see that all the eminent counsel engaged showed a decided repugnance to coming in contact with him, even to receive his "retainers," and paltry ones they were. Some to whom he applied would not take the case from him.

But it was just that we should not evade punishment, and "whom the gods would destroy, they first make mad," taking away their capability of judging aright.

Since the preceding sentence was written, I have been informed by a person just from England, who investigated the matter, that soon after our conviction this unscrupulous shark was expelled from the profession on account of the "legal" swindles perpetrated on us and others.

Chapter XXXVII.

NOW that this extraordinary trial was at last ended, and the sentence of "penal servitude for life" pronounced upon us — strange as it may appear, I felt an immediate relief from the terrible strain of the previous five months. The worst now being known, a great load seemed removed, for the matter was settled — my career on earth finished. Thus I felt, as for the last time we filed out of the dock, down the steps into the corridor shown in the engraving, page 129, and along the subterranean passage leading to the cells in Newgate — a passage which had been trodden by so many thousands of feet, carrying equally hopeless hearts, going mechanically onward to meet their doom. On the way, the accompanying warders tried to cheer us with the hope of a distant pardon; but at that moment I was without hope — rather rejoiced in the prospect of a speedy death that I had already determined upon. During the trial the experienced warders had assured us that, if convicted, we would get at most ten or twelve years. Mr. Freshfield, the bank solicitor, had informed St. John Wontner, McDonald's solicitor, that the bank would be satisfied with a ten years' sentence — but death had seemed preferable to even that. And now it was "For Life!" A thousand times preferable would be a sudden death! Come, ye thunderbolts, and blast me out of existence!

Such was my feeling. Arriving in the ward of Newgate, I gave my brother a last embrace, and he passed up the stairs to the corridor in which his cell was located, as did the others, while I took the way to my own on the lower floor. From that evening of the 25th day of August, 1873, to the time of this writing, I have never had the opportunity of taking him by the hand.

I sat down upon the wooden stool in my dismal cell, and, as I reflected upon the situation, the sense of relief I had experienced faded away, and despair took its place. My past life — my errors, my lost family, friends, country — all rushed through my mind, and overwhelmed me like a tumultuous flood. I felt that my life was ended, and that I could not bear to live to see the light of another day. I picked up a slate and wrote a farewell letter to my wife, and destroyed all letters and papers. I considered the sentence an unmerciful one and worse than death.

Well-nigh maddened by my thoughts, I looked about for some means to end a life now become worthless, and found two large silk handkerchiefs, as previously related. What happened soon after has been briefly described in a former chapter, and I refrain from depicting more fully a frightful incident in my prison life.

Through fear of being discovered by the watchman, I left the prepared noose hanging, and crept into my hammock, but not to sleep. I could exercise no control over my thoughts, and within an hour, I was again tortured into a state of desperation and felt it to be impossible to live; and no less than three times during that fearful night I put my head in the noose, determined to end my misery, but each time, at the last moment, came the voice that recalled me to my senses. Early in the morning I obliterated all traces of the attempted self-murder, erased what I had written on the slate, and no one ever suspected that I had been so near unto death. Among the papers I destroyed were several letters that my brother had received the previous day, which had been handed in to me to read and return the next morning ; and I have no doubt he wonders to this day why I failed to do so.

During the forenoon all my citizen's apparel was taken, and a suit of jail clothes given me ; my hair and beard were cut off, and I was set at work picking oakum.

About 1 o'clock P. M., on the 27th day of August, warders came into my cell, put heavy irons connected by a chain around my ankles, and handcuffs on my wrists. I was then let out into the corridor, where I saw my three companions rigged out in the same graphic style. My mind reverted to the triumphant meeting at the St. James Hotel, previously described, and I could not repress a shudder at the awful contrast.

VISITORS AT NEWGATE STANDING OVER THE BURYING-VAULT.
DOOR LEADING TO THE BLACK-MARIA.

We were all four marched across the open court, beneath the slabs of which is the vault into which are thrown the bodies of all who die or are hanged in Newgate, quick-lime being thrown in, and the vault soon made ready for fresh occupants, which are never lacking. Such is the Newgate burying-ground. For us, surely, a worse fate was reserved. We continued the march toward our living grave, and reached, with chains clanking, an interior court, surrounded by walls thirty feet high, in which stood the black-maria or prison omnibus, shown in illustration, page 113. This we entered, one by one, and were locked into the boxes. Two jail officers then mounted the box with the driver; another stood in the passage between the boxes; the door was banged, and he was locked in with us; the great gate was thrown open, and the vehicle was soon rumbling over the stones toward Pentonville Prison.

PENTONVILLE PRISON.

The following from the *London Times* of September 2d, may be regarded as a finis to that portion of our career:

On Saturday, George and Austin Bidwell, George McDonald, and Edwin Noyes, who were recently convicted at the Central Criminal Court of the great forgeries on the Bank of England, and sentenced by Mr. Justice Archibald to penal servitude for life, were removed from the gaol of Newgate to one of the convict establishments, to undergo a portion of their sentence. Before they left Newgate, they were shorn of their beards and whiskers, and clad in prison garb, and no one, it is said, could have recognized them after this change in their appearance had been effected.

Pentonville Prison, to which we were bound, is on the opposite side of London from Newgate, and in about half an hour the black-maria entered the ponderous gate which closed behind us. The van door was unlocked, as were also the boxes, and all four of us found in safe keeping! We had suffered the worst of all misfortunes, and why the additional humiliation of loading us with chains for a half-hour's ride through the heart of London in a van under lock and guards? The jail officers delivered us over to the prison authorities, one of whom, as we left the van, ordered us to stand in a row while the chains were taken off. My brother happened to place himself two or three inches out of the line, and was given a heavy thump in the breast by an officer who shouted: "Stand back! We'll show you who is master here!" My brother wisely stood back without speaking.

We had been very kindly treated at Newgate, and I had been permitted to take with me in the van two serviceable silk handkerchiefs, a tooth and a nail brush. The same man took away the handkerchiefs, and ordered me to stamp upon the brushes and break them, and none were ever supplied for the use of convicts. We were then marched into a room in which were a great number of baths, sunk below the level of the floor, and ordered to strip and bathe. We were subjected to a disgusting search and inspection of our naked bodies by the warders, to make sure that we had nothing concealed.

After this we were ordered to dress in a suit of convict clothing, consisting of stockings with three red stripes reaching above the knees, a checked cotton shirt, cloth stock, a cap made of three pieces of buff cloth sewed together, corduroy knee-breeches, a vest or waistcoat of the same, and a jacket of buff woolen cloth. (For the costume see illustration, Prisoners at Exercise.)

We were then marched into a corridor, ranged along the wall, and ordered to strip to our shirt (see engraving, Chapter XLVI), ready for examination by the medical officer, each awaiting his turn to pass into the inspection room. After this was over we were marched to cells, each one of our party being put in separate wings, and thenceforth every precaution was taken to prevent us from seeing or speaking to each other. My supper was brought, and consisted of a pint of oatmeal gruel and six ounces of bread.

BIDWELL PICKING OAKUM.

I got scant sleep on the straw pallet till 5 o'clock A.M., and was dreaming of home and family, when

> The cling-clang clanging of the prison bell
> Quick plunged my spirit down from heaven to hell.

Hurrying on my clothes, an assistant warder came in to show me how to fold up the mattress and blankets, and to put them away in a nice heap for the day.

After breakfast — for which see dietary schedules at the end of the next chapter — the assistant warder brought a bundle of short, old tarred ropes, which he said contained two and one-half pounds, and that I must pick it into oakum before night. Well, I sat there, and picked and picked, but the pile did not grow fast, and when I put it out at bedtime, only half was finished.

About 11 A. M. the following day, I was interrupted in the work and ordered into the corridor, where I found my companions. We were marched before Governor Bones (of whom more anon), who, in a menacing voice, read the rules of the prison, a copy of which was hung up in each cell.

Every moment, when not asleep, I was obliged to occupy my mind in some way, or my thoughts instantly reverted to my family, my wasted life, and the awful fate which I had brought upon myself. Even the few minutes between the time I was dressed and breakfast were intolerable, for I could not help thinking. At night I could not sleep until I adopted the device of counting, and this I found necessary to do during every waking moment when I could not see to study. When taking the noose down at Newgate, I had determined to live it out, resolving to devote all my spare time to study, for which I had a natural taste and aptitude.

I was marched into the yard each day for an hour's exercise. At eight o'clock at night I made down my bed, and put the clothes and oakum outside into the corridor. On the morning of the second day I took in the clothes and oakum, dressed, made up the bed, and swallowed the limited breakfast. The assistant warder then came in, looked at the oakum I had picked, and said that I must pick it all over again, and separate every fiber. I told him the dust affected my throat, and he very civilly told me to see the doctor. I saw the medical officer, Dr. Vane C. Clarke, who, in the kindest manner, listened to what I had to say, and ordered my work to be changed from oakum-picking to sewing.

From what I have written, it will be perceived that upon receiving his sentence the convict is taken to the reception cells in Newgate, where he first dons the prison dress. His

hair is cut close, and he is put to oakum-picking until an order
is received to remove him to a prison. If he be a Protestant,
he is sent to the Pentonville; or if a Catholic, to the Millbank
prison — both in the suburbs of London. At either of these
prisons, for nine months he is kept sedulously apart from all
other convicts, and employed at either mat-making, oakum-
picking, carpet-weaving, shoemaking, or tailoring. For the

MAT MAKING AT PENTONVILLE PRISON.

sake of preserving his health it is necessary to give him, daily,
an hour's exercise of pacing round and round a plot of ground
enclosed within the prison walls. (See illustration.) While
grinding away at this monotonous tramp for the preservation
of health, the prisoners must keep three paces apart.

Upon their first reception into a government prison, they
are examined by the medical officer, and any complaint from
which one may be suffering, or from which he claims that he
has previously suffered, is entered on his " medical history or

caption-sheet," together with a full description of all marks, defects, and peculiarities of every kind, however caused; also his height and weight. This medical history sheet is sent with the convict whenever he is transferred from one government prison to another.

This solitary nine months' system was established on the plea that it affords the prison authorities an opportunity of learning the character and disposition of the convicts, thus enabling a better classification when they are sent to the public works prisons. But my experience, and what I have known of its effects on other prisoners, convinces me that it is a bad, and in many cases a fatal system, especially to those who are undergoing their first term of penal servitude; and these are about the only ones who are likely to reform — if such a thing is possible under the present English system. The first nine months bear the hardest on him, and shutting him in solitude so long is apt to drive him into a state of desperation or despair, in which many hundreds of men every year are excited into the commission of some offense, such as striking a warder, attempting to escape, etc., a majority of whom would otherwise get through their term by running smoothly in the even groove of prison life. Should a prisoner lift his hand against any authority, the immediate result would be a severe clubbing, beating, and kicking with heavy boots — punishments not supposed to be permitted by the superior authorities, all under-officers being instructed to use only such force as is sufficient to restrain the prisoner. He would then be taken before the governor (even for a trivial offense, such as talking with or giving a piece of bread to another prisoner), and punished more or less severely, according to the nature of the offense. In my time a flogging with a cat-o'-nine-tails was the most usual sequel to striking an officer, no matter what the provocation.

The prisoner thus acquires a character that follows him to the public works prison, and causes him to be specially watched and reported for every trifle, particularly if he gets his officer down on him ; then he is likely to be in hot water the whole term of his sentence. He loses all his remission, and undergoes punishments which cause his death, unless he has an iron constitution, and even the strongest often succumb.

During this period of his imprisonment, just as he has been judicially choked off from the full supply of food to which he had been accustomed, the prison allowance is less than it is afterwards. It is not a good system — rather, an absurd one — that keeps a prisoner for the first nine months engaged in a sedentary occupation, shut close in a cell, during which time he is not permitted the slightest intercourse with his fellows. He seldom hears a voice except in the chapel on Sundays. Then he is sent to the public works prisons — Dartmoor, Portsmouth, Portland, Chatham, or Wormwood Scrubs — and set to work out of doors, with a party of men who mutually corrupt one another with tales of their knavish adventures, interspersed with the vilest language — for there are some in every gang who cannot open their mouths without giving vent to obscenities and blasphemies.

Under the present English system, the last few months are made as easy and pleasant as possible to the home-going prisoner. This is precisely the portion of his sentence which he should be made to feel acutely as the most severe, in order that when he recovers his liberty, it may be with an abiding sense of the hardships of prison life. It would be a wiser system which gives him at once all the usual prison privileges, and which winds up with putting him, during the last month of his penal term, on a limited diet in solitary confinement.

The following letter from an officer of a banking company embodies a complaint as to the inequality of the sentences passed for crimes, such as forgery. The view of the writer is in a great degree sound, being unquestionably that sentimental or impulsive insinuations are allowed, from the lowest to the highest courts, to influence to a most injurious extent the treatment of criminal cases. When he insists, however, that all cases of forgery being the same in principle, no distinction

AN HOUR'S MONOTONOUS EXERCISE.

should be drawn between any of them, he will find few to concur with him:

LONDON, Sept. 2, 1873.

SIR, — In an article on Friday last *The Times* very properly stated that the recent forgery case has created a very great sensation. The sentence also has taken many people by surprise. Such men, no doubt, deserve to be severely dealt with, but the question arises, are not all cases of forgery the same in principle, and ought not the same punishment to be meted out, whether the Bank of England are prosecutors or other institutions of lesser importance ? Cases of forgery are not uncommon. but the sentences will bear no comparison with the one now referred to. We had within the last six months to prosecute a man for forgery. He had been moving in apparent respectability, and in certain circles was well known and respected, but for some time his success had been the result of forgery. He had not long been a customer of ours when we took the precaution to forward to the acceptor the bill of exchange for verification of signature ; the fraud was thus discov· ered. [If the Bank of England had taken that very necessary precaution, the fraud would have been discovered with the first deposit of forged bills for discount. — G. B.] We afterwards went to the trouble and incurred the expense of the prosecution. The man pleaded guilty and received a sentence of twelve months imprisonment only, the expenses of the prosecution amounting to nearly £50. We need scarcely say had we thought for one moment that such a light sentence would have been passed, we should have saved our money and time also, and our quondam customer might have gone to practice elsewhere. We have before us another case, but we entertain doubts whether it would be worth the annoyance and expense to prosecute, for, comparing the sentence just passed with many others of recent date, I ask: What is forgery ? Is it a thing of degree ? It may be, but between a sentence of twelve months for forgery and a sentence of penal servitude for life for the same thing there is a great gulf. Does the prestige of a great institution fill up the chasm ?

I am sir, yours obediently,

"H." (Bank Manager.)

While not in the least degree wishing to palliate any crime, I cannot let the above letter pass without asking whether, from a moral point of view, the bank forgery was so bad as in the majority of cases when advantage is taken of a confidential position, betraying a confiding employer; or even in the case referred to by the bank manager, where the operator took advantage of a bank whom the manager had trusted on the strength of his known character, obtained in all probability through years of mutual business transactions?

In our case no such advantages were taken, the bank being entire strangers, even to our names.

I know a man, Niblo Clark, who has just completed a term of penal service of fifteen years for stealing two coats. I know another now serving seven years for stealing a shirt. The officers of the Glasgow Bank, who perpetrated the frauds which caused its failure, and the consequent ruin of thousands, many of whom were widows with children, got but one and two years, and while in prison did no work, but had every thing made easy for them by wealthy relatives. Such contrasts are kept constantly before the eyes of prisoners, and they complain bitterly that because they are poor and without friends they get heavy sentences for the least infraction of the law, while those of an opposite social condition can steal on a mammoth scale with comparative immunity from punishment.

See also on the same subject the following from the London *Times* of May 14, 1873:

THE LENGTH OF THE JUDGE'S FOOT.

LONDON, May 13, 1873.

SIR, — Permit me to call attention to the inequality of the sentences passed on two persons charged with the same offense, whose trials were reported in the *Times* on Friday, the 9th of May. William Alexander Roberts, stockbroker, was indicted for forging and uttering a check for £11,500, with intent to defraud the Consolidated Bank.

David Swanson, a merchant, was indicted for forging and uttering two bills of exchange with intent to defraud. In the first case all the facts were disclosed, a verdict of "guilty" was returned, and Mr. Justice Denman observed that "the prisoner had been guilty of a terrible fraud and a most wicked act, for which the sentence must be severe," and ordered the prisoner to be kept in penal servitude for twelve years. In the second case the prisoner pleaded "guilty." The facts therefore were not disclosed in open court, and it is presumable the judge, Mr. Commissioner Kerr, was not acquainted with them, for the prisoner was sentenced to eighteen months hard labor. Mr. Roberts, the stockbroker, forged a check and got money by that means.

Mr. Swanson, the merchant, forged bills of exchange, and, getting them discounted, likewise obtained money. Surely, both men committed the same offense. How can it be reconciled that one of them should remain twelve years in penal servitude, the other escape with eighteen months imprisonment?

Yours faithfully,   H. P.

I became acquainted with the Alexander Roberts referred to in the foregoing letter, in Newgate jail while we were awaiting trial. He appeared to be about twenty-two years of age, well educated, and a well-disposed young man. He was refined in his manners and speech, and had evidently enjoyed the privilege of being brought up surrounded by good associations. During the hour's daily exercise in an inner court of Newgate, as shown in the illustration, I talked with him repeatedly and was quite interested in his story. I will not go into it here farther than to say that it was the usual one of having fallen into bad — genteel bad company — and to keep up "the style" he had been lured on to the result as above detailed by "H. P." But this writer was not aware of the causes which got him the twelve years. These were of a similar nature to those which got us "life," and which have caused the sentences of many a poor wretch to be doubled above what the nature of the case would otherwise have warranted. As I distinctly remember the substance of his account I will let him relate it:

"While awaiting trial here, I was taken several times in

charge of warders, to the law courts, which are some distance away, to give evidence in some suits regarding the settlement of my business. In thinking over the matter I resolved the next time I should be taken out of Newgate that I would make a run for it. Of course before I am tried and convicted I am in citizen's clothes, and I thought if I could dodge around a corner I could have a fair chance of making good my escape. Therefore, yesterday (about the 1st of May, 1873) they put on handcuffs, as before, and sent me out into the streets in charge of warder Smith. At the corner of —— Street I made a dive and got some distance away, but the handcuffs impeded my flight, and as I turned the next corner I ran plump into the arms of a policeman."

That is the true reason why Alexander Roberts received a term of twelve years penal servitude. That is the reason why he was ironed hands and feet; and I saw him walking through the inner open-air court (open to the sky alone) in which I was exercising, with chains clanking at every step. I can never forget the look of mental agony, mingled with a pitiful smile of recognition, which he cast upon me as he passed within a few feet, on his way to undergo the convict's doom — a way which we four Americans followed three months later in exactly the same awful plight, and for the same alleged reason — attempting to escape.

I may add that afterwards at the Pentonville prison I corresponded with him by means of writing on small pieces of slate-stone picked up in the yard; of course this was done at the risk of three days' bread and water.

CHAPTER XXXVIII.

AS before stated, Dr. Vane C. Clarke had relieved me
from oakum-picking, and had me put at sewing, or in
prison parlance, tailoring, which includes patching, and any
work requiring the use of a needle. I had for some years
been troubled with dyspepsia, lumbago, and throat complaint.
The nature of the prison food aggravated the first, and the
damp atmosphere of the English climate, the others. As the
winter approached I became worse. Owing to the complete
and sudden change in my mode of life, in regard to food and
clothing, I suffered extremely from the cold, and was constantly sick from the effects of the food, and after I had been
a few months in Pentonville's solitary cells, I felt sure that I
should soon die, unless I had a change of some kind — and a
change I determined to have. At that period of my imprisonment, I had no knowledge of English prison life, nor of the
severity with which trivial offenses were punished, and especially attempts to escape.

A few days previously, the doctor had ordered me to be
weighed, and the principal warder in charge of the Infirmary,
which was in a separate building, came to my cell in the
prison, and took me out across the yard to a small cottage
where the scales were kept. As I passed back and forth I
observed that this was one of several uninhabited cottages
which had been enclosed within the walls, which were about

(413)

thirty feet in height. One of these passed along near the rear of the cottages. There were a number of long poles lying about near the foot of the wall, such as builders use to support their scaffolds. In crossing the yard, I saw no one, and we entered the cottage, went up stairs, and after being weighed, I was marched back to my cell. The time occupied about fifteen minutes, and I saw no one else during the whole operation, except the warder who was with me. I had no sooner returned to my cell, than my thoughts began to dwell on all I had observed, and I thought to myself: "There are a good many foggy days, and in that isolated cottage it would not be impossible for me to throw dust in the warder's eyes, slip a gag into his mouth, and after having stripped off his clothes for myself, tie his elbows behind his back, and his feet to the scales or stair-railings. In the fog, I could easily place one of the poles against the wall unobserved, climb to the top, and drop into the street."

Sometimes there was little or no sewing to be done, and the bundle of oakum had been left that I might pick away upon it during such intervals, but I could not, according to the doctor's order, be compelled to do that work. I selected a suitable piece of dry, old tarred rope, six inches long, that I thought would answer for a gag. Out of the picked-rope fibre, I made stout strings, and fastened two on the ends of the gag, so that they could be tied behind the warder's neck, and thus secure the gag in his mouth. I also saved some of the strings for the purpose of binding his hands and feet, and collected a quantity of rope tar-dust to throw in his eyes. I concealed all but the gag-piece in the toes of my brogans, which were of so unfashionable a size that this pound of stuffing made them fit perfectly. I then waited for a favorable opportunity — that is to say, a dark foggy day, of which there are plenty in London, especially in the winter. On the morning of just such a day, I put my name down for the doctor, and when he came I complained about my food causing me so much distress, and that I was losing weight. As I anticipated, he ordered the warder to weigh me. I instantly prepared every thing and held my right hand full of dust.

About eleven o'clock he came, and as before we passed through the yard toward the cottage, I peering into the fog to see if the coast was clear — which it appeared to be — and I began saying to myself: "Courage, George! within ten minutes you will be a free man or a corpse! This warder seems a very nice fellow, and I must be careful not to make the mistake that O'Neil and his party did at Sing Sing, and choke him to death by drawing the gag-strings unintentionally too tight around his neck." In the midst of this soliloquy, just as we neared the cottage, something caught my eye, and on looking again I saw the indistinct form of a guard standing under the wall near the spot where I had intended to scale it.

I comprehended that it was customary to put on a guard during foggy weather, and it was fortunate that I caught sight of him before entering the cottage. After having perpetrated an outrage on the warder, even if successful, I should have been obliged to surrender to the guard, and besides a flogging with the cat-o'-nine-tails (which many prisoners who have undergone it informed me took off a strip of skin at each stroke), I should have been put in chains and kept under punishment of some sort as long as I lived.

My only anxiety now was that the warder should not discover, while weighing me, anything to arouse his suspicion; for I had sufficient contraband articles about me to insure the yellow dress and chains for six months. Even the sight of my closed hand might cause him to order it opened, and the dust therein lead to further search. I had to take my shoes off to be weighed, and as the other articles had been transferred from them to my pockets, I took occasion to empty the dust into my shoe, and got back to my cell without discovery.

I have since thought that had the guard escaped my notice, the attempt might have led to murder; for in cases of that kind the aggressor, through excitement and fear of consequences, frequently goes farther than he originally

intended. Burglars do not usually — perhaps never — intend
the murders they commit; and all such serve to show that
there is no knowing how far the least coquetting with evil
may lead. In this case, I had got my mind fixed on freedom,
and of course the overthrow of my hopes cast me for a time
back into despair.

Among those who were sent out into the same yard to
exercise, I noticed a youth of about sixteen, who appeared
to be almost a complete imbecile. Instead of turning out
through the door, he would continue to walk straight up the
ward until an officer caught and turned him in the right
direction. Every day when the exercise was over, and the
order given to march in, he would continue marching around
the small circle until an officer turned him into the path that
led to the entrance. One day he and I were the last to start,
and an old assistant warder, supposing that all were on the
way in with their faces turned away, went to him and began
kicking him with his heavy, hob-nailed boots. Could this
act have been proved against him to the satisfaction of the
superior authorities, he would have been discharged from the
service. But these are bound to take the word of a prison
warder rather than that of prisoners, and the moral level of
very many is such that they do not scruple to make such
statements as are necessary to clear themselves. This will
appear more fully as my narrative proceeds.

About the middle of January, 1873, my sufferings from
cold became so clear to the observation of the experienced
and noble-hearted medical officer, Dr. Vane C. Clarke, that
he ordered me to be put into a cell, one of the inner walls of
which formed a portion of the flue which led from the boiler
furnace beneath my cell. Here I was very comfortable as
regards warmth, but suffering greatly from dyspepsia, constantly aggravated by the prison food.

Convicts during the first year are in the probation class,
nine months of it at the solitary confinement prisons, Pentonville or Millbank, during which time they are allowed no

remission. At the expiration of that time they are removed to the public works prisons before named, and in case they have been well conducted are promoted to the third class, which is distinguished by black facings around the cuffs and collar of the jacket. The diet is unchanged, except that they are allowed an increase of two ounces of bread daily, and they can receive a visit for twenty minutes, and write a letter once in six months.

After being a year in the third, if well conducted, they are promoted into the second class, which is distinguished by yellow facings. In this class they are allowed one pint of tea *vice* gruel, two ounces of bread extra, and also a visit of thirty minutes, and may write a letter once in four months. After another year, with good conduct, they are promoted into the first class, which is distinguished by blue facings, and carries with it the maximum amount of bread, twenty-four ounces per day, an increase of two ounces in each class.

Every prisoner has a letter and numbers on his arm. The letter represents the year in which he was convicted; thus " Z 1084. 20," in a circle, on the arm above the elbow (see cut Prisoners at Exercise), denote the year 1873, the wearer being the 1084th man convicted that year, and his sentence twenty years.

Those whom the authorities suppose never to have had another conviction wear a red star above the circle on the arm, and are kept apart from old " lags." In this the intention is good, but a great many of the younger succeed, through the changes of appearance as they grow older, in concealing their former convictions, and mingling with the genuine " star " men render futile most of the precautions adopted for their protection against the contagion of the ordinary English prison associations.

By this system each man can, by good conduct and hard labor, earn eight marks a day; or, deducting the first nine months (upon which no remission is allowed), one quarter of his sentence. Six of the eight marks represent his full sentence, so that if he is credited with seven marks a day he gets one month of every eight remission; if eight, then two of every eight. Thus, a man with a sentence of four years and nine months, would get remission on the four years. Light work would give seven marks a day or six months, and hard work eight marks, or twelve months' remission. It will be perceived that the two marks a day are all that can be gained, the other six counting for nothing.

The official punishments were flogging with the cat-o'-nine tails and birch rods, chains, the crank, the tread-mill, straight-jackets, galvanic battery, and another very shocking, the shower-bath, also bread and water, and penal-class diet. This diet consisted of one pint of good oatmeal porridge for breakfast and supper, and one pound of boiled potatoes for dinner. In case a man received a sentence of bread and water (only one pound of bread per day) for more than three days, every fourth day he must have this diet. If the offense consisted in tearing up either his wearing apparel or bedding, besides the chance of a flogging and the punishment of bread and water, he would lose from eighty to two hundred and fifty marks, representing from forty to one hundred and twenty-five days' remission, at two marks per day; also to wear the parti-colored dress, one side from top to toe black and the other buff. In case he tore these up, he was then forced to wear a suit made of double-sewed heavy sail canvas, that he could not tear.

Any attempt to escape brought bread and water, heavy band-irons riveted on the ankles and connected by a chain three feet long, the whole weighing from eight to sixteen pounds — and also the parti-colored dress of yellow and buff.

The punishment for violence against any prison authority, striking a warder, or any like offense, incurred a terrible penalty: bread and water — six or twelve months (perhaps more) penal-class diet — three dozen strokes of the flesh-cutting cat-o'-nine tails, and very likely the ankle-irons for six or twelve months, besides the *ex officio* preliminary "doing" by the warders.

<u>L. P.</u>   ABSTRACT OF THE REGULATIONS
<u>D. 20.</u>   RELATING TO THE
TREATMENT AND CONDUCT OF CONVICTED
CRIMINAL PRISONERS.

1. Prisoners shall not disobey the orders of the governor or of any officer of the prison, nor treat them with disrespect.

2. They shall preserve silence, and are not to cause annoyance or disturbance by making unnecessary noise.

3. They shall not communicate, or attempt to do so, with one another, or with any strangers or others who may visit the prison.

4. They shall not disfigure any part of their cells, or damage any property, or deface, erase, destroy, or pull down any rules or other papers hung up therein, or commit any nuisance, or have in their cells or possession any article not sanctioned by the orders and regulations.

5. They shall not be idle nor feign sickness to evade their work.

6. They shall not be guilty of profane language, of indecent or irreverent conduct, nor shall they use threats towards, or commit assaults upon officers or one another.

7. They shall obey such regulations as regards washing, bathing, hair-cutting, and shaving as may from time to time be established with a view to the proper maintenance of health and cleanliness.

8. They shall keep their cells, utensils, clothing, and bedding clean and neatly arranged, and shall, when required, clean and sweep the yards, passages, and other parts of the prison.

9. If any prisoner has any complaint to make regarding the diet, it must be made immediately after a meal is served, and before any portion of it is eaten. Frivolous and groundless complaints repeatedly made will be dealt with as a breach of prison discipline.

10. A prisoner may, if required for purposes of justice, be photographed.

11. Prisoners shall attend Divine Service on Sundays and other days when such service is performed, unless they receive permission to be absent. No prisoner shall be compelled to attend the religious services of a Church to which he does not belong.

12. The following offenses committed by male prisoners con-

victed of felony or sentenced to hard labor will render them liable
to corporal punishment [meaning birch or cat-o'-nine-tails]: —

1st. Mutiny or open incitement to mutiny in the prison, personal
violence to any officer of the prison, aggravated or repeated
assault on a fellow-prisoner, repetition of insulting or threatening language to any officer or prisoner.

2d. Willfully or maliciously breaking the prison windows, or
otherwise destroying prison property.

3d. When under punishment willfully making a disturbance
tending to interrupt the order and discipline of the prison,
and any other acts of gross misconduct requiring to be suppressed by extraordinary means.

13. A prisoner committing a breach of any of the regulations
is liable to be sentenced to confinement in a punishment cell, and
such dietary and other punishments as the rules allow.

14. Any gratuity granted to a prisoner may be paid to him
through a prisoners' aid society, or in such way as the commissioners may direct.

15. Prisoners may, if they desire it, have an interview with
the governor or superior authority to make complaints and prefer
requests, and the governor shall redress any grievance, or take such
steps as may seem necessary.

16. Any prisoners wishing to see a member of the visiting committee, shall be allowed to do so on the occasion of his next occur-
ring visit to the prison.

Printed at H. M. Convict Prison, Millbank.   9—7.   (621.)

L. P.   SYSTEM OF PROGRESSIVE STAGES
D. 76.   FOR MALE PRISONERS
            SENTENCED TO HARD LABOR.

1. A prisoner shall be able to earn on each week-day 8, 7, or 6
marks, according to the degree of his industry; and on Sundays
he shall be awarded marks according to the degree of his industry
during the previous week.

2. There shall be four stages, and every prisoner shall pass
through them, or through so much of them as the term of his
imprisonment admits.

3. He shall commence in the first stage, and shall remain in the

first stage until he has earned 28 × 8 or 224 marks; in the second stage until he has earned 224 more marks, or 448 in the whole; in the third stage until he has earned 224 more marks, or 672 in the whole; in the fourth stage during the remainder of his sentence.

4. A prisoner whose term of imprisonment is twenty-eight days, or less, shall serve the whole of his term in the first stage.

5. A prisoner who is idle, or misconducts himself, or is inattentive to instruction, shall be liable : —

(1.) To forfeit gratuity earned or to be earned.

(2.) To forfeit any other stage privileges.

(3.) To detention in the stage in which he is until he shall have earned in that stage an additional number of marks.

(4.) To degradation to any lower stage (whether such stage is next below the one in which he is, or otherwise), until he has earned in such lower stage a stated number of marks. As soon as the prisoner has earned the stated number, then, unless he has in the meantime incurred further punishment, he shall be restored to the stage from which he was degraded, and be credited with the number of marks he had previously earned therein.

6. None of the foregoing punishments shall exempt a prisoner from any other punishment to which he would be liable for conduct constituting a breach of prison regulations.

7. A prisoner in the first stage will

(a) Be employed ten hours daily, in strict separation, on first class hard labor, of which six to eight hours will be on crank, treadwheel, or work of a similar nature.

(b) Sleep on a plank-bed, without mattress.

(c) Earn no gratuity.

8. A prisoner in the second stage will

(a) Be employed as in the first stage until he has completed one month of imprisonment, and afterwards on hard labor of the second class.

(b) Sleep on a plank-bed, without a mattress, two nights weekly, and have a mattress on the other nights.

(c) Receive school instruction.

(d) Have school-books in his cell.

(*e*) Have exercise on Sunday.

(*f*) Be able to earn a gratuity, not exceeding one shilling.

(*g*) The gratuity to a prisoner in this stage, whose sentence is not long enough for him to earn 244 marks in it, may be calculated at one penny for every 20 marks earned.

9. A prisoner in the third stage will

(*a*) Be employed on second class hard labor.

(*b*) Sleep on a plank-bed, without a mattress, one night weekly, and have a mattress on other nights.

(*c*) Receive school instruction.

(*d*) Have school-books in his cell.

(*e*) Have library-books in his cell.

(*f*) Have exercise on Sunday.

(*g*) Be able to earn a gratuity, not exceeding 1*s*. 6*d*.

(*h*) The gratuity to a prisoner in this stage, whose sentence is not long enough for him to earn 244 marks in it, may be calculated at one penny for every 12 marks earned.

10. A prisoner in the fourth stage will

(*a*) Be eligible for employment of trust in the prison.

(*b*) Sleep on a mattress every night.

(*c*) Receive school instruction.

(*d*) Have school-books in his cell.

(*e*) Have library-books in his cell.

(*f*) Have exercise on Sunday.

(*g*) Be allowed to write and receive a letter, and receive a visit of twenty minutes, and in every three months afterwards to receive and write a letter and receive a visit of half an hour.

(*h*) Be able to earn a gratuity not exceeding two shillings.

(*i*) The gratuity to a prisoner in this stage, whose sentence is not long enough for him to earn 244 marks in it, may be calculated at one penny for every 10 marks earned.

(*j*) The gratuity to a prisoner in this stage, whose sentence is long enough to enable him to earn more than 896 marks, may be calculated at the same rate, provided that it shall not in any case exceed ten shillings.

(620) Printed at H. M. Convict Prison, Millbank.   9—7.

DIETARY FOR CONVICTED CRIMINAL PRISONERS.

MEALS.	NUMBER 1.			NUMBER 2.			
	When Issued.	Article.	Men, Women, and Boys under 16 years of age, with or without Hard Labor.	When Issued.	Article.	Men with Hard Labor.	Men without Hard Labor. Women and Boys under 16 years of age.
Breakfast.	Daily.	Bread.	8 oz.	Daily.	Bread. Gruel.	6 oz. 1 Pint.	5 oz. 1 Pint.
Dinner.	Daily.	Stirabout (containing 3 oz. Indian Meal and 3 oz. Oatme'l).	1½ Pints.	Sunday and Wednesd'y.	Bread. Suet Pudding	6 oz. 8 oz.	5 oz. 6 oz.
				Monday and Friday.	Bread. Potatoes.	6 oz. 8 oz.	5 oz. 8 oz.
				Tuesday, Thur., and Saturday.	Bread. Soup.	6 oz. ½ Pint.	5 oz. ½ Pint.
Supper.	Daily,	Bread.	8 oz.	Daily.	Bread. Gruel.	6 oz. 1 Pint.	5 oz. 1 Pint.

DIETARY FOR CONVICTED CRIMINAL PRISONERS —(CONTINUED).

NUMBER 3.

MEALS.	When Issued.	Article.	Men with Hard Labor.	Men without Hard Labor. Women and Boys under 16 years of age.
Breakfast.	Daily.	Bread. Gruel.	8 oz. 1 Pint.	6 oz. 1 Pint.
Dinner.	Sunday and Wednesd'y.	Bread. Potatoes Suet Puddi'g	4 oz. 8 oz. 8 oz.	4 oz. 6 oz. 6 oz.
	Monday and Friday.	Bread. Potatoes. Cooked Beef (without Bone).	8 oz. 8 oz. 3 oz.	6 oz. 8 oz. 3 oz.
	Tuesday, Thursday, and Saturday.	Bread. Potatoes. Soup.	8 oz. 8 oz. ¼ Pint.	6 oz. 6 oz. ¼ Pint.
Supper.	Daily,	Bread. Gruel.	6 oz. 1 Pint.	6 oz 1 Pint.

NUMBER 4.

MEALS.	When Issued.	Article.	Men with Hard Labor.	Men without Hard Labor. Women and Boys under 16 years of age.
Breakfast.	Daily,	Bread. Porridge. Gruel.	8 oz. 1 Pint.	6 oz. 1 Pint.
Dinner.	Sunday and Wednesd'y.	Bread. Potatoes. Suet Puddi'g	6 oz. 8 oz. 12 oz.	4 oz. 8 oz. 10 oz
	Monday and Friday.	Bread. Potatoes. Cooked Beef (without Bone).	8 oz. 12 oz. 4 oz.	6 oz. 10 oz. 3 oz.
	Tuesday, Thursday, and Saturday.	Bread. Potatoes. Soup.	8 oz. 8 oz. 1 Pint.	6 oz. 8 oz. 1 Pint.
Supper.	Daily.	Bread. Porridge. Gruel.	8 oz. 1 Pint.	6 oz. 1 Pint.

On Mondays, Beans and Fat Bacon may be substituted for Beef.

TABLE OF SUBSTITUTES FOR COOKED ENGLISH BEEF AND POTATOES, WHICH MAY BE ISSUED IF DEEMED NECESSARY BY THE AUTHORITIES.

	Colonial Beef or Mutton, Preserved by Heat. (Served cold).	Beans and Fat Bacon, both weighed after cooking.	American or other Foreign Beef, Preserved by Cold, weighed after cooking.	Cooked Fresh Fish.	Cooked Salt Meat.	Cooked Salt Fish.
	Ounces.	Ounces.	Ounces.	Ounces.	Ounces.	Ounces.
In lieu of 4 oz. Cooked English Beef,	5	Beans, 9. Fat Bacon, 1.	4	8	6	12
In lieu of 3 oz. Cooked English Beef,	3¾	Beans, 7. Fat Bacon, ¾.	3	6	4½	9

(All Meats to be weighed without Bone.)

	Cabbage or Turnip-Tops.	Parsnips, Turnips, or Carrots.	Preserved dried Potatoes.	Leeks.	Rice steamed till tender.
	Ounces.	Ounces.	Ounces.	Ounces.	Ounces.
In lieu of 12 oz. of Potatoes, ...	8	12	12	8	12
In lieu of 10 oz. of Potatoes, ...	7	10	10	7	10
In lieu of 8 oz. of Potatoes, ...	6	8	8	6	8
In lieu of 6 oz. of Potatoes, ...	4	6	6	4	6

(All weighed after Cooking.)

At the expiration of nine months, one pint of cocoa with two ounces extra bread may be given at breakfast three days in the week, in lieu of one pint of porridge or gruel, if preferred.

The following will be the terms to which the above diets will be applied:

Prisoners sentenced to seven days and under, ... } No. 1 diet for whole term.

Prisoners sentenced to more than seven days, and not more than one month, ... } No. 1 diet for seven days, and No. 2 for remainder of term.

Prisoners sentenced to more than one month, and not more than four months, ... } No. 2 diet for one month, and No. 3 for remainder of term.

Prisoners sentenced to more than four months, ... } No. 3 diet for four months, and No. 4 for remainder of term.

CHAPTER XXXIX.

MY narrative has now reached a point where my actual
penal servitude begins, and it will be well to present
here some account of those who were to rule my life for so
many years.

The Board of Prison Commissioners have their headquarters at the Home Office in Parliament Street, London,
and are under the control of the Home Secretary of State.
One of these visits each of her Majesty's convict establishments once a month, in order to try any cases of insubordination which are of too serious a nature for the governor of the
prison to adjudicate upon, he not being permitted to order
any penalty beyond a few days of bread and water, and loss
of a limited number of remission marks.

The head authority at each prison is the governor, of
whom the largest establishments, like Portland, have two; the
smaller one; and the smallest none. Next comes the deputy
governors — the medical officer and an assistant doctor; the
chaplains and schoolmasters, Protestant and Catholic. There
are four grades of prison warders, viz., the chief warder,
principal warders, warders, and assistant warders. The chief
warder of course stands first in the list, and his duties, if honestly executed, render him the most important, as he is the
most responsible of the prison officials, save, perhaps, the med-

ical officer, who is the autocrat of the place.   But, in case anything goes wrong, he is the man who gets all the blame, and
when matters run smoothly and well, the governor gets all the
thanks.   During the absence of the governor, the deputy takes
his place, and in turn the chief warder performs the duties
of the deputy governor's office.   As all business passes through
the chief's hands, he must be a fair scholar, though sometimes
a principal warder who understands book-keeping is detailed
to assist him.   He must be of strict integrity, a thorough dis-
ciplinarian, and of a character to make him respected both
by his superiors and inferiors in position.   The warders of
all grades are under his command, and must fear him for his
inflexibility in punishing any breach of regulations, and have
confidence in his disposition to act justly toward them, he
being the one on whom the governor relies for all information
regarding their conduct.   It is on the reports of the chief
warder that the governor acts in all cases involving their promotion, reprimands, or fines, and their applications for leave
of absence must be approved of and signed by him.   It is
clear that unless he is very straight in the performance of his
duties, he would soon place himself in the power of some of
the warders, who would not fail to take advantage of any
knowledge of his derelictions to benefit themselves, and to the
detriment of discipline and good order.   Under the English
government, the salary of a man possessing these superior
qualifications, is between five and six hundred dollars a year
and his uniform.   This is of blue cloth, the sleeves and collar
of the coat and his cap embroidered with gold lace.   On alter-
nate days, at the prison where I was confined, he came on
duty at 5 A. M. in summer, and 5.30 in winter, and left the
prison at 4 P. M., leaving in charge a principal warder, coming on duty the following morning at 7 A. M.   At 6 o'clock
P. M., after receiving the reports from the ward officers, stating the number of prisoners each has just locked up, and
thus seeing that all are safe, he locks with his master-key the
gates and outer doors of the main buildings, and before finally

retiring for the night he must lock the outer gate, so that no one but the governor can get in or out—each watchman being locked into the ward which he is set to guard. There are bells in his room connecting with the various wards, and in case of sickness or any other emergency, he is the man who is aroused. It is the chief warder who keeps everything connected with the prison in running order, and whatever goes wrong the cry is for the chief, and he is sent for be it day or night.

In a large convict establishment there are a dozen or more principal warders. These are the lieutenants of the chief, and have general supervision of the working parties. Their pay is about four hundred dollars a year and uniforms. There are of the other two grades, warders and assistant warders, from two to three thousand employed in all her Majesty's prisons in Great Britain and Ireland. Warders and assistant warders are provided with a short, heavy truncheon, which each carries in his hand, or in a leather sheath which hangs from his belt, to which is also attached a sort of cartouch-box in which he keeps the keys, which are fastened to a chain, the other end to his belt. When about to leave the prison, on going off duty, he must hang up the belt and attachments in the chief warder's office. Their pay, besides uniforms, which are of blue cloth, is three hundred and fifty dollars a year for warders, and three hundred for assistant warders. All promotions are by seniority. In case of transfer by the authorities to any other prison, they retain their position in the line of promotion, but if they volunteer or make application to be transferred, they have to begin at the bottom in reckoning the length of service for promotion. When the authorities wish to transfer warders, it is usual for them to call for volunteers, of whom they find a sufficient number anxious for a change, unless the transfer is to an unpopular station, such as Dartmoor, which is among the bogs, and a lonely, bleak place.

Warders are exempted from doing night duty, which is all

done by the assistant warders, who are on that service one week out of three. Although, when on night duty, they had the day for sleep and recreation, I never saw one who did not detest it, because they must remain on duty continuously for twelve hours, and must not read, sit down, nor lean against anything, nor have their hands behind them, but must remain standing upright. These military regulations apply as well to the whole time they are on duty in the prison, day or night. A few years ago the time of daily duty was reduced to twelve hours, with one hour at noon for dinner. Besides this, at times they must do a good deal of extra duty. Each is allowed ten days annual holiday, but is frequently obliged to take it piecemeal, a day or two at a time, so that he cannot go far away from the scene of his servitude. Their duties require unflagging attention, and never-ceasing vigilance, which must be a heavy tax on the brain, and the twelve hours must be passed in standing or walking about. In fact, they are subjected to military discipline, or rather despotism, and any known infraction of the rules subjects them to penalties according to the nature of the offense. Leaning against a wall, sitting down, etc., for a first offense, they are mulcted in a small sum — twelve to sixty cents, usually — and are put back in the line of promotion. The fines go to the Officer's Library fund. I knew one officer, Joseph Matthews, who had been assistant warder twenty years, and being frequently set back for doing some small favor to prisoners, was discharged from the service in 1886, without a pension, for some slight breach of regulations. He had a wife and six children, and had worked twenty years for less than seven dollars per week. For giving a convict a small bit of tobacco, a heavy fine, suspension, and in case it was not the first offense, expulsion from the service without a pension. For acting the go-between, and facilitating correspondence with the friends of convicts, expulsion — possibly imprisonment. One of the assistant warders, who was convicted of having received a bribe of one hundred pounds from one of us at Newgate, was expelled from the service and imprisoned eighteen months. Another at Portsmouth prison underwent the same fate, save that his term was but six months, for sending and receiving letters for a prisoner, and similar cases are of frequent occurrence.

The warders and assistant warders are the ones who come in direct and constant contact with prisoners, and when the eye of no superior authority is on them, or nothing else to deter, they are "hail fellow well met" with such of the convicts as are unprincipled enough to curry favor with and assist them in covering up their peccadilloes from their superiors. They naturally recoil at the hardness and parsimony of the government toward them, evading the performance of duties when they can; and I have heard more than one say, substantially, in reply to a remark that I was surprised that they dared be so lax in their duties and permit prisoners to carry on as they did: "Why should we care what prisoners do, so long as we don't get into trouble? The government grind us down to twelve hours' daily duty on just pay enough to keep body and soul together; then, if we complain, tell us that we can leave if we like, as there are others ready to step into our places. Bah! what do we care for the government? It is of no benefit to us; the big-guns get big pay, and the higher up the office the more the pay and the less the work. To be sure, we can go out of the prison to sleep, but otherwise we are bound down as closely as the convicts," etc., etc. Yet these very warders, the moment any superior authority appears on the scene, are as obsequious and fawning as whipped dogs, and recoup themselves for this forced humiliation by "taking it out" of such of the convicts as fail to curry their favor, or offend, or make them trouble. Surely their office is a very responsible one, and it is blind, false economy to retain low-priced men in such a position. The present English system of penal servitude is perfect on paper, and so far as regards cleanliness, clothing, and quality (not quantity) of food, there is no just ground for fault-finding;

but the moral qualities of most of the warders and assistant warders precludes all possibility of the reformation of those in their charge.

Notwithstanding the expositions of the English delegates at the international meetings, prison reform *has never yet been tried in Great Britain and Ireland*. In other words, all efforts in that direction have been defeated by placing convicts in the immediate charge of a class of men who by education and training possess none of the qualifications requisite for such a responsible position.

In so far as forms are concerned, the business of the prison is carried on most systematically. There are blank forms which cover everything, from provisioning the prison to bathing the men, and these must be filled in and signed by the warder in charge of the particular work being done. For example: every two weeks — those in the Infirmary every week — he must fill in the proper form, and certify that every man in his ward has had a bath, unless exempted by the doctor. At Woking prison I have known men to go unbathed for many months, simply because they did not wish to bathe, and it saved the warder trouble — nearly all others in the ward only bathed about once a month, and yet at the stated times the officer filled up and signed the form, certifying to the superior authorities that those in his ward had been bathed at the regulation times.

A great majority of the officers employed in the prisons and jails of Great Britain and Ireland are soldiers who have been invalided or pensioned off after doing the full term for which they enlisted — twelve years — and of sailors in the same condition. In order to encourage enlistment into the army and navy, the government gives discharged soldiers and sailors the preference in the civil service, apparently heedless as to their moral qualifications. Indeed, it would be difficult, if not impossible, to ascertain about these, for the very nature and present requirements of those services tend to harden and make men conscienceless, subservient, and fawning toward their superiors, and tyrannical to those in their power.

PRINCIPAL WARDERS, WOKING PRISON.
No. 1. Scott.
No. 2. Metherell.

ASSISTANT WARDERS, DARTMOOR PRISON.

As to those in the prison service, there are many who would be good men in a situation suited to their acquirements, and there are but a few of those who are brought into immediate contact with the convicts — who, in fact, virtually hold the power of life and death over them — whose influence is of an elevating or reforming kind. Indeed, I have heard many of them telling or exchanging obscene stories with prisoners, and using the vilest language and bandying thieves' slang, in which they become proficients. I am bold to say that at least one-half of all I have known are in morals on a level with the average convict, or, as I have heard more than one assistant warder say, "too much of a coward to steal, ashamed to beg, and too lazy to work" — therefore became a soldier, then a prison warder. This may, at the moment, have been spoken in a jesting way, but it is none the less true.

What can be expected, in the way of refinement and good morals, from a class of men who entered the army or navy, coming, as they did in most cases, from the untaught and mind-debased multitude with which that land of drink and debauchery swarms ?

It will be seen from the foregoing that very much *is* expected from them, and in order to fulfill the very hard terms of their contract with the government, and keep their places, they are forced to resort to trickery, deception, and perjury, until these, in their attitude toward their employer, the government, become second-nature, readily resorting to lies to clear themselves from blame, even in trivial matters, to save themselves from a sixpence fine. There are jealousies among themselves, but when it is a question of deceiving, or keeping any neglect of duties or violences against prisoners from the superior authorities, they all unite as one man, and affirm or swear to anything they think the position requires

For example: A convict named Robinson was kicked in the lower ribs and abdomen so that he died within a few days. I have heard officers assert that they could "kill a man without leaving a mark." In the case of Robinson a large surface turned purple, so that the doctor saw that fatal violence had been used. The patient's parents were sent for, to whom he related the occurrence, inculpating certain officers of Woking prison. An officer of unusual bravery and moral courage — as his conduct in this affair showed — had seen the violence done to Robinson and exposed it to the superior authorities, his account corroborating the dying declaration of the convict Robinson. When he died, the doctor made the usual *post-mortem* examination, ascertaining the exact causes of his death. The coroner's jury, as usual in all cases of death of convicts, was impaneled and evidence taken. One or two prisoners known to me wished to go before the jury to give their evidence, but they were not called. The officer before referred to made oath to the facts. Those who did the violence came forward with their friends and rebutted his evidence in so firm, conclusive, and brazen a way, that this noble-hearted officer *was discharged from the service as a lunatic*, because he had dared to state the truth as it was well known to many officers and prisoners. I am quite aware that the foregoing, and many other things yet to be drawn from my memory, will appear incredible; but if the English government will grant me the necessary facilities, I think it in my power to produce persons and papers which shall prove that all I write is strictly true.

Although prison officers are not supposed to use more force than is absolutely necessary for self-protection, in practice they operate in quite a different manner and on another principle, shocking instances being not infrequent. Numerous cases of cruelty have come under my notice, and I have seen several prisoners die from the neglect and ill-treatment of brutal warders.

Prisoners have little chance of getting their grievances redressed, because they are forced to make their complaints, in the presence of warders, to the governor, or to the government commissioners on their periodical visits.

A "new chum"—and he must be excessively "fresh"—

may dare to make complaints against warders; but it is well known among old "lags" that they may as well cut their own throats as to do *that*. Indeed, there is a general understanding between these and the warders that the latter are to be upheld under all circumstances. For example, I have known instances where men were brutally kicked and beaten for some trifle which made the warder lose his temper. In the excitement of the moment the victim would declare that he would tell the governor. "Tell the governor, will you! You ———— scoundrel! I'll teach you to complain!" And amid a volley of vile language the warder would repeat the ill-treatment, well knowing the governor was bound by law to believe *official* evidence in preference to the word of any prisoner, and that his own unblushing denial must be accepted. It is a frequent occurrence that the officer turns the tables on the complaining convict, and gets him punished for making false statements when he had but told the simple truth.

Surely, the reformation of the criminal must become the one great object in any system of imprisonment. As a rule, prison life is begun when young in years, and, though tainted, they are not so deeply immersed in vice but that there is a good prospect of reformation. Most certainly it will not cost society a thousandth part as much to rescue a child as will be the expense of maintaining him in prison — though I will leave out that factor, and say, as the sum of his depredations during the varying periods when he is outside of a prison.

The fact is that the majority of prisoners would die in a short time if left at liberty, their mode of life and dissipations wearing out their constitutions rapidly. By the time they are shattered or on the brink of the grave, they get into "trouble," are sent to prison, where the regular mode of life restores them to vigor; then they are at liberty long enough, usually, to have committed a considerable amount of depredations and used up that vigor, about which time they are again in "trouble"; and so they revolve — a certain class have the designation of "revolvers" — through life, dying in either prisons or workhouses. I have heard more than one clever professional say something like this: "To be sure, I am doing my second (third or fourth) term, but then I shall have lived longer, and have been free a longer time in all, than if I had never been in prison, for in that case I should have gone to the devil flying!"

In the words of one of America's greatest authors — Charles Dudley Warner — spoken to me not long after my arrival from England: "There will never be any success in reforming criminals until the prison officers with whom they are in immediate contact are gentlemen."

CHAPTER XL.

I NOW come to an important epoch in my prison life. After the failure of my plan to escape, dyspeptic troubles prevented me from retaining or getting the necessary amount of nutriment from the ordinary prison diet. I had spoken to the medical officer on several occasions, and he had said that they did not put those suffering from rheumatism or dyspepsia under hospital treatment. It occurred to me that the penal-class diet would be better for my case, and I applied to him, explaining that I had always been fond of porridge, and felt sure the two pints per day allowed as part of that diet would do me more good than all the other prison food. He replied: " I would like to give you porridge, but cannot do so except as a penalty or punishment diet."

My mind was so unbalanced by the mental and physical troubles of the past few months that I at once resolved to do something by which I should incur a sufficient penalty to ensure my being put on porridge. Therefore, on returning to my cell I began to study upon a plan to bring about the desired result. In my then state of ignorance regarding the severe penalties inflicted for slight irregularities, I imagined that three days bread and water in a dark cell without a bed, was a severe punishment.

(437)

Owing to my sufferings from cold, Dr. Clarke had ordered me to be removed into a cell next to the large flue which led from the furnace beneath. The cell wall which formed one side of the flue was always so hot that it was not comfortable to hold the hand against it very long, and on close examination I noticed that some of the bricks did not appear to be well cemented. "Here goes for some porridge," thought I. I therefore took my tin knife and worked out the plaster around the top and ends of one brick, then watching an opportunity when a gang of men were coming in from exercise, I knocked it, and a second, loose with a few blows of the three-legged stool, and at once set the table in front of the hole and sat down pretending to read. I was no sooner seated than a warder came to the door, looked through the spy-hole, and, seeing me quiet, evidently thought his ears must have deceived him, and passed along to the next cell. My original plan had been to let the warder "cop" me in the act, but as soon as I saw the bricks come loose so easily, it flashed through my mind that I might get up the flue after the fire was extinguished in the spring; therefore, I took precautions not to be discovered until I had satisfied myself if such a plan was among the possibilities. After all was quiet again I removed the two bricks and covered them up under the pile of oakum. My slate had a wooden frame, and with a slate pencil I drove the peg out of one corner, removed the slate, and pulled the four pieces out straight, by which means I had a good measuring rod. Within the first course of bricks was an inch of air space, then came the wall of the flue which was composed of a layer of fire-brick. There were some crevices in this, and I pushed the rod through until it touched the opposite side, which proved the flue to be fifteen inches inside. I had no sooner put the frame back on the slate than steps approached my door. I shoved the table in front of the hole, picked up a book as the door was thrown open, and the assistant doctor came in, followed by the usual retinue of warders. After asking me a few questions as to my health, food, etc., he departed, much to my relief, for while he was speaking I cast a furtive glance at the oakum and I saw one corner of a brick protruding. I put the bricks back in their place, filled bread dough into the crevices in lieu of mortar, then with whitewash scraped from the walls I whitened it so that it looked the same as the rest of the wall.

When in the yard at exercise I calculated the height of the chimney, which was about sixty feet. For several days I turned the matter over in my mind but could come to no conclusion. At the best it would be a "forlorn hope" affair. There was scarce an hour in the day that some one did not look in the spy-hole to see what I was at, as the Newgate affair previously described had made me a suspicious character in the way of escapes. At night the warder on duty was supposed to peer into my cell every hour. The gas was left burning above the door for that purpose.

Under such circumstances I should have been obliged to dig out two layers of brick and make a hole large enough to let me into the flue, ascending which I would perhaps be stopped by iron bars laid across at the level of each story and at the top of the chimney. But if the flue should be unobstructed so that I reached the roof, I must descend about fifty feet into the yard which a watchman patroled, cross this and scale a brick wall thirty feet high, from which I must drop into the street — into the arms of a policeman! Besides, I must not wear the prison clothes, but make some sort of garments out of my bed blankets or sheets beforehand, and conceal them in my cell until the moment for action. To accomplish all this I had a strip of tin for a knife, a wooden spoon, and a needle with plenty of thread. My sufferings and solitary confinement had brought me to that desperate state in which I was willing to risk my life for a change — a change at any price, even for the worst. After revolving the subject for some days I determined that there was a chance of success, for at night the watchman did not peer through the spy-hole sometimes from midnight until 4 A. M., and I thought probable that the yard patrol would be snug in a corner fast asleep; for as a rule prison warders take it easy and shirk every duty they safely can in revenge for being paid but a mere pittance. It is very difficult to catch one of these old soldiers or sailors asleep on duty. I have known a number who would sleep hours in an upright position, and one at Dartmoor Prison — an old soldier of the Indian mutiny — named Varney, who while on night duty in my ward used to sleep, snoring so loudly as to awaken me. Suddenly he would break off in the middle of a snore and shout, "All right, sir!" to the governor, chief, or orderly officer, as either made the customary rounds. Within a minute I would hear him snoring as if he had not been disturbed. It was well-known to the authorities that old Varney slept on duty, and for years they had been trying to "cop" him; they could get near enough to hear him snore, but instantly came the "All right, sir," he giving the customary military salute without moving from his upright position.

But to return from my digression. I determined to attempt to carry out the plan of escape as soon as the furnace fire was put out in the spring, provided I could get the layer of fire-bricks loosened. In order to set my mind at rest on this point, I removed the two bricks and tried to work one of the small crevices between the fire-brick larger with my tin knife. This would not make the least impression on them, and on closer examination I saw that the extreme heat had baked the fire-brick together so that it looked to be nearly as hard and impenetrable as a wall of iron.

At once I abandoned all hope of escape in that direction, and reverted to the plan of procuring porridge by letting them discover the loosened bricks. I had no idea as to the penalty for attempting to escape, but was satisfied that no one could suspect me of being simple enough to get into a red-hot flue. Taking out the two bricks I thought would be a sufficient offense to get me put on the porridge diet. I therefore laid the bricks back in the hole and sat on my stool by the side of it and picked at it with my tin knife.

BIDWELL SIX MONTHS IN SIXTEEN-POUND CHAINS FOR ATTEMPT TO ESCAPE

Shortly I heard the slide over the spy-hole move, and felt that the warder was peering into my cell. He left, and in five minutes came with the principal warder, who unlocked the door and came in. Seeing the bricks loose he pulled them out on the floor to make the thing look as bad as possible, and asked me what made me do it. I told him what the doctor had said in reply to my application for porridge. They went away, locking me in again, and in about ten minutes I heard a heavy tramping over the stone floor of the corridor. My cell door was flung open as the warder shouted " Attention!" and in came the governor, followed by the chief and several other warders.

" What do you mean by this sort of work ?" the governor demanded.

I answered the same as I had done to the warder. He stepped outside of the cell and told the warder to bring me along, and started up the corridor. I followed in escort of the warders, and was locked up in another cell. I had been under the doctor's care on what is called prison treatment, and the next morning the assistant doctor came in, had me stripped, and then sounded my lungs and made some examination of my legs. I was too " fresh " then to know that such an examination was to enable him to report to the governor how much punishment I could endure. During this examination the doctor said :

" Well, you have done it this time ; what made you act so foolish ?"

I told him I was suffering so much from the good-conduct diet, and knowing that the penal-class or porridge diet would be much better for me, I had determined to get it at all hazards, for I could not go on as at present.

" Well," he replied, " I am sorry for you ; but your chest and legs are sound, and it is not in my power to save you from going before the director [designated in the United States state prison inspector]."

I did not, through ignorance, appreciate the gravity of his

last remark, but was soon put in the way of doing so. About noon my cell door was thrown open, I was ordered to " come on," and taken to what proved to be the governor's office. But it was not that official who was to do for me, his accustomed place being occupied by the director. The governor, his clerk, and the deputy governor, were seated near by, while the chief warder, one or two principals, and several warders of a lower grade were standing in waiting, besides three or four who surrounded me to protect their superiors from so desperate a character as myself; at least, that is just how it looked and appeared to be, in order to give color to the false trash with which I have reason to believe the director had been stuffed full. I had been on one occasion taken before the governor, who warned me that I should be severely punished unless I picked more oakum than it was possible for me to pick, but I was totally unprepared to meet so potent an authority as the director, and what followed remains indelibly imprinted in my memory.

" You are charged with attempting to escape. What have you to say for yourself ? " asked the director.

I repeated what I had said to the governor, and added that if he would examine the condition of the flue, he would ascertain that it was constantly so hot that anyone getting into it would be burned to death, also that it would require a sledge-hammer to break through the fire-brick lining — that even if such obstacles were overcome, and there were no gratings in the flue to prevent me from gaining the top, I must get from the roof into the yard, and scale the wall unobserved by the watchmen — and finally assured him that any man in his senses, after having removed the outer course of bricks, would see that escape in that way was not among the possibilities.

No heed was paid to this, but the director immediately sentenced me as follows :

"I ought to have you flogged, but as the doctor says you are not in a state of health to permit, I sentence you to undergo ten days bread-and-water diet, six months chains and ankle-irons [see illustration in explanatory chapter] and to wear the yellow parti colored dress during the period of six months."

I was led from his presence stupefied. I had obtained the porridge diet with a vengeance! Without delay I was inducted into the yellow and buff dress; the blacksmith came and riveted heavy band-irons around my ankles, and did not do his work any too gently. These were connected by a heavy chain, about a yard in length, and the whole weighed some sixteen pounds. I was then put into a cell in the basement, which had nothing within the bare whitewashed walls save a raised bench on one side, with a wooden head-piece for a pillow at one end, and the smoothed section of a tree imbedded on end in the asphalted floor at the other for a table. I thought my condition bad enough before, but now I felt that I had reached the very last stage of degradation except flogging — and I am free to say that, had they flogged me, there is no doubt I should have been put into a state of mind that would have led to murder. I paced restlessly about the cell, dragging the clanking chain. I felt that my ankles were disgraced; the irons gnawed into my soul, as they soon did into my flesh. I dashed my head, in wild despair, against the wall, and madly raved at such injustice. The solid walls, before my wavering sight, appeared unrolled, and showed me mocking demons, to whom my mental pangs gave fresh delight. I shook my clenched hands on high, and cursed these and the Ruler of the Universe for having permitted me to come into existence.

The assistant warder, a kind man, came at regular hours with the few ounces of bread (one pound per day) and to see if the water-jug was empty. On these occasions he tried to cheer me up, but I paid no heed, and for four days I ate none of the bread, and did not even moisten my lips with water.

The warder afterwards told me that on the fifth day he found me lying senseless on the floor, and that I did not show any signs of life except faint breathing for the next week, and that they kept me alive by pouring beef-tea down my throat through a rubber tube. About this time I remember seeing the medical officer, Dr. Vane C. Clarke, leaning over and looking at me with eyes expressive of pity and sympathy. Gradually I recovered my powers of observation, and found that they were giving me a shock of. electricity from a powerful battery, which had no effect on my legs, but as they applied it to other parts of the body it caused the most excruciating pain, and shook me as if it would tear every bone out of my body. The irons and chain were still on. The legs of the breeches which are worn with irons are open on the outside, and when on are fastened by buttoning up both sides, so that they are easily taken off at night without removing the irons, and the stockings can be slipped down inside the iron bands and taken off. As these, and every article of clothing and underclothing, except shirt, must be put outside of the cell at night, the unfortunate wretch must sleep, if he can, with the iron bands against his bare ankles.

There are constantly so many convicts shamming sickness in order to escape hard labor and to obtain admission to the Infirmary, that they may have better food, and the doctors have been so often deceived, that they are forced to be very circumspect, and, except in cases where the disease manifests itself unmistakably, they are obliged to subject every applicant to severe and sometimes terrible ordeals in order to test the genuineness of the case. Indeed, it not infrequently happens that men get no help until (excuse the "bull") they prove that they are really sick by dying. I have known several such cases.

For the reasons above referred to I was subjected to applications of the battery and various other tests for three weeks, when, to my inexpressible relief, the blacksmith came and with a cold-chisel and hammer cut the rivets and removed the irons, although in doing it he nearly broke my ankles. As soon as these were off. the warder of the Infirmary came and removed me to that place, when I was put in one of the observation-cells, on a wide bedstead which contained a good spring-bed.

This observation-cell was about ten by twelve feet square, with the usual spy-hole in the door. In the ceiling was fixed a plate of glass, and the room overhead was so arranged that persons there could see all that passed below, but the man in the observation-cell beneath could not see them nor know when he was being watched. Indeed, any queries as to what the glass was in the ceiling for, elicited the false information that it was originally intended to light the cell with a gas-light above the plate, but it was found it did not work as well as the old plan. This was to allay any suspicions and put the occupant off his guard.

At Woking the ward in which I stayed for a year was in charge of Assistant Warder Joseph Matthews. At the time of which I am writing he was located at the Pentonville prison, and he used to tell me about what happened while I was in that observation cell. He said that he was put on night duty in the room above me, and for six weeks from 6 P. M. till 6 A. M., his eyes were constantly fixed on me, and that another assistant warder was on duty for the same purpose daytimes. Nothing having been reported to the medical officer regarding me that was inconsistent with the nature of my reputed malady, at the end of that time the special watching was given up. He said my case attract-ed much attention among the prison authorities, and that frequently the governor, doctors, and others would come in and peer down on me and ask him how I was going on. During all this time I was subjected to daily shocks with the battery, causing unspeakable torture.

One day the doctor came and (unknown to me) had the bath-tub which was next door filled with hot water, which, by a thermometer, was but a degree or two below the scalding point. In the meantime the assistant warders had stripped me naked, and then picking me up by the shoulders and feet, carried and dropped me like a lobster into the hot bath, in the hope that if I were shamming inability to walk, the sudden scald would make me jump out. I felt as if every inch of skin was coming off, and made out to raise myself into a sitting posture, and there I sat in the hottest spot I had ever known. The doctor made these tests more to satisfy the governor than himself, and seeing that this had failed, I was lifted out and placed in a chair with my back to the door, and instantly there came crashing into the small of my back from a hose-pipe a stream of ice-cold water — for it was in January. After it was played on till I felt myself congealing into solid ice, I was put back to bed. The medical officer having now satisfied all possible requirements, gave me every attention. I had eaten next to nothing for some weeks, although ever since the chains had been removed he had ordered whatever he thought I could relish.

The Governor of Pentonville in 1873 bore the patronymic of Bones, but as he was disgusted with being called "Old Bones," he had taken his wife's name, which I cannot now recall. At this prison I had little opportunity of taking his measure, except to notice his pompous manner, his fondness for the title of Colonel — he had filled that office in the *militia* — and his haughty, overbearing, and despotic demeanor towards prisoners. I was transferred from Dartmoor to Woking prison in November, 1881, where I saw a good deal and heard more of him for some years until he quit the service.

I have said elsewhere that all prisoners were sent away from Pentonville and Millbank prisons at the expiration of their nine months' probation. Therefore, on the 20th of February, 1873, I was handcuffed and taken from the observation-cell, driven in a cab to the station, put into a car, and after an all-night ride, arrived in Portsmouth, where a conveyance was waiting in which I was transported about sixteen miles to Dartmoor prison. About 9 o'clock A. M. the 'bus stopped at a small wayside inn long enough for the warders to breakfast. On the whole journey the warders treated me very kindly, and here they took me into the inn, and out of his own purse the principal paid for a pint of hot milk to wash down the dry bread which had been brought for my breakfast, also giving me three or four lumps of loaf sugar left over from their breakfast, the last that I tasted for the ensuing fourteen years. Had those acts of kindness to a suffering man become known, the warder might have been punished by fine or expulsion from the service. When arrived within the walls of Dartmoor the handcuffs were removed, and I was taken into the reception-room, a dreary-looking place, where, after waiting two or three hours, the doctor came in and ordered me to bed in the Infirmary.

CHAPTER XLI.

THE Dartmoor convict establishment is composed of eight
large prisons, surrounded by a stone wall twenty-five or
thirty feet high, each prison being also separately enclosed.
Dartmoor, in Devonshire, consists of a large tract of treeless,
boggy land, which until within a few years was considered
worthless for farming purposes. I was informed that it
belonged to the Prince of Wales. During the wars with
Napoleon the First, several buildings, with a capacity for
10,000 men, were erected on the site of the present convict
establishment for the incarceration of French prisoners of war.
The story told me about the establishment of a station for
convicts here is that it was done in order to make the property owned by the Prince of Wales valuable without expense
to him. The site on which the prisons are located is on the
highest part of the moor, about seventeen hundred feet above
the sea, and is an extremely desolate place. Westerly winds
bring the clouds saturated with warm moisture from the gulf
stream, which strike this high land and empty floods of rain,
hail, snow, or sleet, according to the season, and at times all
within the same day, so that clear weather is the exception.
The prisoners who work on the bogs are provided with two
suits of clothes, so that when they come in from work, soak-
ing wet, they may have a dry suit. These are employed on
the bog in ditching, draining, and burying the great rocks and

DARTMOOR CONVICT ESTABLISHMENT.—ABOUT 2000 PRISONERS.

boulders with which its surface is covered. If my memory is not at fault these prisons were opened in 1852, and since then the labor of the convicts has made many hundreds of acres of valuable farming land out of a tract supposed to be worthless. It is an inhospitable climate, and the worst possible place for a convict establishment. With the exception of a short time in the summer, there are frequent dense fogs which prevent the men from being taken out to work, the expenses going on just the same when the warders and convict workers are idle.

The bog for some distance around the prisons having been reclaimed, some of the gangs work one to two miles distant. Oftentimes the weather is clear in the morning, and the warders march their parties out as usual, only to find a few hours later themselves and their men enveloped in a dense fog. Each party is accompanied by three or four men known as " civil guards," who are armed with repeating carbines. The guards are posted around the convict laborers who are, at times, scattered some distance apart. As soon as the principal in charge sees a fog coming he collects his men and calls the guards near, but at times the fog sweeps along before this can be accomplished.

That is an opportunity that some men cannot resist, and they make a run for liberty, sometimes getting clear off, in most cases, to be picked up a few days later half starved. Sometimes, indeed, they are forced by hunger to give themselves up. What makes it so difficult for prisoners (even under such apparently favorable conditions) to escape is, that every inhabitant in the surrounding country is on the lookout, in the hope of gaining the standing offer of £5 reward for the recapture of escaped convicts.

Some who had friends arranged with a warder to see or correspond with them, who for a small sum would assist in preparing an escape. I knew a man at Dartmoor, by the name of Britain, for whom an assistant warder secreted a suit of citizen's clothes out on the bog. One morning, a few days later, he and another man started, both disappearing like phantoms in the fog before the guards could fire. Instead of making directly for his secreted clothes, Britain crept under a small bridge, where he was soon discovered and marched into his cell, which was next to mine, and gave me full particulars. Two days later the other man came back to the prison, having been all that time wandering over Dartmoor bogs without food.

The Dartmoor infirmary is in No. 1, the oldest of the buildings, having been built by the French prisoners of war. In the basement and first floor are cells about ten feet square which are used for hospital patients, who from any cause are not permitted to be placed in the large association rooms overhead. Nothwithstanding my physical state, on account of my alleged attempts to escape I was placed in one of the cells.

All association of convicts with each other is destructive. At the time to which I have brought my narrative I had but a dim idea of the important bearing which this fact has on the possibility of reforming convicts; still I was of the impression that under the circumstances it would be best for me to have nothing whatever to do with my fellow-prisoners. It is clear to me, and the sequel will show that had I rigidly adhered to this resolution, there is little doubt but that I would have been sent home many years before I was.

In the corridor where I was located the cells had sheet-iron partitions, the upper two feet of which were perforated with one-quarter inch holes to give a good circulation through the whole tier; and any occupant had only to stand on his deal table and peer through these holes to see all that was going on in the adjoining cells. They could also whisper with each other, and at certain times, or when either one of certain assistant warders was in charge, they could and did talk and shout to each other all down the corridor.

My cell was at the far end of the corridor, and the man in the next cell, Niblo Clark, was a " character." I was no sooner locked in my cell and left on my bed in solitude, as I supposed, than I heard a voice in suppressed tones, say : " Hello ! where did you come from ? Are you a new chum, and how long have you got ?" and a dozen other questions in a breath. I did not answer, nor did I respond to his numerous attempts the ensuing five or six weeks to open conversation. As I was never taken out of my cell, except to the bath-tub close by, and the cell was so dark that I could not see to read when the sun did not shine, the solitude became unbearable, so much so that my resolution of non-intercourse gave way, and I replied to him. The ice once broken there was no end, and he jabbered nearly every moment when he was not asleep, relating every event of his life, a sketch of which may not be uninteresting here, as he is a representative of a large class who fill the prisons.

Niblo Clark was the son of " poor but respectable parents," who lived in London. From early childhood he had been permitted to play in the street, and by the time he was eight or nine years of age he used to run away from home for two or three days at a time, sleeping with his chums in any nook or corner they could find, and pilfering to appease their hunger. At about fourteen, his father procured him a place in a small drug shop, which he did not retain long before he was detected by his master appropriating

ESCAPED FROM A REFORMATORY.

small sums. For this he was brought before a magistrate and sent to a reformatory school, from which he escaped within a few months. While at the reformatory he had learned nothing but evil, and on his return to London he plunged at once into, what was at the time a favorite haunt for thieves, Drury Lane. He was soon arrested for sneaking something from a shop door, and sent to jail for six months. He said they set him at picking oakum, and pun-

ished him on bread and water for not doing the allotted task, till he was nearly dead from starvation, and that the ordinary allowance of food for full labor was only half enough. However, he lived it through, and at fifteen was discharged with a few shillings. He then took up thieving as a profession, and would not have earned an honest living had he the opportunity.

Within a few weeks he received his first penal term, which was five years at Chatham, where he divided his time between the punishment cells and the hospital, preferring to " do" bread and water till so sick or exhausted that the doctor was obliged to take him in and put him on hospital diet for a few days. This he regarded as a full compensation for his sufferings in the punishment-cells, and from that time on for twenty-seven years, until the completion of his last term in 1887, an imprisonment of three penal terms — five, seven, and fifteen years each — he had kept on that plan of shamming and deception which had become to him second nature.

He got his third penal term of fifteen years in 1873, for stealing two coats a few months previous to my trial. His account of his last arrest, the general correctness of which I have no doubt, was substantially as follows:

" I was going along Cheapside late one night, and came to where a new building was being erected, next to which was a tailor's shop. I climbed over the boarding and up into the second story of the new building, from which I got upon the roof of an addition to the tailor's shop. I found a window opening on the roof which was not fastened, and creeping through I got down into the front shop, and by the dim light reflected from the street lamps I collected a lot of things and tied them up in a bundle, which I put up within reach of the window. Seeing two nice coats hanging on a nail, I thought they were just what I wanted — put them both on and climbed up through the window. As I turned to reach in for the bundle, I saw a man come into the shop from a side door, he having been aroused by some noise. Upon seeing me in the

window, he shouted : ' Hello ! what are you doing there ? '
Without stopping to answer or to get the bundle, I scrambled
back into the new building and got safely into the street with
both the coats still on.   I had not gone far before I met two
bobbies, and like a fool as soon as I was past them got frightened and began to run.   This they noticed, and at once gave
chase.   I ran into a back alley, and climbed over into the back-
yard of one of a block of dwelling-houses.   The policemen got
around the corner soon enough to see me disappear over the
fence, so I climbed on top of a great water-cistern, raised a
window through which I climbed, and then shutting, passed
up to the roof through the skylight.   From behind a chimney
I watched the movements of the bobbies who could not see
me, but knowing I was in the block one of them remained on
guard while the other went for assistance, and soon returned
with a number who surrounded the block.   After searching
all the back yards until nearly daylight, they concluded I
must have got into one of the houses, and as it grew light,
these were searched in vain.   I had retired to the far end,
where the block of houses bordered in a narrow lane, which
obstructed further progress in that direction.   While considering what to do in such an emergency, some one in the street
caught sight of me, and soon I saw a policeman's head pop-
ping up through the trap-door.   In a moment several were
on the roof and advancing toward me.   I got close to the end,
and saw a window open in a house on the opposite side of the
lane, a few feet lower than the spot on which I stood.   Without hesitation I leaped, luckily reaching the window-sill, and
swung myself in.   There were hundreds watching me, and
when they saw me make the fearful leap, they no doubt
expected to see me dashed to pieces on the pavement.   As I
entered the room in this unusual manner, an old woman who
was in bed began to scream ; I hastened down the stairs, but
before I had got far a bobby met and collared me."

Strange as it may seem, all this time Niblo Clark had not
attempted to get rid of the stolen coats, but had them on

when arrested! The officers who pursued him had no idea of what he had done, and had a long hunt before they found the owner to identify the garments. I asked him why he did not throw them away, and he replied that they were the best he had ever "owned," and fitted him so nicely he could not bear to part with them — another instance to prove that "something" always happens.

On account of his previous convictions the judge gave him ten years, but as Clark began at once to "cheek" him, he withdrew that sentence and raised it to fifteen years, every day of which he served and completed in the spring of 1887. I have as little doubt that he is now doing his fourth term as I have that he will die the same wretched death in prison as others whom I have known.

It was very amusing to see Niblo Clark, sitting at work or marching at exercise, about three times a minute give his head and neck a peculiar twist, like that of a hen with the pips. He claimed to have the asthma and a combination of all throat and chest diseases, of which this twist was the external sign — certainly the doctors had never been able to discover an interior sign of any complaint save that he appeared to be "constitutionally tired." Niblo was a sort of prison newspaper, for, according to his own accounts, he knew all that had happened, all that was going to happen, and many things that could never happen, about the prison. The authorities might as well try to stop the wind from blowing as to stop his tongue. He would shout to a friend at the other end of the ward, telling him all his secrets, and how he imposed on the doctors, with no thought as to whether any authority was listening or not.

One evening the medical officer happened to come into the ward, and, hearing Niblo's voice, he walked lightly and stopped in front of my cell, which was next to Niblo's, but out of his sight. There he stood, hearing Niblo relate to his friend down the ward all about how he had taken the doctors in for the previous ten years. When there came a pause the doctor suddenly put in his oar: "Well, Niblo," said he, "You have been giving me an interesting story, but it is quite unlike what you tell me ordinarily," and the doctor went tramping out of the ward, leaving Niblo in a state of speechless consternation. After a few minutes he recovered his tongue, and remarked: "By jingo! who'd have thought the doctor was there!" "I did," said I, "for I had to stuff a sheet into my mouth to keep from roaring while I saw him listening."

CHAPTER XLII.

DR. POWER — GOVERNOR HARRIS — HARD LIFE AND TERRIBLE DEATH OF AN ITAL-
IAN CONVICT — LORD KIMBERLY IN MY CELL — PHILLIPS, THE CONVICT IMPOS-
TOR — A PERAMBULATOR — INGRATITUDE — ANOTHER IMPOSTOR "RAISED" BY
GALVANIC SHOCKS — BOOZER'S STORY — SOAP AS AN ARTICLE OF DIET — HOW
CONVICTS GET INTO THE HOSPITAL — BEEFSTEAKS AS BREASTPLATES — "RE-
LIABLE" CONVICTS ON THE LOCK-OUT — "WHOPPER" — HOW TO GET A GOOD
DINNER IN PRISON — SACRIFICING AN EYE FOR A FEW WEEKS IN HOSPITAL —
TAGGART, A PRISON "FAKER" — AN INCURABLE ABSCESS.

WITH one exception I never saw among prison authorities a nobler-hearted Christian gentleman than Dr. P.
Power, the medical officer in charge of Dartmoor prison at
the time of my arrival there. He remained until the beginning of 1878, when he got transferred to Portsmouth prison,
where he still was up to the time I left England, scattering
benefits on all the *miserables* with whom he came in contact, either in or out of prison.

One thing is certain: Dr. Power was not cruel enough to
the prisoners to suit some warders and others. This truly
Christian medical officer never resented anything. On one
occasion a prisoner, to whom he had refused some application,
struck him a heavy blow between the eyes, which blackened
both. Every one expected that the offender would be flogged
and put in chains. But no; the doctor said that the man who
would strike one who was acting for his benefit could not be
in his right mind, and that he should not be punished.

In the second cell from mine — the one adjoining Niblo
Clark's — was an Italian, who, when I arrived, was raving
night and day. His right arm had been cut off at the elbow,
and he was serving out a term of twenty-five years. The fol-

(456)

lowing is the story of his prison life as I had it from various sources :

Some years previously he had been convicted of an attempt to stab some person in an affray, and received a sentence of five years' penal servitude. Upon the completion of his nine months' probation at Millbank prison, on account of the state of his health he was sent to the invalid station, Woking prison. Here he under-went a great deal of pun-ishment, which is almost certain to be the case with foreigners who c a n n o t speak the language. Eng-lishmen of the class from which warders are usually taken are ignorant, preju-diced, and narrow-minded, as a matter of course. They think the customs and man-ners of their own country must be right, and anything

LORD KIMBERLY.

different wrong, in consequence of which they are not capa-ble of making any allowance for the idiosyncrasies of a man who has been brought up in another land, amid surroundings totally unlike their own.

In consequence of this, the treatment of the Italian (who was not a habitual criminal) in the rough, arbitrary, and overbear-ing way to which the great majority of English convicts have been accustomed, would incite him to violence. If, under a feeling that he was being grossly insulted without cause, any prisoner once gave way and lifted his hand, woe to him; his time on earth would not be long, or he would be served as this Italian was.

However it came about, he believed that an official had caused him to undergo great suffering. This injustice, as he deemed it, continued for years, and worked him up to a state of mind which made him resolve to have revenge in true Italian style. By some means he procured a rusty nail, ground it to a point, and tied it on a stick. With this impromptu dagger, while on parade, he rushed up to the offending officer and struck him a blow in the chest which penetrated through his clothes and pricked the skin.

At the time when this mad freak was perpetrated he had but a few months to serve in order to complete his five years. But now he was taken out, tried, convicted, and sentenced to twenty-five years penal servitude, and was serving it out when I first saw him at Dartmoor.

Deputy Governor Harris was appointed Governor of Dartmoor, and some of the warders had a fancy that they would curry favor by making it hot for the Italian. However this may be, it was not long before they twisted his arm — a trick they have — so that the doctor had to amputate it, as stated, at the elbow. At the time I arrived he was a raving maniac, and should have been sent, as were many not so crazy, to a prison lunatic asylum. I do not *know* the reason this was not done, but it certainly was a remarkable circumstance that he was not sent. Influences were brought to bear so that concealments, backed by misrepresentations, ended in inducing the doctor to order him sent to the punishment-cells, where, not long after, he died. Judging by my knowledge of the doctor's character, I do not believe that he ever discharged the man out of the hospital, and I am more inclined to give credence to the other account which was current, viz., that some officer either gave the order himself or procured it from higher quarters.

Throughout the few months during which I had nothing to do with my fellow prisoners, the doctor treated me most kindly and continued to do so. The second summer I was taken for a month into the yard an hour each day, the rest of the time I lay prostrate in bed, my shoulders, knees, and thighs swollen to nearly double their ordinary size. For many months I lay at the point of death, no one believing it possible that I could recover. The fact that the doctor certified that my case was genuine was reason enough why some warders, who were at loggerheads with him, should declare that I was shamming, and sufficient to cause them to make misstatements as to my words and acts, in order to favor that side of the question and influence the doctor against me.

In the meantime a prisoner named Phillips was constantly running the doctor down to me, till, without the slightest real ground, I began to think he was my enemy. Phillips finally led me to believe that the doctor was doing me some injury. The governor on his rounds came in to see me every day, and was always very polite and smiling, and in my weak condition I began to make complaints to him against the doctor, there being no foundation for them but the fancies put in my head by Phillips — the weak state of mind to which I was reduced, making me a fit subject for such as he to operate upon. The governor directed that a statement-sheet should be given me, so that I could write out my complaints for the director, and this I did.

Despite my complaints against him the doctor continued to treat me in the best manner, and matters run on until the winter of 1876–7, when one day I heard a great clattering of feet coming down the stone-paved corridor, and presently the cell door was thrown open and " Attention " shouted. I saw in the corridor the doctor, governor, deputy-governor, chief warder, and a retinue of warders, who all formed the suite of a large, fine-looking man, whom I afterwards discovered was no less a personage than the Earl of Kimberly, after whom the Kimberly diamond mine in South Africa was named, and who, at the time of which I am writing, held the office of Colonial Secretary of State. My lord entered the cell — he had to bend his head — closed the door behind him, came to the side of my bed, and in a pleasant tone of voice asked me how I was, and if I had any complaints to make. I saw that he must be some dignitary, and that the governor had brought him for the purpose of letting him hear my grumbles against

the doctor. Really fancying at the time that I had grounds
for complaints, I went on to state them. His manner was
kind, and his demeanor the same as that of all other true gentlemen, however high their station, towards the unfortunate.

Aside from his position as Colonial Secretary of State, he
had been appointed one of three special commissioners to
examine into the state of the convicts in Her Majesty's
prisons. I have regretted to this day, and it has been a matter of wonder to me how my mind could have been so acted
upon as to make me complain against such a noble-hearted
man as Dr. Power, a skillful physician, who, in addition to his
duties in the prison, had a large practice which frequently
took him out of bed among the poverty-stricken wretches
which abound every where in England, the direct effect of a
cause that fills the prisons, viz., the legalized trade in beer
and spirits.

Phillips had been in the army, and for the offense of striking an officer had been court-martialed and sentenced to
undergo seven years penal servitude. After doing his nine
months' probation at Brixton, the place where military and
naval convicts were sent to do it, he was sent to Chatham to
complete the term. As labor, and in fact any employment,
had never agreed with him, he suddenly became "paralyzed"
in the whole right side, and pretended that he could not
move the right arm and leg. The usual tortures were applied, the battery, straight-jacket, shower-bath, etc., and as
he stood all these for three or four months without wincing,
or showing any other sign which would enable the doctors to
penetrate the deception, he was sent to the Woking invalid
station and put into the same corridor in a cell near mine.
I have said elsewhere that there was little restraint on talking, and we could give food to one another, or write notes
on slates and send by the "cleaner," who would watch an
opportunity to shove them under the door, there having
been left a space of four inches by the width of the door for
the purpose of ventilation.

Phillips made all the trouble he could, depending on his supposed physical state to escape the punishment he deserved. I will not relate further particulars, but conclude by relating that when his time was nearly served the kind-hearted doctor very considerately had a perambulator made, in which he could get about after being discharged from prison. An officer named Nichols, an ex-marine, was sent with him and assisted in lifting him into the train. On their arrival at Birmingham this scamp stood up on his feet, and pointing to the wheeled chair, said: "Take that thing back to Dr. Power, and tell him to —— " (an expression of course too vile to bear repetition). Phillips then walked out of the car and disappeared among the crowd on the station platform. On his return with the chair, assistant warder Nichols, being on duty in my ward, gave me the particulars.

Think what effect such an occurrence would be likely to have on the doctor, and what the higher authorities would think of him, when they were informed of the occurrence. It is such cases, often recurring, which cause the doctors to inflict, in the way of tests, unbounded sufferings on many genuine cases; and this one caused several invalids, of whom I was one, to be put through a series of fresh tests, and it caused me several years of horrors.

As an instance of how the doctors are imposed on, I give the following: A young man of eighteen years was suddenly prostrated, or, rather, prostrated himself, giving the impression that he had a stroke of paralysis, and as he stood the usual torture tests his case was considered genuine, and he remained in hospital, in the next cell to me. After he had lain in bed without speaking for six months, the medical officer left, and Dr. Reid, an old army doctor, came to fill the vacant post till a new appointment should be made. In the meantime the man had been shifted into a cell lower down the ward.

One morning I heard the buzz of the battery, and said to myself: "That fellow is getting a shock." Presently I heard some one rushing down the ward, followed by another, and, looking through the four-inch strips of glass, I saw the "paralyzed" young man going past at high speed, and Dr. Reid close after him. Just past my cell the doctor caught him and asked him why he had tried to impose on the doctors. The young man told him in reply that the warder over his gang had a grudge against him, and constantly reported and had him punished for every trifling infraction of the rules, and that those whom he liked did still worse things with impunity. Dr. Reid listened to him, and after a moment said, as near as I remember: "You are young, and I will give you a chance. You know that if I discharged you from the Infirmary you would be severely flogged, but if you will promise me to go on right, I will have you sent away to another station, where you will have an opportunity for a fresh start." I did not doubt the young man's story, and thought this a just and humane conclusion.

Cases of imposture were of constant occurrence while I was at Dartmoor. In order to get into the hospital, men would bring on incurable diseases by swallowing pounded glass; eating soap, to bring on an appearance of atrophy; pushing small pieces of copper wire into the flesh, and leaving them there until the blood was poisoned; putting lime in the eyes, to bring on inflammation, etc.

A young man known by the flash name of "Boozer," on account of continual boozing at the public houses whenever he was out of jail or prison, was in the next cell to the one occupied by me. It will be remembered that these had sheet-iron partitions, so that whispering and talk could be carried on with impunity. Boozer was born in the London slums, of drunken parents. He said he did not remember when he first began to drink. He went through the usual course of London children, who, from the time they can toddle, are left to gutter influences. At first, thieving for food and, as he grew up, to obtain the means for indulging in the accumulating vices, he had continued the routine through reformatory and jail, and was now doing his third term of penal servitude. He was up to all the tricks and ways of how to get on through his period of incarceration with the performance of as little labor as possible.

On arrival at Dartmoor he had been put at work in the quarry, but finding that too hard for him, he dropped a heavy stone on his foot and injured it so that the doctor was obliged to take him into the hospital. While there, by the time his foot was healed, he had eaten so much soap that he was gradually wasting away to a skeleton, and the doctor could not tell what ailed him. He finally told the doctor that he did not get enough to eat, and wanted to be put in the cook-house to work. The doctor was glad to get rid of him at any price, for he was pretty certain that the man was maltreating, or in prison slang, "faking" himself. Accordingly he was sent into the kitchen, and I saw no more of him for three months. One day I was sitting in the exercising-ground when a party of men harnessed to a cart full of coke passed by, and one of them — a big, burly, red-cheeked fellow, whom I failed to recognize on account of his fatness — bowed to me. I asked another man who it was. "Why, that is Boozer," he replied.

A few days later he was again put in the next cell, and on asking him why he was in hospital again he said that he had "faked" his leg and it was badly swollen. I asked him how he did it, and he explained that he had with a needle drawn a thread through the flesh in his knee, and had left it until it had become so bad he could not bear it longer, then he had drawn out the thread and shown the sore to the doctor.

He had a great deal to say about the abuses that he saw going on in the kitchen, and as what he said corroborates what I had been told by other prisoners who had worked there, I will give the substance of his remarks. The bread was supposed to be made from unbolted wheat flour, or what in the United States is called graham flour. Instead of this, he said they mixed bran, middlings, and flour, some of which was generally musty. Having had a long experience of the virtue of graham bread, in America, and knowing that all English prisons were to be supplied with it by order of the chief authorities, I had often wondered why the brown bread actually supplied was not up to the mark, and had taken pains to learn all I could as to how business was carried on in that most important department — that of feeding the twenty-five thousand, more or less, of wretches in English prisons who were deprived of all opportunity of getting food for themselves. The warder in charge of the cook-house is called the head-cook, although he does no cooking—that being done by prisoners who in all probability never had any experience in cookery. He oversees the ten to twenty who do the work, and these must be what he calls reliable men — that is to say, men who are devoted to him, who will watch for him, assist him in his peccadilloes, and help to swear him out of any difficulty with his superiors when anything goes wrong. The governor, the doctors, deputy governor, and chief warder are the authorities whom he and his helpers fear, and one of the latter is always on the watch to give the signal when either of those are coming toward the cook-house. "Here comes the chief!" etc., and instantly all spring around lively to set everything to rights and conceal any evidences of irregularities and peculations.

There is a considerable quantity of eggs, butter, sugar, etc., allowed by the orders of the doctors to make puddings for the hospital. As I said, from information derived from independent sources — that of several prisoners who worked in the Dartmoor kitchen at various periods — it is a regular thing for at least one-half of those prison dainties to be made away with by the warder and his helpers. More than one of these has assured me that the warder used to cut off thick steaks from the best beef—that allowed for hospital beef-tea —and when he was ready to go home, lay them on his breast and button his overcoat, and thus "get away" with five or six pounds. I have been told that, before the cells were lighted with gas, certain warders would frequently fill the

CONVICTS AT LABOR.

coat-tail pockets of their overcoats with candles. When I was in the dormitory at Woking prison, one Whopper sent word to a friend of his, who was working in the kitchen, where he was located. The consequence was, that the tray which contained our four dormitory dinners had the very best quality of prison rations, and on the four meat days an extra quantity of meat, with half a pound to a pound of melted fat. The dozen dinners in that tray were all alike, thus ensuring Whopper a "square meal" however they might be distributed. To do this a hundred other men were robbed of some portion of their share. A quantity of cocoa was allowed sufficient to make a good three-quarters of a pint for each, but chunks of cocoa were secretly passed all over the prison to the many favored ones who had a friend at court, in consequence of which the cocoa was weaker.

But I have wandered from the subject of impositions on the doctors. Another man, whose name I cannot recollect, but will call Brown, was for a time in the next cell at Dartmoor. Upon inquiring, I ascertained from him that he had put lime in his right eye, and this had brought on something like a cataract, at least that was what the doctor told him it was. I heard the doctor order the warder to see that Brown had no food before the operation was performed, telling him that this would prevent him from being sick with the consequence of losing the eye. The warder forgot his instructions, and the next morning gave him his breakfast. Brown had heard the doctor's orders, and after he had eaten, asked me what I thought of it. I replied, that he had done very foolishly, and that he must tell the doctor ; but the warder would not allow him to do so, well knowing that he would be fined half a crown for breach of orders.

About ten o'clock, he was removed from the cell into the large hospital dormitory where the doctor operated for the cataract, but during the operation, Brown was taken sick at the stomach, and the strain caused the eye to burst and run out. This warder, rather than get the operation adjourned at

30

the risk of losing thirty cents out of his inadequate salary, caused Brown to lose his eye. A week after the operation, he was discharged from the hospital, and I saw nothing more of him for some months, at the end of which, he was again in the hospital totally blind. This young man of twenty, who had only a seven years' term, to escape hard labor in the quarry deliberately risked his eyesight. This was his first term and he appeared to be above the average intelligence of prisoners.

Another young man, named Taggart, was doing his second penal term, the first of five and this of seven years. He was in the hospital in a cell opposite mine for a number of years. When I left Dartmoor he was on his last year. Despite every effort to prevent it, he had managed to "fake" a sore on his left knee-joint, and to keep it open until the leg had become permanently crooked and stiff. In order to give the sore a chance to heal, he had been for months in an observation cell, like the one described in a former chapter, under watch day and night, but *that* sore would not get well.

At other times he had been kept in a straight-jacket for the same purpose, but even that would not cure *that* abscess. One night he got off the straight-jacket and pushed it out through the open ventilator into the yard. He boasted to his fellow prisoners and told all about how he managed, and hardly denied when the doctor charged him with "faking" it. The authorities had such good proofs that he did tamper with it, that he was brought before the director and flogged with a cat-o'-nine-tails, but his back had become so tough and seamed by former floggings that even this extreme measure failed to cure his sore.

Years after, while I was at Woking, I heard that after he had been set at liberty, it was not long before he was in again, serving a third term of ten or fifteen years, and in the Infirmary because of *that* abscess.

Chapter XLIII.

A FEW hours after my interview with Lord Kimberly, after he had left the prison, an order was given to transfer me to the punishment-cells in prison number seven. After having complained against the doctor, the governor took my case in his own hands, believing that his method would soon cure me. These punishment-cells contain nothing in the way of furniture except a raised platform of hard wood on one side large enough for the occupant to lie down on, with a piece of wood fastened at one end for a pillow. Most of these cells are changed into dungeons, having sheet-iron nailed over the windows, shutting out the light. I was put in one which contained a mattress and bed-blankets, a tin knife, a wooden spoon, a deal table, and a bench. I was put on the ordinary prison diet. An order was given by the governor that I was to be carried to the tailor shop and set to work as an able-bodied man. At 7 o'clock the next morning a warder appeared with two men from the tailor shop; one of these took me on his shoulders and started; half way he put me down, and the other took me, reached a flight of steps, and at last landed me on the shop floor. Having been for nearly five years almost continuously shut in a cell, this change

(467)

was very grateful to me. Some articles of clothing being given me, I sewed away as though I had been a born tailor. At noon I was carried back to my cell, and, as I had been unable to swallow any breakfast gruel, I was obliged to eat the prison dinner, though from former experience I had some misgivings as to my stomach's ability to digest it. At 1 o'clock I was again taken to the shop, and went on all right for two or three hours, by which time I became so sick that I could no longer retain the food eaten, as it had turned excessively acid. Seeing my state, the master tailor, Mr. Rayford, who had charge of the shop, sent me back to my cell, but the warder was obliged to report me for idleness, that affording a legal pretext for taking the next step in the drama. Accordingly the next morning two warders came to my cell, and, each grasping an ankle, dragged me fifty yards over the flag-stones of the court to the door of the governor's office. After lying on the stones for some time the door was thrown open and I was carried into his presence, when about the following occurred:

Governor — "You are charged with idleness. What have you to say for yourself?"

"Nothing, beyond what you know from the doctor," I replied.

Governor — "Three days bread and water and eighty-four remission marks."

As these words left his lips, I was seized by the jacket collar and dragged outside, then two assistant warders seized me, one by the ankles the other by the wrists, and carried me along head-first, face upward, lifting me up and bumping me down on the pavement at every step, at the same time the one behind giving me a "helper" in the rear every time he brought his right foot forward. In this way they conveyed me into one of the cells with the window darkened as described, and I was thrown down to lie on the bare boards until night, when a thin mattress and blanket were put in. Bread and water was no punishment to me, for I could not eat without distress even the pound of bread per day.

When the three days were up I was taken back into the former cell and put on prison diet again ; and again I was carried to the tailor shop to go through the same routine, including the bread and water.

A third time I was brought before the governor, and he now tried a new plan of cure. As I had good use of my hands and arms he sentenced me to the crank, and I was taken to still another cell, and placed on a stool by the crank. I began turning away for dear life, and there the reader may leave me for the present to read a description of that wind-grinding instrument.

The crank consists of a circular plate of iron fixed in the wall of the cell ; through the center of this plate runs a spindle to which is attached a crank something like, only longer than that of a grindstone. Just above the center is a dial-plate about four inches in diameter, which shows the number of the revolutions, having different pointers for the tens, hundreds, and thousands. Before the occupant can have his breakfast he must turn the handle 1,875 revolutions. His dinner must be earned with 5,000, and his supper with 4,000 turns. If any one of my readers wishes to experiment on what amount of labor those figures represent, let him get some one to grind an old axe, bearing on pretty hard, while he turns the grindstone and counts.

There is a loaded brake attached to the handle, so that it requires the application of considerable power and great endurance to make it spin thirty-five times a minute in order to earn the food in time. Few men possess patience sufficient to enable them to hold their temper when, after turning until they are breathless, they look at the dial and see that it has moved so very short a space of its journey around. Certainly it is the only example on record by which men literally earn their bread by *grinding the wind*.

Outside of the cell, fixed in the wall, is a dial also connected with the crank, so that the warder can see at a glance how industriously the wind-grinder is working. In case he fails to make the required number of turns, 10,875 in the course of the day, the warder reports him for idleness, and the result is three days' bread and water, with loss, less or greater, of remission marks, at the discretion of the governor, up to a certain number.

After my time on the crank had expired, I was put back in my cell and then taken to the tailor-shop again. Under this treatment, daily becoming weaker, and obliged to continue swallowing the prison diet, the same cause produced like effects, and for some weeks following I was revolving through a circle of punishments, of which one station was the tailor-shop. Work was then brought to my cell, but I had become so weakened that I could only sew while lying on my back on the floor. Under these circumstances I could not do much, and the principal warder, Westlake, who had charge of the punishment-cells, reported me for idleness; and as the doctor would not permit even the governor to put me on bread and water again, when I was brought before him he put me on penal-class diet—porridge at last! the very diet I had four years previously failed to obtain at Pentonville, getting chains instead.

Ever since I had been transferred from the hospital, every article of bedding had been removed from my cell, so that I was obliged to lie all day on the planks; and the warders all having "got the tip," judging from my treatment, it is not surprising that in other respects they were not as gentle as they might have been. At all events, I had got into a state of mind and body which made me feel that death was far preferable to such a life. In my desperation and despair I took the tin strip used for a knife, and after sharpening it against the stone wall, I tried to cut my throat, but discovered that it was tough—so tough that I sawed away with all my force for some minutes, when, by the rate at which it bled, I thought it was enough to put an end to my troubles. I lost consciousness, and when I came to myself the doctor was pushing a needle through to sew up the gash, the cicatrice of which is still visible.

A few days later, in Westlake's presence, I gave utterance to long-repressed words expressive of my opinion regarding his treatment of me. He left the cell without a word, and shortly returned with a couple of warders to assist him to handcuff my hands behind my back, in which condition — a horrible one for a man crippled in the legs to try to sleep in — he left me until the next morning, when the assistant doctor came, Dr. Power being absent. He now had the effrontery to tell the doctor, in my presence, that he had been obliged to handcuff me to prevent me from doing myself another injury! It was impossible to sleep in the handcuffs, and I had not a wink for three days, nor did I eat one mouthful of food or moisten my lips with a drop of water, while undergoing so unjust a punishment.

At this time Mr. Rickards, the excellent chaplain of Dartmoor prison, was absent on his annual holiday, and the Rev. Mr. Ferris, rector of Charlestown in Cornwall, was officiating in his stead. On the morning of the fourth day he was passing my cell and heard groans. He stopped, and after looking through the spy-hole, unlocked the door and came in — the chaplain being allowed a key. Upon seeing my condition he was horrified, being an outsider and not hardened to such sights, and went at once to see Governor Harris, expostulating with him for permitting such cruelty to a man in

REV. A. H. FERRIS.

my condition. The governor sent over an order that the handcuffs were to be at once removed, which of course warder Westlake was obliged to do, very much to his chagrin. To take it out in another way, he had me stripped, put into the bath, and scrubbed with a splint-broom brush, until I was pretty well skinned.

The accompanying memorandum letter from Governor Harris may perhaps be read with interest, as a genuine prison document; it will certainly convince the reader that my correspondence was not excessive:

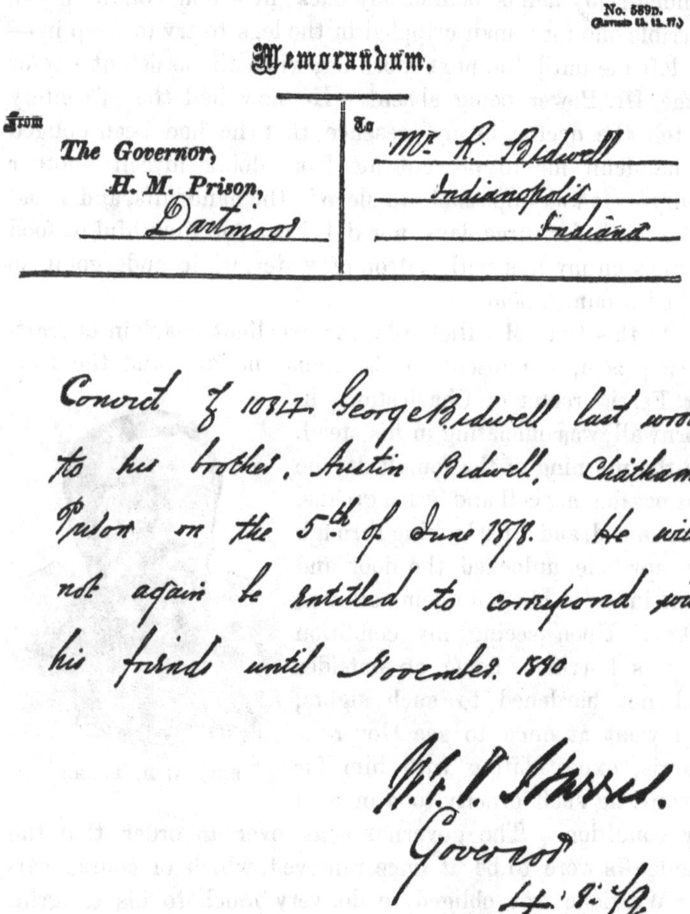

No. 589D.
(Barrack 13. 13. 77.)

Memorandum.

From	To
The Governor, H. M. Prison, *Dartmoor*	*Mr. R. Bidwell, Indianapolis, Indiana*

Convict ℨ 10347 George Bidwell last wrote to his brother, Austin Bidwell, Chatham Prison on the 5th of June 1878. He will not again be entitled to correspond with his friends until November 1890

W. I. V. Starves.
Governor
4. 9. 79

I regard it an honor to be able to present in this volume a letter from so good a man as the Rev. A. H. Ferris, accompanied by a truthful portrait. Readers have here an opportunity to look a true English Samaritan in the face.

BEFORE THE GOVERNOR — ASSISTANT WARDER REPORTING A PRISONER FOR TALKING.

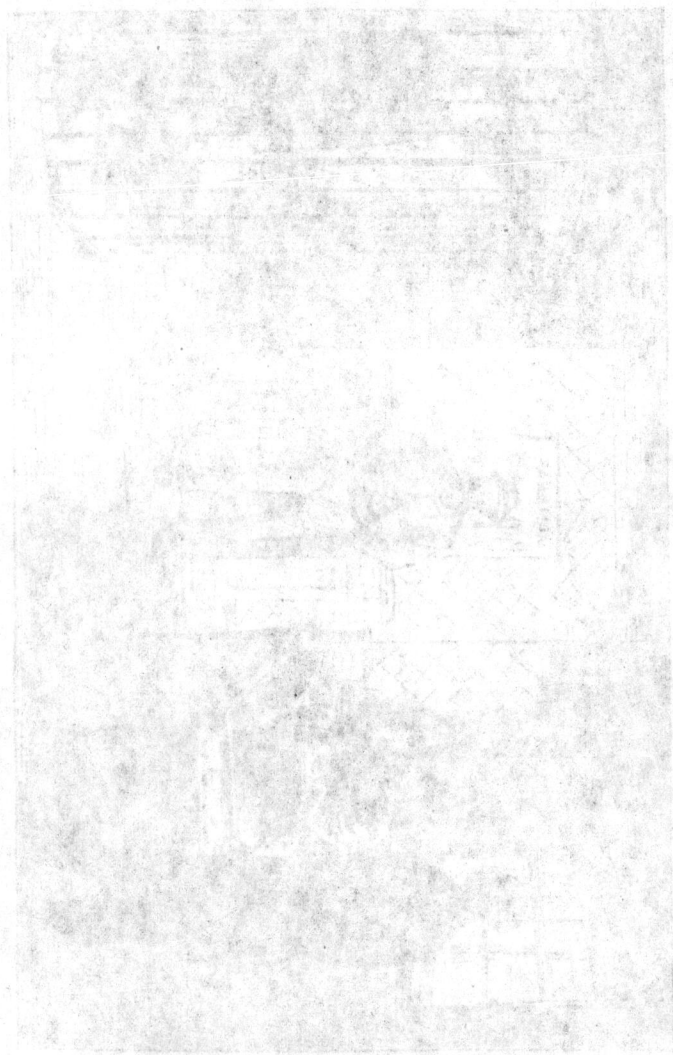

JAN: 3,   ST. ANSTELL,
   1888.   CORNWALL.

MY DEAR BIDWELL, — Your letter came upon me like a resurrection. I had quite given you up to the great majority, after
reading the sad accounts of your treatment in the various newspapers. I am so glad you have recovered your health after all the
troubles and afflictions laid upon you. How thankful you must feel
now you are once more allowed to rest in the bosom of your own
family and amongst your own friends. I have often thought of
you, talked of you, and prayed for you ; but I never expected to
hear that you were liberated, they all seemed so embittered against
you.

Thank you very much for your kind offer of a bed at your
house. I wish I could accept it ; it would give me a great deal of
pleasure to do so, but I am sorry to say I am in great pecuniary
difficulties just now — a friend (?) has cheated me out of £150,
and as I am not a rich man, the loss has caused and will cause me
great trouble. I am afraid I shall not be able to meet my liabilities this year. God help me ! — but I must not enter into my own
troubles.

I am afraid your book will be rather personal if you insert my
photo, letter, and several lines of "abuse," in explanation. Plain
facts and statements of your prison experience will fetch English
people more than anything else. The true story of your sufferings
would create deep feelings of sympathy and interest and do more to
sell the book than whole heaps of parsons' letters and photos.

I am glad to be able to tell you that we have at last succeeded
in getting that man Watson released. I do not know whether
you will remember him. He was a lifer; a painter and glazier
by trade ; crime, writing threatening letters. Twenty years the
poor fellow has been shut up at Dartmoor, a thoroughly well
behaved man. Never had more than one bad report, and then he
was badgered by one of the warders. I am so thankful he is out
at last. How like a poor little mouse just liberated from a trap he
must feel. Please send me a copy of the book as soon as it is out.
I dare say I could sell a few copies down here.

You seem to be highly favoured at Hartford in having two
such shining lights (C. D. Warner and S. L. Clemens) of the

literary world living there. I should like to meet Mr. S. L. Clemens. I always enjoy his quaint, dry humor.

I inclose photo of myself and shall be glad to have one of you. Don't forget the story of the mouse, the galvanic battery torture, the handcuffs and chains. Above all, don't forget to send me a copy of the book.

With kind regards and all good wishes, believe me,

Yours faithfully,

(The Reverend) A. H. FERRIS.

The man Watson referred to in the foregoing letter never missed an opportunity to correspond with the beloved Chaplain Ferris, after his retirement from the service. The following letter, written in 1884, I am kindly permitted to publish:

DEAR SIR, — I received your very kind and ever welcome letter and was very pleased to hear from you. I hope you are quite restored to health again, my letter being lost and my daughter being in a hurry to answer the governor's inquiry, forgot to mention in her letter that you wrote a few lines to me and that it was sent in the letter that was lost. Therefore, I thought you might perhaps be offended with me, but my mind is at rest now I have heard from you. You tell me not to give up all hope yet, but my hope is almost dead, but still I clutch to the least hope whatever. I think sometimes they may perhaps liberate me when I am old and worn out and no one will employ me, and only fit to go from a prison to a union, but they will never do men any good by keeping them in prison all the best of their days, for I believe the longer they keep men in prison the more hardhearted they make them, for I believe if men were shown more mercy and kindness there would not be so many in prison as there are at the present time. I know you have tried your utmost to get me home to my beloved children, and I do most heartily thank you for your great kindness towards me. for it is a great comfort to me to know that I have one true and kind friend in this world I must now say farewell, and may God bless you and grant you a long and happy life in his service in this world and everlasting happiness in the next, is the sincere prayer of your unhappy but ever faithful and hopeful friend Robert Watson. Sir, would you please to acknowl edge the receipt of this letter to my daughter with a few lines for myself (if not giving too much trouble, for your letters seem to cheer me up). Good by, and God bless you.

Yours faithfully,

ROBERT WATSON.

As a further evidence that the Rev. Ferris was notably the prisoner's friend upon all occasions, I insert here another letter from one who was a prisoner at Dartmoor, written shortly after his release, which also shows conclusively that it is possible for a man to get into prison, and afterward become a useful member of society and continue to follow an honorable occupation.

—, EASTCHEAP,

LONDON, E. C., 24th Feb'ry, 1885.

DEAR SIR, — You will best remember me as William ———, formerly one of your correspondents from Dartmoor, and much indebted to you for your kind search and inquiries respecting my dear mother, who, upon my arrival in London last December, I found had died only *last summer*, anxious to the last to hear or see something of me, and wondering why she had not done so. Possibly you will be able now to recall the circumstances under which you became so interested on my behalf. . . .

My mother was in the full possession of her senses, and comparatively, for her years, well to the last. Had it not been for the inexcusable blunder of the authorities at Dartmoor in giving me the address of the Rev'd Mr. ———, then residing at No. —, Frederick Crescent, Clapham Road, instead of that of my mother, at whose instance he wrote to me, all would have gone well, and I should have been in communication with her, and she free from the doubts and misgivings arising naturally from my silence. It is a most painful subject to me to dwell upon, especially too as I never could account for the silence with which you treated my letters for the last few years, the more so on account of the friendly interest you took in me. It is the remembrance of this latter feeling. that induces me again to intrude on your notice. I think you will be glad to hear how I am progressing, and how I am getting on, since my return to London. It has pleased God to help in a manner and to a degree I could never have expected. The son of an old friend has taken an office in the city for me, furnished it, and is helping me to establish myself as an accountant. It is hard, uphill work to secure a connexion, for all my old city friends are dead or retired, and a new generation has risen up, which I know not. And then, too, commercial matters generally are in a stagnant state, and very little business stirring. However, I have secured a standing and a start, and with industry and perseverance, in addition to my experience, with full trust in God, I look hopefully to the future. The circumstance of my having assumed my mother's maiden name when the trouble fell upon me, now stands me in good stead, for no one here in the city knows of my fall. Though technically my business is that of an accountant, I am open to transact all kinds of Agency business, and I shall be very thankful if you can give me any introductions to Solicitors, Tradesmen, or Commercial men, with a view of my establishing a connexion. Further, a parcel of old clothes, linen, &c., which I could get mended up, would be very acceptable, as I have not been able to find a rag, paper, or relic of any kind belonging to my mother or myself. All seems to have been made away with. Hoping to hear from you in reply, and trusting you are in good health,   Believe me faithfully yours,

The Rev'd A. H. FERRIS,
    CHARLESTOWN,
        CORNWALL.

It will be seen that one of the writers of the above letters was in prison for life, on the charge of writing threatening letters; and the other is an educated man who is striving to redeem his character and lost position.

Their experience with this clergyman was the same as my own, and it seems very hard that one who devotes his life to works of piety and charity, should have to struggle years to replace £150 of his small income, out of which he has been swindled.

Oliver Goldsmith's brother was " passing rich on £40 a year." I suppose it is much the same with another country parson—the Rev. A. H. Ferris, my benefactor.

The following letter is from the present chaplain at the Dartmoor convict establishment, whose name has been previously mentioned:

PRINCETOWN,
EASTER MONDAY,
1888.

DEAR BIDWELL, — I was very glad to receive your letter and to hear so favourable an account of you. Long may you live to enjoy your long lost liberty. The contrast between your life here when I knew you, and what you are now having must indeed make you thankful. I don't think any prisoner I ever knew had such a bad time of it as you had, and the wonder to me is that you are alive to tell the tale. I was very glad when I heard you were once more safe at home. Here, you see, I still abide — men may come and men may go, but I stop on, and make the best of it ; although I am beginning to feel a little tired of it, and the next offer I get of a living, I think I shall take it. You old doctor, Power, is, I believe, still at Portsmouth prison, but I seldom hear from him now. Thank you for the photos of yourself — what a contrast ! They show what fifteen years in prison will do for a man *not trained to the business*. I have no newspaper cuttings that would interest you. The only thing I ever read was that after you landed in America you were arrested on some trumpery charge, and that the detectives themselves got a good wigging from the magistrate for their interference !

I shall be pleased to hear from you from time to time, and will not keep you waiting so long for an answer as I have done this time.

With very best wishes,
Believe me to remain,
Your sincere friend,
(The Reverend) CLIFFORD RICKARDS.

Once on a time some prisoner or other cut his throat with a razor, and an order was issued from the Home Office that razors were to be abolished in all Her Majesty's prisons, since which time the warders and assistant warders have had to clip the hair and beard of all convicts once a week. Westlake placed a small bench outside of the door and ordered me to come out and sit on it to be clipped (shaved with shears), though he well knew that at the time I could scarcely hold myself in a sitting posture. But the order was only a pretext for what followed. Two of them came in, seized me by the ankles, dragged me out, and threw me on the stool, from which I fell heavily. Four then seized and held me in the manner shown in the "photographic" picture, which will be found opposite page 33, while a fifth clipped me. Of course, my ears, nose, and mouth (their thumbs being inserted into my cheeks) did not have a comfortable time of it for the next half hour.

A short time previous I had been, by some customary abuse, driven into a state which made me give Westlake " a piece of my mind," and for this result of his own acts he brought me before the governor, who gave me the usual " three days bread and water," and fined me eighty-four remission marks. Of course I could not have been quite right in my mind, and this treatment made me resolve to keep silent, for at the moment I believed they could have no right to punish me for not talking. I therefore refused to speak or answer any question, and lay in sullen despair on the planks by day and on a pallet by night.

As it became noised about that I would not speak, the governor and others came and vainly questioned me, until, at last, the chaplain, Mr. Rickards, came in, but could not with the kindest persuasion get me to open my mouth. Westlake suggested to the assistant doctor that the battery would make me talk or scream. Accordingly, the next day he came in, accompanied by warders, and put it on almost every square inch of my body, causing most indescribable torture, especially when applied to the nerve centers, the eyes, mouth, and ears. This last was horrible, and while the poles of the battery were being applied to my ears, it seemed to me that ten thousand cannon were being exploded inside of my head, since which I have had a ringing in the left ear which became quite deaf. When the current was caused to pass through my arms and legs, it would twist and cramp the muscles until I was in agony. After a half hour of this work he gave it up, and I then said to him that I had been punished for talking, and now he had tortured me for keeping silence. Of course I was in the wrong, but I did not think so then.

The master tailor who had perceived and pitied the state in which I had been sent to his shop, came in at times to see me, and on the last occasion that I saw the good man, he said: " My poor fellow, you must prepare for eternity ; you are not long for this world," etc.

I replied, thanking him for his consideration and kindness while I was in the shop, and remarked that the sooner the end came the better — that I did not think the Almighty would be an unrelenting judge against one who had suffered so much in this life as myself. He shook hands with me, and we parted forever.

Even principal Westlake became satisfied in his own mind that I would not survive ; therefore, the next morning (the medical officer, Dr. Power, being still absent) he brought in the assistant doctor and said : " This man is very bad, sir." The doctor had my shirt taken off, and after a short examination he ordered me to be taken back to my old ward in the hospital.

I will conclude this chapter by giving an incident which proves that the treatment of prisoners by principal Westlake caused the death of one and the serious wounding of another. Governor Harris had been transferred to Chatham. Captain Avery had received the appointment and was, at the time (1881) of the occurrence I am about to relate, the head governor. He was truly a noble-hearted man, and, after leaving the army, had been deputy governor of the convict establishment at Gibraltar. I have on several occasions heard prisoners, who had served a term of penal servitude at that place, relate incidents concerning himself and his benevolent wife, of which the following is an example :

A convict, who was one of those concerned, said that the day before the Christmas holidays Mrs. Avery procured for her ten-year-old son a loose coat, with a number of large pockets, and stowing them full of packages of cake, came to where his party were at work. Of course the warder in charge would feel highly honored at being noticed by the governor's lady, and she skilfully drew his attention away, while her little boy went around and hid the bundles in various nooks and corners, the prisoners of course furtively watching his erratic movements. When his pockets were emptied the men found opportunities for possessing themselves of these angel's gifts — an angel's gifts, indeed! for in British prisons there is no change of food at Christmas-time, and nothing to remind the imprisoned wretches that Christ died as much for them as the more fortunate of mankind.

Another told me how, after he had served his time at Gibraltar, Governor Avery and lady came home on the same ship, and she used to go forward among those who where about to become free men, exhorting them to be good citizens, and shaking hands at parting.

This Governor Avery had not been long at Dartmoor before he detected Westlake in the perpetration of some cruelty, and had him transferred to the stone quarry. Here he made himself so obnoxious by his petty tyrannies that three or four of the men determined to make an attempt to escape. The plan was to knock down Westlake, and make a run for it through the line of the three or four guards who stood at a considerable distance apart. As the quarry was outside of the prison walls, the conspirators believed some of them might succeed, each one, of course, thinking that he would be the lucky man.

This plan was divulged to Westlake, who, instead of taking measures to prevent the attempt, laid his plans to kill the ringleaders, who were serving terms of twenty and twenty-five years respectively.

At the appointed time Westlake pretended to be off his

STONE QUARRY GANG, PORTLAND PRISON.

guard, and the ringleader sprang towards him with a drilling-bar. Westlake whirled and ran out of the quarry, followed by the two ringleaders. The men expected to find the guards at their usual stations, but these were waiting near the outlet of the quarry. The convicts then made a rush, but had not gone far before both were brought down, one shot in the chest, and the other in the legs. This last was the twenty-five-year man who had attempted to knock Westlake down. As he lay on the ground Westlake ordered one of the guards to shoot him, which he did, putting a charge of shot into his chest.

That is the story as told to me by one who was working in the quarry at the time, though I do not vouch for it. At any rate about 4 P. M. of that day a man was carried, groaning horribly, past my cell into the adjoining one, and as the partition was only of sheet-iron, I plainly heard his groans. After about two minutes all became silent, and I knew the man must be dead, although I knew nothing of what had happened.

When he was put in I heard the iron door slammed and locked. After he was still I heard the door opened and a warder say: "He is dead." The door was again locked. In a few moments I heard the clatter of steps and the cell door opened again. Then I heard the doctor's voice. Now what followed I have tried to convince myself that I do not remember distinctly, but it is impressed on my mind that in reply to the doctor's questions the warder said that the man had been shot dead in attempting to escape from the quarry, and that his body had been brought from there.

CHAPTER XLIV.

IN 1878 Dr. Power exchanged to Portsmouth, as elsewhere related, and was replaced by a new medical officer, Dr. Smalley. As Dr. Power's treatment of the previous eighteen months had done me some good, Dr. Smalley thought I was well enough to sew and to be put on the ordinary first-class prison diet.

As Dr. Smalley was a new broom, and felt himself obliged to sweep out of the Infirmary all who could crawl about, he endeavored, by the usual test-tortures, to ascertain who were really unable to do so. Therefore I was subjected to electric applications — or I may better characterize them as bombardments — during a period of five or six months, at the end of which time he was satisfied that my debility was genuine; and I believe, among all whom Dr. Power had left in the Infirmary, the fresh tests by this new doctor did not expose a single case of imposition — a remarkable proof of the former's skill and medical judgment.

I was still kept in the same Infirmary cell, where Dr. Smalley visited me on his daily round. Some patching work was now brought to me from the tailor-shop, and I soon became expert at it, and as it occupied my mind when there was not light enough to study, this part of my imprisonment would not have been so unhappy, had I not been obliged to

(482)

live solely on bread, twenty-four ounces per day, which was the only part of the prison diet that I could possibly digest, in consequence of which I became worse; and as the doctor did not consider it necessary to give me any other food, I lingered along in a very weak state until I was transferred to Woking prison.

During the eight years I had been at Dartmoor, there had been a railway constructed from Portsmouth to Tavistock. In cold weather all convicts are provided with an ulster for their journey — a merciful provision, as their ordinary suit is inadequate. At 5 o'clock on the morning of November 3, 1881, I was carried and placed, without fetters, in a large omnibus; in a moment I heard the clanking of chains, and looking out saw a gang of a dozen men chained together, as shown in the illustration. These were pressed into the omnibus, and a half-hour's drive brought us to Tavistock station. Here we were transferred to the cars, and in another half-hour were put out on the platform of the Plymouth station to wait for the London train. As we passed through the concourse of people, many of them gazed upon the line of chained men with looks expressive of mingled curiosity, astonishment, and compassion. As we were passing to the third-class compartment, three ex-convicts [see cut, " Convicts at Railway Station "] in citizen's clothes, who had just been released, rushed forward and tried to get the three warders who were doing escort duty to bring us into the compartment where they had seats, so that they could have a chat with me. Of course this was refused.

As I had been kept in solitude for eight years, during which I had scarcely a glimpse of the sky, this first unobstructed view of the country from the car window filled me with delight. I gazed with rapture at the shifting panorama of hills, valleys, meadows, herds of cattle, and at the cozy-looking farmsteads in the midst of orchards, beneath the trees of which lay heaps of red-cheeked apples waiting to be eaten. This was a sight which reminded me of Tantalus, only instead of water there I saw millions of apples, and not one for us *miserables*. Potatoes were the only "fruit" I had seen through all those years.

I was very kindly treated by the warders on the journey to Woking station, from which we were taken in an omnibus to the so-called convicts' palace.

Woking convict establishment occupies a fine situation on a hill two miles from Woking railway station, which is twenty-two miles from London. This establishment consists of a male and female prison. They are palatial-looking structures, from the railway station presenting an imposing appearance, and are the chief feature of that part of Surrey county. From the prison windows nothing can be finer than the view of the surrounding country which can be seen for a circle of ten or fifteen miles, in all its variety of undulating hills and valleys, interspersed with farmsteads, hamlets, and villages.

The male prison was planned by Major-General Sir Joshua Jebb, one of Her Majesty's most distinguished prison commissioners. Filled with philanthropic ideas regarding prisons and prisoners, in advance of his time, he had seen enough of the terrible state in which invalid convicts were placed at the

MAJ.-GEN. SIR JOSHUA JEBB.

regular public works prisons, to assure him of the necessity of a special institution where such as were doubly unfortunate could be sent, and receive the special attention and treatment not to be had otherwise. If I was not misinformed, the prison in question cost between a million and a million and a half dollars, and has become famous as the "Woking Palace." The carping of press and public at Gen. Jebb for being instrumental in the erection of so fine a structure for convicts — the cost having exceeded his estimate nearly one-half — finally broke his heart, and he died in 1863, lamented by all his acquaintances and by all the imprisoned wretches in England.

When I arrived I was put in a cell of the Infirmary, where the next forenoon the medical officer, Doctor Campbell, came to examine into my physical condition. He found that the sinews of my legs were so contracted that they were very crooked, and there was not much but skin and bone left, being quite atrophied. After that when going his daily morning round, the warder would throw open my door and shout "Attention," the doctor glancing in as he passed, there being nothing that he could do for me except to order the kind of food my condition required, and, from all I heard *that* was something not to be expected from him, as he in no case prescribed but just sufficient of what was required to save appearances.

Any man, whether in the infirmary or prison, who made application to see the doctor, was usually greeted thus: "Well my man, what do you want?" The "man" would state his complaint, and request that something should be done for him, on conclusion of which the doctor wound up the interview with the clincher, in his high squeaking tones: "Well, my man, you know you were sent here to die, so you must not make any trouble, for there is nothing I can do for you." This was his stereotyped reply, no matter what the case or the nature of the disease, which had usually been aggravated or brought on by hard work with insufficient food.

ALMOST STARVED IN JAIL.

RELEASE OF TWO MEMBERS OF THE HOUSE OF COMMONS FROM PRISON.

LONDON, February 18th.

R. Cunninghame Graham, Member of Parliament for Lanarkshire, and John Burns, the Socialist leader, who were sentenced to six weeks imprisonment each, were released from the Pentonville prison to-day. When the men emerged they were given an ovation. Upon being set at liberty both rushed to an obscure coffee-house and ate an enormous breakfast. They declared that they were almost starved while in prison.

While at Pentonville prison I was on the same dietary on which the Messrs. Graham and Burns "were almost starved."

DRAWING STONE.

At the Pentonville prison the labor was all performed in the cells, and the food was better than at Dartmoor, where the labor was mostly ditching, and other work on the bogs. Some parts of this chapter will give the reader a faint idea what it was at Chatham; though at present at that and the Wormwood Scrubs prisons brickmaking is the work. At Portland prison it is stone-cutting and quarrying.

While in prison I heard that Sir Edmund du Cane, chairmen of the board of prison commissioners — whose pet scheme is the present code for the government of Her Majesty's prisons in Great Britain and Ireland — in order to prove that prisoners' complaints about insufficiency of food had no foundation, conceived the idea of making a party of "navvies" work for a few days on the prison diet. These declared themselves quite satisfied, and of course no change was made. I do not know under what conditions that trial took place, but it is reasonable to suppose that they had the full weight of the best portions of prison food — such a day's rations as the one laid out in each prison kitchen every morning by the head-cook for the inspection (and edification) of the upper authorities and visitors during the day. Not a prisoner except the cooks, but would like to get that ration for his day's supply of food. And in regard to the navvies: Unless Mr. du Cane, or some other superior authority, had his eyes constantly on them, those who are aware of the low moral level and the special characteristics of that class of the British population, will not easily believe that they deprived themselves of their beer and stronger stimulants, or even abstained from getting both food and drink surreptitiously.

I have spoken elsewhere about "gangs of living skeletons," reduced to that condition while at work excavating the chain of vast artificial lakes at Chatham, as shown in the engraving further on. There is ample room within these basins to float all the na-

A SENTRY.

vies of the world. During the working hours sentries were placed around the works at frequent intervals, and their orders were to shoot down any convicts who should endeavor to escape. Some of these were placed on raised platforms so that they could see over any inequalities of the ground, rendering it extremely difficult for a convict to get out of sight of some one of the numerous guards. In the illustration, one of the convicts is depicted working in chains on the wall of the basin. These have been riveted on his ankles for attempting to escape, or some other serious act of insubordination. Another at the bellows, is growing his beard, which is permitted for three months before he is to be set at liberty.

This spot was, during the wars with France, the place where French prisoners of war were buried, large numbers of whom perished in the virulent epidemics which raged on board the old floating hulks in which these unfortunate victims of kingly greeds were confined.

From the opening of Chatham prison in 1859, 1,500 to 2,000 convicts were constantly employed on these basins. Fighting against the tides with dykes and dams, excavating half immersed in mud, making millions of bricks, brick-laying, stone-cutting, mason work, wheeling clay up narrow planks, are a few of the items constituting the daily, unceasing round of labors, which proved to them that "the way of the transgressor is hard." Incessant toil is the requirement.

The "crook," too lazy to work when free, here handles the tools as deftly as he picked a pocket or handled a "jimmy." The miscreant who committed the most revolting crime, becomes, in prison, by force of discipline, a valuable workman in many cases, and while thus beyond temptation displaying some of the best attributes of manhood. The hope of earning his "remission" often makes him a willing if not a cheerful worker.

In 1859 the convict establishment at Bermuda was broken up, the transportation system abolished, and solitary confinement recognized to be a salutary punishment. The "model prison" at Pentonville [see engraving, page 402] was the first erected in Great Britain, as an experiment to carry out that principle in practice. Soon the hulks, which had been stationed at the various government dock-yards and arsenals for the reception of convicts awaiting transportation, became disused. All authorities describe these as sinks of iniquity, abodes of horrors, where reigned the foulest abuses. After Millbank and Pentonville, Portland was the first on the new system. Dartmoor followed, then came Woking, Chatham, Parkhurst, Brixton, and Wormwood Scrubs.

Gangs of men were sent to Woking, who had been employed in excavating the great ship-docks at Chatham, to recover or die — often the latter — after they had been worked there as long as they could stand on their feet for an hour. When such gangs arrived they were living skeletons, and

A GANG IN BLOUSES MARCHING OUT.

excited the commiseration of even the hardened warders. Some of them informed me that they had been obliged to work up to their knees or middle in clay mud. I have seen men who, to escape the labor, have lost a leg or arm by putting it under a railway truck, having been driven to desperation by hunger and bad treatment.

If such was the state of affairs in 1881, what a den of horrors must Chatham prison have been previous to the famous rebellion of the convicts, in the beginning of the year 1861. This occurred before my advent in England. I have succeeded in procuring two illustrations from photographs taken at the time. In one of the cuts may be seen the mess-house where the revolt began, and a party of prisoners in working blouses marching in double file, which is the custom at English prisons. This mess-house is situated on low, swampy ground, separated at that time from the main land by a small creek, the place being called St. Mary's Island, and containing about two hundred and fifty acres. Since 1861 a great part of this has been excavated sixty feet below watermark, and now forms a part of the great basins for the use of the British navy. There was no vegetation save a few dwarfed specimens, rooted in the mud.

A MONTH OUT OF PRIS-ON, SEEKING WORK.

In March, 1861, between three and four hundred convicts were employed in the construction of a solid sea-wall of stone-work around the entire island. This wall, while improving navigation of the River Medway, was intended to form a portion of the basins since constructed in connection with it.

On the morning of the 18th of March the prisoners at work here began to show rebellious signs of discontent. At first no particular attention was paid to their conduct, as there had been a good deal of grumbling for a long time.

When the men were assembled for dinner in the large room of the mess-house, they became openly violent, and the warders, of whom there were about twenty, were seriously alarmed; and perceiving that an outbreak was imminent, they locked the doors on those who were in the mess-room, some two hundred, and those who were in the other part of the building could not be prevented from going out to the bank of the river. At this juncture the men, seeing they had matters for the moment in their own hands, proceeded to a general revolt; those who were on the bank of the river throwing stones into it, while those confined in the mess-room kept up a continuous yelling. There appeared to be no ringleaders and no concerted plan of action. The consciousness that there was not the slightest chance of ultimate success restrained them from using their temporary advantage to perpetrate any act of personal violence, they only giving ebullition to their angry feelings, in the manner above described. Had this been otherwise the few warders would have fared hard in the midst of this " brutal, hooting crowd." Assistance soon arriving from the dockyard just opposite, the prison officials took prompt measures to squelch this uprising; the revolters were called out one by one and taken across to the dockyard. Those who seemed to be the instigators were now separated and put in chains and sent back to the prison.

This convict prison will lodge 1,200 persons. It is built of brick, the interior being principally composed of iron, the cells lighted from side windows, and the interior from skylights and large windows in the ends of the corridors. There are four tiers of cells opening from galleries running along on each side, as shown in the illustration. The parade is a large courtyard running the entire length of the prison.

Next morning the men were mustered on this parade-ground for roll-call, as usual before being marched to their work. Suddenly they began hooting, howling, and throwing their caps into the air, acting very much as on the previous occasion, but soon proceeding to greater lengths, broke ranks and rushed tumultuously into the prison, breaking and destroying everything possible that came in their way, upseting the stoves, strewing the hot ashes over the stone slabs, dismantling the warder's room, smashing the clocks, tearing out the baths and gas piping, cleared out the apothecary shop, and pitched the medicine bottles crashing about — of course swallowing everything that smelled of spirits, by which many of them must have got some queer doses.

As it was found that the force of warders could do nothing towards reducing the rioters to order, the military were called for and marched promptly to the assistance of the prison authorities. The warders had all left the prison and now formed in a body in front of the main entrance, with the soldiers drawn up in the rear, as shown in the illustration. Then the great door was thrown open, the warders with truncheons drawn marched in, the soldiers following, while the bugles at the same moment sounded a charge.

Upon seeing this on-rush of assailants the convicts took to flight, the most of them scampering away to their cells, those who were cut off from that refuge seeking shelter in any nook and corner where there appeared to be a chance of safety. Those who were overtaken had a hot time of it — some were killed, others wounded, and many terribly injured.

Later, forty-eight of the ringleaders were flogged with the cat-o'-nine-tails, one hundred and five were chained together and forced to stand out in the yards all day and sleep on the planks at night. However, on account of their general excellent conduct, after a time Captain Powell ordered the chains removed and the men to return to their cells, with the exception of twenty-five who were made an example of to terrify the others. Many others were deprived of the remission marks for good conduct already earned, and forced to serve their full term.

In compiling the account up to the point of the suppression of the revolt I have omitted many of the harsh terms applied to the rioters. It is apparent that the matter for all the accounts was obtained from the prison authorities, and as there are two sides to all questions, the other side has never had a hearing. These convicts had been worked month after month in winter's cold and summer's heat, amidst slush and mud, or the trying work of wheeling clay up narrow planks, and this on an insufficient quantity of food, so that large men dwindled away to skeletons, the ration being the same whether the prisoner be dwarf or giant, and in case the dwarfs are detected in giving a six-ounce loaf or any other food to the starving giants — I mean men five feet six and upward — they would soon find themselves doing penance on bread and water in a dark cell. They had complained to the proper authorities, and had time and again been turned off with evasive answers. Some had committed suicide rather than drag out a horrid existence, finally to die or to be discharged helpless into the workhouse. Still others through sheer weakness had fallen off the planks while wheeling heavy barrows of clay up an incline, and had been killed or crippled.

One of the Chatham victims was in my ward at Woking, and beside his own first-class prison diet, and some food given him by other invalids who could not eat it, I used to give him forty ounces of bread, which he would devour at once. It was a regularly recognized thing among the invalid prisoners at Woking, that when a skeleton gang arrived from Chatham to "sneak" all the food possible to them until they had a "fill up," which took a month or two, many depriving themselves for that purpose, for they had been through the same course of starvation.

Crime deserves punishment; but the common instincts of humanity demand that it should be administered wisely, and with due regard to the true interests of both society and offenders.

Chapter XLV.

THE handle of the cat-o'-nine-tails varies in length from
two to three feet, and an inch and a half or two inches
in diameter at the butt. This is usually covered with baize
or other suitable material, and ornamented in the center and
at each end with bright yellow whip-cord. On the butt-end
are impressed the royal arms and the words "H. M. Prison
Commissioners" in a circle of scroll-work. The lashes are
arranged in a circle around the top, and are about three feet
and a half in length. They are about the size of the cord
used for carpenter's chalk-lines, and are whipped at the ends
with colored silk, to prevent them from fraying when used.
I have talked with many men who have been flogged, and am
satisfied that it is an instrument of fearful torture. It always
cuts into the flesh so that the cicatrices never disappear, and
the doctors always look at a prisoner's back the first thing
to see if he has been flogged, in which case they know he is
not a "first-timer."

Still, I do not think this instrument does so much permanent injury as the birch, with which boys and those who
have committed acts of a less grave nature are flogged, on
supposition that it is a lighter punishment. This, in my
opinion, is owing to an utterly erroneous conception of the
working of these two instruments of torture. Even if true,

(494)

there is no guide to their respective use, save the will of the
director, of whom one like Squire Morris would punish a man
with the cat for an offense that another would consider amply
punished by what he thought a lighter punishment — the
birch, or even bread and water.

The "birch" is a rod about six feet long, the branch of a
birch tree, one to two inches in diameter at the butt. The

THEY DO IT DIFFERENTLY IN CHINA.

manner of using the cat-o'-nine-tails is as follows: the
man is stripped naked to the thighs, and then bound, hands
and feet, to the triangle. Some of the most powerful warders
are selected as floggers. One of them now strips to the shirt,
the sleeves of which he rolls above the elbows. He now
grasps the cat (or birch, as the case may be,) in both hands,

stands at a distance of five or six feet, and rising to his full
height, brings it down on the prisoner's back with all his
might. At the same instant the principal warder shouts out
"One"; at the next blow he shouts "Two," and so on until
the three dozen, more or less, is completed. If it is to be
three dozen, then it is usual for the first flogger to strike
eighteen blows, then resign the weapon to a second, who com-
pletes the job, unless they have a special grudge against the
man, in which case three floggers "do" a dozen each — so
those who were thus served have informed me; it is also said
that the floggers sometimes grasp the birch by the thin instead of the thick end. However this may be, I never heard
a prisoner complain of *that*.

There may be brutes whose feelings can be touched in no
other way, but it is possible that former floggings, inflicted
from boyhood in various reformatories and jails, helped to
make them what they have become; for there is no doubt in
my mind but that flogging of any description is an unnecessary and a brutalizing punishment. I have heard, from an
authentic source, of cases in which a single flogging with the
birch had brought on incurable atrophy. I refer especially to
the cases of two big, hardy, powerful seamen of the Royal
Navy, named Fitz Gibbon and Austin, who received a term of
a few months in a county jail. These were aggravated by
the warder into a state of mind which made them threaten
personal violence against him, for which offense they received
two dozen strokes of the birch. Five months later they
were liberated, on the recommendation of the surgeon, who
certified that they were both suffering from atrophy, without
the slightest hope of ultimate recovery, and they were accordingly sent home to their friends to save the prison authorities
the expense of burying them.

Flogging, and riveting irons on a prisoner's ankles, making him drag about a heavy ball and chain, or chaining him
in any manner, are the chief, but not the sole means by
which all hope and human feelings are crushed out.

While I was in the punishment-ward of prison number seven at Dartmoor, there were a number of men flogged. The commissioner who visited Dartmoor once a month was known as Squire Morris. Many years ago, when the Queen was in danger from a rusty old unloaded pistol pointed at her by a crazy fool named Edward Oxford, Squire Morris, then a policeman, struck up his arm just in time, and bravely arrested the would-be assassin! This occurred on the occasion of a grand parade, and the knowledge of how promotion is sometimes obtained gives rise to the suspicion that Squire Morris might have done as one of great swimming notoriety did some years since. He induced a friend to jump over London Bridge, then plunged in after him and saved his life! This repeated at intervals made him famous. The above is the version current among prisoners, and whether their experience of defective human nature is at fault in this instance or not, the unfortunate Edward Oxford was declared insane and confined in the Royal Hospital at Bethlem, where he remained until 1864, at which time he was removed to the then new Broadmoor Criminal Lunatic Asylum at Sandhurst, Berkshire, where he is still confined, unless dead.

However this may have been, Squire Morris was rewarded with the gift of an office in the convict service, and in the usual course became a commissioner, or director, as they are called by prisoners. I have heard very many prisoners speak of him as a " relentless, cruel brute," etc. At all events, during the six months I was in the punishment-ward, I think I am correct in saying that not a month passed that he did not have men flogged. The morning after one of his visits the triangle was brought out and four men in succession were flogged for making threats ; and it is as well-known a characteristic among prisoners, as outside the bars, that " the barking dog never bites."

In several places I have made mention of the tests and torture-tests employed by the doctors to ascertain whether any case is genuine, or if it is one in which the man is " put-

32

ting on the balmy." The two most powerful agents used by
them for this purpose are the straight-jacket and the battery.
Most of my readers have doubtless experienced a slight shock
from one of the latter. I call a light shock one during which
the handles can be dropped by opening the hands, and for
medical purposes it is, if I am not in error, never used above
that power; but the object for which it is used by prison
doctors is torture. So powerful a current is used that the
handles, once grasped, cannot be relinquished, for the muscles
become cramped around them as rigid as iron, doubling up
the arms, twisting and wrenching at the nerves and tendons,
cords and muscles, and throwing the victim into an agony
of pain which continues as long as the doctor directs. Except
in heart-disease, there is no permanent injury (unless, as in
my case, it is put on the ears) attending the application of
this most exquisite torture, and in this alone it differs from
those of the Spanish Inquisition of the fifteenth century. The
doctors apply this a half-hour daily, until they feel assured
that the man must have been forced to "chuck it up" in
order to escape the torture. It was applied to me two or
three hundred times, and when, each day, I heard them coming with the battery, I began to tremble despite myself, then
set my teeth to bear it, while the agony caused the perspira-
tion to start from every pore of the body.

The battery is bad enough, but at the worst the pain is over
as soon as it is removed; but the straight-jacket is horrible
when applied in the way and for the purpose it is used in
prison by the warders, who, at Woking, under Governor Bones,
required but a light pretext to put it on.

The ostensible object of a straight-jacket is merely to confine the hands and prevent the person from injuring himself
or others. It is supposed by outsiders to be used without
causing the wearer pain or other inconvenience than confinement of the hands.

The prison straight-jacket is made from doubled, heavy,
No. 1 sail-duck, quilted together with waxed shoe-thread;

MILITARY SUPPRESSING REVOLT OF CONVICTS AT CHATHAM.

the edges and around the neck are bound with leather, some of them having a large circular piece of heavy sole-leather sewed on the front, to make it still more stiff and unyielding. Inside are pockets into which the arms are inserted up to the shoulders. These pockets are usually of heavy upper-leather, but some are made of sole-leather ; in either case it becomes hard, especially at the bottom, against which the hands are jammed.

Straight-jackets are supposed by the general public to be made large enough, so that they may be worn without painful compression of the body ; also that they are long enough to permit the arms being extended full length, with the hands open, and room enough to move them in the pockets. With the exception of *the one they had for show*, at Woking, of single canvas, this is an erroneous supposition, in so far as it regards the several that I saw in use there. Unless the prisoner who is ordered to be put in a jacket has " squared the warder " — *i. e.*, curried favor with him in some way, or by getting money from his friends — one of the jackets weighing from twenty to thirty pounds is selected, care being taken that it is too small by six or eight inches to come together at the back, and as much too short to let the arms remain straight in the pockets. It is fastened by five heavy straps — one each at the neck, across the shoulders, at the waist, the bottom of the jacket, and the fifth is fastened in front at the bottom and passes beneath, being buckled behind so that the jacket cannot, even if loosely put on, be pushed off over the head. The following is a description of the way in which I have repeatedly seen this fearful instrument of torture put on:

The two warders, assisted by their devotee and factotum, the cleaner, thrust the patient's arms into the leathern pockets, then throw him down prostrate on his side. The upper strap is first buckled tight up around the neck, so that on account of the shortness of the jacket the arms are forced to bend at the elbows and the doubled fists pressed with great

force against the bottoms of the pockets, in which the arms
remain immovable; then one of the heaviest sits on the
prisoner's shoulders to compress his chest, while the others
pull up the shoulder-strap until the edges of the six-or-
eight-inches-too-small jacket come together, at the same time
giving him an occasional kick in the stomach or rear. I have
seen three stout straps broken off a jacket in hauling it tight.
Next the lower straps are drawn tight, the one which passes
between the thighs being drawn so tight as to chafe into the
flesh within twenty-four hours. It was a standing order,

THEY DON'T USE STRAIGHT-JACKETS IN PERSIA.

frequently violated by the warders Vile and James, that the
jacket must be taken off every morning, and left off for the
space of twenty minutes, during which the man in the jacket
was permitted to eat his day's supply of twelve ounces of
bread, and a pint of milk, and he was given the opportunity
of doing so unless the cleaner or the warders had a grudge
against him, in which case by the time he had it half eaten
came the cry: "Time's up! On with the jacket! Screw him
up!"—and on it went instanter, in some such mode as

described. At noon he was fed a half pound of rice-pudding, which was stuffed into his mouth by the cleaner with a wooden spoon, and this as fast as it could be shoveled in, the man simply swallowing all he could, the remainder being plastered over his face, while the warders stood in the doorway laughing at the cleaner's performance. At night a pint of milk was poured into his mouth — or down the outside of his neck — twelve ounces of bread, two pints of milk, and a rice pudding comprising a day's ration.

I have known many men who have described all I have written as practiced on themselves, and I have been subjected to the worst of it myself under Dr. Braine, who is known to be a humane physician and a gentleman — only he depended on the warders, who too frequently abused his confidence.

Trussed up like a Christmas turkey, the chest compressed so that breathing is impeded, the hands, wrists, and arms contorted, I have on two occasions seen a man lie four days and nights in such an agony of pain that he never slept one moment. The knuckles, jammed hard against the sole-leather, were soon denuded of the skin, inflamed, and swollen. Each day when Dr. Braine made his daily round, the sufferer complained, but warder Vile or James told him there was nothing the matter with his hands, nor could he induce the doctor to have the jacket removed long enough to see the hands himself. This is no proof that he winked at the torture, but many would believe so.

Principal warder Fry was in charge of the extensive hospital department, and having observed him for more than three years I am satisfied that he may be counted among the considerable number of just, straightforward, and, I may add, humane officers in the convict service. It was one among his multifarious duties to lock up all the hospital wards with his master-key at 6 o'clock. The man of whom I am speaking, having been in unbearable pain all day, would appeal to Mr. Fry not to go away to his own comfortable bed and leave him in such agony, to pass a sleepless and horrible night, but in the name of all he held dear to loosen the neck and shoulder straps. Mr. Fry seldom failed to comply, and during the two months this man was trussed up day and night, this alone enabled him to obtain a little sleep.

At the end of this two months even Governor Bones, the pompous and cruel, was disgusted, and one day while going his round he looked at the man as usual, and I heard him say to warder Vile:

"How long has that man been in the jacket?"

"Two months, sir," replied the warder.

"There is such a thing as overdoing it," said the governor, as he tramped away.

Warder Vile reported this speech of the governor's to Mr. Fry, and he to Dr. Braine, who, in his turn, came at once and ordered the jacket to be taken off. The man's right hand was the worst, and the skin had all come off or hung in great rags; the hand was closed and much swollen. This the doctor took hold of, and, inserting his own under the patient's fingers, he gave a sudden and powerful wrench to open the fingers, but as these had become permanently crooked it could not be done, the inflamed state of the joints caused the man a pang that he remembers vividly to this day. Very lately, and the last time I saw that hand, it was still crooked, and all the joints permanently enlarged, and the left hand still showed marks of the torture. [I may as well state that those hands belong to me.] Permanent pains in the shoulder joints also remind him of their compression in a Woking prison straight-jacket.

I believe that the members of the Spanish Inquisition after torturing their victim for a while let him have a rest, but once "screwed up" in a straight-jacket, there was no getting away from the pain as long as it remained on, and that was usually as long as the warders wished. Indeed, I have heard one of them say to Dr. Braine, "I think this man better have on a jacket," and an order to that effect would be given. All this is a still further proof that only men of a high moral order should be employed as warders, but as this means higher pay for them and less servility in the presence of their superiors, it will be many years before such a change is adopted, it being the present policy of the British Government to get the whole of *the work* done by a class of men who can live and bring up families on a pittance, reserving all the " big-pay-and-little-work " places for themselves, their friends, and relatives, who have inherited the knowledge of " how not to do it," and do *that* to perfection.

In 1884, some time after the events described in this chapter, warder Vile, with three assistant warders, was sent to escort a party of prisoners to one of the hard-labor stations, and before the end of the journey they all became more or less intoxicated — not an unusual or hazardous occurrence, except in case a knowledge of it reached the authorities. This happened, and they were all discharged from the service, since which time I have heard that Vile succeeded in getting into a menial situation where he can no more knock about at his will and lord it over convicts.

The cleaner in the B ward was a prisoner named Mackey, and I have seen him beat a man in the presence of the two warders; but it is only one of the many instances in which certain prisoners were permitted to tyrannize over their fellows by certain warders. This Mackey was in the habit of taking out of the can half the milk and replacing it with water; of course the milk was stolen for the use of himself and the warders.

No doubt when I was sent out of A ward, Abbott informed Vile and James that I was a man who would complain to the governor, and these accordingly made it hot for me all the time I was under their charge, especially as I had complained to Dr. Braine against one of them for beating and kicking me shortly after I came into their ward.

Chapter XLVI.

IN juxtaposition with the chapter showing the worst
features of life in a prison, I will now present one of an
opposite character.

When brought to the Infirmary from the punishment-
ward, I was so nearly dead that I could not turn myself in
bed, and lay for eighteen months before I began to rally,
and then very slowly. Years of suffering were imposed
upon me, as well as hundreds of other genuine invalids,
because the wretch Phillips gloried in having successfully
deceived the good doctor. Day after day, long, dreary,
sleepless nights, dragged along monotonously and slowly into
weeks, months, and years, with little to occupy the mind,
save to stare at the blank, cold walls, and let the thoughts
wander aimlessly, or surge tumultuously as some picture of
the happy past flashed across the mental vision and plunged
the writhing soul into an agony of remorse.

Books were served out but once a week, and most of those
were of an indifferent character, or unsuited to my taste;
besides, the light was bad, and to read or study much meant
ruin to the eyesight. The plan of distribution of the library
books was arranged according to the usual official red-tape
stupidity, by which the largest amount of work is consumed
to produce the least possible result. In case a man wished
to have his book exchanged, on the appointed day he must

put it down at his door before he goes out to his work. In the course of the day a schoolmaster comes around, followed by a prisoner carrying a tray containing a number of books, one of which the prisoner picks up and drops at the cell door, and puts the one returned in with the others. The book left may be one that the man had a week or a fortnight before, and if he has been long there he is quite sure to have had it at some previous time.

A real pleasure was derived from those prisoners' friends, the rats and mice. I have no doubt but that for what is left of my mind I am indebted to those animals, which I easily tamed, and taught to be my companions.

Not long after my arrival at Dartmoor, a prisoner gave me a young rat which became the solace of an otherwise miserable existence. Nothing could be cleaner in its habits, or more affectionate in disposition, than this pet member of a despised race of rodents. It passed all its leisure time in preening its fur, and after eating always most scrupulously cleaned its hands and face. It was easily taught, and in course of time it could perform many surprising feats. I made a small trapeze, the bar being a slate-pencil about four inches long, which was wound with yarn, and hung from strings of the same; and on this the rat would perform like an acrobat, appearing to enjoy the exercise as much as the performance always delighted me. I made a long cord out of yarn, on which it would climb exactly in the manner in which a sailor shins up a rope; and when the cord was stretched horizontally, it would let its body sway under and travel along the cord, clinging by its hands and feet like a human performer.

A rat's natural position when eating a piece of bread is to sit on its haunches, but I had trained this rat to stand upright on his feet, with his head up like a soldier. Placing him in front of me on the bed, I would hand him a piece of bread, which he would hold up to his mouth with his hands while standing erect. Keeping one sharp eye on me and the other on his food, the moment he noticed that I was not looking at him he would gradually settle down upon his haunches. When my eyes turned on him he would instantly straighten himself up like a school-boy caught in some mischief. He always showed great jealousy of my tame mice, and I had to be very careful not to let him get a chance to "go for" one. On one occasion I was training one of the mice, and did not notice that the rat was near. Suddenly, like a flash, he leaped nearly two feet, seizing the mouse by the neck precisely as a tiger seizes its prey. Although I instantly snatched him away, it was too late, the one fierce bite having severed the jugular.

I also made a good many experiments to test my rat's reasoning powers, one of which I will describe, referring to the accompanying diagram, which represents two uprights with the cords *a*, *b*, *c*, running back and forth between them. Placing the rat on the cord at *a*, he went like a sailor to the point *b*, then started toward the point *c*, but had not proceeded far before he appeared to realize that the cord he was on did not lead directly to the floor. He now returned to the point *b*, resting himself upon the cross-piece. From that favorable position he "considered the matter," and then took the cord that led directly to the floor.

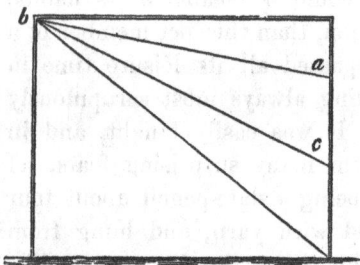

I have mentioned mice, and indeed they were most interesting pets, easily trained, and as scrupulously clean and neat as any creature of a higher race could be. I at times had a half dozen of them, which I had caught in the following simple way: I first stuck a small bit of bread on the inside of my pint tin cup, about half way down; then turning it bottom up on the floor, I raised one edge just high enough so that a mouse could enter, and let the edge of the cup rest on a splinter. It would not be long before one would enter, and as it could not reach the bread otherwise, it stood up, putting its hands against the sides of the cup, thus overbalancing it, causing the cup to drop, and simple mousie would find itself also a prisoner.

Although there was an order that no prisoner should be permitted to have any kind of pets, especially rats and mice, and as the prison swarmed with these, the warders had become tired of being obliged to "turn over" the cells and prisoners daily in search of these contraband favorites, the loss of which generally provoked the owners to insubordination; in consequence of which there was a tacit understanding that they were not to be interfered with, provided they were kept out of sight when the governor made his rounds.

Nothing could overcome the jealousy of my otherwise gentle rat when he saw me petting a mouse; and he would watch for an opportunity to spring upon his diminutive rival and put a speedy end to his career.

I had one mouse which to his other accomplishments added the following: he would lie in the palm of my open hand, with his four legs up in the air, pretending to be dead, only the little creature kept his bright eyes wide open, fixed on my face. As soon as I said "Come to life!" he would spring up, rush along my arm and disappear into my bosom like a flash.

Some years later (about 1883) at Woking prison, I had a mouse trained the same as the one above described, and was in dread lest warder Abbot should see and destroy it. Therefore, in the hope of getting a guarantee for its safety, one day when the medical officer, Dr. Braine, on his round came into my cell with his retinue, I put my mouse through the "dead dog" performance. The little fellow lay exposed in my hand with one of his twinkling eyes fixed on me, and the other on these strangers. Such was his confidence in me that he went through the performance perfectly, and when I gave the signal in an instant he was in my (as the poor thing believed) protecting bosom. The doctors laughed, and the retinue of course followed suit — if they had frowned the latter would have done likewise. The doctors appeared so pleased that I felt certain they would order the warder, as was in their power, to let me keep my harmless pet, the sole companion of my solitude and misery, unmolested.

They went outside the cell and lingered; in a moment Abbot, the warder, came in, and after a struggle got the mouse out of my bosom and put his heel upon it. I am not ashamed to confess that I cried over the loss of this poor little victim of over-confidence in human beings.

At the same prison, where I remained from November 8, 1881, until my release in July, 1887, I once procured a beetle with red stripes across his wing-sheaths, and trained him to show some degree of intelligence. This was for months the sole companion of my helpless solitude, but it was at last discovered in my possession and taken away.

At another time, when I was for more than a year without any means of occupying my mind, I made friends with the flies, and found that they displayed no small degree of intelligence. I soon had a dozen tamed, and in the course of my long observations I discovered, among other things, that the males were very tyrannical over the fair sex, and tried to prevent them from getting any of the food. In the summer mornings at daylight they would gather on the wall next my bed and wait patiently until I had washed, sat up in bed, and finished breakfast; then I placed a little chewed bread on the back of my hand, when instantly there was a rush, and the first one who got possession, if a male, tried to prevent the rest from alighting, and would dart at the nearest, chasing it in zig-zags far away. In the meantime another would have attained possession, and he "went for" the next comer, and for a long time there would be a succession of fierce encounters, until at last all had made good their footing and feasted harmoniously; for as fast as one succeeded in alighting it was let alone. Sometimes a male would take possession of my forehead, and, in case I left him unmolested, he would keep off all intruders on what he evidently considered his domain, by darting at them in a ferocious manner. On one occasion I noticed a fly that had one of his hind legs turned up, apparently out of joint. At it was feeding on my hand I tried to put my finger on the leg to press it down. During three or four such attempts he moved away, after which he appeared to recognize my kind intention and stood perfectly still while I pressed on the leg. It may be unnecessary to add that I failed in performing a successful surgical operation.

As the winter approached the flies began to lose their legs and wings; those that lost their wings would walk along the wall until they came to the usual waiting spot, and as soon as I put a finger against the wall the maimed creature would crawl to the usual place on my hand for breakfast. Indeed, the long years of solitude had produced in me such an unutterable longing for the companionship of something which had life, that I never destroyed any kind of insect which found its way into my cell — even when mosquitoes lit on my face I always let them have their fill undisturbed, and felt well repaid by getting a glimpse of them as they flew, and with the music of their buzzing.

There appears to be a preponderating opinion that the lives of prisoners must be made as wretched as possible while in prison, and the more degrading and terrible the punishments inflicted on them in English prisons, the more spontaneous the verdict, " Served him right." The great body of " revolvers," or convicts who return again and again, began their criminal career in reformatories and jails. The very first time they are locked behind the bars is the only time in their lives when they feel keenly the degradation of their condition. Ever after they have lost all sense that any stigma attaches to imprisonment; for they see so many others there of all classes of society, at the same time practicing the thieves' code of morals : That every man is dishonest, but that the mass of every community keep within the limits of the law, many of them because they lack the courage to brave it, as do thieves. Therefore, when they get into prison, they regard it not as a degradation, but solely as a misfortune.

From the first hour that any man spends in prison, to the last, if he is subjected to degrading punishments like those described in the previous chapter, *he becomes more obdurate and farther removed from the possibility of reformation.* What the prisoner feels most is his loss of liberty. When once the ponderous gates close behind him, and he feels himself cut off from participation in all that is going on in the world — its pleasures and associations — the iron enters his soul and rusts its way deeper and deeper. Now if this man is to be acted on for good it must be by doing him good. Give him every privilege consistent with his safe keeping, and if occasion arises that there is a real necessity for punishing him, let it be by the temporary loss of some of those privileges. When educated men — I mean gentlemen — of a high moral standard are appointed as warders, with adequate pay befitting the great responsibility of their positions, such deprivations will, in my humble opinion, be found amply sufficient to keep up the required discipline. Among these privileges small animals should be allowed the prisoners, to be kept in cages while the men are absent from their cells at work or otherwise, of course under proper regulations. On the expiration of the prisoner's term of servitude he should be permitted to take his cage of pets with him to keep as a reminder that the wages of wrong-doing is suffering in some form. The domestic influence of such pets would be likely to prove a restraint, and do much to prevent their owner's relapse into crime.

Certainly, prisoners should be allowed every means of mental and physical improvement. The English prison educational system, as it came under my notice, which gives but a single hour in a week to the school, is simply a farce.

CHAPTER XLVII.

THE two preceding chapters will enable the reader to understand more clearly much of what follows.

As usual, I remained day and night in the solitude of my cell until the medical officer, Dr. Campbell, resigned from the service and retired to private life with a pension and the inexpressible hatred and contempt of all prisoners who ever had the misfortune to come under his treatment.

He had been a medical officer for more than thirty years. The doctors in the prison service, as a rule, are kind and just to prisoners. Under the system of employing a cheap class of men for warders, the brutal element would have a still greater ascendency than at present, the prisons would become slaughter-houses, notwithstanding the rules laid down for their guidance, and the higher authorities would be kept in still greater ignorance regarding most of the brutalities perpetrated, were it not for the doctors.

In my animadversions concerning the warders, so far as I am conscious of it, I am actuated only by the desire to let the truth be known. Notwithstanding the fact that some who were brutal in their treatment of others, were personally

(511)

kind to me, I do not on that account paint them as excep-
tional angels; and I trust the time is not far distant when
the necessity of employing a higher class of men in that
capacity will be recognized, and changes for the better made.

After Dr. Campbell left, the assistant doctor, Von Martin,
took charge pending the appointment of another medical
officer, which did not take place until a year later. During
this interval he always treated me with the utmost personal
kindness. Believing that eight years in the solitude of a cell
was quite sufficient, he had me located in a small, four-bedded
dormitory on the ground floor, with three other cripples.
Here we were comfortable as long as the warm weather
lasted; but as this dormitory had an air space of four inches
under the door — for the closing of which there had been no
provision made — also a large transom-window, which was
always open, it was a cold place for the winter quarters of
invalids. When it became unbearably cold, one of us would
place our pillows or a blanket to stop the opening below, and
with a cane close the transom; but as soon as the warder,
Abbot, noticed this (not feeling the cold through his heavy
overcoat) he at once opened both, besides taking pains to
keep the outer door, just opposite, wide open, so that the
temperature was about the same as it was in the open air.

After enduring this as long as possible I explained the
matter to Dr. Von Martin, who had us removed to warm
cells on the floor above, but of course I was again in solitude. I was in the dormitory more than six months, with
three men as unlike in character, natural traits, and antecedents as it would be possible to bring together.

One of these was the son of respectable parents, who lived
and died within eight miles of Woking prison, where their
son Selwin was now on the last half of a term of ten
years for stealing some linen from a clothes-line, his first
term having been for five years. He was a very small man,
and had been an unruly small boy, and it was this circumstance which attracted the attention of a tramping chimney-

CONVICTS EXCAVATING CHATHAM BASIN.

sweep, who excited his imagination to such an extent with the wonders to be seen in the great world, that he ran away in his company, and adopted the profession of " climbing-boy," as young sweeps are designated in England. He had gradually fallen into " cadging " ways, and for twenty years had been an inveterate cadger, tramp, and vagabond. He had served more than fifty short terms of imprisonment in the county jails of every shire in England before incurring penal servitude. During the whole time I was in the dormitory he would go on for hours relating his adventures, telling not too re-fined stories to the man in the opposite bed — a fair example of the mutually de-basing influence of prison association.

THE CADGER.

Now for the astonishing side of this man Selwin's character. During all his imprisonments he had studied a great deal, especially figures, till he had become a fair arithmetician, and in algebra he had no difficulty with quadratics. A stranger con-versing with him, who knew nothing of his antecedents, would have no reason to sus-pect that he was other than a respectable, fairly-educated man.

This man had claimed to be incapable of walking, having lain in bed for two or three years ; but Dr. Von Martin put the battery on him until he promised to try crutches, on which he just managed to shuffle along in a queer way and unlike any genuine cripple I had ever seen — although I do not think he was an out and out impostor, but only an individual ex-ample of the many invalid prisoners who fail to get anything done for themselves unless they pretend to be much worse than they actually are. Of course, in such cases disease or ailment is not readily apparent, and causes great perplexity to the doctors. Selwin was forty years of age, twenty-five of which he had passed in durance.

Another character in the dormitory, who was serving a term of seven years, having served one of five previously, out of respect for his children, I will designate by his " flash " name, " Whopper."

He was born in London, his parents being trades-people, who permitted him to roam the streets, and as often as he could obtain the required funds he visited the " penny-gaff " (two-cents-admission theater), and other places where London children are corrupted. Whopper at an early age became very expert at picking pockets, and at sixteen he had become very proud of the peculiar reputation acquired in that " business." He had been regarded as one of the smartest crooks in London, and at forty years of age had for many years been known by the above sobriquet, on account of the " whopping" amount of money he obtained, and the skill and boldness in pocket-picking which he displayed. His plan was to dress like a gentleman — he being a handsome fellow — and by some stratagem get admission as a guest at aristocratic weddings. As soon as he saw any signs of commotion he departed with his booty.

I am now about to make a statement that may appear a strange one to some readers. It is that this pickpocket — this jail and prison-bird — *was a man of honor.* He had adopted crime as a profession, and was as proud of it as any honest tradesman is of his own occupation. Outside of that he was perfectly reliable, his advice being sought by those in his own line, who placed unbounded confidence in his honesty. He was very particular to conceal his mode of life from his family, to whom he was a kind husband and father, having taught his children to be scrupulously honest; and they are to-day respectable and thriving tradesmen in London. They never discovered, until after I became acquainted with him, that their father had been engaged in any dishonorable business, or had been in jail and prison. One day he received a letter from one of his sons, who had in some way ascertained his whereabouts. Whopper showed the letter to me, and in it the son wrote that he was sure of the falsity of the charge against his father, and that in any case he would make application for leave to bring him home.

At the time of his first five years' penal servitude, his wife had deserted him and her children for another man, and after his release he had paid for their board in a respectable family. He remarked that for his children he felt that it was a question of school and a trade, or jail. He had served

SCHOOL AND A TRADE, OR JAIL.

his first term at working in the mud at Chatham, as described elsewhere, until he had been stricken down by *locomotor ataxy*, or inability to guide his legs unless he was looking at them. If he had hold of another man's arm and looked at his feet, he could walk very well; but if he turned his eyes away, and then attempted to walk, he had no idea of the direction in which his legs were moving, and they would sprawl about loose like those of a jumping-jack. He completed his first term in 1876, and was discharged a helpless, incurable cripple, and of course had to abandon the profession of pocket-picking.

He then became a middle-man or agent between thieves and the receivers of stolen goods, sometimes purchasing stolen watches, jewelry, and diamonds on his own account, and disposing of them, after changing the numbers of the watches, melting the gold settings, etc., so that the property could not be identified by the legal owners. His reputation for probity, skill, and promptitude in negotiating stolen goods was so great among the London "crooks," that he soon had all the work of that kind he wanted. While engaged in this business, he had himself wheeled about in a sedan-chair, employing a man to push it and assist him generally.

Whopper was rather polished in his manners, of pleasing address, and I never heard him relate any of the vile tales or make use of the filthy language usual among English prisoners, and too frequently heard from the mouths of warders in their conversations with them. He was a natural actor, and afforded us in the dormitory no end of amusement, some of his comic recitations, as he reclined in bed, causing convulsions of laughter. Altogether, I take him to be the most contradictory and remarkable character I ever met, and one more example of the ruin which awaits all who once enter into a career of crime.

We had been employed at knitting, and after I was removed from the dormitory for the reasons given, I continued that work in my cell, and was getting along as well as could be expected for one who was shut up all day and night in solitude — pet animals being prohibited.

In the early summer of 1882, Dr. Braine came as the new medical officer; but after Dr. Von Martin's administration for one year, he had not much to do in the way of clearing out impostors; and owing to the warders reporting a good many genuine cases as able-bodied men, forty had been sent away previously to other stations, and I heard later that twenty-two of these had died — a further example of how certain of the most cunning and determined prisoners injure and cause the death of many others, by feigning maladies to escape labor, thus imposing on the doctors.

The first day the new medical officer made his round, warder Abbot threw open the door of my cell and shouted, "Attention!" Doctor Braine, on seeing me, asked the warder how I was getting on. "Very bad, sir," he answered; "he makes us all the trouble he can." The fact is, I had been in the habit of ringing for the warder but once in the day. This is an example of how prisoners are prejudiced in the eyes of the authorities, and the best qualification a prison-doctor can have is that of ability to read under the surface and penetrate the tough shell of the various deceptions beneath which the truth is hidden. Dr. Vane C. Clarke possessed this qualification in an eminent degree, and the lack of it, as in Dr. Braine's case, renders them but tools in the hands of unscrupulous warders.

During the warm weather we were put out with the stocking-knitting party under a long open gallery which commanded a far-extended view of the beautiful country. Though we were hemmed in by high walls our longing eyes could roam at will over a space of country that was *free*. The fleecy clouds floating so lazily aloft made us long for liberty. The soft summer breeze blowing from the distant hills was untainted with the breath of slaves, and spoke to our hearts of freedom.

It was here that I first saw D———, who was serving a life sentence for a series of forgeries that carried ruin to many people, including widows and orphans. I was seated beside him on the same bench — a row extending down the gallery on which were seated about one hundred men engaged in knitting stockings and in furtive whispering. It was rather amusing to see the warder march slowly up and down in front of the line of knitters, who, as he got a little past, would cease work and begin whispering eagerly to their neighbors. The warder turning saw every eye fixed intently on the work, the fingers making the needles fly as if their owners' lives were at stake. In this way I had a great deal of stolen conversation with D———. At this time, August, 1882, he was fifty-five, and had completed five years of his term — was crippled in one thigh by sciatica, and compelled to use crutches. He had been a London solicitor and contractor — one of his jobs having been the construction of the very canal which ran past within sight of where we sat, and the view must have awakened in him sharp pangs as he compared his former prosperity with his present wretched condition. "Here by my side," I reflected, "sits a man who has had every worldly advantage that money could give. From birth he has been surrounded with friends, received a good education, and the polish which only association with cultured people can confer ; and yet he has arrived at the same goal as the pickpocket who is sitting next to him, and who started from the gutter."

D——— appeared to me a very nice, well-disposed gentleman, and, although he was the cause of much ruin, I have no doubt that when he first found himself in financial difficulties he resorted to fraudulent practices believing he was as certain to extricate himself as I was when I retained, temporarily, ten dollars of my employer's cash. At the time of his disaster he had a wife and seven grown children, of whom he was very proud, often referring to them and to the fine education they had received. His great sorrow was that, through his business troubles, they had been obliged to forsake their former residence in the " West End " of London, to give up their horses and carriage, and to be deprived of association with the society to which they had been accustomed. He could not have been a very bad man, for they still loved him and did all in their power to procure a pardon, coming to visit him every three months, and occasionally getting a special visiting-order from the Home Office. When arrested he was a strong, healthy, active man of fifty, but these five years of retribution had changed him into an old, decrepit valetudinarian. Petition after petition was refused, but at last his faithful wife had the satisfaction of bringing him the glad tidings that the sentence had been reduced to ten years, and he was discharged shortly before myself.

Here was a case where ruin had been wrought on many helpless persons, and his friends obtained his release from a life sentence after serving ten years — while my friends had a petition refused when I had done thirteen, and only succeeded in getting me home in the fifteenth year by bringing to bear the most powerful influence. Others, who were guiltless as compared with myself, are still held crushed within the Lion's jaws; but then, we were Americans, and charged with putting our hands in the plethoric money-bags of the wealthiest corporation in the world.

It was very pleasant sitting beneath the shade of the gallery engaged in knitting, whispering, and gazing out at the extended landscape, or watching the fleecy clouds floating so majestically in the dull-blue English sky — so different from the cerulean of my own lost native land. I was incessantly repeating: "Sail on, O fleecy clouds, you at least are free!" How often have I asked a fellow prisoner if he would like to lie upon one of them and sail away *anywhere,* so it should convey him into liberty! Alas! this relief to my long period of solitude in cells was too short; the summer was over, and the knitting-party was sent to the close shop, and we cripples kept in separate cells.

Dr. Braine discharged four cripples from the Infirmary — had them placed in the same fireless dormitory where I had suffered so much the previous winter, and ordered that I should be put into it to work with the others during the working hours, and then taken back to my cell. One of the new occupants of the dormitory was the ex-solicitor. During these working hours I suffered with cold. It was in vain that I explained this to Dr. Braine; his orders were like those of the Medes, unchangeable.

In consequence, I became cold and benumbed. I lived entirely on bread (twenty-two ounces per day), and by the middle of January I had become unable to sit up, and I begged of the doctor to let me work in my cell. Dr. Braine would no longer believe the false reports of warder Abbot, and permitted me to remain in my own cell to work.

On several occasions this warder, Abbot, had dragged me about by the collar, and given me kicks in the side with his heavy, hob-nailed boots. On the first of these occasions, when the governor (Bones) made his round, I complained of the violence in Abbot's presence. When I had made the complaint, Governor Bones said: "You are telling lies; no officer would dare do such a thing. You had better be careful how you make any such complaints against officers, or you will be severely punished,"— and away he tramped.

When the irons and chains were put on me at Pentonville, Bones was governor there; and it was my misfortune, and that of hundreds of others, that he had been transferred to Woking. He could not do so much mischief at Pentonville, as the men were only there for nine months; but Woking — where a great many men were sent as invalids from the hard-labor stations of Chatham, Portland, Portsmouth, Dartmoor, and Wormwood Scrubs — became, under his supervision, an unrestricted place of torture, and warders were not long in discovering that they could commit any brutality on prisoners, save for the doctors, without fear of punishment.

It was this governor who manipulated the Robinson murder, previously mentioned, in a way to clear the guilty warders and get the honest, humane one discharged from the service as a lunatic. But within eighteen months of the period to which I have brought my story, there was to be a resurrection at Woking of long-buried humanity, for it was already on the books that the governorship would then be transferred to the able hands of Dr. Vane C. Clarke.

I cannot leave this part of my subject without recording that Abbot was a cavalryman, who was in the "Charge of the Light Brigade" in the Crimea, and for that reason alone he had received the appointment of warder in the prison service.

Across the corridor, opposite our dormitory, there was a three-bedded one, in which were confined three other cripples. Two of these were taken to work in the tailors' shop, and that the third might not be locked up in solitude all day — excepting the hour's exercise — he was brought to sit with us during working hours, in consequence of which I became well-acquainted with him. This was in 1882, and he had then been in prison without a break for twenty-nine years. His name was Pennock, and he was serving a "life" sentence for the murder of a youth, the crime being perpetrated in his eighteenth year. [A "life" sentence is one in which the convict was, previous to 1864, discharged after serving twelve years. Since 1864 a new act of Parliament has extended it to twenty years. A "natural life" sentence is only given in cases of murder or like enormities, and the convict has no hope of release except by death.] When Pennock had served eleven years and nine months he was permitted to grow his hair and beard, as usual, three months before being set at liberty. When the twelve years were fully expired he was dressed in citizen's clothes and sent in charge of a warder to his former home. On making inquiries the warder ascertained that all his friends were dead. He applied to the town authorities for a permit to leave him at the workhouse, but was refused, and as he was a paralytic, unable to earn a livelihood save by begging, he was obliged to take him back to the prison, where he has since remained. In this year of our Lord Christ the Merciful, 1888, he will be serving his thirty-fourth year in prison, twenty-two of it since he was by law entitled to his liberty, and this because he is buried in a living grave and has had no means of making his condition known. Surely there are thousands who would rejoice to assist him to the opportunity of drawing a full breath of God's free air before he dies. And this the more when they read the following account of his birth, and the circumstances under which he committed the crime.

In addition to his infirmities, Pennock was born with an

immense club-foot, the shoe I saw him have on being eight inches in diameter. By the use of a crutch he could walk after a fashion. While in the dormitory he would drop off into epileptic fits several times a day, and he informed me that he had been subject to them from birth, his general appearance bearing out the statement. Every one knows what kind of a life such a deformed boy would have among other boys of whom he would be the butt.

One of the neighboring boys plagued him so persistently for years, that at last Pennock conceived a deadly hatred against him and thirsted for that revenge which his physical debilities precluded him from taking with his fists. One day, when he was about eighteen, a friend of his married sister called at the house, leaving his loaded gun in the kitchen. Pennock had just returned fuming from fresh hectorings of his enemy, and spying the gun, he took it unobserved, went and hid himself in a hedge, and had but just concealed himself when his foe appeared, whom he shot dead.

That is his own version, and it is clear that there must have been very extenuating circumstances, or he would never have been let off for so execrable a crime with a sentence which the judge knew was equivalent to twelve years.

He appeared to me a well-disposed man, of a peaceful, quiet disposition and religiously inclined, though he made no hypocritical professions in that direction.

Although at the time I was myself almost hopeless of regaining my liberty, I vowed that if such an event ever came about I would make his case known where there are so many noble-hearted benefactors of the unfortunate. And here indeed is the *miserable* of *miserables!*

Despite my own black prospects I tried to console the poor fellow, and told him that if I lived to be freed and he was still alive, a breath of free air should expand his lungs before he died. Six years have passed since that promise was given, and now it stands as deeply in my heart as when it was given. He is at the Parkhurst prison on the Isle of Wight.

Chapter XLVIII.

IT was a merciful act to send those convicts who were
really insane to a specially prepared prison where they
could receive the care their condition deserved, for at the
regular prisons they were unavoidably subjected to severe
discipline, and consequent mistreatment, which aggravated
their malady and gave little chance for improvement or
recovery. Had it been possible to keep out the impostors,
this would have accomplished the humane purpose intended
by the board of prison commissioners; but this proved to
be beyond the power of the most skilled and experienced
doctors. It will be seen that scores of convicts "put on the
balmy" so skillfully, and carried the imposture through with
such perseverance, as to undergo successfully every test
known to medical science, as well as the most terrible punishments inflicted on them by the other prison authorities to
break up their imposture.

The first insane convicts who were sent to the criminal
lunatic asylum in 1864, were either cured and sent back to
finish their term of penal servitude, or on its completion
were sent to the lunatic asylum of the county where they had
been convicted. At all events, a large proportion eventually
recovered their liberty, and it was not long before they were
arrested in the commission of some crime, tried, convicted,

(523)

and returned to the public works prisons or convict establishments. Here their talk, or rather whispering, with their fellow-prisoners naturally turned on their experiences at the prison lunatic asylum, then recently established at Broadmoor; and it soon became known to the convicts throughout all Her Majesty's prisons that those among them who were declared to be insane were sent to a place of comparative freedom, where they could act about as they pleased, perform little or no labor, or, in other words, receive the humane treatment which the better feeling prevalent in our time requires toward those unfortunates who have from any cause become irresponsible for their acts. As soon as this became known, numbers of men feigned insanity (in prison parlance, "put on the balmy"), and as the doctors were then unsuspicious, the tests applied were very easily borne, and after remaining in the hospital under observation for two or three weeks only, they were certified to be insane and sent away to Broadmoor.

Cases of insanity now multiplied so rapidly that suspicion of imposture became a certainty, and the doctors gradually became more rigorous and applied tests which tried the physical powers and determination of the most case-hardened and obstinate; so that by the time to which I have brought my personal history, 1883, those who were really insane, or who were feigning to be so, were subjected to the most terrible tests during three, six, twelve, or eighteen months, and few of the attempted impostors were able to withstand the ordeal.

The penalty for "putting on the balmy" was usually a flogging with the cat-o'-nine-tails, provided the doctor gave them over to the *un*tender mercies of the other prison authorities; but unless the man was a very hard nut indeed, the doctors would not let him be reported, for in most cases, before he could be made to desist, he had undergone an amount of deprivation and suffering that should have been sufficient to satisfy the most rigorous martinet.

The foregoing brief sketch will enable the reader to better

understand the whys and wherefores of the various incidents referred to.

In the last chapter I had brought my story up to the spring of 1883, when I had been reduced very low by the peculiar attentions of warder Abbot, the ex-cavalry private. I was then sent up-stairs into B ward, the cells of which were used for hospital patients who for any reason were not allowed to remain in one of the large hospital wards — the former charges of attempting to escape from Newgate and Penton-ville being the alleged reason for my confinement in cells since March, 1873 — ten long years. B ward was in charge of Vile and assistant warder James; the one Vile by name, both utterly vile and corrupt by nature. Some of the cells were also used for "observation" of those who were suspected of feigning insanity; and under the warders named, all such, genuine cases or otherwise, truly had a hard road to travel.

When a new patient was sent into the ward, a scene very much like the following was enacted:

Vile (*to prisoner, in a loud, menacing voice*) — Stand there against the wall! (*Then standing in front of him.*) What's your name?

Prisoner — John Smith.

Vile (*looks menacingly a moment, then giving him a heavy punch with the fist in the stomach*) — Stand up straight, you scoundrel! What's the matter with you?

Prisoner — Nothing, only those women are following me about day and night!

Vile — Putting on the balmy, you ———! Take that! (*giving him another punch.*) I'll learn you to say "Sir" when you answer me!

And so on, for a half-hour, just outside of my cell door, Vile winding up by pointing to a cell and shouting: "Go in there, you ———!" and as the prisoner turned to go, he received a helper in the rear from the toe of the warder's heavy boot.

I have seen warder Vile strike a man with his fist on the chest and back twenty or thirty heavy blows, and kick him with his hob-nailed boots. I have seen assistant warder James do the same thing, and I have been present when he stripped a patient stark naked, dragged him out of bed, and while he lay nude upon his back on the floor, walk up and down his body, standing full weight with both feet on his chest and abdomen. James weighed one hundred and eighty pounds. All this would be done in a way, well understood by prison warders, that left no external bruise or mark, but was pretty certain to bring on heart, liver, or other complaints, of which the man was likely to die. I have heard one of the men thus treated complain to Dr. Braine in the presence of those warders; but as the doctor, on examination, could discover no marks, he took no notice of the complaint — the warders standing by with such an honest, innocent expression of indignation, apparently, mingled with pity for the mendacity of the prisoner who dared tell the doctor such "audacious falsehoods," that even their victim was abashed, and faltered so that the doctor left with the impression that the warders were much-enduring men of humanity and integrity.

[It may be as well to state that *I* am the man who was "operated" upon, as described.]

In 1884, the board of prison commissioners having decided to break up and do away with the Woking prisons, the convicts able to be removed to other stations were sent away; I being crippled was sent to the west wing, which was used for the confinement of convict lunatics who were to remain until a special wing for their accommodation should be erected at Broadmoor.

In the C hospital ward there were twenty-four beds for patients, twelve of which were in cells, the remainder in an open ward where I was located.

There were three wards, A the lower, B the second floor, and C the upper. The whole prison was surrounded by a brick wall about twenty-five feet in height. The west wing, or lunatic wing, was cut off from the rest of the prison by a cross-wall, and the space around it, within the wall of circumvallation, was divided by walls into three yards, one for dangerous lunatics; the largest, comprising about an acre, was used for a flower and vegetable garden, which some of the inmates could cultivate for themselves.

The prisoners here were all considered patients and were under the special charge of the medical officer and his assistants. When it did not storm the patients were out in the garden two hours in the forenoon, and the same in the afternoon. They were also in the recreation-room from half-past eleven to one o'clock, and from half-past four to six P. M., so that they passed only eighteen

MENDING BELLOWS.

hours out of the twenty-four in their cells or dormitories; those who worked out on the farm or in the wash-house having still less time to pass in them.

When I was for the first time in the recreation-room I at once noticed a set of chess-men, but these had never been used, as no one understood the game. Board and men were brought out, and I soon had so many apt pupils that I was obliged to make three other sets of men. I mixed some porridge, bread, and sand into dough, modeled them into shape, and they answered the purpose admirably.

The place had been fitted for convict-lunatics, and furnished with every facility usually found in free insane asylums for the employment of the minds of the inmates; but the conduct of twenty or thirty of those who had got there by imposing on the doctors had caused a gradual reduction of those facilities and privileges.

These pretended lunatics had taken advantage of the situation and cared for nothing but their own indulgences, at the expense of those who were really insane. They were the most hardened, desperate, and depraved characters that the English system of imprisonment could produce — and that is saying a great deal.

A majority of them had cicatrices on their backs left by the cat-o'-nine-tails. Every day there were ring fights in the yard, which the warders enjoyed, and stood around to see fair play.

MASONS AT WORK.

Within the prison they smashed up the furniture and even destroyed the specialties so humanely provided by the government for those doubly unfortunate wretches, convict lunatics, who were really insane. Billiard and bagatelle tables, books, and pictures, were willfully mutilated by these reckless impostors. They played upon the infirmities of the really insane and imbecile, recking not how much these were injured, provided they themselves had " a lot of fun " out of the poor creatures.

There were some strange characters in this unique institution. One man believed that the prison was Solomon's temple, and himself the high priest. In the course of years he had with infinite labor worked down and polished veined stones, which were common in that part of England, into imitation cameos and other really fine works of art. With these he had made a breast-plate, also imitated all the other parts of the costume of a high priest made from precious stones. In order to keep him quiet the doctor had given him materials, and he had rigged himself out in the full costume of a high priest, except that the hat was ornamented with feathers. Following the doctor's cue, the warders humored his " craze," and every Sabbath formed a body guard for him while he marched in state to the chapel.

Another man, by the name of Dickens, believed himself the greatest poet on earth, and had written a play, showing up the horrors of war. The plot and plan of the play were really good, but it was written without rhyme or reason. He had named it " Life's Action," and this sobriquet had taken the place of his own name. " Life's Action" was continually spouting portions of his drama. He took a particular fancy to me, and used to recite it to me by the hour. At the time I was composing a good deal of rhyme myself, and although he thought his own incomparable, after I had altered a few lines of it for him he was so much pleased that he wished me to go through the whole, but so secretly that no one should suspect that I had a hand in " Life's Action." As it was my custom while among the insane there to do anything in my power to benefit or to give healthy occupation to their diseased minds, of course I acceded to his wishes. He brought me his manuscript book, and I rewrote the whole, following his style in a general way, cutting out incoherencies and filling in where required, so that when it left my hands it certainly possessed some metre, rhyme, and reason. I would write a slate full at a time, this he would take and copy on foolscap which the doctor allowed, while I was filling another slate. When we had completed the job he was so highly delighted, and in the same degree so fearful that any one should discover the changes were not his own, that he took the old manuscript and put it in the stove, so that there could be no comparison of the old and new. This man Dickens had received a sentence of fifteen years' penal servitude for at-

34

tempting to shoot his wife and then himself. He was of a respectable family, a distant cousin of the great novelist.

"While on the public works eleven years," said Dickens, "I composed 'Life's Action' with only a slate to write on, and committed it to memory as fast as it was composed. You see what a splendid work it is, and because I used to recite it, they put me down 'balmy,' and instead of sending me home when I had done eleven and a half years, they are keeping me among these insane people and forcing me to serve the whole fifteen years, thus depriving me of the three and one-half years of fairly earned freedom."

Indeed this last was a real grievance, and the case of Dickens was a type of many other genuine cases of insanity which came under my notice during the three and one-half years that I was located in the lunatic wing. This is the injustice — nay, robbery — which, if perpetrated by a private individual instead of by the British Government, would in the eyes of every right-feeling person be considered not only a base and dishonorable, but a criminal act, which should consign the doer to a period of seeing how the world looked from inside the grates, and long enough to give plenty of time for contemplation of his turpitude.

In the aggregate a large number of men have earned the legal remission of a portion of the original sentence, and on showing signs of hallucination on one subject — though right enough in all others — instead of giving them their liberty at the time stipulated, they are sent from all the convict establishments to the lunatic wing at Woking, where they are kept till the full term of the sentence has expired.

For example, Dickens was as sensible as ordinary men on all subjects save that of his hobby, "Life's Action." He had a good trade, was industrious, and, despite his hallucination, was quite capable of earning a livelihood, and withal was an honest man. His general principles were good; he had been in the lunatic wing some years when I first saw him there, and had seen an unlimited number of the horrible abuses prevalent before and after my arrival. It would require another volume to recount what I saw myself. Dickens was inoffensive, careful not to infringe the rules, and never got into trouble with any one. At the time I first knew him he wore the special blue dress, the possession of which proved that he had earned his three and one-half years remission, therefore entitled to his liberty, also that he bore a good prison character. He fretted constantly at being retained in prison so unjustly, and I am sure it was of great injury to his mind. The reason assigned was that the workhouses or asylums of the places whence the convicts were sent would not receive insane men until they had served out the full term of their sentence, and this because for that length of time the county or township could *throw upon the general government the expense of maintaining them.* A reason indeed for a glaring wrong *against a defenseless class who are additionally punished on account of their infirmities!* And this permitted to go on thirty years by the all-powerful central government!

While on the subject I beg to call the attention of my readers to another almost equal robbery, only the sufferers are not yet lunatics: The doctors have become so skillful, and their tests so thorough, that it is seldom a man can sham sickness so successfully as to obtain admission to the hospital. Yet the moment a sick man is admitted into the hospital his remission marks cease, and I have known instances in which men had to remain in prison eighteen months longer on a seven years' sentence *solely because they were sick.*

During my imprisonment I was occasionally granted a blank form on which I wrote petitions in my own behalf, but invariably the reply was the same as in the *fac-simile* of one of the refusals of the English government to grant my release, the application having been presented by the Hon. John R. Buck, the influential Representative of the First district of Connecticut in Congress.

20568^B

Whitehall,
21st April. 1886.

Sir,

 The Secretary of State having carefully considered the application forwarded by you in behalf of George Bidwell; I am directed to express to you his regret that he is unable to discover any sufficient ground to justify him, consistently with his Public Duty, in advising Her Majesty to interfere in this case

   I am,

    Sir,

    Your obedient Servant

     Godfrey Lushington

J. R. Buck, Esq. M.C.

 House of Representatives.

  Washington.

   United States

    America

Chapter XLIX.

IN the early spring of 1884 I was transferred into an association dormitory of twelve beds—these being about four
feet apart. In the bed next to mine was a prison genius
named Heep, who was one of the most singular characters I
ever met. As I shall have occasion to speak of him frequently up to the time of my release, I may as well give here
a sketch of his life as related to me by himself. He was born
in the town of Macclesfield, near Manchester, in 1852, of respectable mechanics, or trades-people as they are called in
England. His father died when Heep was about five years
of age, and after a time his mother married a carpenter and
joiner of the place.

Young Heep was a lively child, up to all sorts of tricks,
and does not remember the time since he could walk that he
was not in some mischief, and, as he remarked, "took to all
sorts of deviltry as naturally as a duck to water." As long
as his own father lived there was not much check on his mischievous propensities, but his step-father proved to be a severe
and stern judge, and brought him to book for every irregularity, thrashing him most unmercifully for each offense. His
mother could not have filled her maternal duty very judi

ciously, judging from the fact that before he was twelve years old she set him to follow and watch his step-father to the house of a woman of whom she was jealous. The boy possessed great natural abilities, and in good hands would have turned out something different than a life-long prison drudge. He was handsome, genteel in appearance, an apt scholar, though very self-willed and headstrong, and as he grew up his naturally hot temper became uncontrollable. At an early age he had discovered that by threats of self-injury he could bend his parents to his wishes, but found in his step-father one who would put up with no nonsense; even when he cut himself so as to bleed freely, instead of the coveted indulgence it only procured him an additional thrashing.

At fifteen he had become ungovernable at home, and his father had him put in the county insane asylum, where he remained a year and a half. While there he caused so much trouble that the attendants were only too glad when he escaped and went to Liverpool. Here he succeeded in getting a situation with a dealer in bric-a-brac, rare books, and antiquities. In a short time the proprietor placed so much confidence in his integrity that he gave him the charge of his place during his own absences, and young Heep was not long in taking advantage of his position to rob his employer by taking a book or other article which he sold to some one of his master's customers. This went on for some time until on one occasion he took a book to a shop kept by a woman to whom he had previously sold several articles and offered it for a sovereign. She examined it and found that it was an ancient, illuminated Greek manuscript, worth fifty times more than the price young Heep asked for it, and, suspecting something wrong, she told him to come again for the money the next evening. At the appointed time he entered the place and was confronted by his master, who contented himself with upbraiding him for his perfidy, and discharging him from his service.

At this period of his career he had contracted vicious

habits, the most pernicious for him being that of drink, for when sober he was in his right mind, but the moment the drink was in — like Edgar A. Poe — his common sense departed, and he became a raving maniac, ready to fight or perpetrate any other act of folly.

Up to this time he had never associated with thieves, and had been tempted to steal only in order to supply means for improper indulgences.

Not long after being discharged from his situation he was found by the police acting in so insane a manner under the influence of drink, that the magistrate before whom he was taken had him sent to the Raynell lunatic asylum. Here, being perfectly reckless, he carried on all sorts of games which made him obnoxious, although making himself very useful in work which he liked, such as gardening, etc. He also took up fancy painting and soon became a skillful copyist of prints of any description, enlarging or reducing, and painting them in oil or water colors. He also became a good decorator and scene-painter, besides devoting time to various studies, including music.

At last he found means to effect his escape and lay in hiding until night, then as he had on the asylum clothes, which would betray him, he went back and got in through the window of the tailors' shop, which was in an isolated building, and exchanged the clothes he had on for a suit belonging to one of the attendants. Thinking himself now safe from recognition he started off across the country, but had not gone more than twenty miles when, in passing through a small town, a policeman who had just heard of the escape from Raynell, arrested him on suspicion.

The Raynell authorities sent some one to identify him ; he was taken back, tried on the charge of stealing the attendant's suit of clothes, which he still had on, was convicted by the usual "intelligent" jury and sentenced to five years penal servitude.

Let the reader mark this and what follows, then compare

it with the fact that *no person certified by the doctors to be of unsound mind can according to English law be tried for any offense whatever.* He finished his term of imprisonment at Chatham and instead of being set at liberty was sent under guard back to the asylum!

According to English law, if a person confined in a lunatic asylum escapes and keeps away fourteen days he cannot after that be arrested, until he commits fresh acts of insanity.

After several futile attemps he at last made good his escape and obtained work with a farmer, where he remained safe for thirteen days, and was congratulating himself that in less than another day he would be free, when his thoughts were broken off by the appearance of two attendants who seized and carried him back to the asylum.

The events above narrated had driven him into a state of desperation at what he felt to be gross injustice, and he carried on in such a way that the doctor ordered his head to be shaved and blistered as a punishment, the straight-jacket and all other coersive measures having been of no avail. The night watchmen had orders to watch him closely, but he kept so sharp an eye on the watchman that he caught him asleep, and creeping to the closet window, which he had previously tampered with, crept out, and after climbing the low wall found himself on a raw November night, with the rain falling in torrents, a stark-naked, head-shaved-and-blistered, but once more a free man. In this condition he wandered on throughout the night, and just before daylight he entered a cemetery to find that refuge among the dead of which he thought himself so cruelly deprived by the living.

Beneath the entrance to the church there was a passage which led to some family vaults in the basement, and he crept down the passage to seek some shelter for his nude body from the driving rain, which had chilled him through. While groping about in the dark his hand rested on something soft, which, to his unbounded delight, proved to be an old coat which had probably been left there by the sexton, and forgotten. He remained hidden all day, and traveled through the fields all night, during which he found a "scarecrow," from which he transferred to his own person its old hat and trousers.

He said that although so hungry, he never had felt so happy as he did at finding himself once more " dressed up." After proceeding a few miles farther, he ventured into a laborer's cottage in quest of food, which was given him, and with it a pair of old boots. As dilapidated, ragged, vagabond-looking, honest people are common in England, no questions were asked, and he proceeded on his way, rejoicing in that freedom of which he had been deprived for ten years or more.

Amidst all his pranks he had never been charged with idleness, and now worked at odd jobs about the farms until he had procured a decent suit of clothes, when he applied to a master house-painter for work as a journeyman, though he had never done anything of that kind. The master, pleased with his appearance, gave him a trial, but the first job showed such ignorance of the art of house-painting that he was forthwith discharged with a half day's wages. However, he had picked up some valuable hints, and being very apt, by the time he had been more or less summarily discharged from half a dozen places, he had become a good workman, and henceforth had no trouble about retaining any situation as long as he refrained from beer and restrained his temper ; but at the slightest fault-finding on the part of the master, he would fly into a passion and throw up his situation, and this, especially, if he suspected that anything had leaked out about his imprisonment.

While at work with a companion at painting the interior of a gentleman's residence near Bradford, a word or two was dropped which made him believe his fellow-workman had become aware of his being an ex-convict. Quitting work, he went to a public house, passing the rest of the day in carousing. About midnight, while on his way to his boarding-house, it occurred to him that he had noticed a good many valuable things about the gentleman's house which he could obtain. No sooner thought than done; the entrance was in a moment gained; he had just consciousness enough left to gather a few things, then lie down by the side of them and fall into a drunkard's sleep, in which the servants found him when they came down in the morning. A constable was sent for, he was given in charge, tried, convicted of the crime of burglary, and sentenced to seven years penal servitude.

His former term of five years had made him a proficient in all the dodges of prison life, and he felt justified in his own mind in using all his craft in order to put in his seven years as easily as possible. As he had been in Raynell asylum, he knew that by " putting on the balmy " so as to be sent to the lunatic department, he would not be subjected to the prison rules, and be as well off as he had been in the free asylums. Persistent attempts at suicide by cutting himself in the arms and legs with a piece of glass so as to bleed freely, accomplished his purpose. Being placed with the other convict lunatics at Woking, he made himself useful as a gardener, but on account of his bad temper and overbearing, quarrelsome disposition, obnoxious to his fellow-prisoners.

However, when he had served about five years and six months, Dr. Campbell gave him his remission-marks and sent him away, as usual in such cases, to Dartmoor prison a month before the time his ticket-of-leave would be due. From there he was discharged with an eighteen-months ticket-of-leave, and two dollars and fifty cents as capital for a " new departure."

He went to Liverpool, procured a passage on board a freight-steamer to America, which he paid for by working at painting. Landing at New York, he made his way to Norfolk, Va., where he procured work as a painter. Owing to his infirmity of temper he did not keep his place long, and after knocking about for a few months he took a freak to return to England — the last place of all for any man who has once been in prison.

Once more in his native land, he procured work without difficulty at house-painting, but, as usual, remained in one place but a very short time. His earnings, like those of a great majority of the working class in England, were squandered in the public house —

> The glittering rum-shop's legal snare,
> The children's curse and wives' despair.

Soon after the events just recorded, Heep concluded to visit his old home in Macclesfield. He accordingly threw up his situation, and arrived at the railway station an hour before the train was due. In order to while away the time, he entered a public house (as all places retailing spirits and beer are called in England), and drank several glasses of ale. The compartment which he entered happened to be empty, and as usual whenever he indulged his appetite for anything containing alcohol, he was soon quite out of his mind and fancied that some one on the train was coming to murder him, and leaped headlong from the train, which was going at the rate of forty miles an hour. This came to a standstill, he was taken on board again, not seriously injured, and left at Wrexham in Denbighshire, from which he was sent to the Denbigh Insane asylum. This being a Welsh institution, did not, according to Heep, possess those facilities for enjoying life which were so liberally supplied to the inmates of the Raynell asylum near Liverpool. Accordingly he behaved himself with so much propriety that the doctor discharged him as cured.

 Not long after his return he got work near Manchester, at painting in a block of new houses where the plumbers were at work putting in the gas and water pipes. On a Saturday, when he left work at noon, he met a young plumber who was out of a job. This man said he knew where he could earn a sovereign if he had tools to do a job in a butcher-shop, and told Heep that if he would go to the houses where he had been painting, and borrow a few plumbers' tools and assist him, he would divide the amount. Heep went back, but

finding that the master plumber and all his men had gone
(Saturday afternoon in England being a half-holiday for
laborers), he took the few tools required, went and finished
the job by 7 P. M.; then instead of taking the tools back, they
went into a public house where they caroused till midnight,
when they separated, Heep taking the tools to his boarding-
house. On Monday he started early, so as to get the tools
back before the other workmen arrived. On nearing the
houses he passed a policeman who walked a little lame. He
turned his head to look back, and the policeman happened to do
the same thing, and seeing Heep looking at him his suspicions
were aroused. Turning back, he came up and asked him
what he had in the two bosses (tool baskets). Heep informed
him, and on further questioning showed him the key to the
house from which he had taken the tools, and asked him to
accompany him there, which he did. They entered, Heep put
back the tools and showed the policeman where he had been
painting, and wished him to stay until the master came in
half an hour. This the policeman declined to do, and took
the tools and told Heep to come to the police station.

Heep lost his temper, and began cursing him. The policeman went to the door, and seeing another just passing, beckoned him in, and the two marched him to the station. The
plumber was sent for, and was induced to make a charge
against Heep and value the stolen goods at ten shillings.
Seeing that the police were bound to make a case against
him by hook or crook (crook, he says), he seized the
plumber's knife and cut his throat, severing the wind-pipe.
The doctor was sent for, he was transferred to the jail hospital, and in the course of two or three weeks was well
enough to appear before the magistrate, though he could not
speak, and was bound over for trial.

In the meantime the police had discovered that he had
served two penal terms, on the strength of which, when
convicted, the magistrate sentenced him to ten years penal
servitude.

At the trial he had not yet recovered the use of his voice, nor did he have any one to defend him, for at that time, unlike the present, the crown did not furnish a lawyer for the defense of those who were unable to employ one at their own expense. When the magistrate was about to pronounce the sentence, he said that as the prisoner had escaped from ordinary asylums he should send him to a place from which he could not escape — meaning the convict lunatic asylum.

He was in the next bed, confined in a straight-jacket to prevent him from cutting and bleeding himself, which he managed to do despite every precaution. On one occasion, when the jacket was taken off for breakfast, he had torn open a vein of his arm with a broken nail; on another his bed was found saturated with blood, a bit of glass being found at the bottom of one of the pockets of the straight-jacket, with which he had managed to cut himself. All this time he refused to eat any of his regular food so that the doctors were obliged to feed him. To do this it was necessary to lay the patient on his back, and, in this case, to insert the edges of a patent-lever jaw-opener between the molars, then by turning a screw the levers opened, of course forcing apart the jaws of the most determined jaw-shutter. The first time it was applied to Heep he held his jaws so firmly together that one of his teeth broke off. The mouth having been forced wide open, a large iron gag a foot in length is put across the mouth, and a warder stands at his head pressing down heavily on each end, so as to force it down as far as the open jaws will let it go. Next the gutta percha tube ½-inch in diameter is inserted through a hole in the center of the gag and pushed down into the stomach. A funnel is attached to the upper end of the tube and a quart of fluid food poured in; this operation is usually performed twice a day. I saw a number of men fed in that way, one of them named Jack Collins for fourteen months, during which time he never swallowed any food.

The reader will, of course, remember the prison character,

Niblo Clark. Since the chapter in which he is referred to was written an original petition of his, in "prose and poetry," has been forwarded to me. As there is but little in this book of a wholly humorous nature, the accompanying decidedly " original " document cannot fail to counteract the effect of some of the horrors heretofore depicted. The petition is copied *verbatim et literatim :*

Printed at H. M. Convict Prison, }
  Brixton.   **No. 413c**

PETITION.

Register No. Y 19.   *Name,* NIBLO CLARK.
Present Age, 40.   *Confined in Dartmoor Prison.*
          Date of Petition, January 15, 1876.

CONVICTED.		CRIME.	SENTENCE.	REMARKS.
When. 1873.	Where. Old Bailey, London.	Burglary.	15 Years.	In Hospital. Troublesome.

To the Right Honorable R. A. CROSS, Her Majesty's Principal
 Secretary of State for the Home Department.

The Petition of Niblo Clark, a Prisoner in the Dartmoor Prison,
HUMBLY SHEWETH —

The Right Honorable Secretary the great benefit your humble petitioner would derive by a speedy removal from this damp and foggy inhospitable Climate to a milder one ; the atmostphere here his thoroughly prejudicial to your petitioners health and causes me to be a great Sufferer i am Suffering from asthma accompanied with bad attacks of Chronic bronchitis and have been now 3 long years Confined to a bed of Sickness in a Sad and pitiable Condition and upon those Clear grounds and physical proofs your petitioner humbly prays that it may please the Right Honorable Secretary to order my removal to a warmer and milder Climate

necessity also compels me to complain of repeated acts of injustice and Cruely committed again me and which in some respects Might Justly undergo the imputation of ferocity there are numbers and frivolous and false charges conspired against me and every time i am discharged from here the Governor takes them Seperate one each and trys to murder me : i have been No less then Six weeks at one time on bread and Water accompanied with a little penal Class and all the officers are incouraged to practise all kinds of barbarious maltreatment against me and other sick men — theres is one officer here place here for the express purpose of tantelizing me and other his Name is Warder Newcombe this officer sir has barbariously struck and assaulted patients on there Sick bed and Several has complained of it to the Governor — But i am Sorry to say its greatly fostered and incouraged especially upon me it is quite useless to complain of anything to the Governor

Right Honourable Sir i humbly beg that you will listen to my woe
for what i Suffer in dartmoor prison the one half you do not Know
From repeated attacks of this frightful disease i am getting worse each day
So i humbly trust you will have me removed without the least delay

In making my request in poetry Sir i hope you wont think i am Joking
for the greatest favour you can bestowe upon me is to Send me back to Woking
For in this damp and foggy Climate its impossible to ever get better
So i humbly trust in addition to this you will grant me a Special letter

Another little case i wish to State if you Sir will Kindly listen
has it would Cause a Vast amount of talk all round and about the prison
I mean if Niblo Clark Should be sent upon some public Works
it would cause more talk then the late dispute between the russians and the turks

in foggy wheather with my disease it would be impossible to larst one hour
and if you doubt the accuracy of what i say i refere to doctor Power
or any other naval doctor or one from plymouth garrison
they one and all would say the Same and likewise Doctor Harrison

Since my reception in dartmoor prison i have been a most unfortunate man
and i will tell you the why and wherefore as well as i possibly Can
for every time i been in this hospital its the whole truth what i Say
for my medical treatment i assure Sir i have dearly had to pay

A regular marked man i have been for them all its well known to Captain Harris
for the list of reports against me would reach from dartmoor to paris
So i humbly beg Right Honourable Sir you will grant this humble petition
for i am sorry to State i have nothing to pay having lost both health and remission

Such Cruel injustice to poor Sick men is far from being just and right
but to report Sick patients in hospital is the officers Chief delight
But perhaps kind Sir you might imagine that they only do this to a dodger
But its done to all — George Bidwell as well and likewise to poor Sir Roger [Tichborne].

like Savage lions in this infirmary the Officers about are walking
to Catch and report a dying poor man for the frivolous Charge of talking
and when we go out from hospital our poor bodies they try to Slaughter
by taking those reports one at the time and Killing us on bread and water

I am suffering a Chest and throat disease a frightful Chronic disorder
and to go out from hospital is attempting Suicide to get heaps of bread and Water
for it is such cruel treatment made me as i am and brought me to the Verge of the grave
So in conclusion Right Honourable Sir a removal i humbly Crave

if this petition should not be sent prisoners abstains from further writting who will explain his case more Clearly to the Visiting director and i wish to have this petition Submitted to the director Signed Niblo Clark

CHAPTER L.

AS a fitting close to my book I have thought it best to
give some account of the fate of the great modern
forgers who have obtained so many millions of other people's
dollars by dishonesty. It will be found that these millions
have in most cases been dissipated without having conferred
any benefit — rather the reverse — on their short-sighted possessors.

I may, however, note here that the first Bank of England
forgery was in the year 1784. It was done by "Old Patch,"
thus nicknamed because he wore a black patch over one eye
as a disguise. He had been a lottery-office keeper, a stock-
broker, and gambler. To save being hanged at Tyburn he
hanged himself in Newgate.

Wilkes, the forger, was born in Orange County, N. Y., in
1837. At twenty-seven he left the employ of the Erie Railway Company, where he had been seven years. It was not
long after this epoch in his life that I became acquainted with
him through Hilton, followed by the abortive attempt to get
Bowen, McNamee & Co.'s forged acceptances cashed in Wall
Street. He made various trips to England and the Continent
— once with Engles — and not less than one or two millions
of dollars must have been obtained by them in Europe from

THE RIGHT HONORABLE HENRY MATTHEWS, Q. C.
Her Majesty's Home Secretary of State, 1887.

1873 to 1885, while we were kept in prison as scarecrows to frighten them away.

George Engles, after squandering a million dollars or more, died prematurely, leaving his family destitute.

Wilson, one of the Engles and Wilkes gang, is forty-eight years of age, and has not long completed a term of twelve years in Canada, and by the time these lines come under the reader's notice, will in all probability be again in prison.

Vanderpool, *alias* Brockway, is now past sixty-three years of age. He has served three or more terms of imprisonment; the last, which expired in 1886, was eight years for forgery at Providence, R. I.

Charles Becker is, like Engles, a German. He is an expert engraver, and worked for Engles, to my knowledge, as far back as 1871. He tried to "beat" the Turks, was apprehended and sentenced to four years' imprisonment at Smyrna, but not liking the quarters in Constantinople to which he had been consigned, took French leave after a few months' confinement. Returning to America, he has recently completed a term of six and one-half years in the Kings County Penitentiary.

Joe Chapman, who accompanied Engles to Europe, was arrested in London in 1878, and served a five-years' term in England. After serving several terms previously, he was not long since, and may be still, in prison at Munich, Bavaria, for passing Engles's forged paper on bankers.

George Bell is forty-two years of age; also a "layer-down" of forged paper. Bell has served several terms in various prisons, and is now near the completion of a ten-years' sentence in the Maryland state prison.

Robert S. Ballard, fifty-one years of age, a physician by profession, a forger and bigamist by practice, has recently completed a term in prison.

Thomas Ballard was sentenced by a United States court to serve twenty years for forgery of United States bonds. After the expiration of thirteen and a half years, he was pardoned by President Cleveland in 1887 (about the time when I came home from England).

Walter Sheridan was arrested in 1858 for robbing a bank in Chicago, Ill.; also in Toledo, 1869, for robbing the First National Bank of Springfield, Ill., but was acquitted for want of proof. In 1870 he was implicated in the robbery of the Maryland Insurance Company, Baltimore, and of the Mechanics Bank, of Scranton, Pa. In 1873 he defrauded the New York Indemnity and Warehouse Company of $84,000, with which he made good his escape to Europe, taking $200,-000 of forged bonds which were stolen from him by another "crook." Returning to New York, Sheridan was sent to Sing Sing in 1877, for five years. Soon after his term had expired, he was arrested in Philadelphia and sent for a term of three years to the Eastern Penitentiary. His term expired in 1884, and in the latter part of the same year he was again arrested, in St. Louis, and sentenced to two years in State prison.

Little Elliott is thirty-three years of age. He went to Turkey with Becker and Chapman, was sentenced at the same time with them to three and one-half years, and escaped after some months imprisonment. He is now serving a term of eighteen years for forgery on the Flour City Bank, of Rochester, N. Y. It was Engles or Wilkes who prepared the forged paper presented by him to that and other banks.

W. H. Lyman, a notorious forger, died in the Charlestown, Mass., prison in 1883, just before the expiration of his sentence.

Stephen Raymond is fifty-six years of age, and after serving several terms for forgery, was sentenced in New York city to imprisonment for life.

Williamson, or Perrine, is forty-five years of age. He acted as "layer-down," or presenter of papers forged by Engles and others, and succeeded in getting large amounts of such papers cashed, but was finally arrested and sent to

Sing Sing for fifteen years. He escaped from that institution in 1877, and went to London with Engles, where, for presenting forged paper to the London and County Bank, he was convicted and sentenced for ten years. By giving evidence against others of the Engles party, he was released in 1883, after serving about four years, and returned to New York.

Dan Noble is now serving out a twenty years' sentence for presenting paper forged by Engles on a London bank.

Williamson is at present in the Missouri state prison, serving a sentence of ten years for presenting in 1885 to the St. Louis National Bank forged checks prepared by Engles.

Wise, or Rosencranz, is forty-five years old. He has been engaged since 1869 in presenting paper forged by Engles. He has served several terms, and has recently completed five years in Auburn state prison.

Spence Pettis, a well known New York layer-down, after serving several terms, ended his career in Charlestown prison, Mass., by hanging himself from the bars of his cell door in 1874.

George Watson, after ruining his constitution by dissipation, died while serving out a sentence for forgery.

Van Etten, in 1871, received a sentence of ten years for presenting a forged check to the Park National Bank, N. Y. He was pardoned, and while being taken to San Francisco to answer another charge of forgery he killed himself on the train by taking a dose of narcotics, which he by some means obtained.

Lewis Cole, after serving several terms, when he was on the point of being again arrested, shot and killed himself with a revolver.

Charles Lister, who went to England in 1877 with Dan Noble, is now about completing a fifteen years term there, if he is alive.

Johnny Miller was arrested on information given by Lister, and is now serving a term of twenty years in England.

I have always been under the impression that Frank

Kibbe, like Engles, would keep out of prison — both being super-extra cowards.

Since the preceding pages were written it has come to my knowledge that Frank Kibbe served a term in Cherry Hill Penitentiary, Philadelphia.

The following letter is from a prominent citizen of the State of Connecticut, it being one of several received by me on the same subject:

—————, CONN., May 29, 1888.

MR. BIDWELL :

SIR, — Yours of the 14th inst. duly received. I have deferred a reply hoping to learn something of Frank's present whereabouts, but have failed. In 1874 I was associated with Judge H. H. Barbour, of Hartford (now deceased), as State Prison Director. The Judge took a deep interest in prison reform, and at his request we visited several States. It occurred to me that I might run across Frank, who had been missing for some years, and who, in my opinion, was a proper subject for confinement. At Philadelphia after going through the prison, looking at the records, etc., the warden told me there were two Eastern fellows confined there for six years (four of which had passed) — for swindling if I am not mistaken. Their assumed names I cannot recall. I gave a description of Frank. The deputy said at once, "That is Kibbe." He had written to his wife, thus exposing his true name. The warden said, "Perhaps he would like to see you" — and we went to his cell. I remained a few feet back. My name was given him, and in his quick way he said, "No, no, I don't know any such man." That was the last time I heard Frank's voice — is all I know of him. . . . .

Yours,   —— ——

Kibbe had previously been twice arrested in Philadelphia, but had on both occasions been let off by paying for the swindled goods.

During his incarceration his wife, also a native of New England, visited him. She bore an excellent character, was driven mad by her husband's conduct, and died in a lunatic asylum in the vicinity of her native place before the expiration of his term. After being discharged, this man who had for years squandered large sums in high living — this exqui-site, formerly decked out in magnificent style with diamonds flashing, became a common beggar, tramp, and vagabond.

A gentleman who knew Kibbe from childhood, at the time a merchant in Philadelphia, living at the Continental Hotel, said to me lately : " One evening I was standing in the office when a seedy-looking man came along and held out his hand. I paid no attention, but observed that he continued the round of the place, then returning, stopped in front of me and asked :

" ' Don't you know me, James ? '

" I replied : ' No.'

" ' Have you forgotten Frank Kibbe ? ' he queried."

My informant now recognized him, and was told some par-ticulars about his imprisonment — that he had been discharged some weeks previously and had since been begging, etc., etc. The gentleman handed him ten dollars on condition that he should trouble him no more.

For about nine months after the above event Kibbe was cadging about Philadelphia, then disappeared — probably got into prison again, or died in some hospital.

I might add to the list enough names to fill a large book, without exhausting the supply.

Despite all the examples on record, proving the sad results which sooner or later invariably follow wrong-doing, forgeries, defalcations, and frauds committed by men in good positions, are now of daily occurrence. I have not space here to enter into an examination of the causes of this terrible fact. For every case that comes to light there are doubtless a hundred which are hushed up by intercession of employers or friends.

As any person advances, step by step, along the seem-ingly flowery path which leads him first to association, then into confederacy with "crooks," he in the same ratio acquires those prodigal and loose habits which cause him to squander his ill-gotten gains in ways which leave him in a few years a wreck in mind, body, and estate.

Chapter LI.

THOUSANDS of people have attended the play entitled the "Ticket-of-leave Man," and have shown deep interest in the fate of one so placed, though only a fictitious representation of what I actually am at the present moment — a genuine ticket-of-leave man.

During my imprisonment I had opportunities of hearing what a large number of men had to say, who had been out on tickets-of-leave, some of them several times. A small gratuity is allowed to each prisoner upon his discharge, but this is not given into his possession all at once. In case he goes to the "Prisoners' Aid Society," it is sent by the warder who accompanies him to the place of his conviction. If London, the ticket-of-leave man is taken to the society's office and his gratuity handed over to its manager. If his destination is elsewhere in England the gratuity is left with the local agent of the society. In either case the ticket-of-leave man receives a half-a-crown (thirty cents) per day so long as any of the gratuity money is left. In case work is not obtained by that time he is turned adrift, at least I was so informed by prisoners who had been thus treated. The general impression

(550)

among the prisoners who have had experience with the society is that it is conducted in the interest of those who draw salaries from its funds.

"They pretend to furnish work or get us into situations," said one to me, "and I was given a basket of oranges, purchased with a part of my gratuity money, and told to go and hawk them through the streets. Finding they did not 'hawk,' or that I did not understand the business sufficiently, and as the society could or would get me no other situation— my gratuity being all gone — I found I must go hungry or steal. Well, I stole, and am here doing another 'lagging.'"

Two or three months before the expiration of his term, or the date he is to be freed on a ticket-of-leave, the convict must inform the governor if he wishes to join the Prisoners' Aid Society. In case he has "done" above a five years term, and by good conduct has been promoted to the special or blue-dress class, he is entitled to an extra gratuity of £2 from the society. This is a substantial benefit, as in many cases, added to the prison gratuity, it enables the society to send him out as an emigrant to one of the colonies where he can have a fair chance to begin an honest life — it being hardly possible for an ex-convict to have it in England. I have heard a number of prisoners relate their experiences while in search of honest employment.

In Tom Taylor's drama, the ticket-of-leave man is persecuted by his former companions, who attempt by every artifice to force him back into crime. Now, in so far as my experience enables me to judge, this picture is not drawn from life. Professionals are fully aware of the risks they run, and never as a rule attempt any unfair means to induce each other to take part in crime.

"Do you continue to wear the clothes furnished by the prison authorities?" I asked on more than one occasion.

"No," was the reply of one, "I got out of them as soon as possible. When I went up to London after my last 'lagging,' there were four of us who went to the society. All of us wished to exchange our clothes for better, and an agent of the society took us to a Jew clothes-dealer, and, as the society had our money, we were obliged to take new suits at the Jew's own price — he allowing but a trifle for the suits we had worn from prison. I felt pretty certain that the agent had a share in that job."

Of course I vouch for none of this, but where there is smoke there must be some fire.

The ticket-of-leave man must report in person at the police headquarters of the place he lives in once a month; by failing to do so he renders himself liable to be taken back to prison to serve the remainder of his time. He must leave his address, and if he changes his residence, must notify the police so that they can find him at any time in case he should be "wanted".

The accompanying illustration will give an idea of the "hang-dog" feeling it gives one who has not become thoroughly hardened, in being thus obliged to "show up" at police-headquarters each month. Indeed, I have had a number of men tell me that they preferred to "do" the whole of their time rather than be out under the surveillance of the police and obliged to report themselves monthly. This police supervision can be escaped only by emigration, some actually conducting themselves so as to lose their remission and serve their whole term.

I knew one who, on the morning he was to go home after serving his term of ten years, refused to put on citizen's clothes, resisting the officers who put him into them by force. This class of men, of whom I have seen hundreds, know that the only comparative comfort they have had from their birth has been while in jail or prison. With them it has been the ever recurring "move on" of the bobbies or peelers, as they call policemen, and the general wretchedness of their lives while free may be only faintly imagined from a due consideration of the above fact.

I have had a good many tell me how they had been fol-

TICKET-OF-LEAVE-MAN REPORTING MONTHLY AT POLICE HEADQUARTERS.

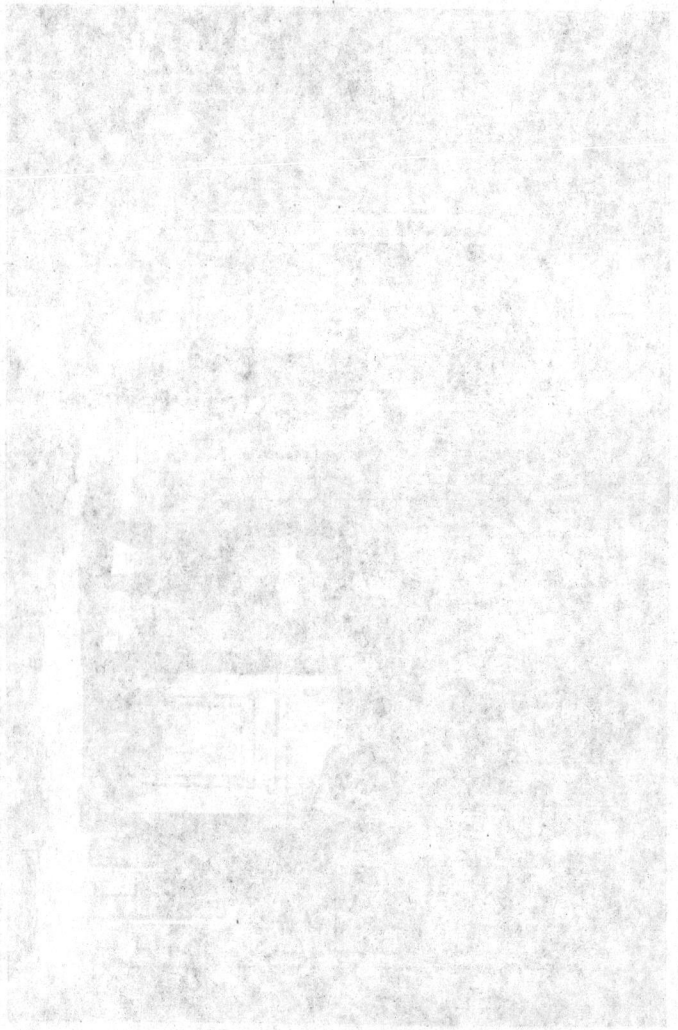

lowed by so-called detectives, when in a situation, and black-mailed, or if they refused to submit to that "tax" were denounced to their masters and discharged to find other work or steal. In other cases charges were trumped up against them, and they were sent back to prison by perjury. At present detectives or policemen who do such dirty work risk imprisonment. A detective in London had acquired the sobriquet of "Truss of straw" from the following circumstance: One day he saw a child some four years of age toddling along the street. Soon the little one's attention was attracted by a small truss of straw at the door of a shop, which it managed to take in its arms and toddle on. Such an opportunity for fame and promotion must not be missed; the detective arrested the child and took him before a magistrate, who, laughing at the zealous guardian of the public, conferred upon him the above title, which stuck to him through life, though his name was Welch. This "Truss of straw" had a partner named Parker, another detective. These precious specimens of justice's aids made a regular business of robbing thieves of their ill-gotten gains, by threatening to "run them in," or in black-mailing ex-convicts who were trying to earn an honest living. These detectives failing to get their demands acceded to by two men, Piper and Shaw, arrested them on a charge of robbery. On their own testimony, aided by that of the person who had been robbed — whom they had induced, by methods elsewhere described, to believe that these were really the men who had robbed him — both the accused were sentenced to fourteen years penal servitude each. A year and a half later Parker was hauled before a magistrate for complicity in some fraud, and the moment he was arrested Welch "went back on him." Parker got out of the scrape with being expelled from the force, and wanted to continue sharing Welch's illicit gains; but refusing to do so, Parker to revenge himself, exposed the plot by which Piper and Shaw had been convicted, and these were set at liberty. Piper had determined to earn an honest living, but failing to obtain employment, and reduced to the point of starvation, he threw himself over London Bridge, but was rescued and taken before a magistrate on the charge of attempted suicide, which crime is severely punished in England. To exonerate himself he told in open court the story of his fourteen years' sentence, out of which he had served eighteen months at Chatham. The magistrate had Shaw hunted up, and having ascertained the truth of Piper's statement, ordered that they should be paid one hundred pounds each, that being the largest sum the law put it in his power to award in such a case. I had the foregoing account from an intelligent prisoner who was acquainted with the men and had heard it from their own lips, which corroborated what I had learned about it from other sources.

The ticket-of-leave and other documents, in the name of "Castro," accompanying this chapter are fac-similes of the originals given to Sir Roger C. D. Tichborne, the world-famed "Claimant," on his discharge from Portsmouth prison, after serving a term of fourteen years. He was at Dartmoor prison during a portion of the time I was there. These documents are the same as are given in all cases, except where the sentence is for "life," as in my case. All others or tickets referring to a limited term of imprisonment, are not signed by the Home Secretary, as is the "ticket-of-leave" at the commencement of this book. That is a fac-simile of the one given to me by the warder who accompanied me to Liverpool, after he had placed me safely on board the steamship *Wisconsin*, as described in the "explanatory" chapter. It is signed by the Right Honorable Henry Matthews, Q. C., Her Majesty's Secretary for Home.

Previous to accepting the eminent office which he holds at the time of this writing, Mr. Matthews had been a barrister of high standing and great ability. He was born in Ceylon in 1826, and educated partly on the Continent, partly in England, having graduated at the University of Paris as bachelor of arts, and in 1849 from the University of London, LL.B., carrying off the University law scholarship of £50 a year for three years. As some of my readers may wish to see the shadow of the man whose name appears on my ticket-of-leave, I have inserted his portrait.

METROPOLITAN POLICE DISTRICT.

To *Thomas Castro* ————— , a *Convict about to be liberated on License, or a Person subject to the Supervision of the Police.*

Under the provisions of the Prevention of Crimes Acts 1871-9, you are required to report yourself personally to the Chief Officer of Police of the District in which you reside, or to a Constable, or person appointed by him.

TAKE NOTICE, THEREFORE, that I, the undersigned, the Commissioner of Police of the Metropolis, being the Chief Officer of Police of the Metropolitan Police District, have appointed the Constable in charge of the Convict Office, Great Scotland Yard, to receive your declaration of residence on liberation, and I require you to report yourself to him personally within 48 hours thereof, at that Office.

If you neglect so to do within 48 hours of the said liberation, you are liable to have your license forfeited or to be sentenced to twelve months' imprisonment with hard labour.

Metropolitan Police Office,
20*th* day of *October* 1882.

[OVER.]

The day before a convict is to be released he is removed to the Millbank prison, London, where the above notice is served on him by a clerk from the Metropolitan Police Headquarters.

No. 300.   (No. 2.)

METROPOLITAN POLICE DISTRICT

To _____*Thomas Carter*_____ a Convict liberated

on LICENSE, or a person subject to the SUPERVISION OF THE POLICE.

Under the provisions of the Prevention of Crimes Acts, 1871 and 1879, you are required to report your *entry into* and *removal from* a Police District to the Chief Officer of Police of the said District, or to such other person as he may appoint, and so long as you remain in the District you must report yourself *personally*, once a month, at such time as may be prescribed by the Chief Officer; and any change of address within the said district must be declared in like manner.

TAKE NOTICE, THEREFORE, that I, the undersigned, the Commissioner of Police of the Metropolis, being the Chief Officer of Police of the Metropolitan Police District, require that you report yourself personally, to the Constable in charge of *the Conard Office* ~~Police Station~~ *fresh Scotland yard* ~~and such Convict being the nearest to your place of abode, between the hours of 9 a.m. and 9 p.m. on the~~ *on the 20th* of each month and any change of residence shall likewise be declared to the said Constable *prior to your removal.*

The Penalty for neglecting to do as above directed, or for leaving the District without declaring your intention so to do, is the forfeiture of your License, or Twelve Months' Imprisonment with Hard Labour.

E.Y.O. Henderson.

Metropolitan Police Office,

22 day of *October* 1884.

NOTE.—If you leave the District and again return to it you must immediately report such return either at the Convict Office, Great Scotland Yard, or at the Police Station nearest to your place of abode.

B. & R. 2000 7-84   [OVER.

FORM—38c.

HANTS CONSTABULARY.

*Notice to be served on License Holder number*_____ *A. 1139*_____

Name *Thomas Castro, alias Tichborne Bart Sir R 6D*

34, 35 Vic., cap. 112.

SECTION 5.—Every holder of a license granted under the Penal Servitude Acts who is at large in great Britain or Ireland shall notify the place of his residence to the chief officer of police of the district in which his residence is situated, and shall, whenever he changes such residence within the same police district, notify such change to the chief officer of police of that district, and whenever he changes his residence from one police district to another shall notify such change of residence to the chief officer of police of the police district which he is leaving, and to the chief officer of police of the police district into which he goes to reside; moreover, every male holder of such a license as aforesaid shall, once in each month, report himself at such time as may be prescribed by the chief officer of police of the district in which such holder may be, either to such chief officer himself or to such other person as that officer may direct, and such report may, according as such chief officer directs, be required to be made personally or by letter.

If any holder of a license who is at large in Great Britain or Ireland, remains in any place for forty-eight hours without notifying the place of his residence to the chief officer of police of the district in which such place is situated, or fails to comply with the requisitions of this section on the occasion of any change of residence, or with the requisitions of this section as to reporting himself once in each month, he shall in every such case, unless he proves to the satisfaction of the court before whom he is tried that he did his best to act in conformity with the law, be guilty of an offence against this Act, and upon conviction thereof his license may in the discretion of the court be forfeited; or, if the term of penal servitude in respect of which his license was granted has expired at the date of his conviction, it shall be lawful for the court to sentence him to imprisonment, with or without hard labour, for a term not exceeding one year, or if the said term of penal servitude has not expired, but the remainder unexpired thereof is a lesser period than one year, then to sentence him to imprisonment, with or without hard labour, to commence at the expiration of the said term of penal servitude, for such a term as, together with the remainder unexpired of his said term of penal servitude, will not exceed one year.

By virtue of the above I hereby direct you to report yourself *by letter* ~~personally~~ on the first Monday in each month to the *officer in charge* of the Hants Constabulary, at the Police Station at *Bitterne,*

J. H. Fn

Chief Constable of Hants.

THIS LICENCE WILL BE FORFEITED IF THE HOLDER DOES NOT OBSERVE THE FOLLOWING CONDITIONS.

CONDITIONS.

1. The Holder shall preserve his Licence, and produce it when called upon to do so by a Magistrate or Police Officer.

2. He shall abstain from any violation of the Law.

3. He shall not habitually associate with notoriously bad Characters, such as reputed Thieves and Prostitutes.

4. He shall not lead an idle and dissolute Life, without visible means of obtaining an honest Livelihood.

If his licence is forfeited or revoked in consequence of a Conviction for any Offence, he will be liable to undergo a ~~Term of Penal Servitude equal to the portion of the term of~~ ~~years which remained unexpired when his~~ ~~Licence was granted, viz., the Term of~~ *for the remainder of his life*

The attention of the Licence-holder is directed to the following provisions of " The Prevention of Crimes Acts, 1871 und 1879."

If it appears from the facts proved before a court of summary jurisdiction that there are reasonable grounds for believing that the convict so brought before it is getting his livelihood by dishonest means, such convict shall be deemed to be guilty of an offence against the Prevention of Crimes Act, and his licence shall be forfeited.

Every holder of a licence granted under the Penal Servitude Acts who is at large in Great Britain or Ireland, shall within 48 hours of his liberation personally *notify the place of his residence to the chief officer of police of the district* in which his residence is situated, or to a constable or person appointed by him, and shall, *whenever he changes such residence within the same police district,* notify such change to the *chief officer of police of that district,* or to a constable or person appointed by him, and *whenever he changes his residence from one police district to another,* shall personally notify such change of residence to the *chief officer of police of the police district* which he is leaving, or to a constable or person appointed by him, and to the *chief officer of police of the police district* into which he goes to reside, or to a constable or person appointed by him; moreover, every male holder of a Licence as aforesaid shall, *once in each month,* report *himself* personally at such time as may be prescribed by the chief officer of police of the district in which such holder may be, either to such chief officer himself or to such other person as that Officer may direct, and such report may, according as such chief officer directs, be required to be made personally or by letter.

If any holder of a licence who is at large in Great Britain or Ireland *remains in any place for forty-eight hours without notifying the place of his residence to the chief officer of police of the district* in which such place is situated, or to a constable or person appointed by him, *or fails to comply with the requisitions of this section* on the occasion of any change of residence, or with the requisitions of this section as to reporting himself once in each month, he shall in every such case unless he proves to the satisfaction of the Court before whom he is tried that he did his best to act in conformity with the law, be guilty of an offence against the Prevention of Crimes Act, and upon conviction thereof *his licence may in the discretion of the Court be forfeited,* or if the term of Penal Servitude in respect of which his licence was granted has expired, at the date of his conviction, it shall be lawful for the court to sentence him to *imprisonment,* with or without Hard Labour, for a term not exceeding *one year,* or if the said term of Penal Servitude has not expired but the remainder unexpired thereof is a lesser period than one year, then to sentence him to imprisonment, with or without Hard Labour, to commence at the expiration of the said term of Penal Servitude, for such a term as, together with the remainder unexpired of his said term of Penal Servitude, will not exceed one year.

Where any person is convicted on indictment of a crime, and a *previous conviction of a crime* is proved against him, he shall, at any time *within seven years* immediately after the expiration of the sentence passed on him for the last of such crimes be guilty of an offence against the Prevention of Crimes Act, and be *liable to imprisonment* with or without Hard Labour, for a term not exceeding *one year,* under the following circumstances or any of them:

FIRST. If, on his being charged by a constable with getting his livelihood by dishonest means, and being brought before a court of summary jurisdiction, it appears to such court that *there are reasonable grounds for believing* that the person so charged is *getting his livelihood by dishonest means,* or,

SECONDLY. If on being charged with any offence punishable on indictment or summary conviction, and on being required by a court of summary jurisdiction to give his name and address, he refuses to do so, or *gives a false name or a false address;* or,

THIRDLY. If he is found in any place, whether public or private, under such circumstances as to satisfy the court before whom he is brought that he was *about to commit or to aid in the commission of any offence* punishable on indictment or summary conviction, or *was waiting for an opportunity to commit or aid in the commission of any offence punishable* on indictment or summary conviction; or,

FOURTHLY. If he is found in or upon any *dwelling-house, or any building, yard, or premises,* being parcel of or attached to such dwelling-house, or in or upon any shop, warehouse, counting-house, or other place of business, or in any garden, orchard, pleasure-ground, or nursery-ground, or in any building or erection in any garden, orchard, pleasure-ground, or nursery-ground, *without being able to account to the satisfaction of the Court* before whom he is brought *for his being found on such premises.*

I have now brought my narrative to the point where it connects with the explanatory chapter, at the beginning of the book.

Good-natured reader — you who have followed my tortuous footsteps almost through a lifetime — a lifetime of experiences the like of which I trust may never fall to the lot of another — the limit of this volume is now reached — the end has come!

The months occupied in the preparation of these pages have been — aside from painful but necessary retrospections — a period of unalloyed happiness. Freedom — home — friends! — why should I not be happy? Instead of the coldness and rebuffs, which the unwarranted proceeding in New York harbor led me to anticipate, I have received only kindness, encouragement, and valued assistance from the best men and women in the world. Fortunate indeed is it that my associations and surroundings have been of so heathful a character. Would that all, in circumstances corresponding with my own, might enjoy like ennobling influences!

What more fitting time than this beautiful day in June for paying my tribute of acknowledgment to those benefactors? Reclining dreamily, my attention is aroused by the hum of bees around my hammock, which swings from the friendly projecting arms of a conical-shaped pine at the foot of the lawn, its myriads of tufts and buds swaying to the summer breeze and filling the air with soft murmurs. Glancing upward, my view is obstructed by majestic ancestral elms, together forming a gigantic bower. The melody among the grand old boughs reveals the nesting-places of many birds. Joyous creatures! Who would not be happy as a bird in June? Alas! my lost — irrevocably lost — score of Junes! How full of life everything appears. Yonder a squirrel scurries circling up the trunk of a poplar. Apple, quince, cherry, and plum trees,

> With flowers and shrubs, here widely spread,
> Shed rich perfumes around my head.

A pair of robin red-breasts are hopping fearlessly about; there to the left, a little jenny-wren is picking at the pea-blossoms, the product of seed planted and tended by my own hands, from which I hope ere long to be rewarded by a feast of green peas — the first in fifteen years! It is too pleasant, the air too delicious, to remain indoors; and seated near me is the modern Penelope — from whom Folly separated me so long — watching the sports of grandchildren. Their merry laughter brings to the youthful-appearing grandmother's lips an answering smile, and a look of the old-time happiness to her still handsome features.

Somehow, I feel that when these closing words of mine are being read, I shall be permitted to regard each reader as a *friend*. To such I say in parting: Come and see me at my pleasant home amid the elms — wife, children, grandchildren, clustering around me. John Howard Payne could never have appreciated "Home, Sweet Home" as I now do.

Good-bye, dear readers — and in the language of Tiny Tim, "God bless us every one!"

"*The Elms,*" *East Hartford, Conn.*